THE LIFE OF JOHN MARSHALL

Standard Library Edition

IN FOUR VOLUMES

VOLUME I

JOHN MARSHALL AT 43
From a miniature painted in Paris

THE LIFE
OF
JOHN MARSHALL

BY

ALBERT J. BEVERIDGE

VOLUME I

FRONTIERSMAN, SOLDIER
LAWMAKER

1755 — 1788

BOSTON AND NEW YORK
HOUGHTON MIFFLIN COMPANY
The Riverside Press Cambridge

COPYRIGHT, 1916, BY ALBERT J. BEVERIDGE

ALL RIGHTS RESERVED

Published October 1916

PREFACE

The work of John Marshall has been of supreme importance in the development of the American Nation, and its influence grows as time passes. Less is known of Marshall, however, than of any of the great Americans. Indeed, so little has been written of his personal life, and such exalted, if vague, encomium has been paid him, that, even to the legal profession, he has become a kind of mythical being, endowed with virtues and wisdom not of this earth.

He appears to us as a gigantic figure looming, indistinctly, out of the mists of the past, impressive yet lacking vitality, and seemingly without any of those qualities that make historic personages intelligible to a living world of living men. Yet no man in our history was more intensely human than John Marshall and few had careers so full of movement and color. His personal life, his characteristics and the incidents that drew them out, have here been set forth so that we may behold the man as he appeared to those among whom he lived and worked.

It is, of course, Marshall's public work with which we are chiefly concerned. His services as Chief Justice have been so lauded that what he did before he ascended the Supreme Bench has been almost entirely forgotten. His greatest opinions, however, cannot be fully understood without considering his previous life and experience. An account of Marshall the frontiersman, soldier, legislator, lawyer, politician, diplomat, and statesman, and of the conditions he faced in each of these capacities, is essential to a comprehension of Marshall the constructive jurist and of the problems he solved.

In order to make clear the significance of Marshall's public activities, those episodes in American history into which his life was woven have been briefly stated. Although to the historian these are twice-told tales, many of them are not fresh in the minds of the reading public. To say that Marshall took this or that position with reference to the events and questions of his time, without some explanation of them, means little to any one except to the historical scholar.

In the development of his career there must be some clear understanding of the impression made upon him by the actions and opinions of other men, and these, accordingly, have been considered. The influence of his father and of Washington upon John Marshall was profound and determinative, while his life finally became so interlaced with that of Jefferson that a faithful account of the one requires a careful examination of the other.

Vitally important in their effect upon the conduct and attitude of Marshall and of the leading characters of his time were the state of the country, the condition of the people, and the tendency of popular thought. Some reconstruction of the period has, therefore, been attempted. Without a background, the picture and the figures in it lose much of their significance.

PREFACE

The present volumes narrate the life of John Marshall before his epochal labors as Chief Justice began. While this was the period during which events prepared him for his work on the bench, it was also a distinctive phase of his career and, in itself, as important as it was picturesque. It is my purpose to write the final part as soon as the nature of the task permits.

For reading one draft of the manuscript of these volumes I am indebted to Professor Edward Channing, of Harvard University; Dr. J. Franklin Jameson, of the Carnegie Foundation for Historical Research; Professor William E. Dodd, of Chicago University; Professor James A. Woodburn, of Indiana University; Professor Charles A. Beard, of Columbia University; Professor Charles H. Ambler, of Randolph-Macon College; Professor Clarence W. Alvord, of the University of Illinois; Professor D. R. Anderson, of Richmond College; Dr. H. J. Eckenrode, of Richmond College; Dr. Archibald C. Coolidge, Director of the Harvard University Library; Mr. Worthington C. Ford, of the Massachusetts Historical Society; and Mr. Lindsay Swift, Editor of the Boston Public Library. Dr. William G. Stanard, of the Virginia Historical Society, has read the chapters which touch upon the colonial period. I have availed myself of the many helpful suggestions made by these gentlemen and I gratefully acknowledge my obligations to them.

Mr. Swift and Dr. Eckenrode, in addition to reading early drafts of the manuscript, have read the last draft with particular care and I have utilized their criticisms. The proof has been read by Mr. Swift and the comment of this finished critic has been especially valuable.

I am indebted in the highest possible degree to Mr. Worthington C. Ford, of the Massachusetts Historical Society, who has generously aided me with his profound and extensive knowledge of manuscript sources and of the history of the times of which this work treats. His sympathetic interest and wholehearted helpfulness have not only assisted me, but encouraged and sustained me in the prosecution of my labors.

In making these acknowledgments, I do not in the least shift to other shoulders the responsibility for anything in these volumes. That burden is mine alone.

I extend my thanks to Mr. A. P. C. Griffin, Assistant Librarian, and Mr. Gaillard Hunt, Chief of the Manuscripts Division, of the Library of Congress, who have been unsparing in their efforts to assist me with all the resources of that great library. The officers and their assistants of the Virginia State Library, the Boston Public Library, the Library of Harvard University, the Manuscripts Division of the New York Public Library, the Massachusetts Historical Society, the Pennsylvania Historical Society, and the Virginia Historical Society have been most gracious in affording me all the sources at their command.

I desire to express my appreciation for original material furnished me by several of the descendants and collateral relatives of John Marshall. Miss

PREFACE

Emily Harvie, of Richmond, Virginia, placed at my disposal many letters of Marshall to his wife. For the use of the book in which Marshall kept his accounts and wrote notes of law lectures, I am indebted to Mrs. John K. Mason, of Richmond. A large number of original and unpublished letters of Marshall were furnished me by Mr. James M. Marshall, of Front Royal, Virginia, Mr. Robert Y. Conrad, of Winchester, Virginia; Mrs. Alexander H. Sands, of Richmond, Virginia; Miss Sallie Marshall, of Leeds, Virginia; Mrs. Claudia Jones, and Mrs. Fannie G. Campbell of Washington, D.C.; Judge J. K. M. Norton, of Alexandria, Virginia; Mr. A. Moore, Jr., of Berryville, Virginia; Dr. Samuel Eliot Morison, of Boston, Massachusetts, and Professor Charles William Dabney, of Cincinnati, Ohio. Complete copies of the highly valuable correspondence of Mrs. Edward Carrington were supplied by Mr. John B. Minor, of Richmond, Virginia, and by Mr. Carter H. FitzHugh, of Lake Forest, Illinois. Without the material thus generously opened to me, this narrative of Marshall's life would have been more incomplete than it is and many statements in it would, necessarily, have been based on unsupported tradition.

Among the many who have aided me, Judge James Keith, of Richmond, Virginia, until recently President of the Court of Appeals of Virginia; Judge J. K. M. Norton and the late Miss Nannie Burwell Norton of Alexandria, Virginia; Mr. William Marshall Bullitt, of Louisville, Kentucky; Mr. Thomas Marshall Smith, of Baltimore, Maryland; Mr. and Mrs. Alexander H. Sands; Mr. W. P. Taylor and Dr. H.

PREFACE

Norton Mason, of Richmond, Virginia; Mr. Lucien Keith, Mr. William Horgan, and Mr. William C. Marshall, of Warrenton, Virginia; Judge Henry H. Downing and Mr. Aubrey G. Weaver, of Front Royal, Virginia, have rendered notable assistance in the gathering of data.

I am under particular obligations to Miss Emily Harvie for the use of the striking miniature of Marshall, the reproduction of which appears as the frontispiece to the first volume; to Mr. Roland Gray, of Boston, for the right to reproduce the portrait by Jarvis as the frontispiece of the second volume; to Mr. Douglas H. Thomas of Baltimore, Maryland, for photographs of the portraits of William Randolph, Mary Isham, and Mary Randolph Keith; and to Mr. Charles Edward Marshall, of Glen Mary, Kentucky, for permission to photograph the portrait of Colonel Thomas Marshall.

The large number of citations has made abbreviations necessary. At the end of each volume will be found a careful explanation of references, giving the full title of the work cited, together with the name of the author or editor, and a designation of the edition used.

The index has been made by Mr. David Maydole Matteson, of Cambridge, Massachusetts, and his careful work has added to whatever of value these volumes possess.

ALBERT J. BEVERIDGE

CONTENTS

I. ANCESTRY AND ENVIRONMENT **1**

The defeat of Braddock — Influence on American opinion — Washington's heroism — Effect on Marshall's parents — Marshall's birth — American solidarity the first lesson taught him — Marshall's ancestry — Curious similarity to that of Jefferson, to whom he was related — The paternal line: the "Marshall legend" — Maternal line: the Randolphs, the Ishams, and the Keiths — Character of Marshall's parents — Colonial Virginia society — Shiftless agriculture and abundant land — Influence of slavery — Jefferson's analysis — Drinking heavy and universal — Education of the gentry and of the common people — The social divisions — Causes of the aristocratic tone of Virginia society — The backwoodsmen — Their character — Superiority of an occasional frontier family — The Marshalls of this class — The illustrious men produced by Virginia just before the Revolution.

II. A FRONTIER EDUCATION **33**

Marshall's wilderness birthplace — His father removes to the Blue Ridge — The little house in "The Hollow" — Neighbors few and distant — Daily life of the frontier family — Marshall's delight in nature — Effect on his physical and mental development — His admiration for his father — The father's influence over and training of his son — Books: Pope's Poems — Marshall commits to memory at the age of twelve many passages — The "Essay on Man" — Marshall's father an assistant of Washington in surveying the Fairfax grant — Story of Lord Fairfax — His influence on Washington and on Marshall's father — Effect on Marshall — His father elected Burgess from Fauquier County — Vestryman, Sheriff, and leading man of his county — He buys the land in "The Hollow" — John Thompson, deacon, teaches Marshall for a year — His father buys more land and removes to Oak Hill — Subscribes to the first American edition of Blackstone — Military training interferes with Marshall's reading of Blackstone — He is sent to Campbell's Academy for a few months — Marshall's father as Burgess supports Patrick Henry, who defeats the tidewater aristocracy in the Robinson loan-office contest — Henry offers his resolutions on the Stamp Act: "If this be treason, make the most of it" — Marshall's father votes with Henry — 1775 and Henry's "Resolutions for Arming and Defense" — His famous speech: "Give me liberty or give me death" — Marshall's father again supports Henry — Marshall learns from his father of these great events — Father and son ready to take the field against the British.

CONTENTS

III. A SOLDIER OF THE REVOLUTION . . . **69**

The "Minute Men" of Virginia — Lieutenant John Marshall drills his company and makes a war speech — His appearance in his nineteenth year — Uniforms of the frontier — The sanguinary fight at Great Bridge — Norfolk — The Marshalls in the Continental service, the father as major, the son as lieutenant — Condition of the army — Confusion of authority — Unreliability of militia "who are here to-day and gone to-morrow" — Fatal effect of State control — Inefficiency and powerlessness of Congress — Destitution of the troops: "our sick naked and well naked" — Officers resign, privates desert — The harsh discipline required: men whipped, hanged, and shot — Impression on Marshall — He is promoted to be captain-lieutenant — The march through disaffected Philadelphia — Marshall one of picked men forming the light infantry — Iron Hill — The battle of the Brandywine — Marshall's father and his Virginians prevent entire disaster — Marshall's part in the battle — The retreat — The weather saves the Americans — Marshall one of rear guard under Wayne — The army recovers and tries to stop the British advance — Confused by false reports of the country people who are against the patriots "almost to a man" — Philadelphia falls — The battle of Germantown — Marshall at the bloodiest point of the fight — The retreat of the beaten Americans — Unreasonable demands of "public opinion" — Further decline of American fortunes — Duché's letter to Washington: "How fruitless the expense of blood" — Washington faces the British — The impending battle — Marshall's vivid description — The British withdraw.

IV VALLEY FORGE AND AFTER **108**

The bitter winter of 1777 — The British in Philadelphia: abundance of provisions, warm and comfortable quarters, social gayeties, revels of officers and men — The Americans at Valley Forge, "the most celebrated encampment in the world's history": starvation and nakedness — Surgeon Waldo's diary of "camp-life": "I'll live like a Chameleon upon Air" — Waldo's description of soldiers' appearance — Terrible mortality from sickness — The filthy "hospitals" — Moravians at Bethlehem — The Good Samaritans to the patriots — Marshall's cheerfulness: "the best tempered man I ever knew" — His pranks and jokes — Visitors to the camp remark his superior intelligence — Settles disputes of his comrades — Hard discipline at Valley Forge: a woman given a hundred lashes — Washington alone holds army together — Jealousy of and shameful attacks upon him — The "Conway Cabal" — His dignity in the face of slander — His indignant letter to Congress — Faith of the soldiers in Washington — The absurd popular demand that he attack Philadelphia — The amazing inferiority of Congress — Ablest

CONTENTS

men refuse to attend — Washington's pathetic letter on the subject: "Send your ablest men to Congress; Where is Jefferson" — Talk of the soldiers at Valley Forge — Jefferson in the Virginia Legislature — Comparison of Marshall and Jefferson at this period — Marshall appointed Deputy Judge Advocate of the army — Burnaby's appeal to Washington to stop the war: efforts at reconciliation — Washington's account of the sufferings of the army — The spring of 1778 — Sports in camp — Marshall the best athlete in his regiment: "Silver Heels" Marshall — The Alliance with the King of France — Rejoicing of the Americans at Valley Forge — Washington has misgivings — The services of Baron von Steuben — Lord Howe's departure — The "Mischianza" — The British evacuate Philadelphia — The Americans quick in pursuit — The battle of Monmouth — Marshall in the thick of the fight — His fairness to Lee — Promoted to be captain — One of select light infantry under Wayne, assigned to take Stony Point — The assault of that stronghold — Marshall in the reserve command — One of the picked men under "Light Horse Harry" Lee — The brilliant dash upon Powles Hook — Term of enlistment of Marshall's regiment expires and he is left without a command — Returns to Virginia while waiting for new troops to be raised — Arnold invades Virginia — Jefferson is Governor; he fails to prepare — Marshall one of party to attack the British — Effect of Jefferson's conduct on Marshall and the people — Comment of Virginia women — Inquiry in Legislature as to Jefferson's conduct — Effect of Marshall's army experience on his thinking — The roots of his great Nationalist opinions run back to Valley Forge.

V. MARRIAGE AND LAW BEGINNINGS . . . 148

Marshall's romance — Visits his father who is commanding at Yorktown — Mythical story of his father's capture at Charleston — The Ambler family — Rebecca Burwell, Jefferson's early love — Attractiveness of the Amblers — The "ball" at Yorktown — High expectations of the young women concerning Marshall — Their disappointment at his uncouth appearance and rustic manners — He meets Mary Ambler — Mutual love at first sight — Her sister's description of the ball and of Marshall — The courtship — Marshall goes to William and Mary College for a few weeks — Description of the college — Marshall elected to the Phi Beta Kappa Society — Attends the law lectures of Mr. Wythe — The Ambler daughters pass though Williamsburg — The "ball" at "The Palace" — Eliza Ambler's account: "Marshall was devoted to my sister" — Marshall leaves college and follows Mary Ambler to Richmond — Secures license to practice law — Resigns his command — Walks to Philadelphia to be inoculated against smallpox — Tavernkeeper refuses to take him in because of his appearance — Returns to Virginia and resumes his courtship of Mary Ambler — Marshall's account of his love-making — His sister-in-law's description

CONTENTS

of Marshall's suit — Marshall's father goes to Kentucky and returns — Marshall elected to the Legislature from Fauquier County — He marries Mary Ambler: "but one solitary guinea left" — Financial condition of Marshall's father at this time — Lack of ready money everywhere — Marshall's account — He sets up housekeeping in Richmond — Description of Richmond at that time — Brilliant bar of the town — "Marshall's slender legal equipment" — The notes he made of Mr. Wythe's lectures — His Account Book — Examples of his earnings and expenditures from 1783 until 1787 — Life of the period — His jolly letter to Monroe — His books — Elected City Recorder — Marshall's first notable case: Hite *vs.* Fairfax — His first recorded argument — His wife becomes an invalid — His tender care of her — Mrs. Carrington's account: Marshall "always and under every circumstance, an enthusiast in love."

VI. IN THE LEGISLATURE AND COUNCIL OF STATE   200

In the House of Delegates — The building where the Legislature met — Costumes and manners of the members — Marshall's popularity and his father's influence secure his election — He is appointed on important committees — His first vote — examples of legislative business — Poor quality of the Legislature: Madison's disgust, Washington's opinion — Marshall's description and remarkable error — He is elected member of Council of State — Pendleton criticizes the elevation of Marshall — Work as member of Council — Resigns from Council because of criticism of judges — Seeks and secures reëlection to Legislature from Fauquier County — Inaccuracy of accepted account of these incidents — Marshall's letter to Monroe stating the facts — Becomes champion of needy Revolutionary soldiers — Leads fight for relief of Thomas Paine — Examples of temper of the Legislature — Marshall favors new Constitution for Virginia — The "Potowmack Company" — Bills concerning courts — Reform of the High Court of Chancery — The religious controversy — State of religion in Virginia — Marshall's languid interest in the subject — Great question of the British debts — Long-continued fight over payment or confiscation — Marshall steadily votes and works for payment of the debts — Effect of this contest on his economic and political views — His letter to Monroe — Instability of Legislature: a majority of thirty-three changed in two weeks to an adverse majority of forty-nine — No National Government — Resolution against allowing Congress to lay any tax whatever: "May prove destructive of rights and liberties of the people" — The debts of the Confederation — Madison's extradition bill — Contempt of the pioneers for treaties — Settlers' unjust and brutal treatment of the Indians — Struggle over Madison's bill — Patrick Henry saves it — Marshall supports it — Henry's bill for amalgamation of Indians and whites — Marshall regrets its defeat — Anti-National sentiment of the people —

CONTENTS

Steady change in Marshall's ideas — Mercantile and financial interests secure the Constitution — Shall Virginia call a Convention to ratify it? — Marshall harmonizes differences and Convention is called — He is in the first clash over Nationalism.

VII. LIFE OF THE PEOPLE: COMMUNITY ISOLATION 250

The state of the country — A résumé of conditions — Revolutionary leaders begin to doubt the people — Causes of this doubt — Isolation of communities — Highways and roads — Difficulty and danger of travel — The road from Philadelphia to Boston: between Boston and New York — Roads in interior of New England, New York, Philadelphia, and New Jersey — Jefferson's account of roads from Richmond to New York — Traveler lost in the "very thick woods" on way from Alexandria to Mount Vernon to visit Washington — Travel and transportation in Virginia — Ruinous effect on commerce — Chastellux lost on journey to Monticello to visit Jefferson — Talleyrand's description of country — Slowness of mails — Three weeks or a month and sometimes two months required between Virginia and New York — Mail several months in reaching interior towns — News that Massachusetts had ratified the Constitution eight days in reaching New York — Ocean mail service — letters opened by postmasters or carriers — Scarcity of newspapers — Their untrustworthiness — Their violent abuse of public men — Franklin's denunciation of the press: he advises "the liberty of the cudgel" to restrain "the liberty of the press" — Jefferson's disgust — The country newspaper: Freneau's "The Country Printer" — The scantiness of education — Teachers and schools — The backwoodsmen — The source of abnormal American individualism — The successive waves of settlers — Their ignorance, improvidence, and lack of social ideals — Habits and characteristics of Virginians — Jefferson's harsh description of them — Food of the people — Their houses — Continuous drinking of brandy, rum, and whiskey — This common to whole country — Lack of community consciousness — Abhorrence of any National Government.

VIII. POPULAR ANTAGONISM TO GOVERNMENT 288

Thomas Paine's "Common Sense" — Its tremendous influence: "Government, even in its best state, is but a necessary evil" — Popular antagonism to the very idea of government — Impossibility of correcting falsehoods told to the people — Popular credulity — The local demagogue — North Carolina preacher's idea of the Constitution — Grotesque campaign story about Washington and Adams — Persistence of political canard against Levin Powell — Amazing statements about the Society of the Cincinnati: Ædanus Burke's pamphlet; Mirabeau's pamphlet; Jefferson's

CONTENTS

denunciation — Marshall and his father members of the Cincinnati — Effect upon him of the extravagant abuse of this patriotic order — Popular desire for general division of property and repudiation of debts — Madison's bitter comment — Jay on popular greed and "impatience of government" — Paper money — Popular idea of money — Shays's Rebellion — Marshall's analysis of its objects — Knox's report of it — Madison comes to the conclusion that "the bulk of mankind" are incapable of dealing with weighty subjects — Washington in despair — He declares mankind unfit for their own government — Marshall also fears that "man is incapable of governing himself" — Jefferson in Paris — Effect on his mind of conditions in France — His description of the French people — Jefferson applauds Shays's Rebellion: "The tree of liberty must be refreshed by the blood of patriots and tyrants" — Influence of French philosophy on Jefferson — The impotence of Congress under the Confederation — Dishonorable conduct of the States — Leading men ascribe evil conditions to the people themselves — Views of Washington, Jay, and Madison — State Sovereignty the shield of turmoil and baseness — Efforts of commercial and financial interests produce the Constitution — Madison wants a National Government with power of veto on all State laws "whatsoever" — Jefferson thinks the Articles of Confederation "a wonderfully perfect instrument" — He opposes a "strong government" — Is apprehensive of the Constitution — Thinks destruction of credit a good thing — Wishes America "to stand with respect to Europe precisely on the footing of China" — The line of cleavage regarding the Constitution — Marshall for the Constitution.

IX. THE STRUGGLE FOR RATIFICATION . . . 319

The historic Convention of 1788 assembles — Richmond at that time — General ignorance of the Constitution — Even most members of the Convention poorly informed — Vague popular idea of Constitution as something foreign, powerful, and forbidding — People in Virginia strongly opposed to it — The Virginia debate to be the greatest ever held over the Constitution — The revolutionary character of the Constitution: would not have been framed if the people had known of the purposes of the Federal Convention at Philadelphia: "A child of fortune" — Ratification hurried — Pennsylvania Convention: hastily called, physical violence, small number of people vote at election of members to Pennsylvania Convention — People's ignorance of the Constitution — Charges of the opposition — "The humble address of the *low born*" — Debate in Pennsylvania Convention — Able "Address of Minority" — Nationalism of the Constitution the principal objection — Letters of "Centinel": the Constitution "a spurious brat" — Attack on Robert Morris — Constitutionalist replies: "Sowers of sedition" — Madison alarmed — The struggle in

CONTENTS

Massachusetts — Conciliatory tactics of Constitutionalists — Upper classes for Constitution — Common people generally opposed — Many towns refuse to send delegates to the Convention — Contemporary descriptions of the elections — High ability and character of Constitutionalist members — Self-confessed ignorance and incapacity of opposition: Madison writes that there is "Scarcely a man of respectability among them" — Their pathetic fight against the Constitution — Examples of their arguments — The bargain with Hancock secures enough votes to ratify — The slender majority: one hundred and sixty-eight vote against ratification — Methods of Constitutionalists after ratification — Widgery's amusing account: hogsheads of rum — Gerry's lament — Bribery charged — New Hampshire almost rejects Constitution — Convention adjourned to prevent defeat — "Little information among the people," but most "men of property and abilities" for Constitution — Constitution receives no deliberate consideration until debated in the Virginia Convention — Notable ability of the leaders of both sides in the Virginia contest.

X. IN THE GREAT CONVENTION 357

Virginia the deciding State — Anxiety of Constitutionalists in other States — Hamilton writes Madison: "No hope unless Virginia ratifies" — Economic and political importance of Virginia — Extreme effort of both sides to elect members to the Convention — Preëlection methods of the Constitutionalists — They capture Randolph — Marshall elected from opposition constituency — Preëlection methods of Anti-Constitutionalists — The Convention meets — Neither side sure of a majority — Perfect discipline and astute Convention tactics of the Constitutionalists — They secure the two powerful offices of the Convention — The opposition have no plan of action — Description of George Mason — His grave error in parliamentary tactics — Constitutionalists take advantage of it: the Constitution to be debated clause by clause — Analysis of the opposing forces: an economic class struggle, Nationalism against provincialism — Henry tries to remedy Mason's mistake — Pendleton speaks and the debate begins — Nicholas speaks — His character and personal appearance — Patrick Henry secures the floor — Description of Henry — He attacks the Constitution: why "*we the people* instead of *we* the States"? Randolph replies — His manner and appearance — His support of the Constitution surprises the opposition — His speech — His about-face saves the Constitution — The Clinton letter: if Randolph discloses it the Anti-Constitutionalists will win — He keeps it from knowledge of the Convention — Decisive importance of Randolph's action — His change ascribed to improper motives — Mason answers Randolph and again makes tactical error — Madison fails to speak — Description of Edmund Pendleton — He addresses the Convention: "the war is between government and licentiousness" — "Light Horse Harry" Lee — The ermine and the sword — Henry secures the floor — His great speech: the Constitution "a revolution as radical as that which separated us from Great Britain" — The proposed National Government something foreign and monstrous — "This government is not a Virginian but an American government" — Marshall studies the arguments and methods of the debaters — Randolph answers Henry: "I am a child of the Revolution" — His error concerning Josiah Philips — His speech ineffective — Description of James Madison — He makes the first of his powerful expositions of the Constitution, but has little or no effect on the votes of the members — Speech of youthful Francis Corbin — Randolph's futile effort — Madison makes the second of his masterful speeches — Henry replies — His wonderful art — He attacks Randolph for his apostasy — He closes the first week's debate with the Convention under his spell.

XI. THE SUPREME DEBATE 401

Political managers from other States appear — Gouverneur Morris and Robert Morris for the Constitutionalists and Eleazer Oswald for the opposition — Morris's letter: "depredations on my purse" — Grayson's letter: "our affairs suspended by a thread" — Opening second week of the debate — The New Academy crowded — Henry resumes his speech — Appeals to the Kentucky members, denounces secrecy of Federal Convention, attacks Nationalism — Lee criticizes lobbying "out of doors" and rebukes Henry — Randolph attacks Henry: "If our friendship must fall, *let it fall like Lucifer, never to rise again*" — Randolph challenges Henry: a duel narrowly averted — Personal appearance of James Monroe — He speaks for the Revolutionary soldiers against the Constitution and makes no impression — Marshall put forward by the Constitutionalists — Description of him: badly dressed, poetic-looking, "habits convivial almost to excess" — Best-liked man in the Convention; considered an orator — Marshall's speech: Constitutionalists the "firm friends of liberty"; "we, sir, idolize democracy"; only a National Government can promote the general welfare — Marshall's argument his first recorded expression on the Constitution — Most of speech on necessity of providing against war and inspired by his military experience — Description of Benjamin Harrison — Mason attacks power of National taxation and sneers at the "well-born" — He denounces Randolph — Lee answers with a show of anger — William Grayson secures the floor — His character, attainments, and appearance — His learned and witty speech: "We are too young to know what we are good for" — Pendleton answers: "government necessary to protect liberty" — Madison makes his fourth great argument — Henry replies: "the tyranny of Philadelphia [National Government] may be like the tyranny of George III, a horrid, wretched, dreadful picture";

CONTENTS

Henry's vision of the West — Tremendous effect on the Convention — Letter of Gouverneur Morris to Hamilton describing the Convention — Madison's report to Hamilton and to Washington: "the business is in the most ticklish state that can be imagined" — Marshall speaks again — Military speech: "*United we are strong, divided we fall*" — Grayson answers Marshall — Mason and Henry refer to "vast speculations": "we may be taxed for centuries to give advantage to rapacious speculators" — Grayson's letter to Dane — The advantage with the Anti-Constitutionalists at the end of the second week.

XII. THE STRATEGY OF VICTORY 444

The climax of the fight — The Judiciary the weakest point for the Constitutionalists — Reasons for this — Especially careful plans of the Constitutionalists for this part of the debate — Pendleton expounds the Judiciary clause — Mason attacks it — His charge as to secret purpose of many Constitutionalists — His extreme courtesy causes him again to make a tactical error — He refers to the Fairfax grant — A clever appeal to members from the Northern Neck — Madison's distinguished address — Henry answers Madison — His thrilling speech: "Old as I am, it is probable I may yet have the appellation of *rebel*. As to this government [the Constitution] I despise and abhor it" — Marshall takes the floor — Selected by the Constitutionalists to make the principal argument for the Judiciary clause — His speech prepared — The National Judiciary "will benefit collective Society"; National Courts will be as fair as State Courts; independence of judges necessary; if Congress should pass an unconstitutional law the National Courts "*would declare it void*"; they alone the only "protection from an infringement of the Constitution"; State courts "crowded with suits which the life of man will not see determined"; National Courts needed to relieve this congestion; under the Constitution, States cannot be sued in National Courts; the Constitution does not exclude trial by jury: "Does the word *court* only mean the judges?"; comparison with the Judiciary establishment of Virginia; reply to Mason's argument on the Fairfax title; "what security have you for justice? The independence of your Judiciary!" — Marshall's speech unconnected and discursive, but the Constitutionalists rest their case upon it — Madison's report to Hamilton: "If we can weather the storm against the Judiciary I shall hold the danger to be pretty well over" — Anti-Constitutionalists try to prolong debate until meeting of Legislature which is strongly against the Constitution — Secession threatened — Madison's letter to Hamilton — Contest so close that "ordinary casualties may vary the result" — Henry answers Marshall — His compliment to the young lawyer — His reference to the Indians arouses Colonel Stephen who harshly assails Henry — Nicholas insults Henry, who demands an explanation — Debate draws to a close — Mason intimates forcible resistance to the Constitution — Lee rebukes him — The Constitutionalists forestall Henry and offer amendments — Henry's last speech: "Nine-tenths of the people" against the Constitution; Henry's vision of the future; a sudden and terrific storm aids his dramatic climax; members and spectators in awe — The Legislature convenes — Quick, resolute action of the Constitutionalists — Henry admits defeat — The Virginia amendments — Absurdity of some of them — Necessary to secure ratification — Marshall on the committee to report amendments — Constitutionalists win by a majority of only ten — Of these, two vote against their instructions and eight vote against the well-known desires of their constituents — The Clinton letter at last disclosed — Mason's wrath — Henry prevents Anti-Constitutionalists from talking measures to resist the new National Government — Washington's account: "Impossible for anybody not on the spot to conceive what the delicacy and danger of our situation have been."

APPENDIX 481

   I. WILL OF THOMAS MARSHALL, "CARPENTER" . . 483

  II. WILL OF JOHN MARSHALL "OF THE FOREST" . . 485

 III. DEED OF WILLIAM MARSHALL TO JOHN MARSHALL "OF THE FOREST" 487

 IV. MEMORIAL OF THOMAS MARSHALL FOR MILITARY EMOLUMENTS 489

WORKS CITED IN THIS VOLUME 491

ILLUSTRATIONS

JOHN MARSHALL AT 43 . . . . . *Colored Frontispiece*

    From a miniature painted on ivory by an unknown artist. It was executed in Paris in 1797–98, when Marshall was there on the X. Y. Z. Mission. It is now in the possession of Miss Emily Harvie, of Richmond, Virginia. It is the only portrait in existence of Marshall at this period of his life and faithfully portrays him as he was at the time of his intellectual duel with Talleyrand.

COLONEL WILLIAM RANDOLPH 10

    From a copy in the possession of Mr. Douglas H. Thomas, of Baltimore, after the original portrait in the possession of Mr. Edward C. Mayo, of Richmond. The painter of the original is unknown. It was painted about 1673 and has passed down through successive generations of the family. Mr. Thomas's copy is a faithful one, and has been used for reproduction here because the original is not sufficiently clear and distinct for the purpose.

MARY ISHAM RANDOLPH, WIFE OF COLONEL WILLIAM RANDOLPH 10

    From a copy in the possession of Mr. Douglas H. Thomas, of Baltimore, after the original in the possession of Miss Anne Mortimer Minor. The original portrait was painted about 1673 by an unknown artist. It is incapable of satisfactory reproduction.

COLONEL THOMAS MARSHALL, THE FATHER OF JOHN MARSHALL 14

    From a portrait in the possession of Charles Edward Marshall, of Glen Mary, Kentucky. This is the only portrait or likeness of any kind in existence of John Marshall's father. It was painted at some time between 1790 and 1800 and was inherited by Charles Edward Marshall from his parents, Charles Edward and Judith Langhorne Marshall. The name of the painter of this unusual portrait is not known.

MARY RANDOLPH (KEITH) MARSHALL, WIFE OF THOMAS MARSHALL AND MOTHER OF JOHN MARSHALL 18

    From a portrait in the possession of Miss Sallie Marshall, of Leeds, Virginia. The portrait was painted at some time between 1790 and 1800, but the painter's name is unknown. The reproduction is from a photograph furnished by Mr. Douglas H. Thomas.

ILLUSTRATIONS

"THE HOLLOW" 36

> The Blue Ridge home of the Marshall family where John Marshall lived from early childhood to his eighteenth year. The house is situated on a farm at Markham, Va. From a photograph.

OAK HILL 56

> From a water-color in the possession of Mr. Thomas Marshall Smith, of Baltimore. The small house at the rear of the right of the main building was the original dwelling, built by John Marshall's father in 1773. The Marshall family lived here until after the Revolution. The large building was added nearly forty years afterward by Thomas Marshall, son of the Chief Justice. The name of the painter is unknown.

OAK HILL 64

> This is the original house, built in 1773 and carefully kept in repair. The brick pavement is a modern improvement. From a photograph.

FACSIMILE OF THE LAST PAGE OF A LETTER FROM JOHN MARSHALL TO HIS WIFE, DESCRIBING THEIR COURTSHIP 152

> This letter was written at Washington, February 23, 1824, forty-one years after their marriage. No part of it has ever before been published.

MARY AMBLER MARSHALL, THE WIFE OF JOHN MARSHALL 168

> A crayon drawing from the original painting now in the possession of Mrs. Carroll, a granddaughter of John Marshall, living at Leeds Manor, Va. This is the only painting of Mrs. Marshall in existence and the name of the artist is unknown.

RICHMOND IN 1800 184

> From a painting in the rooms of the Virginia Historical Society.

FACSIMILE OF A PAGE OF MARSHALL'S ACCOUNT BOOK, MAY, 1787 198

> In this book Marshall kept his accounts of receipts and expenses for twelve years after his marriage in 1783. In the first part of it he also recorded his notes of law lectures during his brief attendance at William and Mary College. The original volume is owned by Mrs. John K. Mason, of Richmond.

ILLUSTRATIONS

FACSIMILES OF SIGNATURES OF JOHN MARSHALL AT TWENTY-NINE AND FORTY-TWO AND OF THOMAS MARSHALL 210

These signatures are remarkable as showing the extreme dissimilarity between the signature of Marshall as a member of the Council of State before he was thirty and his signature in his mature manhood, and also as showing the basic similarity between the signatures of Marshall and his father. The signature of Marshall as a member of the Council of State in 1784 is from the original minutes of the Council in the Archives of the Virginia State Library. His 1797 signature is from a letter to his wife, the original of which is in the possession of Miss Emily Harvie, of Richmond. The signature of Thomas Marshall is from the original roster of the officers of his regiment in the Manuscripts Division of the Library of Congress.

FACSIMILE OF THE FIRST PAGE OF A LETTER FROM MARSHALL TO JAMES MONROE, APRIL 17, 1784 . 212

From the original in the Manuscript Division of the New York Public Library. This letter has never before been published. It is extremely important in that it corrects extravagant errors concerning Marshall's resignation from the Council of State and his reëlection to the legislature.

JOHN MARSHALL 294

From a profile drawing by Charles Balthazar Julien Fèvre de Saint Mémin, in the possession of Miss Emily Harvey of Richmond, Va., a granddaughter of John Marshall. Autograph from manuscript collection in the Library of the Boston Athenæum.

GEORGE WYTHE 368

From an engraving by J. B. Longacre after a portrait by an unknown painter in the possession of the Virginia State Library. George Wythe was Professor of Law at William and Mary College during Marshall's brief attendance.

JOHN MARSHALL 420

From a painting by J. B. Martin in the Robe Room of the Supreme Court of the United States, Washington, D.C.

PATRICK HENRY 470

From a copy (in the possession of the Westmoreland Club, of Richmond) of the portrait by Thomas Sully. Sully, who never saw Patrick Henry himself, painted the portrait from a miniature on ivory done by a French artist in Richmond about 1792. John Marshall, under date of December 30, 1816, attested its excellence as follows: "I have been shown a painting of the late Mr. Henry, painted by Mr. Sully, now in possession of Mr. Webster, which I think a good likeness."

LIST OF ABBREVIATED TITLES MOST FREQUENTLY CITED

All references here are to the List of Authorities at the end of this volume.

Beard: *Econ. I. C. See* Beard, Charles A. Economic Interpretation of the Constitution of the United States.

Beard: *Econ. O. J. D. See* Beard, Charles A. Economic Origins of Jeffersonian Democracy.

Bruce: *Econ. See* Bruce, Philip Alexander. Economic History of Virginia in the Seventeeth Century.

Bruce: *Inst. See* Bruce, Philip Alexander. Institutional History of Virginia in the Seventeeth Century.

Cor. Rev.: Sparks. *See* Sparks, Jared. Correspondence of the Revolution.

Eckenrode: *R. V. See* Eckenrode, H. J. The Revolution in Virginia.

Eckenrode: *S. of C. and S. See* Eckenrode, H. J. Separation of Church and State in Virginia.

Jefferson's *Writings:* Washington. *See* Jefferson, Thomas. Writings. Edited by H. A. Washington.

Monroe's *Writings:* Hamilton. *See* Monroe, James. Writings. Edited by Stanislaus Murray Hamilton.

Old Family Letters. See Adams, John. Old Family Letters. Edited by Alexander Biddle.

Wertenbaker: *P. and P. See* Wertenbaker, Thomas J. Patrician and Plebeian in Virginia; or the Origin and Development of the Social Classes of the Old Dominion.

Wertenbaker: *V. U. S. See* Wertenbaker, Thomas J. Virginia Under the Stuarts, 1607–1688.

Works: Adams. *See* Adams, John. Works. Edited by Charles Francis Adams.

Works: Ford. *See* Jefferson, Thomas. Works. Federal Edition. Edited by Paul Leicester Ford.

Works: Hamilton. *See* Hamilton, Alexander. Works. Edited by John C. Hamilton.

Works: Lodge. *See* Hamilton, Alexander. Works. Federal Edition. Edited by Henry Cabot Lodge.

Writings: Conway. *See* Paine, Thomas. Writings. Edited by Moncure Daniel Conway.

Writings: Ford. *See* Washington, George. Writings. Edited by Worthington Chauncey Ford.

Writings: Hunt. *See* Madison, James. Writings. Edited by Gaillard Hunt.

Writings: Smyth. *See* Franklin, Benjamin. Writings. Edited by Albert Henry Smyth.

Writings: Sparks. *See* Washington, George. Writings. Edited by Jared Sparks.

THE LIFE OF JOHN MARSHALL

THE LIFE OF JOHN MARSHALL

CHAPTER I

ANCESTRY AND ENVIRONMENT

Often do the spirits of great events stride on before the events and in to-day already walks to-morrow. (Schiller.)

I was born an American; I will live an American; I shall die an American. (Webster.)

"THE British are beaten! The British are beaten!" From cabin to cabin, from settlement to settlement crept, through the slow distances, this report of terror. The astounding news that Braddock was defeated finally reached the big plantations on the tidewater, and then spread dismay and astonishment throughout the colonies.

The painted warriors and the uniformed soldiers of the French-Indian alliance had been growing bolder and bolder, their ravages ever more daring and bloody.[1] Already the fear of them had checked the thin wave of pioneer advance; and it seemed to the settlers that their hereditary enemies from across the water might succeed in confining British dominion in America to the narrow strip between the ocean and the mountains. For the royal colonial authorities had not been able to cope with their foes.[2]

[1] For instance, the Indians massacred nine families in Frederick County, just over the Blue Ridge from Fauquier, in June, 1755. (*Pennsylvania Journal and Weekly Advertiser*, July 24, 1755.)

[2] Marshall, i, 12–13; Campbell, 469–71. "The Colonial contingents were not nearly sufficient either in quantity or quality." (Wood, 40.)

But there was always the reserve power of Great Britain to defend her possessions. If only the home Government would send an army of British veterans, the colonists felt that, as a matter of course, the French and Indians would be routed, the immigrants made safe, and the way cleared for their ever-swelling thousands to take up and people the lands beyond the Alleghanies.

So when at last, in 1755, the redoubtable Braddock and his red-coated regiments landed in Virginia, they were hailed as deliverers. There would be an end, everybody said, to the reign of terror which the atrocities of the French and Indians had created all along the border. For were not the British grenadiers invincible? Was not Edward Braddock an experienced commander, whose bravery was the toast of his fellow officers?[1] So the colonists had been told, and so they believed.

They forgave the rudeness of their British champions; and Braddock marched away into the wilderness carrying with him the unquestioning confidence of the people.[2] It was hardly thought necessary for any Virginia fighting men to accompany him; and that haughty, passionate young Virginia soldier, George Washington (then only twenty-three years of age, but already the chief military figure of the Old Dominion), and his Virginia rangers were invited to

[1] Braddock had won promotion solely by gallantry in the famous Coldstream Guards, the model and pride of the British army, at a time when a lieutenant-colonelcy in that crack regiment sold for £5000 sterling. (Lowdermilk, 97.)

[2] "The British troops had been looked upon as invincible, and preparations had been made in Philadelphia for the celebration of Braddock's anticipated victory." (*Ib.*, 186.)

ANCESTRY AND ENVIRONMENT

accompany Braddock more because they knew the country better than for any real aid in battle that was expected of them. "I have been importuned," testifies Washington, "to make this campaign by General Braddock, . . . conceiving . . . that the . . . knowledge I have . . . of the country, Indians, &c. . . . might be useful to him." [1]

So through the ancient and unbroken forests Braddock made his slow and painful way.[2] Weeks passed; then months.[3] But there was no impatience, because everybody knew what would happen when his scarlet columns should finally meet and throw themselves upon the enemy. Yet this meeting, when it came, proved to be one of the lesser tragedies of history, and had a deep and fateful effect upon American public opinion and upon the life and future of the American people.[4]

Time has not dulled the vivid picture of that disaster. The golden sunshine of that July day; the pleasant murmur of the waters of the Monongahela; the silent and somber forests; the steady tramp,

[1] Washington to Robinson, April 20, 1755; *Writings:* Ford, i, 147.
[2] The "wild desert country lying between fort Cumberland and fort Frederick [now the cities of Cumberland and Frederick in Maryland], the most common track of the Indians, in making their incursions into Virginia." (Address in the Maryland House of Delegates, 1757, as quoted by Lowdermilk, 229–30.) Cumberland was "about 56 miles beyond our [Maryland] settlements." (*Ib.*) Cumberland "is far remote from any of our inhabitants." (Washington to Dinwiddie, Sept. 23, 1756; *Writings:* Ford, i, 346.) "Will's Creek was on the very outskirts of civilization. The country beyond was an unbroken and almost pathless wilderness." (Lowdermilk, 50.)
[3] It took Braddock three weeks to march from Alexandria to Cumberland. He was two months and nineteen days on the way from Alexandria to the place of his defeat. (*Ib.*, 138.)
[4] "All America watched his [Braddock's] advance." (Wood, 61.)

tramp of the British to the inspiriting music of their regimental bands playing the martial airs of England; the bright uniforms of the advancing columns giving to the background of stream and forest a touch of splendor; and then the ambush and surprise; the war-whoops of savage foes that could not be seen; the hail of invisible death, no pellet of which went astray; the pathetic volleys which the doomed British troops fired at hidden antagonists; the panic; the rout; the pursuit; the slaughter; the crushing, humiliating defeat! [1]

Most of the British officers were killed or wounded as they vainly tried to halt the stampede.[2] Braddock himself received a mortal hurt.[3] Raging with battle lust, furious at what he felt was the stupidity and cowardice of the British regulars,[4] the youthful Washington rode among the fear-frenzied Englishmen, striving to save the day. Two horses were shot under him. Four bullets rent his uniform.[5] But, crazed with fright, the Royal soldiers were beyond human control.

Only the Virginia rangers kept their heads and their courage. Obeying the shouted orders of their young commander, they threw themselves between the terror-stricken British and the savage victors;

[1] For best accounts of Braddock's defeat see Bradley, 75-107; Lowdermilk, 156-63; and Marshall, i, 7-10.

[2] "Of one hundred and sixty officers, only six escaped." (Lowdermilk, footnote to 175.)

[3] Braddock had five horses killed under him. (*Ib.*, 161.)

[4] "The dastardly behavior of the Regular [British] troops," who "broke and ran as sheep before hounds." (Washington to Dinwiddie, July 18, 1755; *Writings:* Ford, i, 173-74.)

[5] Washington to John A. Washington, July 18, 1755. (*Ib.*, 176.)

ANCESTRY AND ENVIRONMENT 5

and, fighting behind trees and rocks, were an ever-moving rampart of fire that saved the flying remnants of the English troops. But for Washington and his rangers, Braddock's whole force would have been annihilated.[1] Colonel Dunbar and his fifteen hundred British regulars, who had been left a short distance behind as a reserve, made off to Philadelphia as fast as their panic-winged feet could carry them.[2]

So everywhere went up the cry, "The British are beaten!" At first rumor had it that the whole force was destroyed, and that Washington had been killed in action.[3] But soon another word followed hard upon this error — the word that the boyish Virginia captain and his rangers had fought with coolness, skill, and courage; that they alone had prevented the extinction of the British regulars; that they alone had come out of the conflict with honor and glory.

Thus it was that the American colonists suddenly came to think that they themselves must be their own defenders. It was a revelation, all the more impressive because it was so abrupt, unexpected, and dramatic, that the red-coated professional soldiers were not the unconquerable warriors the colonists

[1] "The Virginia companies behaved like men and died like soldiers ... of three companies ... scarce thirty were left alive." (Washington to Dinwiddie, July 18, 1755; *Writings:* Ford, i, 173-74.)

[2] Lowdermilk, 182-85; and see Washington's *Writings:* Ford, i, footnote to 175. For account of battle and rout see Washington's letters to Dinwiddie, *ib.*, 173-76; to John A. Washington, July 18, 1755, *ib.*; to Robert Jackson, Aug. 2, 1755, *ib.*, 177-78; also see Campbell, 472-81. For French account see Hart, ii, 365-67; also, Sargent: *History of Braddock's Expedition.*

[3] Washington to John A. Washington, July 18, 1755; *Writings:* Ford, i, 175.

had been told that they were.[1] From colonial "mansion" to log cabin, from the provincial "capitals" to the mean and exposed frontier settlements, Braddock's defeat sowed the seed of the idea that Americans must depend upon themselves.[2]

As Bacon's Rebellion at Jamestown, exactly one hundred years before Independence was declared at Philadelphia, was the beginning of the American Revolution in its first clear expression of popular rights,[3] so Braddock's defeat was the inception of that same epoch in its lesson of American military self-dependence.[4] Down to Concord and Lexington, Great Bridge and Bunker Hill, the overthrow of the King's troops on the Monongahela in 1755 was a theme of common talk among men, a household legend on which American mothers brought up their children.[5]

Close upon the heels of this epoch-making event, John Marshall came into the world. He was born in

[1] "The Defeat of Braddock was totally unlooked for, and it excited the most painful surprise." (Lowdermilk, 186.)

[2] "After Braddock's defeat, the Colonists jumped to the conclusion that all regulars were useless." (Wood, 40.)

[3] See Stanard: *Story of Bacon's Rebellion.* Bacon's Rebellion deserves the careful study of all who would understand the beginnings of the democratic movement in America. Mrs. Stanard's study is the best brief account of this popular uprising. See also Wertenbaker: *V. U. S.*, chaps. 5 and 6.

[4] "The news [of Braddock's defeat] gave a far more terrible blow to the reputation of the regulars than to the British cause [against the French] itself." (Wood, 61.)

[5] "From that time [Braddock's defeat] forward the Colonists had a much less exalted opinion of the valor of the royal troops." (Lowdermilk, 186.) The fact that the colonists themselves had been negligent and incompetent in resisting the French or even the Indians did not weaken their newborn faith in their own prowess and their distrust of British power.

ANCESTRY AND ENVIRONMENT 7

a little log cabin in the southern part of what now is Fauquier County, Virginia (then a part of Prince William), on September 24, 1755,[1] eleven weeks after Braddock's defeat. The Marshall cabin stood about a mile and a half from a cluster of a dozen similar log structures built by a handful of German families whom Governor Spotswood had brought over to work his mines. This little settlement was known as Germantown, and was practically on the frontier.[2]

Thomas Marshall, the father of John Marshall, was a close friend of Washington, whom he ardently admired. They were born in the same county, and their acquaintance had begun, apparently, in their boyhood.[3] Also, as will presently appear, Thomas Marshall had for about three years been the companion of Washington, when acting as his assistant in surveying the western part of the Fairfax estate.[4] From that time forward his attachment to Washington amounted to devotion.[5]

Also, he was, like Washington, a fighting man.[6] It seems strange, therefore, that he did not accom-

[1] *Autobiography.*
[2] Campbell, 494. "It is remarkable," says Campbell, "that as late as the year 1756, when the colony was a century and a half old, the Blue Ridge of mountains was virtually the western boundary of Virginia." And see Marshall, i, 15; also, *New York Review* (1838), iii, 330. For frontier settlements, see the admirable map prepared by Marion F. Lansing and reproduced in Channing, ii.
[3] Humphrey Marshall, i, 344-45. Also Binney, in Dillon, iii, 283.
[4] See *infra*, chap. II.
[5] Humphrey Marshall, i, 344-45.
[6] He was one of a company of militia cavalry the following year, (Journal, H.B. (1756), 378); and he was commissioned as ensign Aug. 27, 1761. (Crozier: *Virginia Colonial Militia*, 96.) And see *infra*, chaps. III and IV.

pany his hero in the Braddock expedition. There is, indeed, a legend that he did go part of the way.[1] But this, like so many stories concerning him, is untrue.[2] The careful roster, made by Washington of those under his command,[3] does not contain the name of Thomas Marshall either as officer or private. Because of their intimate association it is certain that Washington would not have overlooked him if he had been a member of that historic body of men.

So, while the father of John Marshall was not with his friend and leader at Braddock's defeat, no man watched that expedition with more care, awaited its outcome with keener anxiety, or was more affected by the news, than Thomas Marshall. Beneath no rooftree in all the colonies, except, perhaps, that of Washington's brother, could this capital event have made a deeper impression than in the tiny log house in the forests of Prince William County, where John Marshall, a few weeks afterwards, first saw the light of day.

Wars and rumors of wars, ever threatening danger, and stern, strong, quiet preparation to meet whatever befell — these made up the moral and intellectual atmosphere that surrounded the Marshall cabin before and after the coming of Thomas and Mary

[1] Paxton, 20.
[2] A copy of a letter (MS.) to Thomas Marshall from his sister Elizabeth Marshall Martin, dated June 15, 1755, referring to the Braddock expedition, shows that he was at home at this time. Furthermore, a man of the quality of Thomas Marshall would not have left his young wife alone in their backwoods cabin at a time so near the birth of their first child, when there was an overabundance of men eager to accompany Braddock.
[3] Washington MSS., Lib. Cong.

Marshall's first son. The earliest stories told this child of the frontier[1] must have been those of daring and sacrifice and the prevailing that comes of them.

Almost from the home-made cradle John Marshall was taught the idea of American solidarity. Braddock's defeat, the most dramatic military event before the Revolution,[2] was, as we have seen, the theme of fireside talk; and from this grew, in time, the conviction that Americans, if united,[3] could not only protect their homes from the savages and the French, but defeat, if need be, the British themselves.[4] So thought the Marshalls, father and mother; and so they taught their children, as subsequent events show.

It was a remarkable parentage that produced this child who in manhood was to become the master-builder of American Nationality. Curiously enough, it was exactly the same mingling of human elements that gave to the country that great apostle of the rights of man, Thomas Jefferson. Indeed, Jefferson's mother and Marshall's grandmother were first cousins. The mother of Thomas Jefferson was Jane

---

[1] Simon Kenton, the Indian fighter, was born in the same county in the same year as John Marshall. (M'Clung: *Sketches of Western Adventure*, 93.)

[2] Neither the siege of Louisburg nor the capture of Quebec took such hold on the public imagination as the British disaster on the Monongahela. Also, the colonists felt, though unjustly, that they were entitled to as much credit for the two former events as the British.

[3] The idea of unity had already germinated. The year before, Franklin offered his plan of concerted colonial action to the Albany conference. (*Writings:* Smyth, i, 387.)

[4] Wood, 38-42.

Randolph, daughter of Isham Randolph of Turkey Island; and the mother of John Marshall was Mary Randolph Keith, the daughter of Mary Isham Randolph, whose father was Thomas Randolph of Tuckahoe, the brother of Jefferson's maternal grandfather.

Thus, Thomas Jefferson was the great-grandson and John Marshall the great-great-grandson of William Randolph and Mary Isham. Perhaps no other couple in American history is so remarkable for the number of distinguished descendants. Not only were they the ancestors of Thomas Jefferson and John Marshall, but also of "Light Horse Harry" Lee, of Revolutionary fame, Edmund Randolph, Washington's first Attorney-General, John Randolph of Roanoke, George Randolph, Secretary of War under the Confederate Government, and General Robert E. Lee, the great Southern military leader of the Civil War.[1]

The Virginia Randolphs were one of the families of that proud colony who were of undoubted gentle descent, their line running clear and unbroken at least as far back as 1550. The Ishams were a somewhat older family, their lineage being well established to 1424. While knighthood was conferred upon one ancestor of Mary Isham, the Randolph and Isham families were of the same social stratum, both being of the English gentry.[2] The

[1] For these genealogies see Slaughter: *Bristol Parish*, 212; Lee: *Lee of Virginia*, 406 *et seq.*; Randall, i, 6-9; Tucker, i, 26. See Meade, i, footnote to 138-39, for other descendants of William Randolph and Mary Isham.

[2] *Va. Mag. Hist. and Biog.*, iii, 261; xviii, 86-87.

COLONEL WILLIAM RANDOLPH

MARY ISHAM RANDOLPH

Virginia Randolphs were brilliant in mind, physically courageous, commanding in character, generally handsome in person, yet often as erratic as they were gifted.

When the gentle Randolph-Isham blood mingled with the sturdier currents of the common people, the result was a human product stronger, steadier, and abler than either. So, when Jane Randolph became the wife of Peter Jefferson, a man from the grass roots, the result was Thomas Jefferson. The union of a daughter of Mary Randolph with Thomas Marshall, a man of the soil and forests, produced John Marshall.[1]

Physically and mentally, Peter Jefferson and Thomas Marshall were much alike. Both were powerful men of great stature. Both were endowed with rare intellectuality.[2] Both were hard-working, provident, and fearless. Even their occupations were the same: both were land surveyors. The chief difference between them was that, whereas Peter Jefferson appears to have been a hearty and con-

---

[1] The curious sameness in the ancestry of Marshall and Jefferson is found also in the surroundings of their birth. Both were born in log cabins in the backwoods. Peter Jefferson, father of Thomas, "was the third or fourth white settler within the space of several miles" of his cabin home, which he built "in a small clearing in the dense and primeval forest." (Randall, i, 11.) Here Jefferson was born, April 2, 1743, a little more than twelve years before John Marshall came into the world, under like conditions and from similar parents.

Peter Jefferson was, however, remotely connected by descent, on his mother's side, with men who had been burgesses. His maternal grandfather, Peter Field, was a burgess, and his maternal great-grandfather, Henry Soane, was Speaker of the House of Burgesses. But both Peter Jefferson and Thomas Marshall were "of the people" as distinguished from the gentry.

[2] Morse, 3; and Story, in Dillon, iii, 330.

vivial person,[1] Thomas Marshall seems to have been self-contained though adventurous, and of rather austere habits. Each became the leading man of his county[2] and both were chosen members of the House of Burgesses.[3]

On the paternal side, it is impossible to trace the origin of either Peter Jefferson[4] or Thomas Marshall farther back than their respective great-grandfathers, without floundering, unavailingly, in genealogical quicksands.

Thomas Marshall was the son of a very small planter in Westmoreland County, Virginia. October 23, 1727, three years before Thomas was born, his father, John Marshall "of the forest," acquired by deed, from William Marshall of King and Queen County, two hundred acres of poor, low, marshy land located on Appomattox Creek.[5] Little as the value of land in Virginia then was, and continued to be for three quarters of a century afterwards,[6] this particu-

[1] Randall, i, 7. Peter Jefferson "purchased" four hundred acres of land from his "bosom friend," William Randolph, the consideration as set forth in the deed being, "Henry Weatherbourne's biggest bowl of arrack punch"! (*Ib.*)

[2] Peter Jefferson was County Lieutenant of Albemarle. (*Va. Mag. Hist. and Biog.*, xxiii, 173–75.) Thomas Marshall was Sheriff of Fauquier.

[3] Randall, i, 12–13; and see *infra*, chap. II.   [4] Tucker, i, 26.

[5] Records of Westmoreland County, Deeds and Wills, viii, 1, 276.

[6] *Ib.* Seventy years later La Rochefoucauld found land adjoining Norfolk heavily covered with valuable timber, close to the water and convenient for shipment, worth only from six to seven dollars an acre. (La Rochefoucauld, iii, 25.) Virginia sold excellent public land for two cents an acre three quarters of a century after this deed to John Marshall "of the forest." (Ambler, 44; and see Turner, Wis. Hist. Soc., 1908, 201.) This same land which William Marshall deeded to John Marshall nearly two hundred years ago is now valued at only from ten to twenty dollars an acre. (Letter of Albert Stuart,

ANCESTRY AND ENVIRONMENT

lar tract seems to have been of an especially inferior quality. The deed states that it is a part of twelve hundred acres which had been granted to "Jno. Washington & Thos. Pope, gents . . . & by them lost for want of seating."

Here John Marshall "of the forest" [1] lived until his death in 1752, and here on April 2, 1730, Thomas Marshall was born. During the quarter of a century that this John Marshall remained on his little farm, he had become possessed of several slaves, mostly, perhaps, by natural increase. By his will he bequeaths to his ten children and to his wife six negro men and women, ten negro boys and girls, and two negro children. In addition to "one negro fellow named Joe and one negro woman named Cate" he gives to his wife "one Gray mair named beauty and side saddle also six hogs also I leave her the use of my land During her widowhood, and afterwards to fall to my son Thomas Marshall and his heirs forever." [2] One year later the widow, Elizabeth Marshall, deeded half of this two hundred acres to her son Thomas Marshall.[3]

Deputy Clerk of Westmoreland County, to author, Aug. 26, 1913.) In 1730 it was probably worth one dollar per acre.

[1] A term generally used by the richer people in referring to those of poorer condition who lived in the woods, especially those whose abodes were some distance from the river. (Statement of W. G. Stanard, Secretary of the Virginia Historical Society and Dr. H. J. Eckenrode of Richmond College, and formerly Archivist of the Virginia State Library.) There were, however, Virginia estates called "The Forest." For example, Jefferson's father-in-law, John Wayles, a wealthy man, lived in "The Forest."

[2] Will of John Marshall "of the forest," made April 1, 1752, probated May 26, 1752, and recorded June 22, 1752; Records of Westmoreland County, Deeds and Wills, xi, 419 *et seq.* (Appendix II.)

[3] *Ib.*, 421.

Such was the environment of Thomas Marshall's birth, such the property, family, and station in life of his father. Beyond these facts, nothing positively is known of the ancestry of John Marshall on his father's side. Marshall himself traces it no further back than his grandfather. "My Father, Thomas Marshall, was the eldest son of John Marshall, who intermarried with a Miss Markham and whose parents migrated from Wales, and settled in the county of Westmoreland, in Virginia, where my Father was born." [1]

It is probable, however, that Marshall's paternal great-grandfather was a carpenter of Westmoreland County. A Thomas Marshall, "carpenter," as he describes himself in his will, died in that county in 1704. He devised his land to his son William. A William Marshall of King and Queen County deeded to John Marshall "of the forest," for five shillings, the two hundred acres of land in Westmoreland County, as above stated.[2] The fair inference is that this William was the elder brother of John "of the forest" and that both were sons of Thomas the "carpenter."

Beyond his paternal grandfather or at furthest his great-grandfather, therefore, the ancestry of John Marshall, on his father's side, is lost in the fogs of uncertainty.[3] It is only positively known that

[1] *Autobiography*. Marshall gives the ancestry of his wife more fully and specifically. See *infra*, chap. v.

[2] Will of Thomas Marshall, " carpenter," probated May 31, 1704; Records of Westmoreland County, Deeds and Wills, iii, 232 *et seq.* (Appendix I.)

[3] Most curiously, precisely this is true of Thomas Jefferson's paternal ancestry.

THOMAS MARSHALL

ANCESTRY AND ENVIRONMENT

his grandfather was of the common people and of moderate means.[1]

[1] There is a family tradition that the first of this particular Marshall family in America was a Royalist Irish captain who fought under Charles I and came to America when Cromwell prevailed. This may or may not be true. Certainly no proof of it has been discovered. The late Wilson Miles Cary, whose authority is unquestioned in genealogical problems upon which he passed judgment, decided that "the Marshall family begins absolutely with Thomas Marshall, 'Carpenter.'" (The Cary Papers, MSS., Va. Hist. Soc. The *Virginia Magazine of History and Biography* is soon to publish these valuable genealogical papers.)

Within comparatively recent years, this family tradition has been ambitiously elaborated. It includes among John Marshall's ancestors William le Mareschal, who came to England with the Conqueror; the celebrated Richard de Clare, known as "Strongbow"; an Irish king, Dermont; Sir William Marshall, regent of the kingdom of England and restorer of Magna Charta; a Captain John Marshall, who distinguished himself at the siege of Calais in 1558; and finally, the Irish captain who fought Cromwell and fled to Virginia as above mentioned. (Paxton, 7 *et seq.*)

Senator Humphrey Marshall rejected this story as "a myth supported by vanity." (*Ib.*) Colonel Cary declares that "there is no evidence whatever in support of it." (Cary Papers, MSS.) Other painstaking genealogists have reached the same conclusion. (See, for instance, General Thomas M. Anderson's analysis of the subject in *Va. Mag. Hist. and Biog.*, xii, 328 *et seq.*)

Marshall himself, of course, does not notice this legend in his *Autobiography*; indeed, it is almost certain that he never heard of it. In constructing this picturesque genealogical theory, the kinship of persons separated by centuries is assumed largely because of a similarity of names. This would not seem to be entirely convincing. There were many Marshalls in Virginia no more related to one another than the various unrelated families by the name of Smith. Indeed, *maréchal* is the French word for a "shoeing smith."

For example, there lived in Westmoreland County, at the same time with John Marshall "of the forest," another John Marshall, who died intestate and the inventory of whose effects was recorded March 26, 1751, a year before John Marshall "of the forest" died. These two John Marshalls do not seem to have been kinsmen.

The only prominent person in Virginia named Marshall in 1723-34 was a certain Thomas Marshall who was a member of the colony's House of Burgesses during this period; but he was from Northampton County. (Journal, H.B. (1712-23), xi; *ib.* (1727-40), viii, and 174.) He does not appear to have been related in any way to John "of the forest."

Concerning his paternal grandmother, nothing definitely is established except that she was Elizabeth Markham, daughter of Lewis Markham, once Sheriff of Westmoreland County.[1]

John Marshall's lineage on his mother's side, however, is long, high, and free from doubt, not only through the Randolphs and Ishams, as we have seen, but through the Keiths. For his maternal grand-

There were numerous Marshalls who were officers in the Revolutionary War from widely separated colonies, apparently unconnected by blood or marriage. For instance, there were Abraham, David, and Benjamin Marshall from Pennsylvania; Christopher Marshall from Massachusetts; Dixon Marshall from North Carolina; Elihu Marshall from New York, etc. (Heitman, 285.)

At the same time that John Marshall, the subject of this work, was captain in a Virginia regiment, two other John Marshalls were captains in Pennsylvania regiments. When Thomas Marshall of Virginia was an officer in Washington's army, there were four other Thomas Marshalls, two from Massachusetts, one from South Carolina, and one from Virginia, all Revolutionary officers. (*Ib.*)

When Stony Point was taken by Wayne, among the British prisoners captured was Lieutenant John Marshall of the 17th Regiment of British foot (see Dawson, 86); and Captain John Marshall of Virginia was one of the attacking force. (See *infra*, chap. IV.)

In 1792, John Marshall of King and Queen County, a boatswain, was a Virginia pensioner. (*Va. Hist. Prs.*, v, 544.) He was not related to John Marshall, who had become the leading Richmond lawyer of that time.

While Hamilton was Secretary of the Treasury he received several letters from John Marshall, an Englishman, who was in this country and who wrote Hamilton concerning the subject of establishing manufactories. (Hamilton MSS., Lib. Cong.)

Illustrations like these might be continued for many pages. They merely show the danger of inferring relationship because of the similarity of names, especially one so general as that of Marshall.

[1] The Cary Papers, *supra*. Here again the Marshall legend riots fantastically. This time it makes the pirate Blackbeard the first husband of Marshall's paternal grandmother; and with this freebooter she is said to have had thrilling and melancholy experiences. It deserves mention only as showing the absurdity of such myths. Blackbeard was one Edward Teach, whose career is well authenticated. (Wise, 186.) Colonel Cary put a final quietus on this particular tale, as he did on so many other genealogical fictions.

ANCESTRY AND ENVIRONMENT 17

father was an Episcopal clergyman, James Keith, of the historic Scottish family of that name, who were hereditary Earls Marischal of Scotland. The Keiths had been soldiers for generations, some of them winning great renown.[1] One of them was James Keith, the Prussian field marshal and ablest of the officers of Frederick the Great.[2] James Keith, a younger son of this distinguished family, was destined for the Church;[3] but the martial blood flowing in his veins asserted itself and, in his youth, he also became a soldier, upholding with arms the cause of the Pretender. When that rebellion was crushed, he fled to Virginia, resumed his sacred calling, returned to England for orders, came back to Virginia[4] and during his remaining years performed his priestly duties with rare zeal and devotion.[5] The motto of the Keiths of Scotland was "Veritas Vincit," and John Marshall adopted it. During most of his life he wore an amethyst with the ancient Keith motto engraved upon it.[6]

When past middle life the Scottish parson married Mary Isham Randolph,[7] granddaughter of William Randolph and Mary Isham. In 1754 their

[1] See Douglas: *Peerage of Scotland* (1764), 448. Also Burke: *Peerage* (1903), 895; and *ib.* (1876). This peerage is now extinct. See Burke: *Extinct Peerages*.

[2] For appreciation of this extraordinary man see Carlyle's *Frederick the Great*.

[3] Paxton, 30.

[4] From data furnished by Justice James Keith, President of the Court of Appeals of Virginia.

[5] Paxton, 30; and see Meade, ii, 216.

[6] Data furnished by Thomas Marshall Smith of Baltimore, Md.

[7] With this lady the tradition deals most unkindly and in highly colored pictures. An elopement, the deadly revenge of outraged brothers, a broken heart and resulting insanity overcome by gentle

daughter, Mary Randolph Keith, married Thomas Marshall and became the mother of John Marshall. "My mother was named Mary Keith, she was the daughter of a clergyman, of the name of Keith, who migrated from Scotland and intermarried with a Miss Randolph of James River" is Marshall's comment on his maternal ancestry.[1]

Not only was John Marshall's mother uncommonly well born, but she was more carefully educated than most Virginia women of that period.[2] Her father received in Aberdeen the precise and methodical training of a Scottish college;[3] and, as all parsons in the Virginia of that time were teachers, it is certain that he carefully instructed his daughter. He was a deeply religious man, especially in his latter years, — so much so, indeed, that there was in him a touch of mysticism; and the two marked qualities of his daughter, Mary, were deep piety and strong intellectuality. She had, too, all the physical hardiness of her Scottish ancestry, fortified by the active and useful labor which all Virginia women of her class at that time performed.

treatment, only to be reinduced in old age by a fraudulent Enoch Arden letter apparently written by the lost love of her youth — such are some of the incidents with which this story clothes Marshall's maternal grandmother. (Paxton, 25–26.)

[1] *Autobiography.*

[2] In general, Virginia women at this time had very little education (Burnaby, 57.) Sometimes the daughters of prominent and wealthy families could not read or write. (Bruce: *Inst.*, i, 454–55.) Even forty years after John Marshall was born, there was but one girls' school in Virginia. (La Rochefoucauld, iii, 227.) In 1789, there were very few schools of any kind in Virginia, it appears. (Journal, H.B. (Dec. 14, 1789), 130; and see *infra*, chap. vi.)

[3] Paxton, 30. Marischal College, Aberdeen, was founded by George Keith, Fifth Earl Marischal (1593).

MARY RANDOLPH KEITH MARSHALL
(Mrs. Thomas Marshall)

So Thomas Marshall and Mary Keith combined unusual qualities for the founding of a family. Great strength of mind both had, and powerful wills; and through the veins of both poured the blood of daring. Both were studious-minded, too, and husband and wife alike were seized of a passion for self-improvement as well as a determination to better their circumstances. It appears that Thomas Marshall was by nature religiously inclined;[1] and this made all the greater harmony between himself and his wife. The physical basis of both husband and wife seems to have been well-nigh perfect.

Fifteen children were the result of this union, every one of whom lived to maturity and almost all of whom rounded out a ripe old age. Every one of them led an honorable and successful life. Nearly all strongly impressed themselves upon the community in which they lived.

It was a peculiar society of which this prolific and virile family formed a part, and its surroundings were as strange as the society itself. Nearly all of Virginia at that time was wilderness,[2] if we look upon it with the eyes of to-day. The cultivated parts were given over almost entirely to the raising of tobacco, which soon drew from the soil its virgin strength; and the land thus exhausted usually was abandoned to the forest, which again soon covered it. No use was made of the commonest and most

---

[1] See *infra*, chap. II. When Leeds Parish was organized, we find Thomas Marshall its leading vestryman. He was always a stanch churchman.

[2] Jones, 35; Burnaby, 58. But see Maxwell in *William and Mary College Quarterly*, xix, 73–103; and see Bruce: *Econ.*, i, 425, 427, 585, 587.

obvious fertilizing materials and methods; new spaces were simply cleared.[1] Thus came a happy-go-lucky improvidence of habits and character.

This shiftlessness was encouraged by the vast extent of unused and unoccupied domain. Land was so cheap that riches measured by that basis of all wealth had to be counted in terms of thousands and tens of thousands of acres.[2] Slavery was an even more powerful force making for a kind of lofty disdain of physical toil among the white

---

[1] "Though tobacco exhausts the land to a prodigious degree, the proprietors take no pains to restore its vigor; they take what the soil will give and abandon it when it gives no longer. They like better to clear new lands than to regenerate the old." (De Warville, 439; and see Fithian, 140.)

The land produced only "four or five bushels of wheat per acre or from eight to ten of Indian corn. These fields are never manured, hardly even are they ploughed; and it seldom happens that their owners for two successive years exact from them these scanty crops. . . . The country . . . everywhere exhibits the features of laziness, of ignorance, and consequently of poverty." (La Rochefoucauld, iii, 106–07; describing land between Richmond and Petersburg, in 1797; and see Schoepf, ii, 32, 48; and Weld, i, 138, 151.)

[2] Burnaby, 45, 59. The estate of Richard Randolph of Curels, in 1742 embraced "not less than forty thousand acres of the choicest lands." (Garland, i, 7.) The mother of George Mason bought ten thousand acres in Loudoun County for an insignificant sum. (Rowland, i, 51.) The Carter plantation in 1774 comprised sixty thousand acres and Carter owned six hundred negroes. (Fithian, 128.) Compare with the two hundred acres and few slaves of John Marshall "of the forest," *supra*.

Half a century later the very best lands in Virginia with valuable mines upon them sold for only eighteen dollars an acre. (La Rochefoucauld, iii, 124.) For careful account of the extent of great holdings in the seventeenth century see Wertenbaker: *P. and P.*, 34–35, 97–99. Jefferson in 1790 owned two hundred slaves and ten thousand acres of very rich land on the James River. (Jefferson to Van Staphorst, Feb. 28, 1790; *Works:* Ford, vi, 33.) Washington owned enormous quantities of land, and large numbers of slaves. His Virginia holdings alone amounted to thirty-five thousand acres. (Beard: *Econ. I. C.*, 144.)

ANCESTRY AND ENVIRONMENT

people.[1] Black slaves were almost as numerous as white free men.[2] On the great plantations the negro quarters assumed the proportions of villages;[3] and the masters of these extensive holdings were by example the arbiters of habits and manners to the whole social and industrial life of the colony. While an occasional great planter was methodical and industrious,[4] careful and systematic methods were rare. Manual labor was, to most of these lords of circumstance, not only unnecessary but degrading. To do no physical work that could be avoided on the one hand, and on the other hand, to own as many slaves as possible, was, generally, the ideal of members of the first estate.[5] This spread to the classes below, until it became a common ambition of white men throughout the Old Dominion.

While contemporary travelers are unanimous upon this peculiar aspect of social and economic conditions in old Virginia, the vivid picture drawn by Thomas Jefferson is still more convincing. "The whole com-

[1] Burnaby, 54.

[2] In the older counties the slaves outnumbered the whites; for instance, in 1790 Westmoreland County had 3183 whites, 4425 blacks, and 114 designated as "all others." In 1782 in the same county 410 slave-owners possessed 4536 slaves and 1889 horses. (*Va. Mag. Hist. and Biog.*, x, 229–36.)

[3] Ambler, 11. The slaves of some planters were valued at more than thirty thousand pounds sterling. (Fithian, 286; and Schoepf, ii, 38; also, Weld, i, 148.)

[4] Robert Carter was a fine example of this rare type. (See Fithian, 279–80.)

[5] Burnaby, 53–54 and 59. "The Virginians ... are an indolent haughty people whose thoughts and designs are directed solely towards p[l]aying the lord, owning great tracts of land and numerous troops of slaves. Any man whatever, if he can afford so much as 2–3 [two or three] negroes, becomes ashamed of work, and goes about in idleness, supported by his slaves." (Schoepf, ii, 40.)

merce between master and slave," writes Jefferson, "is a perpetual exercise of the most boisterous passions, the most unremitting despotism on the one part, and degrading submissions on the other. Our children see this and learn to imitate it. . . . Thus nursed, educated, and daily exercised in tyranny ... the man must be a prodigy who can retain his manners and morals undepraved. . . . With the morals of the people their industry also is destroyed. For in a warm climate, no man will labour for himself who can make another labour for him. . . . Of the proprietors of slaves a very small proportion indeed are ever seen to labour." [1]

Two years after he wrote his "Notes on Virginia" Jefferson emphasized his estimate of Virginia society. "I have thought them [Virginians] as you found them," he writes Chastellux, "aristocratical, pompous, clannish, indolent, hospitable . . . careless of their interests, . . . thoughtless in their expenses and in all their transactions of business." He again ascribes many of these characteristics to "that warmth of their climate which unnerves and unmans both body and mind." [2]

From this soil sprang a growth of habits as noxious as it was luxuriant. Amusements to break the monotony of unemployed daily existence took the form of horse-racing, cock-fighting, and gambling.[3]

[1] "Notes on Virginia"; *Works:* Ford, iv, 82–83. See La Rochefoucauld, iii, p. 161, on Jefferson's slaves.

[2] Jefferson to Chastellux, Sept. 2, 1785; *Thomas Jefferson Correspondence,* Bixby Collection: Ford, 12; and see Jefferson's comparison of the sections of the country, *ib.* and *infra,* chap. vi.

[3] "Many of the wealthier class were to be seen seeking relief from the vacuity of idleness, not merely in the allowable pleasures of the

ANCESTRY AND ENVIRONMENT

Drinking and all attendant dissipations were universal and extreme;[1] this, however, was the case in all the colonies.[2] Bishop Meade tells us that even the clergy indulged in the prevailing customs to the neglect of their sacred calling; and the church itself was all but abandoned in the disrepute which the conduct of its ministers brought upon the house of God.[3]

---

chase and the turf, but in the debasing ones of cock-fighting, gaming, and drinking." (Tucker, i, 18; and see La Rochefoucauld, iii, 77; Weld, i, 191; also *infra*, chap. VII, and references there given.)

[1] Jones, 48, 49, and 52; Chastellux, 222–24; also, translator's note to *ib.*, 292–93. The following order from the Records of the Court of Rappahannock County, Jan. 2, 1688 (*sic*), p. 141, is illustrative:—
"It having pleased Almighty God to bless his Royall Mahst. with the birth of a son & his subjects with a Prince of Wales, and for as much as his Excellency hath sett apart the 16th. day of this Inst. Janr'y. for solemnizing the same. To the end therefore that it may be don with all the expressions of joy this County is capable of, this Court have ordered that Capt. Geo. Taylor do provide & bring to the North Side Courthouse for this county as much Rum or other strong Liquor with sugar proportionable as shall amount to six thousand five hundred pounds of Tobb. to be distributed amongst the Troops of horse, Compa. of foot and other persons that shall be present at the Sd. Solemnitie. And that the said sum be allowed him at the next laying of the Levey. As also that Capt. Samll. Blomfield provide & bring to the South side Courthouse for this county as much Rum or other strong Liquor Wth. sugar proportionable as shall amount to three thousand five hundred pounds of Tobb. to be distributed as above att the South side Courthouse, and the Sd. sum to be allowed him at the next laying of the Levey."
And see Bruce: *Econ.*, ii, 210–31; also Wise, 320, 327–29. Although Bruce and Wise deal with a much earlier period, drinking seems to have increased in the interval. (See Fithian, 105–14, 123.)

[2] As in Massachusetts, for instance. "In most country towns . . . you will find almost every other house with a sign of entertainment before it. . . . If you sit the evening, you will find the house full of people, drinking drams, flip, toddy, carousing, swearing." (John Adams's *Diary*, describing a New England county, in 1761; *Works*: Adams, ii, 125–26. The Records of Essex County, Massachusetts, now in process of publication by the Essex Institute, contain many cases that confirm the observation of Adams.)

[3] Meade, i, 52–54; and see Schoepf, ii, 62–63.

Yet the higher classes of colonial Virginians were keen for the education of their children, or at least of their male offspring.[1] The sons of the wealthiest planters often were sent to England or Scotland to be educated, and these, not infrequently, became graduates of Oxford, Cambridge, and Edinburgh.[2] Others of this class were instructed by private tutors.[3] Also a sort of scanty and fugitive public instruction was given in rude cabins, generally located in abandoned fields. These were called the Old Field Schools.[4]

More than forty per cent of the men who made deeds or served on juries could not sign their names, although they were of the land-owning and better educated classes;[5] the literacy of the masses, especially that of the women,[6] was, of course, much lower.

An eager desire, among the "quality," for reading brought a considerable number of books to the homes of those who could afford that luxury.[7] A few

[1] Wise, 317-19; Bruce: *Inst.*, i, 308-15.

[2] Bruce: *Inst.*, i, 317-22; and see especially, *Va. Mag. Hist. and Biog.*, ii, 196 *et seq.*

[3] *Ib.*, 323-30; also Fithian, 50 *et seq.*

[4] Bruce: *Inst.*, i, 331-42. [5] *Ib.*, 452-53.

[6] *Ib.*, 456-57. Bruce shows that two thirds of the women who joined in deeds could not write. This, however, was in the richer section of the colony at a much earlier period. Just before the Revolution Virginia girls, even in wealthy families, "were simply taught to read and write at 25/ [shillings] and a load of wood per year — A boarding school was no where in Virginia to be found." (Mrs. Carrington to her sister Nancy; MS.) Part of this letter appears in the *Atlantic Monthly* series cited hereafter (see chap. v); but the teacher's pay is incorrectly printed as "pounds" instead of "shillings." (*Atlantic Monthly*, lxxxiv, 544-45.)

[7] Bruce: *Inst.*, i, 402-42; and see Wise, 313-15. Professor Tucker says that "literature was neglected, or cultivated, by the small number who had been educated in England, rather as an accomplishment and a mark of distinction than for the substantial benefits it confers." (Tucker, i, 18.)

ANCESTRY AND ENVIRONMENT

libraries were of respectable size and two or three were very large. Robert Carter had over fifteen hundred volumes,[1] many of which were in Latin and Greek, and some in French.[2] William Byrd collected at Westover more than four thousand books in half a dozen languages.[3] But the Carter and Byrd libraries were, of course, exceptions. Byrd's library was the greatest, not only in Virginia, but in all the colonies, except that of John Adams, which was equally extensive and varied.[4]

Doubtless the leisure and wealth of the gentry, created by the peculiar economic conditions of the Old Dominion, sharpened this appetite for literature and afforded to the wealthy time and material for the gratification of it. The passion for reading and discussion persisted, and became as notable a characteristic of Virginians as was their dislike for physical labor, their excessive drinking, and their love of strenuous sport and rough diversion.

There were three social orders or strata, all contemporary observers agree, into which Virginians were divided; but they merged into one another so that the exact dividing line was not clear.[5] First, of course, came the aristocracy of the immense plantations. While the social and political dominance of this class was based on wealth, yet some of its members were derived from the English gentry, with, perhaps, an occasional one from a noble family in the

---

[1] Fithian, 177. [2] See catalogue in *W. and M. C. Q.*, x and xi.
[3] See catalogue in Appendix A to Byrd's *Writings:* Bassett.
[4] See catalogue of John Adams's Library, in the Boston Public Library.
[5] Ambler, 9; and see Wise, 68-70.

mother country.[1] Many, however, were English merchants or their sons.[2] It appears, also, that the boldest and thriftiest of the early Virginia settlers, whom the British Government exiled for political offenses, acquired extensive possessions, became large slave-owners, and men of importance and position. So did some who were indentured servants;[3] and, indeed, an occasional transported convict rose to prominence.[4]

But the genuine though small aristocratic element gave tone and color to colonial Virginia society. All, except the "poor whites," looked to this supreme group for ideals and for standards of manners and conduct. "People of fortune . . . are the pattern of all behaviour here," testifies Fithian of New Jersey, tutor in the Carter household.[5] Also, it was, of course, the natural ambition of wealthy planters and those who expected to become such to imitate the life of the English higher classes. This was much truer in Virginia than in any other colony; for she had been more faithful to the Crown and to the

[1] Trustworthy data on this subject is given in the volumes of the *Va. Mag. Hist. and Biog.*; see also *W. and M. C. Q.*

[2] Wertenbaker: *P. and P.*, 14-20. But see William G. Stanard's exhaustive review of Mr. Wertenbaker's book in *Va. Mag. Hist. and Biog.*, xviii, 339-48.

[3] "One hundred young maids for wives, as the former ninety sent. One hundred boys more for apprentices likewise to the public tenants. One hundred servants to be disposed among the old planters which they exclusively desire and will pay the company their charges." (*Virginia Company Records*, i, 66; and see Fithian, 111.)

[4] For the understanding in England at that period of the origin of this class of Virginia colonists see Defoe: *Moll Flanders*, 65 *et seq.* On transported convicts see *Amer. Hist. Rev.*, ii, 12 *et seq.* For a summary of the matter see Channing, i, 210-14, 226-27.

[5] Fithian to Greene, Dec. 1, 1773; Fithian, 280.

royal ideal than had her sisters. Thus it was that the Old Dominion developed a distinctively aristocratic and chivalrous social atmosphere peculiar to herself,[1] as Jefferson testifies.

Next to the dominant class came the lesser planters. These corresponded to the yeomanry of the mother country; and most of them were from the English trading classes.[2] They owned little holdings of land from a few hundred to a thousand and even two thousand acres; and each of these inconsiderable landlords acquired a few slaves in proportion to his limited estate. It is possible that a scanty number of this middle class were as well born as the best born of the little nucleus of the genuine aristocracy; these were the younger sons of great English houses to whom the law of primogeniture denied equal opportunity in life with the elder brother. So it came to pass that the upper reaches of the second estate in the social and industrial Virginia of that time merged into the highest class.

At the bottom of the scale, of course, came the poverty-stricken whites. In eastern Virginia this was the class known as the "poor whites"; and it was more distinct than either of the two classes above it. These "poor whites" lived in squalor, and without the aspirations or virtues of the superior orders. They carried to the extreme the examples of

[1] Fithian to Peck, Aug. 12, 1774; Fithian, 286-88; and see Professor Tucker's searching analysis in Tucker, i, 17-22; also see Lee, in Ford: *P. on C.*, 296-97. As to a genuinely aristocratic *group*, the New York patroons were, perhaps, the most distinct in the country.

[2] Wertenbaker: *P. and P.*, 14-20; also *Va. Mag. Hist. and Biog.*, xviii, 339-48.

idleness given them by those in higher station, and coarsened their vices to the point of brutality.[1] Near this social stratum, though not a part of it, were classed the upland settlers, who were poor people, but highly self-respecting and of sturdy stock.

Into this structure of Virginia society Fate began to weave a new and alien thread about the time that Thomas Marshall took his young bride to the log cabin in the woods of Prince William County where their first child was born. In the back country bordering the mountains appeared the scattered huts of the pioneers. The strong character of this element of Virginia's population is well known, and its coming profoundly influenced for generations the political, social, industrial, and military history of that section. They were jealous of their "rights," impatient of restraint, wherever they felt it, and this was seldom. Indeed, the solitariness of their lives, and the utter self-dependence which this forced upon them, made them none too tolerant of law in any form.

These outpost settlers furnished most of that class so well known to our history by the term "backwoodsmen," and yet so little understood. For the heroism, the sacrifice, and the suffering of this "advance guard of civilization" have been pictured

[1] For accounts of brutal physical combats, see Anburey, ii, 310 *et seq.* And for dueling, though at an earlier period, see Wise, 329–31. The practice of dueling rapidly declined; but fighting of a violent and often repulsive character persisted, as we shall see, far into the nineteenth century. Also, see La Rochefoucauld, Chastellux, and other travelers, *infra*, chap. VII.

by laudatory writers to the exclusion of its other and less admirable qualities. Yet it was these latter characteristics that played so important a part in that critical period of our history between the surrender of the British at Yorktown and the adoption of the Constitution, and in that still more fateful time when the success of the great experiment of making out of an inchoate democracy a strong, orderly, independent, and self-respecting nation was in the balance.

These American backwoodsmen, as described by contemporary writers who studied them personally, pushed beyond the inhabited districts to get land and make homes more easily. This was their underlying purpose; but a fierce individualism, impatient even of those light and vague social restraints which the existence of near-by neighbors creates, was a sharper spur.[1] Through both of these motives, too, ran the spirit of mingled lawlessness and adventure. The physical surroundings of the backwoodsman nourished the non-social elements of his character. The log cabin built, the surrounding patch of clearing made, the seed planted for a crop of cereals only large enough to supply the household needs — these almost ended the backwoodsman's agricultural activities and the habits of regular industry which farming requires.

While his meager crops were coming on, the backwoodsman must supply his family with food from the stream and forest. The Indians had not yet retreated so far, nor were their atrocities so remote,

[1] Schoepf, i, 261; and see references, *infra*, chap. VII.

that fear of them had ceased;[1] and the eye of the backwoodsman was ever keen for a savage human foe as well as for wild animals. Thus he became a man of the rifle,[2] a creature of the forests, a dweller amid great silences, self-reliant, suspicious, non-social, and almost as savage as his surroundings.[3]

But among them sometimes appeared families which sternly held to high purposes, orderly habits, and methodical industry;[4] and which clung to moral and religious ideals and practices with greater tenacity than ever, because of the very difficulties of their situation. These chosen families naturally became the backbone of the frontier; and from them came the strong men of the advanced settlements.

[1] After Braddock's defeat the Indians "extended their raids... pillaging and murdering in the most ruthless manner... The whole country from New York to the heart of Virginia became the theatre of inhuman barbarities and heartless destruction." (Lowdermilk, 186.)

[2] Although the rifle did not come into general use until the Revolution, the firearms of this period have been so universally referred to as "rifles" that I have, for convenience, adopted this inaccurate term in the first two chapters.

[3] "Their actions are regulated by the wildness of the neighbourhood. The deer often come to eat their grain, the wolves to destroy their sheep, the bears to kill their hogs, the foxes to catch their poultry. This surrounding hostility immediately puts the gun into their hands, ... and thus by defending their property, they soon become professed hunters;... once hunters, farewell to the plough. The chase renders them ferocious, gloomy, and unsociable; a hunter wants no neighbour, he rather hates them.... The manners of the Indian natives are respectable, compared with this European medley. Their wives and children live in sloth and inactivity... You cannot imagine what an effect on manners the great distance they live from each other has.... Eating of wild meat... tends to alter their temper.... I have seen it." (Crèvecœur, 66–68.) Crèvecœur was himself a frontier farmer. (*Writings:* Sparks, ix, footnote to 259.)

[4] "Many families carry with them all their decency of conduct, purity of morals, and respect of religion; but these are scarce." (Crèvecœur, 70.) Crèvecœur says his family was one of these.

Such a figure among the backwoodsmen was Thomas Marshall. Himself a product of the settlements on the tidewater, he yet was the personification of that spirit of American advance and enterprise which led this son of the Potomac lowlands ever and ever westward until he ended his days in the heart of Kentucky hundreds of miles through the savage wilderness from the spot where, as a young man, he built his first cabin home.

This, then, was the strange mingling of human elements that made up Virginia society during the middle decades of the eighteenth century — a society peculiar to the Old Dominion and unlike that of any other place or time. For the most part, it was idle and dissipated, yet also hospitable and spirited, and, among the upper classes, keenly intelligent and generously educated. When we read of the heavy drinking of whiskey, brandy, rum, and heady wine; of the general indolence, broken chiefly by fox-hunting and horse-racing, among the quality; of the coarser sport of cock-fighting shared in common by landed gentry and those of baser condition, and of the eagerness for physical encounter which seems to have pervaded the whole white population,[1] we wonder at the greatness of mind and soul which grew from such a social soil.

Yet out of it sprang a group of men who for ability, character, spirit, and purpose, are not outshone and have no precise counterpart in any other company of illustrious characters appearing in like space of time

[1] This bellicose trait persisted for many years and is noted by all contemporary observers.

and similar extent of territory. At almost the same point of time, historically speaking, — within thirty years, to be exact, — and on the same spot, geographically speaking, — within a radius of a hundred miles, — George Mason, James Madison, Patrick Henry, Thomas Jefferson, John Marshall, and George Washington were born. The life stories of these men largely make up the history of their country while they lived; and it was chiefly their words and works, their thought and purposes, that gave form and direction, on American soil, to those political and social forces which are still working out the destiny of the American people.

CHAPTER II

A FRONTIER EDUCATION

> "Come to me," quoth the pine tree,
> "I am the giver of honor." (Emerson.)

I do not think the greatest things have been done for the world by its bookmen. Education is not the chips of arithmetic and grammar. (Wendell Phillips.)

JOHN MARSHALL was never out of the simple, crude environment of the near frontier for longer than one brief space of a few months until his twentieth year, when, as lieutenant of the famous Culpeper Minute Men, he marched away to battle. The life he had led during this period strengthened that powerful physical equipment which no strain of his later years seemed to impair; and helped to establish that extraordinary nervous equilibrium which no excitement or contest ever was able to unbalance.[1] This foundation part of his life was even more influential on the forming mind and spiritual outlook of the growing youth.

Thomas Marshall left the little farm of poor land in Westmoreland County not long after the death of his father, John Marshall "of the forest." This ancestral "estate" had no attractions for the enterprising young man. Indeed, there is reason for thinking that he abandoned it.[2] He lifted his first

[1] Story, in Dillon, iii, 334.
[2] The records of Westmoreland County do not show what disposition Thomas Marshall made of the one hundred acres given him by his mother. (Letter of Albert Stuart, Deputy Clerk of Westmoreland County, Virginia, to the author, Aug. 26, 1913.) He probably abandoned it just as John Washington and Thomas Pope abandoned one thousand acres of the same land. (*Supra.*)

rooftree in what then were still the wilds of Prince William County.[1] There we find him with his young wife, and there in the red year of British disaster his eldest son was born. The cabin has long since disappeared, and only a rude monument of native stone, erected by college students in recent years, now marks the supposed site of this historic birthplace.

The spot is a placid, slumberous countryside. A small stream runs hard by. In the near distance still stands one of the original cabins of Spotswood's Germans.[2] But the soil is not generous. When Thomas Marshall settled there the little watercourse at the foot of the gentle slope on which his cabin stood doubtless ran bank-full; for in 1754 the forests remained thick and unviolated about his cabin,[3] and fed the waters from the heavy rains in restrained and steady flow to creek and river channels. Amidst these surroundings four children of Thomas Marshall and Mary Keith were born.[4]

The sturdy young pioneer was not content to remain permanently at Germantown. A few years later found him building another home about thirty

[1] Westmoreland County is on the Potomac River near its entrance into Chesapeake Bay. Prince William is about thirty miles farther up the river. Marshall was born about one hundred miles by wagon road from Appomattox Creek, northwest toward the Blue Ridge and in the wilderness.

[2] Campbell, 404-05.

[3] More than forty years later the country around the Blue Ridge was still a dense forest. (La Rochefoucauld, iii, 173.) And the road even from Richmond to Petersburg, an hundred miles east and south of the Marshall cabin, as late as 1797 ran through "an almost uninterrupted succession of woods." (*Ib.*, 106; and see *infra*, chap. VII.)

[4] John, 1755; Elizabeth, 1756; Mary, 1757; Thomas, 1761.

miles farther westward, in a valley in the Blue Ridge Mountains.[1] Here the elder son spent the critical space of life from childhood to his eighteenth year. This little building still stands, occupied by negroes employed on the estate of which it forms a part. The view from it even now is attractive; and in the days of John Marshall's youth must have been very beautiful.

The house is placed on a slight rise of ground on the eastern edge of the valley. Near by, to the south and closer still to the west, two rapid mountain streams sing their quieting, restful song. On all sides the Blue Ridge lifts the modest heights of its purple hills. This valley at that time was called "The Hollow," and justly so; for it is but a cup in the lazy and unambitious mountains. When the eldest son first saw this frontier home, great trees thickly covered mountain, hill, and glade, and surrounded the meadow, which the Marshall dwelling overlooked, with a wall of inviting green.[2]

Two days by the very lowest reckoning it must have taken Thomas Marshall to remove his family to this new abode. It is more likely that three or four days were consumed in the toilsome task. The very careful maps of the British survey at that time show only three roads in all immense Prince William County.[3] On one of these the Marshalls might have made their way northward, and on another, which probably joined, they could have traveled west-

[1] Binney, in Dillon, iii, 284.
[2] The ancient trunks of one or two of these trees still stand close to house.
[3] British map of 1755; Virginia State Library.

ward. But these trails were primitive and extremely difficult for any kind of vehicle.[1]

Some time before 1765, then, rational imagination can picture a strong, rude wagon drawn by two horses crawling along the stumpy, rock-roughened, and mud-mired road through the dense woods that led in the direction of "The Hollow." In the wagon sat a young woman.[2] By her side a sturdy, red-cheeked boy looked out with alert but quiet interest showing from his brilliant black eyes; and three other children cried their delight or vexation as the hours wore on. In this wagon, too, were piled the little family's household goods; nor did this make a heavy load, for all the Lares and Penates of a frontier settler's family in 1760 would not fill a single room of a moderately furnished household in the present day.

By the side of the wagon strode a young man dressed in the costume of the frontier. Tall, broad-shouldered, lithe-hipped, erect, he was a very oak of a man. His splendid head was carried with a peculiar dignity; and the grave but kindly command that shone from his face, together with the brooding thoughtfulness and fearless light of his striking eyes

[1] See La Rochefoucauld, iii, 707. These "roads" were scarcely more than mere tracks through the forests. See chap. VII, infra, for description of roads at the period between the close of the Revolution and the beginning of our National Government under the Constitution. Even in the oldest and best settled colonies the roads were very bad. Chalkley's *Augusta County (Va.) Records* show many orders regarding roads; but, considering the general state of highways (see *infra*, chap. VII) these probably concerned very primitive efforts. When Thomas Marshall removed his family to the Blue Ridge, the journey must have been strenuous even for that hardship-seasoned man.

[2] She was born in 1737. (Paxton, 19.)

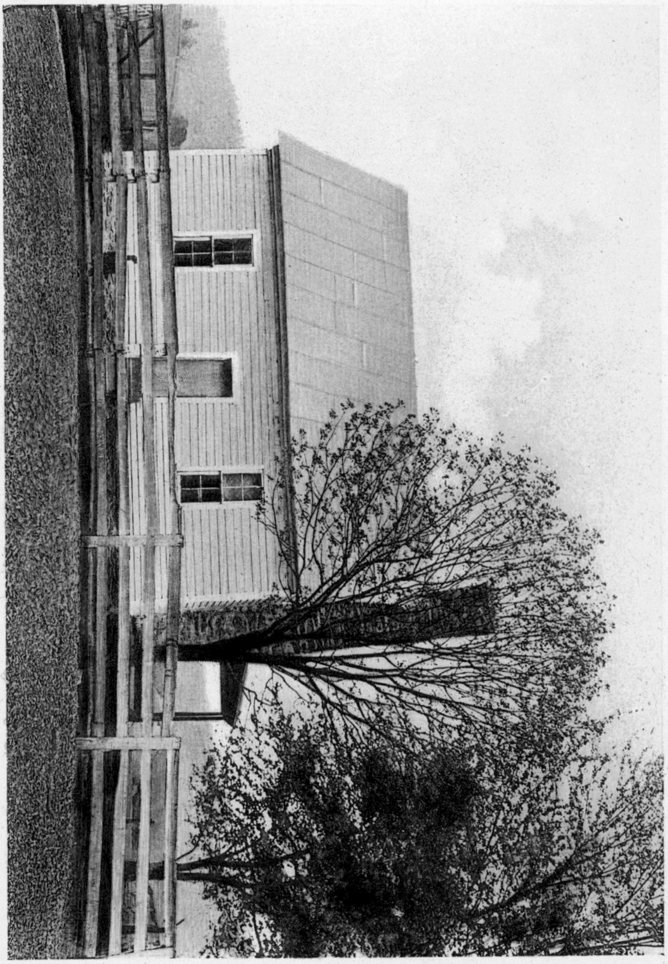

"The Hollow," Markham, Virginia
John Marshall's boyhood home.

would have singled him out in any assemblage as a man to be respected and trusted. A negro drove the team, and a negro girl walked behind.[1]

So went the Marshalls to their Blue Ridge home. It was a commodious one for those days. Two rooms downstairs, one fifteen feet by sixteen, the other twelve by fourteen, and above two half-story lofts of the same dimensions, constituted this domestic castle. At one end of the larger downstairs room is a broad and deep stone fireplace, and from this rises a big chimney of the same material, supporting the house on the outside.[2]

Thomas and Mary Marshall's pride and aspiration, as well as their social importance among the settlers, are strongly shown by this frontier dwelling. Unlike those of most of the other backwoodsmen, it was not a log cabin, but a frame house built of whip-sawed uprights and boards.[3] It was perhaps easier to construct a one and a half story house with such materials; for to lift heavy timbers to such a height required great effort.[4] But Thomas Marshall's social, religious, and political status [5] in the newly organized County of Fauquier were the leading influences that

[1] At this time, Thomas Marshall had at least two slaves, inherited from his father. (Will of John Marshall "of the forest," Appendix I.) As late as 1797 (nearly forty years after Thomas Marshall went to "The Hollow"), La Rochefoucauld found that even on the "poorer" plantations about the Blue Ridge the "planters, however wretched their condition, have all of them one or two negroes." (La Rochefoucauld, iii, 135.)

[2] Personal inspection.

[3] Mill-sawed weather-boarding, held by cut nails, now covers the sides of the house, the original broad whip-sawed boards, fastened by wrought nails, having long since decayed.

[4] Practically all log cabins, at that time, had only one story.

[5] See *infra*.

induced him to build a house which, for the time and place, was so pretentious. A small stone "meat house," a one-room log cabin for his two negroes, and a log stable, completed the establishment.

In such an abode, and amidst such surroundings, the fast-growing family[1] of Thomas Marshall lived for more than twelve years. At first neighbors were few and distant. The nearest settlements were at Warrenton, some twenty-three miles to the eastward, and Winchester, a little farther over the mountains to the west.[2] But, with the horror of Braddock's defeat subdued by the widespread and decisive counter victories, settlers began to come into the country on both sides of the Blue Ridge. These were comparatively small farmers, who, later on, became raisers of wheat, corn, and other cereals, rather than tobacco.

Not until John Marshall had passed his early boyhood, however, did these settlers become sufficiently numerous to form even a scattered community, and his early years were enlivened with no child companionship except that of his younger brothers and sisters. For the most part his days were spent, rifle in hand, in the surrounding mountains, and by the pleasant waters that flowed through the valley of his forest home. He helped his mother, of course, with her many labors, did the innumerable chores which the day's work required, and looked after the

[1] Six more children were born while the Marshalls remained in "The Hollow": James M., 1764; Judith, 1766; William and Charles, 1767; Lucy, 1768; and Alexander, 1770.

[2] Nearly twenty years later, "Winchester was rude, wild, as nature had made it," but "it was less so than its inhabitants." (Mrs. Carrington to her sister Nancy, describing Winchester in 1777, from personal observation; MS.)

A FRONTIER EDUCATION

younger children, as the eldest child always must do. To his brothers and sisters as well as to his parents, he was devoted with a tenderness peculiar to his uncommonly affectionate nature and they, in turn, "fairly idolized" him.[1]

There were few of those minor conveniences which we to-day consider the most indispensable of the simplest necessities. John Marshall's mother, like most other women of that region and period, seldom had such things as pins; in place of them use was made of thorns plucked from the bushes in the woods.[2] The fare, naturally, was simple and primitive. Game from the forest and fish from the stream were the principal articles of diet. Bear meat was plentiful.[3] Even at that early period, salt pork and

---

[1] See Mrs. Carrington to her sister Nancy, *infra*, chap. v.

[2] John Marshall, when at the height of his career, liked to talk of these times. "He ever recurred with fondness to that primitive mode of life, when he partook with a keen relish of balm tea and mush; and when the females used thorns for pins." (Howe, 263, and see *Hist. Mag.*, iii, 166.)

Most of the settlers on the frontier and near frontier did not use forks or tablecloths. Washington found this condition in the house of a Justice of the Peace. "When we came to supper there was neither a Cloth upon ye Table nor a knife to eat with; but as good luck would have it, we had knives of our [own]." (*Writings*: Ford, i, 4.)

Chastellux testifies that, thirty years later, the frontier settlers were forced to make almost everything they used. Thus, as population increased, necessity developed men of many trades and the little communities became self-supporting. (Chastellux, 226-27.)

[3] More than a generation after Thomas Marshall moved to "The Hollow" in the Blue Ridge large quantities of bear and beaver skins were brought from the Valley into Staunton, not many miles away, just over the Ridge. (La Rochefoucauld, iii, 179-80.) The product of the Blue Ridge itself was sent to Fredericksburg and Alexandria. (See Crèvecœur, 63-65.) Thirty years earlier (1733) Colonel Byrd records that "Bears, Wolves, and Panthers" roamed about the site of Richmond; that deer were plentiful and rattlesnakes considered a delicacy. (Byrd's *Writings*: Bassett, 293, 318-19.)

salt fish probably formed a part of the family's food, though not to the extent to which such cured provisions were used by those of the back country in later years, when these articles became the staple of the border.[1]

Corn meal was the basis of the family's bread supply. Even this was not always at hand, and corn meal mush was welcomed with a shout by the clamorous brood with which the little cabin soon fairly swarmed. It could not have been possible for the Marshall family in their house on Goose Creek to have the luxury of bread made from wheat flour. The clothing of the family was mostly homespun. "Store goods," whether food, fabric, or utensil, could be got to Thomas Marshall's backwoods dwelling only with great difficulty and at prohibitive expense.[2]

But young John Marshall did not know that he was missing anything. On the contrary, he was conscious of a certain wealth not found in cities or among the currents of motion. For ever his eye looked out upon noble yet quieting, poetic yet placid, surroundings. Always he could have the in-

[1] See *infra*, chap. VII.
[2] Even forty years later, all "store" merchandise could be had in this region only by hauling it from Richmond, Fredericksburg, or Alexandria. Transportation from the latter place to Winchester cost two dollars and a half per hundredweight. In 1797, "store" goods of all kinds cost, in the Blue Ridge, thirty per cent more than in Philadelphia. (La Rochefoucauld, iii, 203.) From Philadelphia the cost was four to five dollars per hundredweight. While there appear to have been country stores at Staunton and Winchester, over the mountains (Chalkley's *Augusta County (Va.) Records*), the cost of freight to those places was prohibitive of anything but the most absolute necessities even ten years after the Constitution was adopted.

spiring views from the neighboring heights, the majestic stillness of the woods, the soothing music of meadow and stream. So uplifted was the boy by the glory of the mountains at daybreak that he always rose while the eastern sky was yet gray.[1] He was thrilled by the splendor of sunset and never tired of watching it until night fell upon the vast and somber forests. For the boy was charged with poetic enthusiasm, it appears, and the reading of poetry became his chief delight in youth and continued to be his solace and comfort throughout his long life;[2] indeed, Marshall liked to make verses himself, and never outgrew the habit.

There was in him a rich vein of romance; and, later on, this manifested itself by his passion for the great creations of fiction. Throughout his days he would turn to the works of favorite novelists for relaxation and renewal.[3]

The mental and spiritual effects of his surroundings on the forming mind and unfolding soul of this young American must have been as lasting and profound as were the physical effects on his body.[4] His environment and his normal, wholesome daily activities could not have failed to do its work in building the character of the growing boy. These and his sound, steady, and uncommonly strong parentage must, perforce, have helped to give him that courage for action, that balanced vision for judgment, and that serene outlook on life and its

---
[1] *Hist. Mag.*, iii, 166; Howe, 263; also, Story, in Dillon, iii, 334.
[2] Story, in Dillon, iii, 331–32.   [3] *Ib.*
[4] See Binney, in Dillon, iii, 285.

problems, which were so notable and distinguished in his mature and rugged manhood.

Lucky for John Marshall and this country that he was not city born and bred; lucky that not even the small social activities of a country town drained away a single ohm of his nervous energy or obscured with lesser pictures the large panorama which accustomed his developing intelligence to look upon big and simple things in a big and simple way.

There were then no public schools in that frontier [1] region, and young Marshall went untaught save for the instruction his parents gave him. For this task his father was unusually well equipped, though not by any formal schooling. All accounts agree that Thomas Marshall, while not a man of any learning, had contrived to acquire a useful though limited education, which went much further with a man of his well-ordered mind and determined will than a university training could go with a man of looser fiber and cast in smaller mould. The father was careful, painstaking, and persistent in imparting to his children and particularly to John all the education he himself could acquire.

Between Thomas Marshall and his eldest son a mutual sympathy, respect, and admiration existed, as uncommon as it was wholesome and beneficial. "My father," often said John Marshall, "was a far

[1] "Fauquier was then a frontier county ... far in advance of the ordinary reach of compact population." (Story, in Dillon, iii, 331; also see *New York Review* (1838), iii, 333.) Even a generation later (1797), La Rochefoucauld, writing from personal investigation, says (iii, 227-28): "There is no state so entirely destitute of all means of public education as Virginia."

A FRONTIER EDUCATION

abler man than any of his sons." [1] In "his private and familiar conversations with me," says Justice Story, "when there was no other listener ... he never named his father ... without dwelling on his character with a fond and winning enthusiasm ... he broke out with a spontaneous eloquence ... upon his virtues and talents." [2] Justice Story wrote a sketch of Marshall for the "National Portrait Gallery," in which Thomas Marshall is highly praised. In acknowledging the receipt of the magazine, Marshall wrote: "I am particularly gratified by the terms in which you speak of my father. If any contemporary, who knew him in the prime of manhood, survived, he would confirm all you say." [3]

So whether at home with his mother or on surveying trips with his father, the boy continually was under the influence and direction of hardy, clear-minded, unusual parents. Their lofty and simple ideals, their rational thinking, their unbending uprightness, their religious convictions — these were the intellectual companions of John Marshall's childhood and youth. While too much credit has not been given Thomas Marshall for the training of the eldest son, far too little has been bestowed on Mary Randolph Keith, who was, in all things, the equal of her husband.

Although, as we have seen, many books were brought into eastern Virginia by the rich planters, it was difficult for the dwellers on the frontier to secure any reading material. Most books had to be im-

[1] See Binney, in Dillon, iii, 285.   [2] Story, in Dillon, iii, 330.
[3] Marshall to Story, July 31, 1833; Story, ii, 150.

ported, were very expensive, and, in the back country, there were no local sources of supply where they could be purchased. Also, the frontier settlers had neither the leisure nor, it appears, the desire for reading [1] that distinguished the wealthy landlords of the older parts of the colony.[2] Thomas Marshall, however, was an exception to his class in his eagerness for the knowledge to be gathered from books and in his determination that his children should have those advantages which reading gives.

So, while his small house in "The Hollow" of the Blue Ridge probably contained not many more books than children, yet such volumes as were on that frontier bookshelf were absorbed and made the intellectual possession of the reader. The Bible was there, of course; and probably Shakespeare also.[3] The only book which positively is known to have been a literary companion of John Marshall was a volume of Pope's poems. He told Justice Story that, by the time he was twelve years old (1767), he had copied every word of the "Essay on Man" and other of Pope's moral essays, and had committed to memory "many of the most interesting passages." [4] This

[1] See *infra*, chaps. vii and viii.

[2] "A taste for reading is more prevalent [in Virginia] among the gentlemen of the first class than in any other part of America; but the common people are, perhaps, more ignorant than elsewhere." (La Rochefoucauld, iii, 232.) Other earlier and later travelers confirm this statement of this careful French observer.

[3] Story thinks that Thomas Marshall, at this time, owned Milton, Shakespeare, and Dryden. (Dillon, iii, 331.) This is possible. Twenty years later, Chastellux found Milton, Addison, and Richardson in the parlor of a New Jersey inn; but this was in the comparatively thickly settled country adjacent to Philadelphia. (Chastellux, 159.)

[4] Story, in Dillon, iii, 331, and Binney, in *ib.*, 283; *Hist. Mag.*, iii, 166.

would seem to prove that not many other attractive books were at the boyhood hands of so eager a reader of poetry and fiction as Marshall always was. It was quite natural that this volume should be in that primitive household; for, at that time, Pope was more widely read, admired, and quoted than any other writer either of poetry or prose.[1]

For those who believe that early impressions are important, and who wish to trace John Marshall's mental development back to its sources, it is well to spend a moment on that curious work which Pope named his "Essay on Man." The natural bent of the youth's mind was distinctively logical and orderly, and Pope's metred syllogisms could not but have appealed to it powerfully. The soul of Pope's "Essay" is the wisdom of and necessity for order; and it is plain that the boy absorbed this vital message and made it his own. Certain it is that even as a beardless young soldier, offering his life for his country's independence, he already had grasped the master truth that order is a necessary condition of liberty and justice.

It seems probable, however, that other books were brought to this mountain fireside. There was a limited store within his reach from which Thomas Marshall could draw. With his employer and friend, George Washington,[2] he was often a visitor at the

[1] Lang: *History of English Literature*, 384; and see Gosse: *History of Eighteenth Century Literature*, 131; also, Traill: *Social England*, v, 72; Stephen: *Alexander Pope*, 62; and see Cabot to Hamilton, Nov. 29, 1800; *Cabot:* Lodge, 299.

[2] Binney, in Dillon, iii, 283-84; Washington's *Diary;* MS., Lib. Cong.

wilderness home of Lord Fairfax just over the Blue Ridge. Washington availed himself of the Fairfax Library,[1] and it seems reasonable that Thomas Marshall did the same. It is likely that he carried to his Blue Ridge dwelling an occasional Fairfax volume carefully selected for its usefulness in developing his own as well as his children's minds.

This contact with the self-expatriated nobleman had more important results, however, than access to his books. Thomas Marshall's life was profoundly influenced by his early and intimate companionship with the well-mannered though impetuous and headstrong young Washington, who engaged him as assistant surveyor of the Fairfax estate.[2] From youth to manhood, both had close association with Lord Fairfax, who gave Washington his first employment and secured for him the appointment by the colonial authorities as public surveyor.[3] Washington was related by marriage to the proprietor of the Northern Neck, his brother Lawrence having married the daughter of William Fairfax. When their father died, Lawrence Washington took the place of parent to his younger brother;[4] and in his house the great landowner met George Washington, of whom he became very fond. For more than three years the youthful surveyor passed most of his time in the Blue Ridge part of the British nobleman's vast

---

[1] Irving, i, 45; and Lodge: *Washington*, i, 59. Many years later when he became rich, Washington acquired a good library, part of which is now in the Boston Athenæum. But as a young and moneyless surveyor he had no books of his own and his "book" education was limited and shallow.

[2] Binney, in Dillion, iii, 281–84.

[3] Irving, i, 37, 45; and Sparks, 10.   [4] Irving, i, 27.

A FRONTIER EDUCATION

holdings,[1] and in frequent and intimate contact with his employer. Thus Thomas Marshall, as Washington's associate and helper, came under the guidance and example of Lord Fairfax.

The romantic story of this strange man deserves to be told at length, but only a résumé is possible here. This summary, however, must be given for its bearing on the characters of George Washington and Thomas Marshall, and, through them, its formative influence on John Marshall.[2]

Lord Fairfax inherited his enormous Virginia estate from his mother, the daughter of Lord Culpeper, the final grantee of that kingly domain. This profligate grant of a careless and dissolute monarch embraced some five million acres between the Potomac and Rappahannock Rivers back to a straight line connecting the sources of these streams. While the young heir of the ancient Fairfax title was in Oxford, his father having died, his mother and grandmother, the dowager Ladies Fairfax and Culpeper, forced him to cut off the entail of the extensive Fairfax estates in England in order to save the heavily mortgaged Culpeper estates in the same country; and as compensation for this sacrifice, the noble Oxford student was promised the inheritance of this wild Virginia forest principality.

Nor did the youthful baron's misfortunes end there. The lady of his heart had promised to become his bride, the wedding day was set, the prepara-

---

[1] Irving, i, 46.
[2] As will appear, the Fairfax estate is closely interwoven into John Marshall's career. (See vol. II of this work.)

tions made. But before that hour of joy arrived, this fickle daughter of ambition received an offer to become a duchess instead of a mere baroness, and, throwing over young Fairfax without delay, she embraced the more exalted station offered her.

These repeated blows of adversity embittered the youthful head of the illustrious house of Fairfax against mother and grandmother, and, for the time being, all but against England itself. So, after some years of management of his Virginia estate by his cousin, William, who was in Government employ in America, Lord Fairfax himself left England forever, came to Virginia, took personal charge of his inherited holdings, and finally established himself at its very outskirts on the savage frontier. In the Shenandoah Valley, near Winchester, he built a small house of native stone and called it Greenway Court,[1] after the English fashion; but it never was anything more than a hunting lodge.[2]

From this establishment he personally managed his vast estates, parting with his lands to settlers on easy terms. His tenants generally were treated with liberality and consideration. If any land that was leased or sold did not turn out as was expected by the purchaser or lessee, another and better tract would be given in its place. If money was needed for improvements, Lord Fairfax advanced it. His excess revenues were given to the poor. So that the Northern Neck under Lord Fairfax's administration

---

[1] For description of Greenway Court see Pecquet du Bellet, ii, 175.
[2] Washington's *Writings:* Ford, i, footnote to 329.

A FRONTIER EDUCATION 49

became the best settled, best cultivated, and best governed of all the upper regions of the colony.[1]

Through this exile of circumstance, Fate wove another curious thread in the destiny of John Marshall. Lord Fairfax was the head of that ancient house whose devotion to liberty had been proved on many a battlefield. The second Lord Fairfax commanded the Parliamentary forces at Marston Moor. The third Lord Fairfax was the general of Cromwell's army and the hero of Naseby. So the proprietor of the Northern Neck, who was the sixth Lord Fairfax, came of blood that had been poured out for human rights. He had, as an inheritance of his house, that love of liberty for which his ancestors had fought.[2]

But much as he hated oppression, Lord Fairfax was equally hostile to disorder and upheaval; and his forbears had opposed these even to the point of helping restore Charles II to the throne. Thus the Virginia baron's talk and teaching were of liberty with order, independence with respect for law.[3]

[1] For a clear but laudatory account of Lord Fairfax see Appendix No. 4 to Burnaby, 197-213. But Fairfax could be hard enough on those who opposed him, as witness his treatment of Joist Hite. (See *infra*, chap. v.)

[2] When the Revolution came, however, Fairfax was heartily British. The objection which the colony made to the title to his estate doubtless influenced him.

[3] Fairfax was a fair example of the moderate, as distinguished from the radical or the reactionary. He was against both irresponsible autocracy and unrestrained democracy. In short, he was what would now be termed a liberal conservative (although, of course, such a phrase, descriptive of that demarcation, did not then exist). Much attention should be given to this unique man in tracing to their ultimate sources the origins of John Marshall's economic, political, and social convictions.

He loved literature and was himself no mean writer, his contributions while he was in the University having been accepted by the "Spectator."[1] His example instructed his companions in manners, too, and schooled them in the speech and deportment of gentlemen. All who met George Washington in his mature years were impressed by his correct if restricted language, his courtly conduct, and his dignified if rigid bearing. Much of this was due to his noble patron.[2]

Thomas Marshall was affected in the same way and by the same cause. Pioneer and backwoodsman though he was, and, as we shall see, true to his class and section, he yet acquired more balanced ideas of liberty, better manners, and finer if not higher views of life than the crude, rough individualists who inhabited the back country. As was the case with Washington, this intellectual and moral tendency in Thomas Marshall's development was due, in large measure, to the influence of Lord Fairfax. While it cannot be said that George Washington imitated the wilderness nobleman, yet Fairfax undoubtedly afforded his protégé a certain standard of living, thinking, and acting; and Thomas Marshall followed the example set by his fellow surveyor.[3] Thus came into the Marshall household a different atmosphere from that which pervaded the cabins of the Blue Ridge.

[1] Sparks, 11; and Irving, i, 33.
[2] For Fairfax's influence on Washington see Irving, i, 45; and in general, for fair secondary accounts of Fairfax, see *ib.*, 31–46; and Sparks, 10–11.
[3] Senator Humphrey Marshall says that Thomas Marshall "emulated" Washington. (Humphrey Marshall, i, 345.)

A FRONTIER EDUCATION

All this, however, did not make for his unpopularity among Thomas Marshall's distant, scattered, and humbly placed neighbors. On the contrary, it seems to have increased the consideration and respect which his native qualities had won for him from the pioneers. Certainly Thomas Marshall was the foremost man in Fauquier County when it was established in 1759. He was almost immediately elected to represent the county in the Virginia House of Burgesses;[1] and, six years later, he was appointed Sheriff by Governor Fauquier, for whom the county was named.[2] The shrievalty was, at that time, the most powerful local office in Virginia; and the fees and perquisites of the place made it the most lucrative.[3]

By 1765 Thomas Marshall felt himself sufficiently established to acquire the land where he had lived since his removal from Germantown. In the autumn of that year he leased from Thomas Ludwell Lee and Colonel Richard Henry Lee the three hundred and thirty acres on Goose Creek "whereon the said Thomas Marshall now lives." The lease was "for and during the natural lives of ... Thomas Marshall, Mary Marshall his wife, and John Marshall his son and ... the longest liver of them." The consideration was "five shillings current money in

---

[1] See *infra*.
[2] Bond of Thomas Marshall as Sheriff, Oct. 26, 1767; Records of Fauquier County (Va.), Deed Book, iii, 70. Approval of bond by County Court; Minute Book (from 1764 to 1768), 322. Marshall's bond was "to his Majesty, George III," to secure payment to the British revenue officers of all money collected by Marshall for the Crown. (Records of Fauquier County (Va.), Deed Book, iii, 71.)
[3] Bruce: *Inst.*, i, 597, 600; also, ii, 408, 570–74.

hand paid" and a "yearly rent of five pounds current money, and the quit rents and Land Tax." [1]

In 1769 Leeds Parish, embracing Fauquier County, was established.[2] Of this parish Thomas Marshall became the principal vestryman.[3] This office supplemented, in dignity and consequence, that of sheriff; the one was religious and denoted high social status, the other was civil and evidenced political importance.[4] The occupancy of both marked Thomas Marshall as the chief figure in the local government and in the social and political life of Fauquier County, although the holding of the superior office of burgess left no doubt as to his leadership. The vestries had immense influence in the civil affairs of the parish and the absolute management of the practical business of the established (Episcopal) church.[5] Among the duties and privileges of the vestry was that of selecting and employing the clergyman.[6]

The vestry of Leeds Parish, with Thomas Mar-

[1] Records of Fauquier County (Va.), Deed Book, ii, 42. There is a curious record of a lease from Lord Fairfax in 1768 to John Marshall for his life and "the natural lives of Mary his wife and Thomas Marshall his son and every of them longest living." (Records of Fauquier County (Va.), Deed Book, iii, 230.) John Marshall was then only thirteen years old. The lease probably was to Thomas Marshall, the clerk of Lord Fairfax having confused the names of father and son.

[2] Meade, ii, 218.

[3] In 1773 three deeds for an aggregate of two hundred and twenty acres "for a glebe" were recorded in Fauquier County to "Thos. Marshall & Others, Gentlemen, & Vestrymen of Leeds Parish." (Records of Fauquier County (Va.), Deed Book, v, 401, 403, 422.)

[4] The vestrymen were "the foremost men ... in the parish ... whether from the point of view of intelligence, wealth or social position." (Bruce: *Inst.*, i, 62; and see Meade, i, 191.)

[5] Bruce: *Inst.*, i, 62–93; and see Eckenrode: *S. C. & S.*, 13.

[6] Bruce: *Inst.*, i, 131 *et seq.*

A FRONTIER EDUCATION

shall at its head, chose for its minister a young Scotchman, James Thompson, who had arrived in Virginia a year or two earlier. He lived at first with the Marshall family.[1] Thus it came about that John Marshall received the first of his three short periods of formal schooling; for during his trial year the young [2] Scotch deacon returned Thomas Marshall's hospitality by giving the elder children such instruction as occasion offered,[3] as was the custom of parsons, who always were teachers as well as preachers. We can imagine the embryo clergyman instructing the eldest son under the shade of the friendly trees in pleasant weather or before the blazing logs in the great fireplace when winter came. While living with the Marshall family, he doubtless slept with the children in the half-loft [4] of that frontier dwelling.

There was nothing unusual about this; indeed, circumstances made it the common and unavoidable custom. Washington tells us that in his surveying trips, he frequently slept on the floor in the room of a settler's cabin where the fireplace was and where husband, wife, children, and visitors stretched themselves for nightly rest; and he remarks that the person was lucky who got the spot nearest the fireplace.[5]

[1] Meade, ii, 219. Bishop Meade here makes a slight error. He says that Mr. Thompson "lived at first in the family of Colonel Thomas Marshall, of Oak Hill." Thomas Marshall did not become a colonel until ten years afterward. (Heitman, 285.) And he did not move to Oak Hill until 1773, six years later. (Paxton, 20.)

[2] James Thompson was born in 1739. (Meade, ii, 219.)   [3] *Ib.*

[4] Forty years later La Rochefoucauld found that the whole family and all visitors slept in the same room of the cabins of the back country. (La Rochefoucauld, iv, 595-96.)

[5] "I have not sleep'd above three nights or four in a bed, but, after walking ... all the day, I lay down before the fire upon a little hay,

At the end of a year the embryo Scottish clergyman's character, ability, and services having met the approval of Thomas Marshall and his fellow vestrymen, Thompson returned to England for orders.[1] So ended John Marshall's first instruction from a trained teacher. His pious tutor returned the next year, at once married a young woman of the Virginia frontier, and settled on the glebe near Salem, where he varied his ministerial duties by teaching such children of his parishioners as could get to him. It may be that John Marshall was among them.[2]

In the light they throw upon the Marshall family, the political opinions of Mr. Thompson are as important as was his teaching. True to the impulses of youth, he was a man of the people, ardently championed their cause, and was fervently against British misrule, as was his principal vestryman. Five years later we find him preaching a sermon

straw, fodder or bearskin... with man, wife, and children, like a parcel of dogs and cats; and happy is he, who gets the berth nearest the fire." (Washington to a friend, in 1748; *Writings:* Ford, i, 7.)

Here is another of Washington's descriptions of frontier comforts: "I not being so good a woodsman as ye rest of my company, striped myself very orderly and went into ye Bed, as they calld it, when to my surprize, I found it to be nothing but a little straw matted together without sheets or any thing else, but only one thread bear [*sic*] blanket with double its weight of vermin such as Lice, Fleas, &c." (Washington's *Diary*, March 15, 1747; *ib.*, 2.) And see La Rochefoucauld, iii, 175, for description of homes of farmers in the Valley forty years later — miserable log huts "which swarmed with children." Thomas Marshall's little house was much better than, and the manners of the family were far superior to, those described by Washington and La Rochefoucauld.

[1] Meade, ii, 219.

[2] *Ib.* Bishop Meade says that Thomas Marshall's sons were sent to Mr. Thompson again; but Marshall himself told Justice Story that the Scotch parson taught him when the clergyman lived at his father's house.

A FRONTIER EDUCATION

on the subject so strong that a part of it has been preserved.[1]

Thus the years of John Marshall's life sped on until his eighteenth birthday. By this time Thomas Marshall's rapidly growing prosperity enabled him to buy a larger farm in a more favorable locality. In January, 1773, he purchased from Thomas Turner seventeen hundred acres adjacent to North Cobler Mountain, a short distance to the east of his first location in "The Hollow."[2] For this plantation he paid "nine hundred and twelve pounds ten shillings current money of Virginia." Here he established himself for the third time and remained for ten years.

On an elevation overlooking valley, stream, and grove, with the Blue Ridge as a near background, he built a frame house thirty-three by thirty feet, the attic or loft under the roof serving as a second story.[3] The house had seven rooms, four below and three above. One of the upper rooms is, comparatively, very large, being twenty-one by fifteen feet; and, according to tradition, this was used as a schoolroom for the Marshall children. Indeed, the structure was, for that section and period, a pretentious

---

[1] Meade, ii, 219. This extract of Mr. Thompson's sermon was treasonable from the Tory point of view. See *infra*, chap. III.

[2] Records of Fauquier County (Va.), Deed Book, v, 282. This purchase made Thomas Marshall the owner of about two thousand acres of the best land in Fauquier County. He had sold his Goose Creek holding in "The Hollow."

[3] The local legend, current to the present day, is that this house had the first glass windows in that region, and that the bricks in the chimney were imported from England. The importation of brick, however, is doubtful. Very little brick was brought to Virginia from England.

dwelling. This is the famous Oak Hill.[1] The house still stands as a modest wing to the large and attractive building erected by John Marshall's eldest son, Thomas, many years later.

A book was placed in the hands of John Marshall, at this time, that influenced his mind even more than his reading of Pope's poetry when a small boy. Blackstone's "Commentaries" was published in America in 1772 and one of the original subscribers was "Captain Thomas Marshall, Clerk of Dunmore County, Virginia." [2] The youthful backwoodsman read Blackstone with delight; for this legal classic is the poetry of law, just as Pope is logic in poetry. Also, Thomas Marshall saw to it that his son read Blackstone as carefully as circumstances permitted. He had bought the book for John's use as much as or more than for his own information. Marshall's parents, with a sharp eye on the calling that then brought greatest honor and profit, had determined that their eldest son should be a lawyer. "From my infancy," says Marshall, "I was destined for the bar." [3] He did not, we believe, give his attention exclusively to Blackstone. Indeed, it appears certain that his legal reading at this period was fragmentary and interrupted, for his time was taken up and his mind largely absorbed by military exercises

---

[1] Five more children of Thomas and Mary Marshall were born in this house: Louis, 1773; Susan, 1775; Charlotte, 1777; Jane, 1779; and Nancy, 1781. (Paxton.)

[2] This volume is now in the possession of Judge J. K. M. Norton, of Alexandria, Va. On several leaves are printed the names of the subscribers. Among them are Pelatiah Webster, James Wilson, Nathanael Greene, John Adams, and others.

[3] *Autobiography.*

OAK HILL.

From a water-color. The original house, built by Thomas Marshall in 1773, is shown at the right, in the rear of the main building.

A FRONTIER EDUCATION

and study. He was intent on mastering the art of war against the day when the call of patriotism should come to him to be a soldier.[1] So the law book was pushed aside by the manual of arms.

About this time John Marshall was given his second fragment of formal teaching. He was sent to the school of the Reverend Archibald Campbell in Westmoreland County.[2] This embryo "academy" was a primitive affair, but its solitary instructor was a sound classical scholar equipped with all the learning which the Scottish universities could give. He was a man of unusual ability, which, it appears, was the common possession of his family. He was the uncle of the British poet Campbell.[3]

The sons of this colonial parson school-teacher from Scotland became men of note and influence, one of them among the most distinguished lawyers of Virginia.[4] Indeed, it was chiefly in order to teach his two boys that Mr. Campbell opened his little school in Westmoreland.[5] So, while John Marshall attended the "academy" for only a few months, that brief period under such a teacher was worth much in methods of thought and study.

The third scanty fragment of John Marshall's education by professional instructors comes seven years later, at a time and under circumstances which make it necessary to defer a description of it.

---

[1] Binney, in Dillon, iii, 286.
[2] Story and Binney say that Marshall's first schooling was at Campbell's "academy" and his second and private instruction under Mr. Thompson. The reverse seems to have been the case.
[3] Meade, ii, 159, and footnote to 160.
[4] *Ib.*, 161. [5] *Ib.*

During all these years, however, young Marshall was getting another kind of education more real and more influential on his later life than any regular schooling could have given him. Thomas Marshall served in the House of Burgesses at Williamsburg[1] from 1761 until October, 1767, when he became Sheriff of Fauquier County.[2] In 1769 he was again chosen Burgess,[3] and reëlected until 1773, when he was appointed Clerk of Dunmore County.[4] In 1775 he once more appears as Burgess for Fauquier County.[5] Throughout this period, George Washington also served as Burgess from Westmoreland County. Thomas Marshall was a member of the standing committees on Trade, Religion, Propositions and Grievances, and on several special committees and commissions.[6]

[1] Journal, H.B. (1761–65), 3. Thomas Marshall was seldom out of office. Burgess, Sheriff, Vestryman, Clerk, were the promising beginnings of his crowded office-holding career. He became Surveyor of Fayette County, Kentucky, upon his removal to that district, and afterwards Collector of Revenue for the District of Ohio. (Humphrey Marshall, i, 120; and see ii, chap. v, of this work. Thomas Marshall to Adams, April 28, 1797; MS.) In holding offices, John Marshall followed in his father's footsteps.

[2] Journal, H.B. (1766–69), 147 and 257.

[3] His election was contested in the House, but decided in Marshall's favor. (*Ib.* (1761–69), 272, 290, 291.)

[4] *Ib.*, (1773–76), 9. County Clerks were then appointed by the Secretary of State. In some respects the Clerk of the County Court had greater advantages than the Sheriff. (See Bruce: *Inst.*, i, 588 *et seq.*) Dunmore County is now Shenandoah County. The Revolution changed the name. When Thomas Marshall was appointed Clerk, the House of Burgesses asked the Governor to issue a writ for a new election in Fauquier County to fill Marshall's place as Burgess. (*Ib.* (1773–76), 9.)

[5] *Ib.* (1766–69), 163.

[6] *Ib.*, 16, 71, 257; (1770–72), 17, 62, 123, 147, 204, 234, 251, 257, 274, 292; (1773–76), 217, 240.

A FRONTIER EDUCATION

The situations, needs, and interests of the upland counties above the line of the falls of the rivers, so different from those on the tidewater, had made the political oligarchy of the lower counties more distinct and conspicuous than ever. This dominant political force was aristocratic and selfish. It was generally hostile to the opinions of the smaller pioneer landowners of the back country and it did not provide adequately for their necessities. Their petitions for roads, bridges, and other indispensable requisites of social and industrial life usually were denied; and their rapidly growing democratic spirit was scorned with haughty disfavor and contempt.[1]

In the House of Burgesses, one could tell by his apparel and deportment, no less than by his sentiments, a member from the mountains, and indeed from anywhere above the fall line of the rivers; and, by the same tokens, one from the great plantations below. The latter came fashionably attired, according to the latest English mode, with the silk knee breeches and stockings, colored coat, ornamented waistcoat, linen and lace, buckled shoes, garters, and all details of polite adornment that the London fashion of the time dictated. The upland men were plainly clad; and those from the border appeared in their native homespun, with buckskin shirts, coonskin caps, and the queue of their unpowdered hair tied in a bag or sack of some thin material. To this upland class of Burgesses, Thomas Marshall belonged.

He had been a member of the House for four years

[1] Ambler, Introduction.

when the difference between the two Virginia sections and classes suddenly crystallized. The upper counties found a leader and fought and overcame the hitherto invincible power of the tidewater aristocracy, which, until then, had held the Government of Virginia in its lordly hand.

This explosion came in 1765, when John Marshall was ten years old. For nearly a quarter of a century the combination of the great planter interests of eastern Virginia had kept John Robinson Speaker of the House and Treasurer of the Colony.[1] He was an ideal representative of his class — rich, generous, kindly, and ever ready to oblige his fellow members of the ruling faction.[2] To these he had lent large sums of money from the public treasury and, at last, finding himself lost unless he could find a way out of the financial quagmire in which he was sinking, Robinson, with his fellow aristocrats, devised a scheme for establishing a loan office, equipping it with a million and a quarter of dollars borrowed on the faith of the colony, to be lent to individuals on personal security.[3] A bill to this effect was presented and the tidewater machine was oiled and set in motion to put it through.

As yet, Robinson's predicament was known only to himself and those upon whom he had bestowed the proceeds of the people's taxes; and no opposition was expected to the proposed resolution which would extricate the embarrassed Treasurer. But Patrick Henry, a young member from Hanover County, who had just been elected to the House of

[1] Ambler, 17–18.   [2] Henry, i, 71.   [3] Ib., 76–77.

A FRONTIER EDUCATION

Burgesses and who had displayed in the famous Parsons case a courage and eloquence which had given him a reputation throughout the colony,[1] opposed, on principle, the proposed loan-office law. In a speech of startling power he attacked the bill and carried with him every member from the up counties. The bill was lost.[2] It was the first defeat ever experienced by the combination that had governed Virginia so long that they felt that it was their inalienable right to do so. One of the votes that struck this blow was cast by Thomas Marshall.[3] Robinson died the next year; his defalcation was discovered and the real purpose of the bill was thus revealed.[4]

Quick on the heels of this victory for popular rights and honest government trod another event of vital influence on American history. The British Parliament, the year before, had passed resolutions declaring the right of Parliament to tax the colonies without representation, and, indeed, to enact any law it pleased for the government and administration of British dominions wherever situated.[5] The

[1] Henry, i, 39–48.

[2] Wirt, 71 *et seq.* It passed the House (Journal, H.B. (1761–65), 350); but was disapproved by the Council. (*Ib.*, 356; and see Henry, i, 78.)

[3] The "ayes" and "noes" were not recorded in the Journals of the House; but Jefferson says, in his description of the event, which he personally witnessed, that Henry "carried with him all the members of the upper counties and left a minority composed merely of the aristocracy." (Wirt, 71.) "The members, who, like himself [Henry], represented the yeomanry of the colony, were filled with admiration and delight." (Henry, i, 78.)

[4] Wirt, 71. The incident, it appears, was considered closed with the defeat of the loan-office bill. Robinson having died, nothing further was done in the matter. For excellent condensed account see Eckenrode: *R. V.*, 16–17.

[5] Declaratory Resolutions.

colonies protested, Virginia among them; but when finally Parliament enacted the Stamp Act, although the colonies were in sullen anger, they yet prepared to submit.[1] The more eminent men among the Virginia Burgesses were willing to remonstrate once more, but had not the heart to go further.[2] It was no part of the plan or feeling of the aristocracy to affront the Royal Government openly. At this moment, Patrick Henry suddenly offered his historic resolutions, the last one a bold denial of Parliament's right to pass the Stamp Act, and a savage defiance of the British Government.[3]

Cautious members of the tidewater organization were aghast. They did not like the Stamp Act themselves, but they thought that this was going too far. The logical end of it would be armed conflict, they said; or at the very least, a temporary suspension of profitable commerce with England. Their material interests were involved; and while they hazarded these and life itself most nobly when the test of war finally came, ten years later, they were not minded to risk either business or comfort until forced to do so.[4]

But a far stronger influence with them was their hatred of Henry and their fear of the growing power of the up country. They were smarting from the defeat[5] of the loan-office bill. They did not relish the idea of following the audacious Henry and his

---

[1] For the incredible submission and indifference of the colonies before Patrick Henry's speech, see Henry, i, 63–67. The authorities given in those pages are conclusive.
[2] *Ib.*, 67.   [3] *Ib.*, 80–81.   [4] *Ib.*, 82–86.
[5] Wirt, 74–76.

democratic supporters from the hills. They resented the leadership which the "new men" were assuming. To the aristocratic machine it was offensive to have any movement originate outside itself.[1]

The up-country members to a man rallied about Patrick Henry and fought beneath the standard of principle which he had raised. The line that marked the division between these contending forces in the Virginia House of Burgesses was practically identical with that which separated them in the loan-office struggle which had just taken place. The same men who had supported Robinson were now against any measure which might too radically assert the rights of the colonies and offend both the throne and Westminster Hall. And as in the Robinson case so in the fight over Henry's Stamp Act Resolutions, the Burgesses who represented the frontier settlers and small landowners and who stood for their democratic views, formed a compact and militant force to strike for popular government as they already had struck, and successfully, for honest administration.[2]

Henry's fifth resolution was the first written American assertion of independence, the virile seed out of which the declaration at Philadelphia ten years later directly grew. It was over this resolution that Thomas Jefferson said, "the debate was most bloody";[3] and it was in this particular part of the debate that Patrick Henry made his immortal

[1] Eckenrode: *R. V.*, 5–6.
[2] "The members from the upper counties invariably supported Mr. Henry in his revolutionary measures." (Jefferson's statement to Daniel Webster, quoted in Henry, i, 87.)
[3] Henry, i, 86.

speech, ending with the famous words, "Tarquin and Cæsar had each his Brutus, Charles the First his Cromwell, and George the Third —" And as the cries of "Treason! Treason! Treason!" rang from every part of the hall, Henry, stretching himself to the utmost of his stature, thundered, " — *may profit by their example*. If *this* be treason, make the most of it." [1]

Henry and the stout-hearted men of the hills won the day, but only by a single vote. Peyton Randolph, the foremost member of the tidewater aristocracy and Royal Attorney-General, exclaimed, "By God, I would have given one [2] hundred guineas for a single vote!" [3] Thomas Marshall again fought by Henry's side and voted for his patriotic defiance of British injustice.[4]

This victory of the poorer section of the Old Dominion was, in Virginia, the real beginning of the active period of the Revolution. It was more — it

[1] Henry, i, 86, and authorities there cited in the footnote.
[2] Misquoted in Wirt (79) as "500 guineas."
[3] Jefferson to Wirt, Aug. 14, 1814; *Works:* Ford, xi, 404.
[4] It is most unfortunate that the "ayes" and "noes" were not kept in the House of Burgesses. In the absence of such a record, Jefferson's repeated testimony that the up-country members voted and worked with Henry must be taken as conclusive of Thomas Marshall's vote. For not only was Marshall Burgess from a frontier county, but Jefferson, at the time he wrote to Wirt in 1814 (and gave the same account to others later), had become very bitter against the Marshalls and constantly attacked John Marshall whom he hated virulently. If Thomas Marshall had voted out of his class and against Henry, so remarkable a circumstance would surely have been mentioned by Jefferson, who never overlooked any circumstance unfavorable to an enemy. Far more positive evidence, however, is the fact that Washington, who was a Burgess, voted with Henry, as his letter to Francis Dandridge, Sept. 20, 1765, shows. (*Writings:* Ford, ii, 209.) And Thomas Marshall always acted with Washington.

Oak Hill

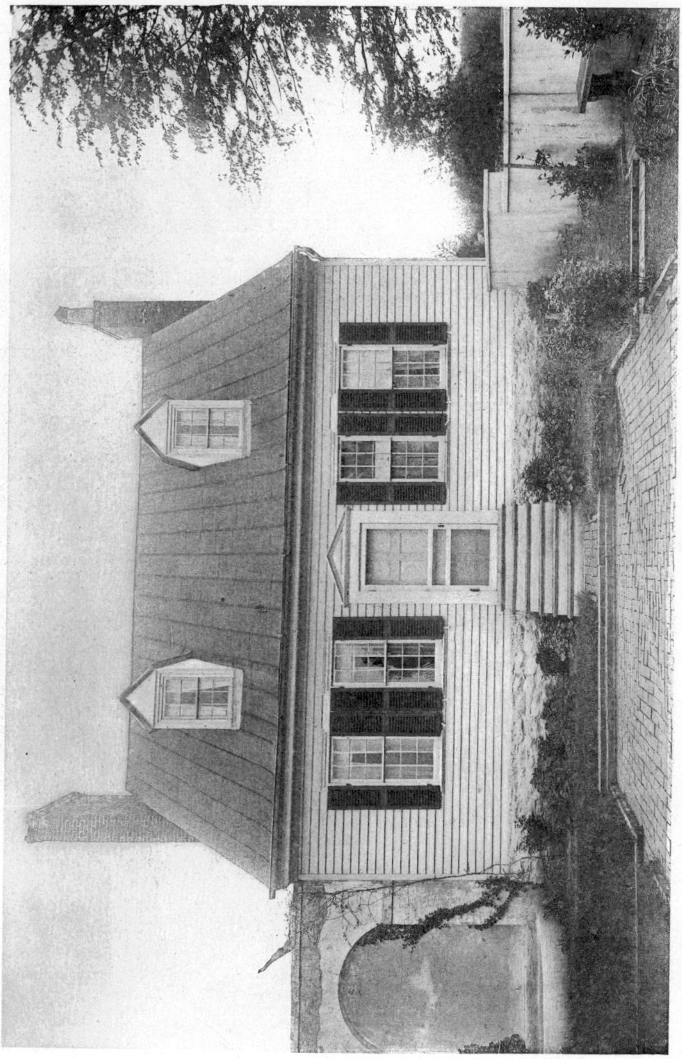

was the ending of the hitherto unquestioned supremacy of the tidewater aristocracy.[1] It marked the effective entrance of the common man into Virginia's politics and government.

When Thomas Marshall returned to his Blue Ridge home, he described, of course, the scenes he had witnessed and taken part in. The heart of his son thrilled, we may be sure, as he listened to his father reciting Patrick Henry's words of fire and portraying the manner, appearance, and conduct of that master orator of liberty. So it was that John Marshall, even when a boy, came into direct and living touch with the outside world and learned at first hand of the dramatic movement and the mighty forces that were about to quarry the materials for a nation.

Finally the epic year of 1775 arrived, — the year of the Boston riots, Paul Revere's ride, Lexington and Concord, — above all, the year of the Virginia Resolutions for Arming and Defense. Here we find Thomas Marshall a member of the Virginia Convention,[2] when once more the radicals of the up country met and defeated the aristocratic conservatives of the older counties. The latter counseled prudence. They argued weightily that the colony was not prepared for war with the Royal Power across the sea. They urged patience and the working-out of the problem by processes of conciliation and moderate devices, as those made timid by their

[1] "By these resolutions, Mr. Henry took the lead out of the hands of those who had heretofore guided the proceedings of the House." (Jefferson to Wirt, Aug. 14, 1814; *Works:* Ford, xi, 406.)
[2] *Proceedings*, Va. Conv., 1775, March 20, 3; July 17, 3, 5, 7.

own interests always do.[1] Selfish love of ease made them forget, for the moment, the lesson of Braddock's defeat. They held up the overwhelming might of Great Britain and the impotence of the King's subjects in his western dominions; and they were about to prevail.

But again Patrick Henry became the voice of America. He offered the Resolutions for Arming and Defense and carried them with that amazing speech ending with, "Give me liberty or give me death,"[2] which always will remain the classic of American liberty. Thomas Marshall, who sat beneath its spell, declared that it was "one of the most bold, animated, and vehement pieces of eloquence that had ever been delivered."[3] Once more he promptly took his stand under Henry's banner and supported the heroic resolutions with his vote and influence.[4] So did George Washington, as both had done ten years before in the battle over Henry's Stamp Act Resolutions in the House of Burgesses in 1765.[5]

Not from newspapers, then, nor from second-hand rumor did John Marshall, now nineteen years old, learn of the epochal acts of that convention. He

[1] Henry, i, 255-61; Wirt, 117-19. Except Henry's speech itself, Wirt's summary of the arguments of the conservatives is much the best account of the opposition to Henry's fateful resolutions.

[2] Wirt, 142; Henry, i, 261-66.   [3] *Ib.*, 271; and Wirt, 143.

[4] In the absence of the positive proof afforded by a record of the "ayes" and "noes," Jefferson's testimony, Washington's vote, Thomas Marshall's tribute to Henry, and above all, the sentiment of the frontier county he represented, are conclusive testimony as to Thomas Marshall's stand in this all-important legislative battle which was the precursor of the iron conflict soon to come in which he bore so heroic a part. (See Humphrey Marshall, i, 344.)

[5] Washington was appointed a member of the committee provided for in Henry's second resolution. (Henry, i, 271.)

heard of them from his father's lips. Henry's inspired speech, which still burns across a century with undiminished power, came to John Marshall from one who had listened to it, as the family clustered around the fireside of their Oak Hill home. The effect on John Marshall's mind and spirit was heroic and profound, as his immediate action and his conduct for several years demonstrate.

We may be sure that the father was not deceived as to the meaning of it all; nor did he permit his family to be carried off the solid ground of reality by any emotional excitement. Thomas Marshall was no fanatic, no fancy-swayed enthusiast resolving highly in wrought-up moments and retracting humbly in more sober hours. He was a man who looked before he leaped; he counted the costs; he made up his mind with knowledge of the facts. When Thomas Marshall decided to act, no unforeseen circumstance could make him hesitate, no unexpected obstacle could swerve him from his course; for he had considered carefully and well; and his son was of like mettle.

So when Thomas Marshall came back to his Fauquier County home from the fateful convention of 1775 at Richmond, he knew just what the whole thing meant; and, so knowing, he gravely welcomed the outcome. He knew that it meant war; and he knew also what war meant. Already he had been a Virginia ranger and officer, had seen fighting, had witnessed wounds and death.[1] The same decision

[1] Thomas Marshall had been ensign, lieutenant, and captain in the militia, had taken part in the Indian wars, and was a trained soldier. (Crozier: *Virginia Colonial Militia*, 96.)

that made him cast his vote for Henry's resolutions also caused Thomas Marshall to draw his sword from its scabbard. It inspired him to do more; for the father took down the rifle from its deerhorn bracket and the hunting-knife from its hook, and placed them in the hands of his first-born. And so we find father and son ready for the field and prepared to make the ultimate argument of willingness to lay down their lives for the cause they believed in.

CHAPTER III

A SOLDIER OF THE REVOLUTION

Our liberties are at stake. It is time to brighten our fire-arms and learn to use them in the field. (Marshall to Culpeper Minute Men, 1775.)

Our sick naked, and well naked, our unfortunate men in captivity naked. (Washington, 1777.)

I have seen a regiment consisting of *thirty men* and a company of *one corporal*. (Von Steuben, 1778.)

THE fighting men of the up counties lost not a minute's time. Blood had been shed in New England; blood, they knew, must soon flow in Virginia. At once Culpeper, Orange, and Fauquier Counties arranged to raise a regiment of minute men with Lawrence Taliaferro of Orange as colonel, Edward Stevens of Culpeper as lieutenant, Thomas Marshall of Fauquier as major.[1] Out over the countryside went the word; and from mountain cabins and huts in forest clearings, from log abodes in secluded valleys and on primitive farms, the fighting yeomanry of northern Virginia came forth in answer.

In the years between Patrick Henry's two epochal appeals in 1765 and 1775, all Virginia, but particularly the back country, had been getting ready to make answer in terms of rifle and lead. "No man should scruple, or hesitate a moment, to use arms," wrote Washington in 1769.[2] Thomas Marshall's

---
[1] Slaughter, 107-08. This was "the first minute battalion raised within this Commonwealth." (Memorial of Thomas Marshall to the Virginia Legislature for military "emoluments"; MS. Archives, Va. St. Lib.) Appendix IV.

[2] Washington to Mason, April 5, 1769; *Writings:* Ford, ii, 263.

minister, Mr. Thompson, preached militant preparation; Parliament had deprived the colonists of "their just and legal rights" by acts which were "destructive of their liberties," thundered the parson; it had "overawed the inhabitants by British troops," loaded "great hardships" upon the people, and "reduced the poor to great want." The preacher exhorted his flock "as men and Christians" to help "supply the country with arms and ammunition," and referred his hearers, for specific information, to "the committee of this county,"[1] whose head undoubtedly was their Burgess and leading vestryman of the parish, Thomas Marshall.

When news of Concord and Lexington finally trickled through to upper Virginia, it found the men of her hills and mountains in grim readiness; and when, soon after, Henry's flaming words came to them, they were ready and eager to make those words good with their lives. John Marshall, of course, was one of the band of youths who had agreed to make up a company if trouble came. In May, 1775, these young frontiersmen were called together. Their captain did not come, and Marshall was appointed lieutenant, "instead of a better," as he modestly told his comrades. But, for his years, "a better" could not have been found; since 1773 John Marshall had received careful military instruction from his father.[2] Indeed, during the two years before his company took the field in actual warfare, the youth had devoted most of his time to preparing himself, by study and practice, for military service.[3] So these

[1] Meade, ii, 219. [2] Binney, in Dillon, iii, 286. [3] *Ib.*

embryo warriors gathered about their leader to be told what to do.[1]

Here we get the first glimpse of John Marshall's power over men. "He had come," the young officer informed his comrades of the backwoods, "to meet them as fellow soldiers, who were likely to be called on to defend their country." Their own "rights and liberties" were at stake. Their brothers in New England had fought and beaten the British; now "it is time to brighten our fire-arms and learn to use them in the field." He would show them how to do this. So the boys fell into line, and John Marshall, bringing his own gun to his shoulder, instructed them in the manual of arms. He first gave the words of command slowly and distinctly and then illustrated the movements with his own rifle so that every man of the company might clearly understand what each order meant and how to execute it. He then put the company through the drill.[2]

On this muster field we learn how John Marshall looked in his nineteenth year. He was very tall, six feet at least, slender and erect. His complexion was dark, with a faint tinge of red. His face was round — "nearly a circle." His forehead was straight and low, and thick, strong, "raven black" hair covered his head. Intense eyes "dark to blackness,"[3] of compelling power, pierced the beholder while they reassured him by the good nature which shone from

[1] Statement of eye-witness. (Binney, in Dillon, iii, 287.)
[2] *Ib.*, 288.
[3] In all descriptions of Marshall, it is stated that his eyes were black and brilliant. His portraits, however, show them as dark brown, but keen and piercing.

them. "He wore a purple or pale blue hunting-shirt, and trousers of the same material fringed with white."[1]

At this point, too, we first learn of his bent for oratory. What his father told him about the debates in the House of Burgesses, the speeches of Wythe and Lee and Randolph, and above all, Patrick Henry; what he had dreamed and perhaps practiced in the silent forests and vacant fields, here now bore public fruit. When he thought that he had drilled his company enough for the time being, Marshall told them to fall out, and, if they wished to hear more about the war, to gather around him and he would make them a speech.[2] And make them a speech he did. Before his men the youthful lieutenant stood, in his hand his "round black hat mounted with a buck's tail for a cockade," and spoke to that company of country boys of the justice of their cause and of those larger things in life for which all true men are glad to die.

"For something like an hour" he spoke, his round face glowing, the dormant lightning of his eye for the time unloosed. Lively words they were, we may be sure; for John Marshall was as ardent a patriot as the colonies could produce. He had learned the elementary truths of liberty in the school of the frontier; his soul was on fire with the burning words of Henry; and he poured forth his immature eloquence not to a company of peaceful theorists, but to a group of youths ready for the field. Its premises were freedom and independence; its conclusion was

[1] Binney, in Dillon, iii, 287-88.   [2] *Ib.*

action. It was a battle speech.[1] This fact is very important to an understanding of John Marshall's character, and indeed of the blood that flowed in his veins. For, as we shall find, he was always on the firing line; the Marshall blood was fighting blood.[2]

But it was not all labor of drill and toil of discipline, heroics of patriotic speech, or solemn preachments about duty, for the youths of John Marshall's company. If he was the most earnest, he was also, it seems, the jolliest person in the whole band; and this deserves especial note, for his humor was a quality which served not only the young soldier himself, but the cause for which he fought almost as well as his valor itself, in the martial years into which he was entering. Indeed this capacity for leavening the dough of serious purpose with the yeast of humor and diversion made John Marshall's entire personal life wholesome and nutritious. Jokes and fun were a part of him, as we shall see, whether in the army, at the bar, or on the bench.

So when, the business of the day disposed of, Lieutenant Marshall challenged his sure-eyed, strong-limbed, swift-footed companions to a game of quoits, or to run a race, or to jump a pole, we find him practicing that sport and comradeship which, luckily for himself and his country, he never outgrew. Pitch quoits, then, these would-be soldiers did, and coursed their races, and vaulted high in

[1] Binney, in Dillon, iii, 288.
[2] Not only do we find Marshalls, father and sons, taking gallant part in the Revolutionary War, but, thereafter, advocates of war with any country when the honor or interest of America was at stake.

their running jumps.[1] Faster than any of them could their commander run, with his long legs out-going and his powerful lungs out-winding the best of them. He could jump higher, too, than anybody else; and from this accomplishment he got his soldier nickname "Silver Heels" in Washington's army a year later.[2]

The final muster of the Culpeper Minute Men was in "Major Clayton's old field" hard by the county seat [3] on September 1, 1775.[4] They were clad in the uniform of the frontier, which indeed was little different from their daily apparel. Fringed trousers often of deerskins, "strong brown linen hunting-shirts dyed with leaves, . . . buck-tails in each hat, and a leather belt about the shoulders, with tomahawk and scalping-knife" made up their warlike costume.[5] By some preconcert, — an order perhaps from one of the three superior officers who had poetic as well as fighting blood in him, — the mothers and wives of this wilderness soldiery had worked on the breast of each hunting-shirt in large white letters the words "Liberty or Death," [6] with which Patrick Henry had trumpeted the purpose of hitherto inarticulate America.

Early in the autumn of 1775 came the expected call. Not long had the "shirt men,"[7] as they were styled, been drilling near the court-house of Cul-

[1] Binney, in Dillon, iii, 288. [2] *Infra*, chap. IV.
[3] Slaughter, 107-08. But Binney's informant says that it was twenty miles from the court-house. (Binney, in Dillon, iii, 286.)
[4] Slaughter, 107-08; and certificate of J. Marshall in pension claim of William Payne; MSS. Rev. War, S. F. no. 8938½, Pension Bureau.
[5] Slaughter, 107-08. [6] *Ib.* [7] Campbell, 607-14.

peper County when an "express" came from Patrick Henry.[1] This was a rider from Williamsburg, mounting swift relays as he went, sometimes over the rough, miry, and hazardous roads, but mostly by the bridle paths which then were Virginia's principal highways of land travel. The "express" told of the threatening preparations of Lord Dunmore, then Royal Governor of Virginia, and bore Patrick Henry's command to march at once for the scene of action a hundred miles to the south.

Instantly the Culpeper Minute Men were on the move. "We marched immediately," wrote one of them, "and in a few days were in Williamsburg." News of their coming went before them; and when the better-settled districts were reached, the inhabitants were in terror of them, for the Culpeper Minute Men were considered as "savage backwoodsmen" by the people of these older communities.[2] And indeed they must have looked the part, striding along armed to the teeth with the alarming weapons of the frontier,[3] clad in the rough but picturesque war costume of the backwoods, their long hair falling behind, untied and unqueued.

---

[1] Slaughter, 107–08; certificate of J. Marshall in pension claim of David Jameson; MSS. Rev. War, S. F. no. 5607, Pension Bureau.

[2] Only the Tories and the disaffected were frightened by these back-countrymen. Apparently Slaughter took this for granted and failed to make the distinction.

[3] "The people hearing that we came from the backwoods, and seeing our savage-looking equipments, seemed as much afraid of us as if we had been Indians," writes the chronicler of that march. But the people, it appears, soon got over their fright; for this frontier soldiery, as one of them relates, "took pride in demeaning ourselves as patriots and gentlemen, and the people soon treated us with respect and great kindness." (Slaughter, 107–08.)

When they reached Williamsburg half of the minute men were discharged, because they were not needed;[1] but the other half, marching under Colonel Woodford, met and beat the enemy at Great Bridge, in the first fight of the Revolution in Virginia, the first armed conflict with British soldiers in the colonies since Bunker Hill. In this small but bloody battle, Thomas Marshall and his son took part.[2]

The country around Norfolk swarmed with Tories. Governor Dunmore had established martial law, proclaimed freedom of slaves, and summoned to the Royal standard everybody capable of bearing arms. He was busy fortifying Norfolk and mounting cannon upon the entrenchments. Hundreds of the newly emancipated negroes were laboring upon these fortifications. To keep back the patriots until this military work should be finished, the Governor, with a force of British regulars and all the fighting men whom he could gather, took up an almost impregnable position near Great Bridge, about twenty miles from Norfolk, "in a small fort on an oasis surrounded by a morass, not far from the Dismal Swamp, accessible on either side by a long causeway." Here Dunmore and the Loyalists awaited the Americans.[3]

When the latter came up they made their camp "within gunshot of this post, in mud and mire, in a village at the southern end of the causeway." Across this the patriot volunteers threw a breastwork. But, having no cannon, they did not attack the British position. If only Dunmore would take the offen-

---

[1] Slaughter, 107–08.   [2] *Ib.*
[3] Campbell, 633–34; Eckenrode: *R. V.*, 81, 82.

sive, the Americans felt that they would win. Legend has it that through a stratagem of Thomas Marshall, the British assault was brought on. He instructed his servant to pretend to desert and mislead the Governor as to the numbers opposing him. Accordingly, Marshall's decoy sought the enemy's lines and told Dunmore that the insurgents numbered not more than three hundred. The Governor then ordered the British to charge and take the Virginians, "or die in the attempt." [1]

"Between daybreak and sunrise," Captain Fordyce, leading his grenadiers six abreast, swept across the causeway upon the American breastworks. Marshall himself tells us of the fight. The shots of the sentinels roused the little camp and "the bravest ... rushed to the works," firing at will, to meet the British onset. The gallant Fordyce "fell dead within a few steps of the breastwork.... Every grenadier ... was killed or wounded; while the Americans did not lose a single man." Full one hundred of the British force laid down their lives that bloody December morning, among them four of the King's officers. Small as was this affair, — which was called "The Little Bunker Hill," — it was more terrible than most military conflicts in loss of life in proportion to the numbers engaged.[2]

This was John Marshall's first lesson [3] in warfare upon the field of battle. Also, the incidents of

[1] Burk, iv, 85; and Lossing, ii, 535-36.
[2] Marshall, i, 69; and Campbell, 635.
[3] Marshall to Samuel Templeman, Richmond, Sept. 26, 1832, supporting latter's claim for pension; MSS. Rev. War, S. F. no. 6204, Pension Bureau.

Great Bridge, and what went before and came immediately after, gave the fledgling soldier his earliest knowledge of that bickering and conflict of authority that for the next four years he was to witness and experience in far more shocking and dangerous guise.[1]

Within a few months from the time he was haranguing his youthful companions in "Major Clayton's old field" in Culpeper County, John Marshall learned, in terms of blood and death and in the still more forbidding aspects of jealousy and dissension among the patriots themselves, that freedom and independence were not to be wooed and won merely by high-pitched enthusiasm or fervid speech. The young soldier in this brief time saw a flash of the great truth that liberty can be made a reality and then possessed only by men who are strong, courageous, unselfish, and wise enough to act unitedly as well as to fight bravely. He began to discern, though vaguely as yet, the supreme need of the organization of democracy.

After the victory at Great Bridge, Marshall, with the Culpeper Minute Men, marched to Norfolk, where he witnessed the "American soldiers frequently amuse themselves by firing" into Dunmore's vessels in the harbor; saw the exasperated Governor imprudently retaliate by setting the town on fire; and beheld for "several weeks" the burning of Virginia's metropolis.[2] Marshall's battalion then

[1] For the conduct of the men then in supreme authority in Virginia see Wirt, 166–81; and Henry, i, 333–36; also, Campbell, 636 *et seq.*; and see Eckenrode: *R. V.*, 75.

[2] Marshall, i, 69; and see Eckenrode: *R. V.*, chap. iii, for the best account that has been given of this important episode. Dr. Ecken-

marched to Suffolk, and was discharged in March, 1776.[1]

With this experience of what war meant, John Marshall could have returned to the safety of Oak Hill and have spent, at that pleasant fireside, the red years that were to follow, as indeed so many in the colonies who then and after merely prated of liberty, actually did. But it was not in the Marshall nature to support a cause with lip service only. Father and son chose the sterner part; and John Marshall was now about to be schooled for four years by grim instructors in the knowledge that strong and orderly government is necessary to effective liberty. He was to learn, in a hard and bitter school, the danger of provincialism and the value of Nationality.

Not for long did he tarry at the Fauquier County home; and not an instant did the father linger there. Thomas Marshall, while still serving with his command at Great Bridge, was appointed by the Legislature major of the Third Virginia Regiment; and at once entered the Continental service;[2] on July 30, 1776, four months after the Culpeper Minute Men, their work finished, had been disbanded by the new State, his son was commissioned lieutenant in the same regiment. The fringed hunting-shirt and leggings, the buck-tail headgear, scalping-knife, and

---

rode's narrative is a complete statement, from original sources, of every phase of this initial armed conflict between the patriots and Royalists in Virginia. Also see affidavit of Marshall in pension claim of William Payne, April 26, 1832; MSS. Rev. War, S. F. no. 8938½, Pension Bureau.

[1] Affidavit of Marshall in pension claim of William Payne, April 26, 1832; MSS. Rev. War, S. F. no. 8938½, Pension Bureau.

[2] Memorial of Thomas Marshall. (*Supra*, and Appendix IV.)

tomahawk of the backwoods warrior now gave place to the buff and blue uniform, the three-cornered hat,[1] the sword, and the pistol of the Continental officer; and Major Thomas Marshall and his son, Lieutenant John Marshall, marched away to the north to join Washington, and under him to fight and suffer through four black and heart-breaking years of the Revolution.

It is needful, here, to get clearly in our minds the state of the American army at this time. What particular year of the Revolution was darkest up almost to the victorious end, it is hard to say. Studying each year separately one historian will conclude that 1776 sounded the depths of gloom; another plumbs still greater despair at Valley Forge; still another will prove that the bottom was not reached until '79 or '80. And all of them appear to be right.[2]

Even as early as January, 1776, when the war was new, and enthusiasm still warm, Washington wrote to the President of Congress, certain States having paid no attention to his application for arms: "I have, as the last expedient, sent one or two officers from each regiment into the country, with money to try if they can buy."[3] A little later he writes: "My situation has been such, that I have been obliged to use art to conceal it from my own officers."[4]

[1] This uniform was rare; it is probable, however, that Thomas Marshall procured it for himself and son. He could afford it at that time, and he was a very proud man.
[2] Chastellux found the army nearly disbanded from necessity in 1782. (Chastellux, translator's note to 60.)
[3] Washington to President of Congress, Jan. 24, 1776; *Writings:* Ford, iii, 372–73.
[4] Washington to Reed, Feb. 10, 1776; *ib.*, 413.

A SOLDIER OF THE REVOLUTION 81

Congress even placed some of Washington's little army under the direction of the Committee of Safety of New York; and Washington thus wrote to that committee: "I should be glad to know how far it is conceived that my powers over them [the soldiers] extend, or whether I have any at all. Sure I am that they cannot be subjected to the direction of both"[1] (the committee and himself).

In September the Commander-in-Chief wrote to the President of Congress that the terms of enlistment of a large portion of the army were about to expire, and that it was direful work "to be forming armies constantly, and to be left by troops just when they begin to deserve the name, or perhaps at a moment when an important blow is expected."[2]

Four days later Washington again told Congress, "beyond the possibility of doubt, . . . unless some speedy and effectual measures are adopted by Congress, our cause will be lost."[3] On December 1, 1776, the army was "greatly reduced by the departure of the Maryland *Flying Camp* men, and by sundry other causes."[4] A little afterwards General Greene wrote to Governor Cooke [of Rhode Island] that "two brigades left us at Brunswick, notwithstanding the enemy were within two hours' march and coming on."[5]

Thirteen days before the Christmas night that

[1] Washington to Committee of Safety of New York, April 27, 1776; *Writings:* Ford, iv, 51–52.
[2] Washington to President of Congress, Sept. 20, 1776; *ib.*, 422.
[3] Washington to President of Congress, Sept. 24, 1776; *ib.*, 439.
[4] Washington to Major-General Lee, Dec. 1, 1776; *ib.*, v, 62.
[5] General Greene to Governor Cooke, Dec. 4, 1776; *ib.*, footnote to 62.

Washington crossed the Delaware and struck the British at Trenton, the distressed American commander found that "our little handful is daily decreasing by sickness and other causes."[1] And the very day before that brilliant exploit, Washington was compelled to report that "but very few of the men have [re]enlisted" because of "their wishes to return home, the nonappointment of officers in some instances, the turning out of good and appointing of bad in others, and the incomplete or rather no arrangement of them, a work unhappily committed to the management of their States; nor have I the most distant prospect of retaining them ... notwithstanding the most pressing solicitations and the obvious necessity for it." Washington informed Reed that he was left with only "fourteen to fifteen hundred effective men. This handful and such militia as may choose to join me will then compose our army."[2] Such was American patriotic efficiency, as exhibited by "State Sovereignty," the day before the dramatic crossing of the Delaware.

A month earlier the general of this assemblage of shreds and patches had been forced to beg the various States for militia in order to get in "a number of men, if possible, to keep up the appearance of our army."[3] And he writes to his brother Augustine of his grief and surprise to find "the different States

[1] Washington to President of Congress, Dec. 12, 1776; *Writings:* Ford, v, 84.
[2] Washington to President of Congress, Dec. 24, 1776; *ib.*, 129-30. While Washington was desperately badly off, he exaggerates somewhat in this despondent report, as Mr. Ford's footnote (*ib.*, 130) shows.
[3] Washington to President of Congress, Nov. 11, 1776; *ib.*, 19.

so slow and inattentive.... In ten days from this date there will not be above two thousand men, if that number, of the fixed established regiments, ... to oppose Howe's whole army." [1]

Throughout the war, the neglect and ineffectiveness of the States, even more than the humiliating powerlessness of Congress, time and again all but lost the American cause. The State militia came and went almost at will. "The impulse for going home was so irresistible, that it answered no purpose to oppose it. Though I would not discharge them," testifies Washington, "I have been obliged to acquiesce, and it affords one more melancholy proof, how delusive such dependencies [State controlled troops] are." [2]

"The Dependence, which the Congress have placed upon the militia," the distracted general complains to his brother, "has already greatly injured, and I fear will totally ruin our cause. Being subject to no controul themselves, they introduce disorder among the troops, whom you have attempted to discipline, while the change in their living brings on sickness; this makes them Impatient to get home, which spreads universally, and introduces abominable desertions. In short, it is not in the power of words to describe the task I have to act." [3]

---

[1] Washington to John Augustine Washington, Nov. 19, 1776; *Writings:* Ford, v, 38–39.

[2] Washington to President of Congress, Sept. 8, 1776; *ib.*, iv, 397.

[3] Washington to John Augustine Washington, Sept. 22, 1776; *ib.*, 429.

Nor was this the worst. Washington thus pours out his soul to his nephew: "Great bodies of militia in pay that never were in camp; ... immense quantities of provisions drawn by men that never rendered ... one hour's service ... every kind of military [discipline] destroyed by them. ... They [the militia] come without any conveniences and soon return. I discharged a regiment the other day that had in it fourteen rank and file fit for duty only. ... The subject ... is not a fit one to be publicly known or discussed. ... I am wearied to death all day ... at the conduct of the militia, whose behavior and want of discipline has done great injury to the other troops, who never had officers, except in a few instances, worth the bread they eat." [1]

Conditions did not improve in the following year, for we find Washington again writing to his brother of "militia, who are here today and gone tomorrow — whose way, like the ways of [Pr]ovidence, are almost inscrutable." [2] Baron von Steuben testifies thus: "The eternal ebb and flow of men ... who went and came every day, rendered it impossible to have either a regiment or company complete. ... I have seen a regiment consisting of *thirty men* and a company of *one corporal*." [3] Even Thomas Paine, the arch-enemy of anything resembling a regular or "standing" army, finally declared that militia "will not do for a long campaign." [4] Marshall thus de-

[1] Washington to Lund Washington, Sept. 30, 1776; *Writings:* Ford, iv, 457–59.

[2] Washington to John Augustine Washington, Feb. 24, 1777; *ib.*, v, 252. The militia officers were elected "without respect either to service or experience." (Chastellux, 235.)

[3] Kapp, 115.   [4] *The Crisis:* Paine; *Writings:* Conway, i, 175.

scribes the predicament in which Washington was placed by the inconstancy of this will-o'-the-wisp soldiery: "He was often abandoned by bodies of militia, before their places were filled by others. ... The soldiers carried off arms and blankets."[1]

Bad as the militia were,[2] the States did not keep up even this happy-go-lucky branch of the army. "It is a matter of astonishment," savagely wrote Washington to the President of Pennsylvania, two months before Valley Forge, "to every part of the continent, to hear that Pennsylvania, the most opulent and populous of all the States, has but twelve hundred militia in the field, at a time when the enemy are endeavoring to make themselves completely masters of, and to fix their winter quarters in, her capital."[3] Even in the Continental line, it appears, Pennsylvania's quota had "never been above one third full; and now many of them are far below even that."[4]

Washington's wrath at Pennsylvania fairly blazed at this time, and the next day he wrote to Augustine Washington that "this State acts most infamously, the People of it, I mean, as we derive little or no assistance from them. ... They are in a manner, totally disaffected or in a kind of Lethargy."[5]

The head of the American forces was not the only patriot officer to complain. "The Pennsylvania Asso-

---

[1] Marshall (1st ed.), iii, 66.
[2] The militia were worse than wasteful and unmanageable; they deserted by companies. (Hatch, 72–73.)
[3] Washington to Wharton, Oct. 17, 1777; *Writings:* Ford, vi, 118–19.
[4] *Ib.*
[5] Washington to John Augustine Washington, Oct. 18, 1777; *ib.,* 126–29.

ciators [militia] . . . are deserting . . . notwithstanding the most spirited exertions of their officers," reported General Livingston in the midsummer of 1776.[1] General Lincoln and the Massachusetts Committee tried hard to keep the militia of the Bay State from going home; but, moaned Lee, "whether they will succeed, Heaven only knows."[2]

General Sullivan determined to quit the service because of abuse and ill-treatment.[3] For the same reason Schuyler proposed to resign.[4] These were not examples of pique; they denoted a general sentiment among officers who, in addition to their sufferings, beheld their future through none too darkened glasses. They "not only have the Mortification to See every thing live except themselves," wrote one minor officer in 1778, "but they see their private fortune wasting away to make fat those very Miscreants [speculators] . . . they See their Country . . . refuse to make any future provision for them, or even to give them the Necessary Supplies."[5]

Thousands of the Continentals were often practically naked; Chastellux found several hundred in an invalid camp, not because they were ill, but because "they were not covered even with rags."[6] "Our sick naked, and well naked, our unfortunate men in captivity naked"! wailed Washington in

[1] Livingston to Washington, Aug. 12, 1776; *Cor. Rev.*: Sparks, i, 275.
[2] Lee to Washington, Nov. 12, 1776; *ib.*, 305.
[3] Sullivan to Washington, March 7, 1777; *ib.*, 353–54.
[4] Schuyler to Washington, Sept. 9, 1776; *ib.*, 287.
[5] Smith to McHenry, Dec. 10, 1778; Steiner, 21.
[6] Chastellux, 44; and see Moore's *Diary*, i, 399–400; and *infra*, chap. IV.

A SOLDIER OF THE REVOLUTION 87

1777.[1] Two days before Christmas of that year he informed Congress that, of the force then under his immediate command, nearly three thousand were "barefoot and otherwise naked."[2] Sickness was general and appalling. Smallpox raged throughout the army even from the first.[3] "The Regimental Surgeons are immediately to make returns . . . of all the men in their Regiments, who have not had the small Pox,"[4] read the orders of the day just after New Year's Day, in 1778.

Six years after Concord and Lexington, three hundred American soldiers, in a body, wished to join the British.[5] Stern measures were taken to prevent desertion and dishonesty and even to enforce the most ordinary duties of soldiers. "In the afternoon three of our reg.^t were flogged; — 2 of them received one hundred lashes apiece for attempting to desert; the other received 80 for enlisting twice and taking two bounties,"[6] Wild coolly enters in his diary. And again: "This afternoon one of our men was hanged on the grand parade for attempting to desert to the enemy";[7] and "at 6 ock P.M. a soldier of Col. Gimatts Battalion was hanged."

Sleeping on duty meant "Twenty Lashes on . . .

---

[1] Washington to Livingston, Dec. 31, 1777; *Writings:* Ford, vi, 272.

[2] Washington to President of Congress, Dec. 23, 1777; *ib.*, 260; and see *ib.*, 267.

[3] *Pa. Mag. Hist. and Biog.*, 1890-91 (2d Series), vi, 79. Most faces among the patriot troops were pitted with this plague. Washington was deeply pockmarked. He had the smallpox in the Barbadoes when he was nineteen years old. (Sparks, 15.)

[4] Weedon, Jan. 6, 1778, 183.   [5] Hatch, 135; and Kapp, 109.

[6] *Proc.*, Mass. Hist. Soc. (2d Series), vi, 93.

[7] *Ib.* Entries of desertions and savage punishment are frequent in Wild's *Diary;* see p. 135 as an example. Also see Moore's *Diary*, i, 405.

[the] bare back" of the careless sentry.[1] A soldier convicted of "getting drunk & losing his Arms" was "Sentenc'd to receive 100 Lashes on his bare back, & pay for his Arms lost."[2] A man who, in action, "turns his back on the Enemy" was ordered to be "instantly put . . . to Death" by the officers.[3] At Yorktown in May, 1781, Wayne ordered a platoon to fire on twelve soldiers who were persuading their comrades not to march; six were killed and one wounded, who was, by Wayne's command, enforced by a cocked pistol, then finished with the bayonet thrust into the prostrate soldier by a comrade.[4]

Such was the rough handling practiced in the scanty and ill-treated army of individualists which Washington made shift to rally to the patriot colors.[5] It was not an encouraging omen. But blacker still was the disorganizing effect of local control of the various "State Lines" which the pompous authority of the newborn "sovereign and independent" Commonwealths asserted.[6]

[1] Weedon, 14.   [2] *Ib.*, Sept. 3, 1777, 30.

[3] *Ib.*, Sept. 15, 1777, 52. And see Sept. 6, p. 36, where officers as well as privates are ordered "instantly Shot" if they are "so far lost to all Shame as basely to quit their posts without orders, or shall skulk from Danger or offer to retreat before orders."

[4] Livingston to Webb, May 28, 1781; *Writings:* Ford, ix, footnote to 267.

[5] One reason for the chaotic state of the army was the lack of trained officers and the ignorance of the majority of common soldiers in regard to the simplest elements of drill or discipline. Many of the bearers of commissions knew little more than the men; and of such untrained officers there was an overabundance. (Hatch, 13–15.) To Baron von Steuben's training of privates as well as officers is due the chief credit for remedying this all but fatal defect. (Kapp, 126–35; also *infra*, chap. IV.)

[6] For statement of conditions in the American army throughout the war see Hatch; also, Bolton.

Into this desperate confusion came the young Virginia lieutenant. Was this the manner of liberty? Was this the way a people fighting for their freedom confronted their enemy? The dreams he had dreamed, the visions he had seen back in his Virginia mountains were clad in glories as enchanting as the splendors of their tree-clad summits at break of day — dreams and visions for which strong men should be glad of the privilege of dying if thereby they might be won as realities for all the people. And indeed at this time, and in the even deadlier days that followed, young John Marshall found strong men by his side willing to die and to go through worse than death to make their great dream come true.

But why thus decrepit, the organization called the American army? Why this want of food even for such of the soldiers as were willing and eager to fight for their country? Why this scanty supply of arms? Why this avoidable sickness, this needless suffering, this frightful waste? What was the matter? Something surely was at fault. It must be in the power that assumed to direct the patriot army. But whence came that power? From Congress? No. Congress had no power; after a while, it did not even have influence. From the States? Yes; that was its source — there was plenty of power in the States.

But what kind of power, and how displayed? One State did one thing; another State did another thing.[1] One State clothed its troops well; another

[1] The States were childishly jealous of one another. Their different laws on the subject of rank alone caused unbelievable confusion. (Hatch, 13–16. And see Watson, 64, for local feeling, and inefficiency caused by the organization of the army into State lines.)

sent no supplies at all.¹ One regiment of Maryland militia had no shirts and the men wrapped blankets about their bare bodies.² One day State troops would come into camp, and the next day leave. How could war be conducted, how could battles be fought and won, through such freakish, uncertain power as that?

But how could this vaunted liberty, which orators had proclaimed and which Lieutenant Marshall himself had lauded to his frontier companions in arms, be achieved except by a well-organized army, equipped, supplied, and directed by a competent central Government? This was the talk common among the soldiers of the Continental establishment in which John Marshall was a lieutenant. In less than two years after he entered the regular service, even officers, driven to madness and despair by the pusillanimous weakness of Congress, openly denounced that body; and the soldiers themselves, who saw their wounds and sufferings coming to naught, cursed that sham and mockery which the jealousy and shallowness of State provincialism had set up in place of a National Government.³

All through the latter half of 1776, Lieutenant

[1] Hatch says that Connecticut provided most bountifully for her men. (Hatch, 87.) But Chastellux found the Pennsylvania line the best equipped; each Pennsylvania regiment had even a band of music. (Chastellux, 65.)

[2] "The only garment they possess is a blanket elegantly twined about them. You may judge, sir, how much this apparel graces their appearance in parade." (Inspector Fleury to Von Steuben, May 13, 1778; as quoted in Hatch, 87.)

[3] Diary of Joseph Clark; *Proceedings*, N.J. Hist. Soc. (1st Series), vii, 104. The States would give no revenue to the general Government and the officers thought the country would go to pieces. (Hatch, 154.)

Marshall of the Third Virginia Regiment marched, suffered, retreated and advanced, and performed his duties without complaint. He did more. At this time, when, to keep up the sinking spirits of the men was almost as important as was ammunition, young Marshall was the soul of good humor and of cheer; and we shall find him in a few months heartening his starving and freezing comrades at Valley Forge with quip and jest, a center from which radiated good temper and a hopeful and happy warmth. When in camp Marshall was always for some game or sport, which he played with infinite zest. He was the best quoit-thrower in the regiment. His long legs left the others behind in foot-races or jumping contests.

So well did he perform his work, so highly did he impress his superior officers, that, early in December, 1776, he was promoted to be captain-lieutenant, to rank from July 31, and transferred to the Fifteenth Virginia Line.[1] Thus he missed the glory of being one of that immortal company which on Christmas night, 1776, crossed the Delaware with Washington and fell upon the British at Trenton. His father, Major Thomas Marshall, shared in that renown;[2] but the days ahead held for John Marshall his share of fighting in actual battle.

Sick, ill-fed, dirty, and ragged, but with a steady nucleus of regular troops as devoted to their great commander as they were disgusted with the hybrid arrangement between the States and Congress, Washington's army worried along. Two months before the battle of the Brandywine, the American

[1] Heitman, 285.   [2] Binney, in Dillon, iii, 284.

General informed the Committee of Congress that "no army was ever worse supplied than ours . . . our Soldiers, the greatest part of last Campaign, and the whole of this, have scarcely tasted any kind of Vegetables; had but little salt and Vinegar." He told of the "many putrid diseases incident to the Army, and the lamentable mortality," which this neglect of soldiers in the field had caused. "Soap," says he, "is another article in great demand," but not to be had. He adds, sarcastically: "A soldier's pay will not enable him to purchase [soap] by which his . . . consequent dirtiness adds not a little to the disease of the Army." [1]

Such was the army of which John Marshall was a part when it prepared to meet the well-fed, properly clad, adequately equipped British veterans under Howe who had invaded Pennsylvania. Even with such a force Washington felt it necessary to make an impression on disaffected [2] Philadelphia, and, for that purpose, marched through the city on his way to confront the enemy. For it was generally believed that the American army was as small in numbers [3] as it was wretched in equipment. A parade of eleven thousand men [4] through the Tory-infested metropolis would, Washington hoped, hearten patriot sympathizers and encourage Congress. He took pains that his troops should make the best appearance possible. Arms were scoured and the men wore

[1] Washington to Committee of Congress, July 19, 1777; *Writings*: Ford, v, 495.

[2] Washington to President of Congress, Aug. 23, 1777; *Writings*: Ford, vi, 50; also see Marshall (1st ed.), iii, 126.

[3] Marshall (1st ed.), iii, 126.   [4] *Ib.*, 127.

sprigs of green in their headgear. Among the orders for the march through the seat of government it was directed: "If any Sold[r]. shall dare to quit his ranks He shall receive 39 Lashes at the first halting place afterwards. . . . Not a Woman [1] belonging to the Army is to be seen with the troops on their March through the City." [2]

The Americans soon came in contact with the enemy and harassed him as much as possible. Many of Washington's men had no guns. Although fewer militia came to his aid than Congress had called for, testifies Marshall, yet "more appeared than could be armed. Those nearest danger were, as usual, most slow in assembling." [3]

Upon Wayne's suggestion, Washington formed "a corps of light infantry consisting of nine officers, eight sergeants, and a hundred rank and file, from each brigade" and placed them under the command of General Maxwell who had acquired a reputation as a hard fighter.[4] Among these picked officers was Captain-Lieutenant John Marshall. Maxwell's command was thrown forward to Iron Hill. "A choice body of men" was detailed from this select light infantry and, during the night, was posted on the road along which it was believed one column of the British army would advance. The small body of Americans had no artillery and its only purpose was to annoy the enemy and retard his progress. The British under Cornwallis attacked as soon as they discovered

---

[1] On this subject see Waldo's poem, *Hist. Mag.*, vii, 274; and Clark's Diary, *Proc.*, N.J. Hist. Soc., vii, 102.
[2] Weedon, Aug. 23, 1777, 19.　　[3] Marshall (1st ed.), iii, 127.
[4] *Ib.*, 128; and see Trevelyan, iv, 226.

Maxwell's troops. The Americans quickly were forced to retreat, having lost forty killed and wounded. Only three of the British were killed and but nineteen were wounded.[1]

This action was the first engagement in which Marshall took part after the battle of Great Bridge. It is important only as fixing the command to which he was assigned. Marshall told Justice Story that he was in the Iron Hill fight;[2] and it is certain, therefore, that he was in Maxwell's light infantry and one of the little band picked from that body of choice troops, for the perilous and discouraging task of checking the oncoming British thousands.

The American army retreated to the Brandywine, where on the 9th of September Washington stationed all his forces except the light infantry on the left of the river. The position was skillfully chosen, but vague and conflicting reports[3] of the movement of the British finally resulted in American disaster.

The light infantry was posted among the hills on the right of the stream along the road leading to Chadd's Ford, in order to skirmish with the British when they approached, and, if possible, prevent them from crossing the river. But the enemy, without much effort, drove the Americans across the Brandywine, neither side suffering much loss.[4]

[1] Marshall (1st ed.), iii, 127-29; *ib.* (2d ed.), i, 154-56; Washington to President of Congress, Sept. 3, 1777; *Writings:* Ford, vi, 64-65.

[2] Story, in Dillon, iii, 335.

[3] Washington to President of Congress, Sept. 11, 1777; *Writings:* Ford, vi, 69.

[4] Marshall (1st ed.), iii, 131; *ib.* (2d ed.), i, 156. Colonel Harrison, Washington's Secretary, reported immediately to the President of Congress that Maxwell's men believed that they killed or wounded

A SOLDIER OF THE REVOLUTION

Washington now made his final dispositions for battle. The command to which Marshall belonged, together with other detachments under the general direction of Anthony Wayne, were placed opposite the British at Chadd's Ford. Small parties of selected men crossed over and attacked the British on the other side of the stream. In one of these skirmishes the Americans "killed a British captain with ten or fifteen privates, drove them out of the wood and were on the point of taking a field piece." But large numbers of the enemy hurried forward and again the Americans were thrown across the river. Marshall was in this party.[1]

Thomas Marshall, now colonel,[2] held the advanced position under Sullivan at the right; and his regiment did the hardest fighting and suffered the heaviest losses on that unhappy day. When Cornwallis, in greatly superior numbers, suddenly poured down upon Sullivan's division, he all but surprised the Continentals and drove most of them flying before him;[3] but Colonel Marshall and his Virginians refused to be stampeded. That regiment "main-

"at least three hundred" of the British. (Harrison to President of Congress, Sept. 11, 1777; *Writings:* Ford, vi, footnote to 68.)

[1] Marshall, i, 156. The fact that Marshall places himself in this detachment, which was a part of Maxwell's light infantry, together with his presence at Iron Hill, fixes his position in the battle of the Brandywine and in the movements that immediately followed. It is reasonably certain that he was under Maxwell until just before the battle of Germantown. Of this skirmish Washington's optimistic and excited Secretary wrote on the spot, that Maxwell's men killed thirty men and one captain "left dead on the spot." (Harrison to the President of Congress, Sept. 11, 1777; *Writings:* Ford, vi, footnote to 68.)

[2] Thomas Marshall was promoted to be lieutenant-colonel Aug. 13, 1776; and colonel Feb. 21, 1777. (Heitman, 285.)

[3] Trevelyan, iv, 230.

tained its position without losing an inch of ground until both its flanks were turned, its ammunition nearly expended, and more than half the officers and one third of the soldiers were killed and wounded." [1] Colonel Marshall had two horses shot under him. But, cut to pieces as they were, no panic appeared in this superb Virginia command and they "retired in good order." [2]

While Thomas Marshall and his Third Virginia Line were thus checking Cornwallis's assault on the right, the British charged, in dense masses, across the Brandywine, at Chadd's Ford, upon Wayne's division, to which Captain-Lieutenant John Marshall had been assigned. The Americans made a show of resistance, but, learning of the rout of their right wing, quickly gave way.[3]

"Nearly six hundred British . . . were killed or wounded; and the Americans lost eleven pieces of artillery and above a thousand men, of whom the third part were prisoners," according to the British

[1] Marshall, i, footnote to 158.
[2] *Ib.* Colonel Thomas Marshall's cool-headed and heroic conduct at this battle, which brought out in high lights his fine record as an officer, caused the Virginia House of Delegates to elect him colonel of the State Regiment of Artillery raised by that Commonwealth three months later. The vote is significant; for, although there were three candidates, each a man of merit, and although Thomas Marshall himself was not an aspirant for the place, and, indeed, was at Valley Forge when the election occurred, twice as many votes were cast for him as for all the other candidates put together. Four men were balloted for, Thomas Marshall receiving seventy-five votes and the other three candidates all together but thirty-six votes. (Journal, H.B. (Nov. 5, 1777), 27.)
[3] Marshall, i, 156; and Trevelyan, iv, 230–31. Washington reported that Wayne and Maxwell's men retreated only "after a severe conflict." (Washington to President of Congress, Sept. 11, 1777; *Writings:* Ford, vi, 69.)

A SOLDIER OF THE REVOLUTION

statement.[1] And by their own account the Americans lost three hundred killed, six hundred wounded, and between three and four hundred prisoners.[2]

Both British and American narratives agree that the conduct of the Continental troops at Brandywine was most unequal in stanchness, discipline, and courage. John Marshall himself wrote: "As must ever be the case in new-raised armies, unused to danger and from which undeserving officers have not been expelled, their conduct was not uniform. Some regiments, especially those which had served the preceding campaign, maintained their ground with the firmness and intrepidity of veterans, while others gave way as soon as they were pressed." [3]

But the inefficiency of the American equipment gave some excuse for the fright that seized upon so many of them. For, testifies Marshall, "many of their muskets were scarcely fit for service; and being of unequal caliber, their cartridges could not be so well fitted, and consequently, their fire could not do as much execution as that of the enemy. This radical defect was felt in all the operations of the army." [4]

So ended the battle of the Brandywine, the third formal armed conflict in which John Marshall took part. He had been in skirmish after skirmish, and in all of them had shown the characteristic Marshall coolness and courage, which both father and son exhibited in such striking fashion on this September day on the field where Lafayette fell

---

[1] Trevelyan, iv, 232. [2] Marshall, i, 157–58.
[3] *Ib.*; and see Irving, iii, 200–09.
[4] Marshall, i, 158–59.

wounded, and where the patriot forces reeled back under the all but fatal blows of the well-directed British regiments.[1]

It is small wonder that the Americans were beaten in the battle of the Brandywine; indeed, the wonder is that the British did not follow up their victory and entirely wipe out the opposing patriots. But it is astonishing that the American army kept up heart. They were even "in good spirits" as Washington got them in hand and directed their retreat.[2]

They were pretty well scattered, however, and many small parties and numerous stragglers were left behind. Maxwell's men, among whom was John Marshall, were stationed at Chester as "a rallying point" for the fragments which otherwise would disperse or be captured. Much maneuvering followed by both British and Americans. At sight of a detachment of the enemy approaching Wilmington, the Delaware militia "dispersed themselves," says Marshall.[3] Soon the two armies again faced one another. Marshall thus describes the situation: "The advanced parties had met, and were beginning to skirmish, when they were separated by a heavy rain, which, becoming more and more violent, rendered the retreat of the Americans a measure of absolute necessity." [4]

Through a cold and blinding downpour, over

[1] Four years afterward Chastellux found that "most of the trees bear the mark of bullets or cannon shot." (Chastellux, 118.)

[2] Washington to President of Congress, Sept. 11, 1777; *Writings:* Ford, vi, 70.

[3] Marshall (1st ed.), iii, 141, and see Washington to President of Congress, Sept. 23, 1777; *Writings:* Ford, vi, 81.

[4] Marshall, i, 160.

roads deep with mud, Captain-Lieutenant Marshall marched with his retreating comrades. All day they struggled forward, and nearly all night. They had no time to eat and little or no food, even if they had had the time. Before the break of a gray, cold, rainy September dawn, a halt was called, and an examination made of arms and ammunition. "Scarcely a musket in a regiment could be discharged," Marshall records, "and scarcely one cartridge in a box was fit for use," although "forty rounds per man had just been drawn" — this because the cartridge boxes had been ill-made and of improper material.

Gun locks were loose, declares Marshall, because flimsily put on; the muskets were scarcely better than clubs. Hardly any of the soldiers had bayonets.[1] "Never" had the patriot army been "in such imminent peril," he asserts — and all because of the inefficiency or worse of the method of supplies. Well might Washington's dilapidated troops thank Providence for the bitter weather that drenched through and through both officers and men and soaked their ammunition, for "the extreme severity of the weather had entirely stopped the British army."[2]

Yet Washington was determined to block the British march on Philadelphia. He made shift to secure some fresh ammunition[3] and twice moved his army to get in front of the enemy or, failing in that,

[1] Marshall, i, 160. When their enlistments expired, the soldiers took the Government's muskets and bayonets home with them. Thus thousands of muskets and bayonets continually disappeared. (See Kapp, 117.)
[2] Marshall, i, 160–61. [3] *Ib.*

"to keep pace with them."[1] To check their too rapid advance Washington detached the troops under Wayne, among whom was John Marshall.[2] They found the "country was so extensively disaffected that Sir William Howe received accurate accounts of his [Wayne's] position and of his force. Major-General Grey was detached to surprise him [Wayne] and effectually accomplished his purpose." At eleven o'clock at night Grey drove in Wayne's pickets with charged bayonets, and in a desperate midnight encounter killed and wounded one hundred and fifty of his men.[3] General Smallwood, who was to have supported Wayne, was less than a mile away, but his militia, who, writes Marshall, "thought only of their own safety, having fallen in with a party returning from the pursuit of Wayne, fled in confusion with the loss of only one man."[4]

Another example, this, before John Marshall's eyes, of the unreliability of State-controlled troops;[5] one more paragraph in the chapter of fatal inefficiency of the so-called Government of the so-called United States. Day by day, week by week, month by month, year by year, these object lessons were witnessed by the young Virginia officer. They made

[1] Washington to President of Congress, Sept. 23, 1777; *Writings:* Ford, vi, 81-82.

[2] This is an inference, but a fair one. Maxwell was under Wayne; and Marshall was one of Maxwell's light infantry of picked men. (*Supra.*)

[3] Marshall, i, 161. "The British accounts represent the American loss to have been much larger. It probably amounted to at least three hundred men." (*Ib.*, footnote.)

[4] *Ib.*, and see *Pa. Mag. Hist. and Biog.*, i, 305.

[5] Marshall repeatedly expresses this thought in his entire account of the war.

a lifelong impression upon him and had an immediate effect. More and more he came to depend on Washington, as indeed the whole army did also, for all things which should have come from the Government itself.

Once again the American commander sought to intercept the British, but they escaped "by a variety of perplexing maneuvers," writes Washington, "thro' a Country from which I could not derive the least intelligence (being to a man disaffected)" and "marched immediately toward Philadelphia."[1] For the moment Washington could not follow, although, declares Marshall, "public opinion" was demanding and Congress insisting that one more blow be struck to save Philadelphia.[2] His forces were not yet united; his troops utterly exhausted.

Marching through heavy mud, wading streams, drenched by torrential rains, sleeping on the sodden ground "without tents ... without shoes or ... clothes ... without fire ... without food,"[3] to use Marshall's striking language, the Americans were in no condition to fight the superior forces of the well-found British. "At least one thousand men are bare-footed and have performed the marches in that condition," Washington informed the impatient Congress.[4] He did his utmost; that brilliant officer, Alexander Hamilton, was never so efficient; but nearly all that could be accomplished was to

[1] Washington to President of Congress, Sept. 23, 1777; *Writings:* Ford, vi, 80.
[2] Marshall, i, 162.   [3] *Ib.*
[4] Washington to President of Congress, Sept. 23, 1777; *Writings:* Ford, vi, 82.

remove the military stores at Philadelphia up the Delaware farther from the approaching British, but also farther from the American army. Philadelphia itself "seemed asleep, or dead, and the whole State scarce alive. Maryland and Delaware the same," wrote John Adams in his diary.[1]

So the British occupied the Capital, placing most of their forces about Germantown. Congress, frightened and complaining, fled to York. The members of that august body, even before the British drove them from their cozy quarters, felt that "the prospect is chilling on every side; gloomy, dark, melancholy and dispiriting."[2] Would Washington never strike? Their impatience was to be relieved. The American commander had, by some miracle, procured munitions and put the muskets of his troops in a sort of serviceable order; and he felt that a surprise upon Germantown might succeed. He planned his attack admirably, as the British afterwards conceded.[3] In the twilight of a chilling October day, Washington gave orders to begin the advance.

Throughout the night the army marched, and in the early morning[4] the three divisions into which the American force was divided threw themselves upon the British within brief intervals of time. All went well at first. Within about half an hour after Sullivan and Wayne had engaged the British left wing, the American left wing, to which John Mar-

---

[1] *Works:* Adams, ii, 437. [2] *Ib.*
[3] *Pa. Mag. Hist. and Biog.*, xvi, 197 *et seq.*
[4] American officer's description of the battle. (*Ib.*, xi, 330.)

A SOLDIER OF THE REVOLUTION 103

shall was now attached,[1] attacked the front of the British right wing, driving that part of the enemy from the ground. With battle shouts Marshall and his comrades under General Woodford charged the retreating British. Then it was that a small force of the enemy took possession of the Chew House and poured a murderous hail of lead into the huzzaing American ranks. This saved the day for the Royal force and turned an American victory into defeat.[2]

It was a dramatic struggle in which John Marshall that day took part. Fighting desperately beside them, he saw his comrades fall in heaps around him as they strove to take the fiercely defended stone house of the Tory Judge. A fog came up so thick that the various divisions could see but a little way before them. The dun smoke from burning hay and fields of stubble, to which the British had set fire, made thicker the murk until the Americans fighting from three different points could not tell friend from foe.[3] For a while their fire was directed only by the flash from what they thought must be the guns of the enemy.[4]

The rattle of musketry and roar of cannon was like "the crackling of thorns under a pot, and incessant peals of thunder," wrote an American officer in an attempt to describe the battle in a letter to his relatives at home.[5] Through it all, the Americans kept up their cheering until, as they fought, the

[1] Marshall, i, 168. [2] Ib., 168–69.
[3] From an American officer's description, in *Pa. Mag. Hist. and Biog.*, xi, 330.
[4] Ib., 331–32. [5] Ib.

defeat was plain to the most audacious of them; and retreat, with which they had grown so familiar, once more began. For nine miles the British pursued them, the road stained with blood from the beaten patriots.[1] Nearly a thousand of Washington's soldiers were killed or wounded, and over four hundred were made prisoners on that ill-fated day, while the British loss was less than half these numbers.[2]

Two months of service followed, as hard as the many gone before with which Fate had blackened the calendar of the patriot cause. Washington was frantically urged to "storm" Philadelphia: Congress wished it; a "torrent of public opinion" demanded it; even some of Washington's officers were carried off their feet and advised "the mad enterprise," to use Marshall's warm description of the pressure upon his commander.[3] The depreciation of the Continental paper money, the increasing disaffection of the people, the desperate plight of American fortunes, were advanced as reasons for a "grand effort" to remedy the ruinous situation. Washington was immovable, and his best officers sustained him. Risking his army's destruction was not the way to stop depreciation of the currency, said Washington; its value had fallen for want of taxes to sustain it and could be raised only by their levy.[4] And "the corruption and defection of the people, and their unwillingness to serve in the army of the United States,

---

[1] "The rebels carried off a large number of their wounded as we could see by the blood on the roads, on which we followed them so far [nine miles]." (British officer's account of battle; *Pa. Mag. Hist. and Biog.*, xvi, 197 *et seq.*)

[2] Marshall, i, 170-71.   [3] *Ib.*, 181.   [4] *Ib.*, 181-82.

were evils which would be very greatly increased by an unsuccessful attempt on Philadelphia." [1]

So black grew American prospects that secret sympathizers with the British became open in their advocacy of the abandonment of the Revolution. A Philadelphia Episcopal rector, who had been chaplain of Congress, wrote Washington that the patriot cause was lost and besought him to give up the struggle. "The most respectable characters" had abandoned the cause of independence, said Duché. Look at Congress. Its members were "obscure" and "distinguished for the weakness of their understandings and the violence of their tempers . . . chosen by a little, low, faction. . . . Tis you . . . only that support them." And the army! "The whole world knows that its only existence depends on you." Consider the situation: "Your harbors are blocked up, your cities fall one after the other; fortress after fortress, battle after battle is lost. . . . How fruitless the expense of blood!" Washington alone can end it. Humanity calls upon him to do so; and if he heeds that call his character "will appear with lustre in the annals of history." [2] Deeply offended, Washington sent the letter to Congress, which, however, continued to find fault with him and to urge an attack upon the British in the Capital.

Although Washington refused to throw his worn and hungry troops upon the perfectly prepared and victorious enemy entrenched in Philadelphia, he was

[1] Marshall (1st ed.), iii, 287. Marshall omits this sentence in his second edition. But his revised account is severe enough.
[2] The Reverend Jacob Duché, to Washington, Oct. 8, 1777; *Cor. Rev.*: Sparks, i, 448-58.

eager to meet the British in the open field. But he must choose the place. So when, early in December, Howe's army marched out of Philadelphia the Americans were ready. Washington had taken a strong position on some hills toward the Schuylkill not far from White Marsh. After much maneuvering by the British and effective skirmishing by detachments of the patriots,[1] the two armies came into close contact. Not more than a mile away shone the scarlet uniforms of the Royal troops. Washington refused to be lured from his advantageous ground.[2] Apparently the British were about to attack and a decisive battle to be fought. After Brandywine and Germantown, another defeat would have been ruinous.

Washington personally animated his men. Marshall, who witnessed it, thus describes the scene: "The American chief rode through every brigade of his army, delivering, in person, his orders respecting the manner of receiving the enemy, exhorting his troops to rely principally on the bayonet, and encouraging them by the steady firmness of his countenance, as well as by his words, to a vigorous performance of their duty."[3]

These words make one see, as one reads, the great Virginian in his noblest aspect — calm in the face of possible disaster, his spirit burning brightest on the

[1] Washington to President of Congress, Dec. 10, 1777; *Writings:* Ford, vi, 238–39.

[2] Clark's Diary, *Proc.*, N.J. Hist. Soc. (1st Series), vii, 102–03. "It seems that the enemy had waited all this time before our lines to decoy us from the heights we possessed." (*Ib.*)

[3] Marshall, i, 184.

A SOLDIER OF THE REVOLUTION 107

very fuel of danger itself, his clear mind unclouded by what was likely to befall.

Each division, each regiment, each company, was given plain and practical orders for the expected conflict. And we may be sure that each man, private as well as officer, took heart as he looked upon the giant figure and listened to the steady directions and undismayed encouragement of his chief. Certain it is that John Marshall so felt and thought. A rare picture, this, full of life and color, that permits us to behold the growth in the young soldier's soul of that faith in and devotion to George Washington, seeds of which had been planted in his childhood days in the Blue Ridge home.

Finally the British, seeing the resolute front of the Americans and already bleeding from the fierce thrusts of Morgan's Virginia riflemen, suddenly withdrew to Philadelphia,[1] and Washington's army went into winter quarters on the hills of Valley Forge.

[1] Marshall, i, 184.

CHAPTER IV

VALLEY FORGE AND AFTER

Unless some great and capital change suddenly takes place . . . this army must inevitably starve, dissolve, or disperse. (Washington, Dec. 23, 1777.)

John Marshall was the best tempered man I ever knew. Nothing discouraged, nothing disturbed him. (Lieutenant Slaughter, of Marshall at Valley Forge.)

GAUNT and bitter swept down the winter of 1777. But the season brought no lean months to the soldiers of King George, no aloes to the Royal officers in fat and snug Philadelphia.[1] It was a period of rest and safety for the red-coated privates in the city, where, during the preceding year, Liberty Bell had sounded its clamorous defiance; a time of revelry and merry-making for the officers of the Crown. Gay days chased nights still gayer, and weeks of social frolic made the winter pass like the scenes of a warm and glowing play.

For those who bore the King's commission there were balls at the City Tavern, plays at the South-Street Theater; and many a charming flirtation made lively the passing months for the ladies of

[1] It appears that, throughout the Revolution, Pennsylvania's metropolis was noted for its luxury. An American soldier wrote in 1779: "Philada. may answer very well for a man with his pockets well lined, whose pursuit is idleness and dissipation. But to us who are not in the first predicament, and who are not upon the latter errand, it is intolerable. . . . A morning visit, a dinner at 5 o'clock — Tea at 8 or 9 — supper and up all night is the round *die in diem*. . . . We have advanced as far in luxury in the third year of our Indepeny. as the old musty Republics of Greece and Rome did in twice as many hundreds." (Tilghman to McHenry, Jan. 25, 1799; Steiner, 25.)

VALLEY FORGE AND AFTER

the Capital, as well as for lieutenant and captain, major and colonel, of the invaders' army. And after the social festivities, there were, for the officers, carousals at the "Bunch of Grapes" and all night dinners at the "Indian Queen." [1]

"You can have no idea," wrote beautiful Rebecca Franks, — herself a keen Tory, — to the wife of a patriot, "you can have no idea of the life of continued amusement I live in. I can scarce have a moment to myself. I spent Tuesday evening at Sir William Howe's, where we had a concert and dance. ... Oh, how I wished Mr. Paca would let you come in for a week or two! ... You'd have an opportunity of raking as much as you choose at Plays, Balls, Concerts, and Assemblies. I have been but three evenings alone since we moved to town." [2]

"My wife writes me," records a Tory who was without and whose wife was within the Quaker City's gates of felicity, "that everything is gay and happy [in Philadelphia] and it is like to prove a frolicking winter." [3] Loyal to the colors of pleasure, society waged a triumphant campaign of brilliant amusement. The materials were there of wit and loveliness, of charm and manners. Such women there were as Peggy Chew and Rebecca Franks, Williamina Bond and Margaret Shippen — afterwards the wife of Benedict Arnold and the probable cause of his fall;[4] such men as Banastre Tarleton of the Dragoons, twenty-three years old, handsome and accomplished;

---

[1] Trevelyan, iv, 279.   [2] *Ib.*, 280.   [3] *Ib.*
[4] The influence of Margaret Shippen in causing Arnold's treason is now questioned by some. (See Avery, vi, 243-49.)

brilliant Richard Fitzpatrick of the Guards; Captain John André, whose graces charmed all hearts.[1] So lightly went the days and merrily the nights under the British flag in Philadelphia during the winter of 1777–78.

For the common soldiers there were the racecourse and the cock-pit, warm quarters for their abodes, and the fatness of the land for their eating. Beef in abundance, more cheese than could be used, wine enough and to spare, provisions of every kind, filled pantry and cellar. For miles around the farmers brought in supplies. The women came by night across fields and through woods with eggs, butter, vegetables, turkeys, chickens, and fresh meat.[2] For most of the farmers of English descent in that section hated the war and were actively, though in furtive manner, Tory. They not only supplied the British larder, but gave news of the condition and movements of the Americans.[3]

Not twenty miles away from these scenes of British plenty and content, of cheer and jollity, of wassail and song, rose the bleak hills and black ravines of Valley Forge, where Washington's army had crawled some weeks after Germantown. On the Schuylkill heights and valleys, the desperate Americans made an encampment which, says Trevelyan, "bids fair to be the most celebrated in the

---

[1] Trevelyan, iv, 281–82.   [2] *Ib.*, 278–80.
[3] *Ib.*, 268–69; also Marshall, i, 215. The German countrymen, however, were loyal to the patriot cause. The Moravians at Bethlehem, though their religion forbade them from bearing arms, in another way served as effectually as Washington's soldiers. (See Trevelyan, iv, 298–99.)

VALLEY FORGE AND AFTER

world's history." [1] The hills were wooded and the freezing soldiers were told off in parties of twelve to build huts in which to winter. It was more than a month before all these rude habitations were erected.[2] While the huts were being built the naked or scarcely clad [3] soldiers had to find what shelter they could. Some slept in tents, but most of them lay down beneath the trees.[4] For want of blankets, hundreds, had "to sit up all night by fires."[5] After Germantown Washington's men had little to eat at any time. On December 2, "the last ration had been delivered and consumed."[6] Through treachery, cattle meant for the famishing patriots were driven into the already over-supplied Philadelphia.[7]

The commissariat failed miserably, perhaps dishonestly, to relieve the desperate want. Two days before Christmas there was "not a single hoof of any kind to slaughter, and not more than twenty-five barrels of flour!" [8] Men died by the score from starvation.[9] Most of the time "fire cake" made of dirty, soggy dough, warmed over smoky fires, and

---

[1] Trevelyan, iv, 290.

[2] The huts were fourteen by sixteen feet, and twelve soldiers occupied each hut. (Sparks, 245.)

[3] "The men were literally naked [Feb. 1] some of them in the fullest extent of the word." (Von Steuben, as quoted in Kapp, 118.)

[4] *Hist. Mag.*, v, 170.

[5] Washington to President of Congress, Dec. 23, 1777; *Writings:* Ford, vi, 260.

[6] Marshall, i, 213.   [7] *Ib.*, 215.

[8] Washington to President of Congress, Dec. 23, 1777; *Writings:* Ford, vi, 258.

[9] "The poor soldiers were half naked, and had been half starved, having been compelled, for weeks, to subsist on simple flour alone and this too in a land almost literally flowing with milk and honey." (Watson's description after visiting the camp, Watson, 63.)

washed down with polluted water was the only sustenance. Sometimes, testifies Marshall himself, soldiers and officers "were absolutely without food."[1] On the way to Valley Forge, Surgeon Waldo writes: "I'm Sick — eat nothing — No Whiskey — No Baggage — Lord, — Lord, — Lord."[2] Of the camp itself and of the condition of the men, he chronicles: "Poor food — hard lodging — Cold Weather — fatigue — Nasty Cloaths — nasty Cookery — Vomit half my time — Smoak'd out of my senses — the Devil's in it — I can't Endure it — Why are we sent here to starve and freeze — What sweet Felicities have I left at home; — A charming Wife — pretty Children — Good Beds — good food — good Cookery — all agreeable — all harmonious. Here, all Confusion — Smoke — Cold, — hunger & filthyness — A pox on my bad luck. Here comes a bowl of beef soup, — full of burnt leaves and dirt, sickish enough to make a hector spue — away with it, Boys — I'll live like the Chameleon upon Air."[3]

While in overfed and well-heated Philadelphia officers and privates took the morning air to clear the brain from the night's pleasures, John Marshall and his comrades at Valley Forge thus greeted one another: "Good morning Brother Soldier (says one to another) how are you? — All wet, I thank'e, hope you are so — (says the other)."[4] Still, these empty, shrunken men managed to squeeze some fun out of it. When reveille sounded, the hoot of an owl would come from a hut door, to be answered by like hoots

---

[1] Marshall (1st ed.), iii, 341.
[2] *Hist. Mag.*, v, 131.
[3] *Ib.*
[4] *Ib.*, 132.

and the cawing of crows; but made articulate enough to carry in this guise the cry of "'No meat! — No meat!' The distant vales Echo'd back the melancholy sound — 'No Meat! — No Meat!' . . . What have you for our Dinners, Boys? [one man would cry to another] 'Nothing but Fire Cake and Water, Sir.' At night — 'Gentlemen, the Supper is ready.' What is your Supper, Lads? 'Fire Cake & Water, Sir.'"

Just before Christmas Surgeon Waldo writes: "Lay excessive Cold & uncomfortable last Night — my eyes are started out from their Orbits like a Rabbit's eyes, occasion'd by a great Cold — and Smoke. What have you got for Breakfast, Lads? 'Fire Cake and Water, Sir.' The Lord send that our Commissary of Purchases may live on Fire Cake & Water till their glutted Gutts are turned to Pasteboard."

He admonishes: "Ye who Eat Pumpkin Pie and Roast Turkies — and yet Curse fortune for using you ill — Curse her no more — least she reduce you . . . to a bit of Fire Cake & a Draught of Cold Water, & in Cold Weather." [1]

Heart-breaking and pitiful was the aspect of these soldiers of liberty. "There comes a Soldier — His bare feet are seen thro' his worn out Shoes — his legs nearly naked from the tatter'd remains of an only pair of stockings — his Breeches not sufficient to cover his Nakedness — his Shirt hanging in Strings — his hair dishevell'd — his face meagre — his whole appearance pictures a person foresaken &

[1] *Hist. Mag.*, v, 132-33.

discouraged. He comes, and crys with an air of wretchedness & despair — I am Sick — my feet lame — my legs are sore — my body cover'd with this tormenting Itch — my Cloaths are worn out — my Constitution is broken — my former Activity is exhausted by fatigue — hunger & Cold! — I fail fast I shall soon be no more! And all the reward I shall get will be — 'Poor Will is dead.'"[1]

On the day after Christmas the soldiers waded through snow halfway to their knees. Soon it was red from their bleeding feet.[2] The cold stung like a whip. The huts were like "dungeons and . . . full as noisome."[3] Tar, pitch, and powder had to be burned in them to drive away the awful stench.[4] The horses "died by hundreds every week"; the soldiers, staggering with weakness as they were, hitched themselves to the wagons and did the necessary hauling.[5] If a portion of earth was warmed by the fires or by their trampling feet, it froze again into ridges which cut like knives. Often some of the few blankets in the army were torn into strips and wrapped around the naked feet of the soldiers only to be rent into shreds by the sharp ice under foot.[6] Sick men lay in filthy hovels covered only by their rags, dying and dead comrades crowded by their sides.[7]

As Christmas approached, even Washington became so disheartened that he feared that "this army

[1] *Hist. Mag.*, v, 131–32.   [2] Trevelyan, iv, 297.
[3] *Ib.* For putrid condition of the camp in March and April, 1778, see Weedon, 254–55 and 288–89.
[4] Trevelyan, iv, 298.   [5] *Ib.*
[6] Personal narrative; Shreve, *Mag. Amer. Hist.*, Sept., 1897, 568.
[7] Trevelyan, iv, 298.

VALLEY FORGE AND AFTER

must dissolve;"[1] and the next day he again warned Congress that, unless the Commissary were quickly improved, "this army must inevitably . . . starve, dissolve, or disperse."[2]

Early in 1778 General Varnum wrote General Greene that "The situation of the Camp is such that in all human probability the Army must soon dissolve. Our desertions are astonishingly great."[3] "The army must dissolve!" "The army must dissolve!" — the repeated cry comes to us like the chant of a saga of doom.

Had the British attacked resolutely, the Americans would have been shattered beyond hope of recovery.[4] On February 1, 1778, only five thousand and twelve men out of a total of more than seventeen thousand were capable of any kind of service: four thousand were unfit for duty because of nakedness.[5] The patriot prisoners within the British lines were in even worse case, if we credit but half the accounts then current. "Our brethren," records Surgeon Waldo in his diary, "who are unfortunately Prisoners in Philadelphia, meet with the most savage & inhumane treatments — that Barbarians are Capable of inflicting. . . . One of these poor unhappy men — drove to the last extreem by the rage of hunger —

---

[1] Washington to President of Congress, Dec. 22, 1777; *Writings*: Ford, vi, 253.

[2] Washington to President of Congress, Dec. 23, 1777; *ib.*, 257.

[3] General Varnum to General Greene, Feb. 12, 1778, Washington MSS., Lib. Cong., no. 21. No wonder the desertions were so great. It was not only starvation and death but the hunger-crazed soldiers "had daily temptations thrown out to them of the most alluring nature," by the British and Loyalists. (Chastellux, translator's note to 51.)

[4] Marshall, i, 227.   [5] *Ib.*

eat his own fingers up to the first joint from the hand, before he died. Others eat the Clay — the Lime — the Stones — of the Prison Walls. Several who died in the Yard had pieces of Bark, Wood, — Clay & Stones in their mouths — which the ravings of hunger had caused them to take in the last Agonies of Life." [1]

The Moravians in Bethlehem, some miles away from Valley Forge, were the only refuge of the stricken patriots. From the first these Christian socialists were the Good Samaritans of that ghastly winter. This little colony of Germans had been overrun with sick and wounded American soldiers. Valley Forge poured upon it a Niagara of starvation, disease, and death. One building, scarcely large enough for two hundred and fifty beds, was packed with nearly a thousand sick and dying men. Dysentery reduced burly strength to trembling weakness. A peculiar disease rotted blood and bones. Many died on the same foul pallet

[1] *Hist. Mag.*, v, 132. This is, probably, an exaggeration. The British were extremely harsh, however, as is proved by the undenied testimony of eye-witnesses and admittedly authentic documentary evidence. For their treatment of American prisoners see Dandridge: *American Prisoners of the Revolution*, a trustworthy compilation of sources. For other outrages see Clark's Diary, *Proc.*, N.J. Hist. Soc., vii, 96; Moore's *Diary*, ii, 183. For the Griswold affair see Niles: *Principles and Acts of the Revolution*, 143–44. For transportation of captured Americans to Africa and Asia see Franklin's letter to Lord Stormont, April 2, 1777; Franklin's *Writings*: Smyth, vii, 36–38; also Moore's *Diary*, i, 476. For the murder of Jenny M'Crea see Marshall, i, 200, note 9, Appendix, 25; and Moore's *Diary*, i, 476; see also Miner: *History of Wyoming*, 222–36; and British officer's letter to Countess of Ossory, Sept. 1, 1777; *Pa. Mag. Hist. and Biog.*, i, footnote to 289; and Jefferson to Governor of Detroit, July 22, 1779; *Cal. Va. St. Prs.*, i, 321. For general statement see Marshall (1st ed.), iii, 59. These are but a few of the many similar sources that might be cited.

before it could be changed. The beds were "heaps of polluted litter." Of forty of John Marshall's comrades from a Virginia regiment, which was the "pride of the Old Dominion," only three came out alive.[1] "A violent putrid fever," testifies Marshall, "swept off much greater numbers than all the diseases of the camp."[2]

Need, was there not, at Valley Forge for men of resolve so firm and disposition so sunny that they would not yield to the gloom of these indescribable months? Need, was there not, among these men, for spirits so bright and high that they could penetrate even the death-stricken depression of this fetid camp with the glow of optimism and of hope?

Such characters were there, we find, and of these the most shining of all was John Marshall of the Virginia line.[3] He was a very torch of warmth and encouragement, it appears; for in the journals and diaries left by those who lived through Valley Forge, the name of John Marshall is singled out as conspicuous for these comforting qualities.

"Although," writes Lieutenant Philip Slaughter, who, with the "two Porterfields and Johnson," was

---

[1] Trevelyan, iv, 299.   [2] Marshall, i, 227.
[3] John Marshall's father was also at Valley Forge during the first weeks of the encampment and was often Field Officer of the Day. (Weedon.) About the middle of January he left for Virginia to take command of the newly raised State Artillery Regiment. (Memorial of Thomas Marshall; *supra*.) John Marshall's oldest brother, Thomas Marshall, Jr., seventeen years of age, was commissioned captain in a Virginia State Regiment at this time. (Heitman, 285.) Thus all the male members of the Marshall family, old enough to bear arms, were officers in the War of the Revolution. This important fact demonstrates the careful military training given his sons by Thomas Marshall before 1775 — a period when comparatively few believed that war was probable.

the messmate of John Marshall, "they were reduced sometimes to a single shirt, having to wrap themselves in a blanket when that was washed"[1] and "the snow was knee-deep all the winter and stained with blood from the naked feet of the soldiers,"[2] yet "nothing discouraged, nothing disturbed" John Marshall. "If he had only bread to eat," records his fellow officer, "it was just as well; if only meat it made no difference. If any of the officers murmured at their deprivations, he would shame them by good-natured raillery, or encourage them by his own exuberance of spirits.

"He was an excellent companion, and idolized by the soldiers and his brother officers, whose gloomy hours were enlivened by his inexhaustible fund of anecdote. . . . John Marshall was the best tempered man I ever knew,"[3] testifies his comrade and messmate.

So, starving, freezing, half blind with smoke, thinly clad and almost shoeless, John Marshall went through the century-long weeks of Valley Forge, poking fun wherever he found despondency, his drollery bringing laughter to cold-purpled lips, and, his light-hearted heroism shaming into erectness the bent backs of those from whom hope had fled. At one time it would be this prank; another time it would be a different expedient for diversion. By some miracle he got hold of a pair of silk stockings and at mid-

---

[1] This was the common lot; Washington told Congress that, of the thousands of his men at Valley Forge, "few men have more than one shirt, many only the moiety of one and some none at all." (Washington to President of Congress, Dec. 23, 1777; *Writings:* Ford, vi, 260.)
[2] Slaughter, 107–08. [3] Howe, 266.

night made a great commotion because the leaves he had gathered to sleep on had caught fire and burned a hole in his grotesque finery.[1]

High spirits undismayed, intelligence shining like a lamp, common sense true as the surveyor's level — these were the qualities which at the famine camp at Valley Forge singled the boyish Virginia officer out of all that company of gloom. Just before the army went into winter quarters Captain-Lieutenant Marshall was appointed "Deputy Judge Advocate in the Army of the United States,"[2] and at the same time, by the same order, James Monroe was appointed aide-de-camp to Lord Stirling, one of Washington's generals.[3]

Such was the confidence of his fellow officers and of the soldiers themselves in Marshall's judgment and fairness that they would come to him with their disputes and abide by his decision; and these tasks, it seems, the young Solomon took quite seriously. He heard both sides with utmost patience, and, having taken plenty of time to think it over, rendered his decision, giving the reasons therefor in writing.[4] So just after he had turned his twenty-second year, we find John Marshall already showing those qualities which so distinguished him in after life. Valley Forge was a better training for Marshall's peculiar abilities than Oxford or Cambridge could have been.

His superiority was apparent, even to casual ob-

[1] Slaughter, 108.
[2] Weedon, 134; also, Heitman, 285. [3] *Ib.*
[4] Description of Marshall at Valley Forge by eye-witness, in *North American Review* (1828), xxvi, 8.

servers, notwithstanding his merriment and waggishness. One of a party visiting Valley Forge said of the stripling Virginia officer: "By his appearance then we supposed him about twenty-two or twenty-three years of age. Even so early in life . . . he appeared to us *primus inter pares,* for amidst the many commissioned officers he was discriminated for superior intelligence. Our informant, Colonel Ball, of another regiment in the same line,[1] represented him as a young man, not only brave, but signally intelligent." [2]

Marshall's good humor withstood not only the horrors of that terrible winter, but also Washington's iron military rule. The Virginia lieutenant saw men beaten with a hundred stripes for attempting to desert. Once a woman was given a hundred lashes and drummed out of the army. A lieutenant was dismissed from the service in disgrace for sleeping and eating with privates, and for buying a pair of shoes from a soldier.[3] Bitter penalties were inflicted on large numbers of civilians for trying to take flour, cattle, and other provisions to the British in Philadelphia;[4] a commissary was "mounted on a horse, back foremost, without a Saddle, his Coat turn'd wrong side out his hands tied behind him & drummed out of the Army (Never more to return) by all the Drums in the Division." [5]

What held the patriot forces together at this time?

[1] Ninth Virginia. (Heitman, 72.)
[2] *North American Review* (1828), xxvi, 8.
[3] Weedon, Feb. 8, 1778, 226–27. Washington took the severest measures to keep officers from associating with private soldiers.
[4] *Ib.,* 227–28.   [5] *Ib.,* Jan. 5, 1778; 180.

VALLEY FORGE AND AFTER

George Washington, and he alone.[1] Had he died, or had he been seriously disabled, the Revolution would have ended. Had typhoid fever seized Washington for a month, had any of those diseases, with which the army was plagued, confined him, the patriot standard would have fallen forever. Washington was the soul of the American cause. Washington was the Government. Washington was the Revolution. The wise and learned of every land agree on this. Professor Channing sums it all up when he declares: "Of all men in history, not one so answers our expectations as Washington. Into whatever part of his life the historian puts his probe, the result is always satisfactory." [2]

Yet intrigue and calumny sought his ruin. From Burgoyne's surrender on through the darkest days of Valley Forge, the Conway cabal shot its filaments through Congress, society, and even fastened upon the army itself. Gates was its figurehead, Conway its brain, Wilkinson its tool, Rush its amanuensis, and certain members of Congress its accessories before the fact. The good sense and devotion of Patrick Henry, who promptly sent Washington the anonymous letter which Rush wrote to the Virginia Governor,[3] prevented that shameful plot from driving Washington out of the service of his country.

Washington had led his army to defeat after de-

---

[1] See Washington's affecting appeal to the soldiers at Valley Forge to keep up their spirits and courage. (Weedon, March 1, 1778, 245-46.)
[2] Channing, ii, 559.
[3] See Rush's anonymous letter to Henry and the correspondence between Henry and Washington concerning the cabal. (Henry, i, 544-51.)

feat while Gates had gained a glorious victory; Gates was the man for the hour — down, then, with the incompetent Virginian, said the conspirators. The Pennsylvania Legislature, wroth that Howe's army had not been beaten, but allowed to occupy the comfortable Capital of the State, remonstrated to Congress. That body, itself, was full of dissatisfaction with the Commander-in-Chief. Why would he not oust the British from Philadelphia? Why had he allowed Howe to escape when that general marched out to meet him? As the first step toward Washington's downfall, Congress created a new Board of War, with Gates as President; Conway was made Inspector-General.[1]

The conspirators and those whom their gossip could dupe lied about Washington's motives. His abilities, it was said, were less than ordinary; and his private conduct, went the stealthy whisper, was so bad as to prove the hypocrisy of his deportment.[2] Nor were Washington's generals spared. Greene was a sycophant, said these assassins of character; Sullivan a braggart; Stirling "a lazy, ignorant drunkard." These poisoners of reputation declared that General Knox and Alexander Hamilton were "paltry satellites" of Washington and flatterers of his vanity.[3] So cunning, subtle, and persistent were these sappers and miners of reputation that even the timely action of Patrick Henry in sending Washington Rush's unsigned attack might not have prevented the great American's overthrow; for envy of Washington's strength, suspicion of his motives, distrust of

[1] Marshall, i, 217. [2] Trevelyan, iv, 301. [3] *Ib.*, 303–04.

his abilities, had made some impression even on men like John Adams.[1]

The great American bore himself with dignity, going hardly further than to let his enemies know that he was aware of their machinations.[2] At last, however, he lashed out at Congress. Let that body look to the provisioning of the army if it expected the soldiers to fight. The troops had no food, no clothing. The Quartermaster-General had not been heard from for five months. Did his critics think "the soldiers were made of stocks and stones?" Did they think an active winter campaign over three States with starving naked troops "so easy and practicable a business? I can assure those gentlemen," writes Washington, "that it is a much easier and less distressing thing to draw remonstrances in a comfortable room by a good fireside, than to occupy a cold, bleak hill, and sleep under frost and snow, without clothes or blankets. . . . I have exposed myself to detraction and calumny" because "I am obliged to conceal the true state of the army from public view. . . . No day nor scarce an hour passes without" an officer tendering his resignation.[3]

Washington was saved finally by the instinctive faith which that part of the common people who

---

[1] "The idea that any one Man Alone can save us is too silly for any Body but such weak Men as Duché to harbor for a Moment." (Adams to Rush, Feb. 8, 1778; *Old Family Letters*, 11; and see Lodge: *Washington*, i, 208; also Wallace, chap. ix.)

[2] Sparks, 252; and Marshall, i, 218.

[3] Washington to President of Congress, Dec. 23, 1777; *Writings:* Ford, vi, 257-65. And see Washington's comprehensive plans for the reorganization of the entire military service. (Washington to Committee of Congress, Jan. 28, 1778; *ib.*, 300-51.)

still supported the Revolution had in their great leader, and by his soldiers' stanch devotion, which defeat after defeat, retreat hard upon the heels of preceding retreat, hunger and nakedness, wounds and sickness could not shake.

"See the poor Soldier," wrote Surgeon Waldo at Valley Forge. "He labours thro' the Mud & Cold with a Song in his mouth, extolling War & Washington." [1]

Congress soon became insignificant in numbers, only ten or twelve members attending, and these doing business or idling as suited their whim.[2] About the only thing they did was to demand that Washington strike Philadelphia and restore the members of this mimetic government to their soft, warm nests. Higher and yet more lofty in the esteem of his officers and men rose their general. Especially was this true of John Marshall for reasons already given, which ran back into his childhood.

In vain Washington implored the various States to strengthen Congress by sending their best men to this central body. Such able men as had not taken up arms for their country refused to serve in Congress. Nearly every such man "was absorbed in provincial politics, to the exclusion of any keen and intelligent interest in the central Government of his nation." [3]

Amidst the falling snow at Valley Forge, Washing-

[1] *Hist. Mag.*, v, 131.
[2] On April 10, 1778, Ædanus Burke of South Carolina broke a quorum and defied Congress. (Secret Journals of Congress, April 10, 11, 24, 25, 1778, i, 62; and see Hatch, 21.)
[3] Trevelyan, iv, 291–92.

VALLEY FORGE AND AFTER

ton thus appealed to Colonel Harrison in Virginia: "America never stood in more eminent need of the wise, patriotic, and spirited exertions of her Sons than at this period. . . . The States, separately, are too much engaged in their local concerns. . . . The States . . . have very inadequate ideas of the present danger."[1] The letter could not be sent from that encampment of ice and death for nearly two weeks; and the harassed commander added a postscript of passionate appeal declaring that "our affairs are in a more distressed, ruinous, and deplorable condition than they have been in since the commencement of the War."[2]

"You are beseeched most earnestly, my dear Colo Harrison," pleaded Washington, "to exert yourself in endeavoring to rescue your Country by . . . sending your best and ablest Men to Congress — these characters must not slumber nor sleep at home in such times of pressing danger — they must not content themselves in the enjoyment of places of honor or profit in their Country [Virginia][3] while the common interests of America are mouldering and sinking into irretrievable . . . ruin, in which theirs also must ultimately be involved."[4]

With such men, Washington asserted, "party disputes and personal quarrels are the great business of the day, whilst the momentous concerns of an

---

[1] Washington to Harrison, Dec. 18, 1778; *Writings:* Ford, vii, 297–98.
[2] *Ib.*
[3] At this period and long after a State was referred to as "the country."
[4] Washington to Harrison, Dec. 18, 1778; *Writings:* Ford, vii, 297–98.

empire [America] [1] . . . are but secondary considerations." Therefore, writes Washington, in angry exasperation, "in the present situation of things, I cannot help asking — Where is Mason — Wythe — Jefferson?" [2]

"Where is Jefferson?" wrote Washington in America's darkest hour, when the army was hardly more than an array of ragged and shoeless skeletons, and when Congress was so weak in numbers and ability that it had become a thing of contempt. Is it not probable that the same question was asked by the shivering soldiers and officers of the Continental army, as they sat about the smoking fires of their noisome huts sinking their chattering teeth into their "Fire Cake" and swallowing their brackish water? If Washington would so write, is it not likely that the men would so talk? For was not Jefferson the penman who had inscribed the Declaration of Independence, for which they were fighting, suffering, dying?

Among the Virginians especially there must have been grave questionings. Just as to John Marshall's army experience the roots of the greatest of his constitutional opinions may clearly be traced, so the beginnings of his personal estimate of Thomas Jefferson may be as plainly found in their relative situations and conduct during the same period.

John Marshall was only a few days beyond his twentieth year when, with his Culpeper Minute Men,

[1] Until after Jefferson's Presidency, our statesmen often spoke of our "empire." Jefferson used the term frequently.

[2] Washington to Harrison, Dec. 18, 1778; *Writings:* Ford, vii, 301-02.

he fought the British at Great Bridge. Thomas Jefferson at that time was thirty-two years old; but the prospect of battle on Virginia's soil did not attract him. At Valley Forge, John Marshall had just entered on his twenty-third year, and Thomas Jefferson, thirty-five years old, was neither in the army nor in Congress. Marshall had no fortune; Jefferson was rich.[1]

So, therefore, when as reserved a man as Washington had finally and with great effort trained himself to be, asked in writing, "Where is Jefferson?" is it not a reasonable inference that the Virginia officers in the familiar talk of comrades, spoke of Jefferson in terms less mild?

And, indeed, where was Thomas Jefferson? After serving in Congress, he refused point-blank to serve there again and resigned the seat to which he had been reëlected. "The situation of my domestic affairs renders it indispensably necessary that I should solicit the substitution of some other person," was the only excuse Jefferson then gave.[2] He wanted to go to the State Legislature instead, and to the State Legislature he went. His "domestic affairs" did not prevent that. In his Autobiography, written forty-four years afterward (1821), Jefferson declares that he resigned from Congress and went to the

[1] "My estate is a large one ... to wit upwards of ten thousand acres of valuable land on the navigable parts of the James river and two hundred negroes and not a shilling out of it is or ever was under any incumbrance for debt." (Jefferson to Van Staphorst and Hubbard, Feb. 28, 1790; *Works:* Ford, vi, 33.) At the time of Valley Forge Jefferson's estate was much greater, for he had sold a great deal of land since 1776. (See Jefferson to Lewis, July 29, 1787; *ib.*, v, 311.)
[2] Jefferson to Pendleton, July, 1776; *ib.*, ii, 219–20.

State Legislature because "our [State] legislation under the regal government had many very vicious points which urgently required reformation and I thought I could be of more use in forwarding that work." [1]

So while the British revels were going on in Philadelphia and the horrors of Valley Forge appeared to be bringing an everlasting night upon American liberty, and when the desperation of the patriot cause wrung from the exasperated Washington his appeal that Virginia's ablest men should strengthen the feeble and tottering Congress, Jefferson was in the State Legislature. But he was not there merely enjoying office and exclusively engaged in party politics as Washington more than intimates. He was starting such vital reforms as the abolition of entails, the revision of the criminal code, the establishment of a free school system, the laying of the legal foundations of religious freedom.[2]

In short, Jefferson was sowing the seeds of liberalism in Virginia. But it is only human nature that breasts bearing the storm of war should not have thrilled in admiration of this civil husbandry. It was but natural that the benumbed men at Valley Forge should think the season early for the planting of State reforms, however needful, when the very ground of American independence was cold and still freezing with patriot misfortune and British success.

[1] Jefferson's *Autobiography; Works:* Ford, i, 57.
[2] Tucker, i, 92 *et seq.*; Randall, i, 199 *et seq.*; *Works:* Ford, ii, 310, 323, 324.

Virginia's Legislature might pass all the so-called laws it liked; the triumph of the British arms would wipe every one of them from the statute books. How futile, until America was free, must all this bill-drafting and reforming have appeared to the hard-driven men on the Schuylkill's Arctic hills! "Here are we," we can hear them say, "in worse case than most armies have been in the whole history of the world; here are we at Valley Forge offering our lives, wrecking our health, losing the little store we have saved up, and doing it gladly for the common American cause; and there, in safe and comfortable Williamsburg or at sumptuous Monticello, is the man who wrote our Declaration of Independence, never venturing within the sound of cannon or smell of powder and even refusing to go to Congress."

The world knows now that Jefferson was not to be blamed. He was not a man of arms, dreaded the duties of a soldier, had no stomach for physical combat.[1] He was a philosopher, not a warrior. He loved to write theories into laws that correct civil abuses by wholesale, and to promote the common good by sweeping statutes. Also, he was a born politician, skillful and adroit in party management above any man in our history.[2]

But as a man of action in rough weather, as an executive in stern times, he himself admitted his deficiency.[3] So we know to-day and better understand this great reformer, whose devotion to human

---

[1] Bloodshed, however, Jefferson thought necessary. See *infra*, vol. II, chap. I.

[2] See vol. II of this work.

[3] Jefferson's *Autobiography; Works:* Ford, i, 79.

rights has made men tolerant of his grave personal shortcomings. Nothing of this, however, could have occurred to the starving, shivering patriot soldiers in their awful plight at Valley Forge. Winning the war was their only thought, as always is the soldier's way.

Early in April, 1778, when, but for the victory at Saratoga, the Revolution seemed well-nigh hopeless to all but the stoutest hearts, an old and valued English friend begged Washington to give up the apparently doomed American cause. The Reverend Andrew Burnaby appealed to him for American and British reunion. "Must the parent and the child be forever at variance? And can either of them be happy, independent of the other?" The interests of the two countries are the same; "united they will constitute the fairest and happiest state in the world; divided they will be quite the reverse. It is not even possible that America should be happy, unconnected with Great Britain." In case America should win, the States will fall asunder from civil discord. The French, "that false and treacherous people," will desert the Americans. Great Britain and America have "the same interest, the same lineage, the same language, the same liberty, the same religion, connecting them." Everybody in England wants reunion; even the Government is anxious to "rectify ... errors and misunderstandings." It is time to "heal the wounds on both sides." Washington can achieve this "divine purpose" and "thereby acquire more glory and confer more real and lasting service, both to your own country and to mankind in general than ... ever yet happened to the lot of any one man." [1]

This subtle plea, designed to prepare the way for the British "Commission of Conciliation," neither flattered nor tempted Washington. It insulted him. He acted more vigorously than ever; and, soon afterward, his answer was delivered with cannon and bayonet on the field of Monmouth.[2]

When the winter had passed, Washington once more appealed to Congress to cease its bickering and indecision. That body was jealous of the army, he declared, whereas, said he, "We should all be considered, Congress and Army, as one people, embarked in one cause, in one interest; acting on the same principle, and to the same end" — a philosophy which a young Virginia officer was then absorbing and continued to absorb, until it became the ruling force in his life.

"No history extant," continues Washington, "can furnish an instance of an army's suffering such uncommon hardships ... and bearing them with the same patience and fortitude. To see men without clothes to cover their nakedness, without blankets to lie on, without shoes, by which their marches might be traced by the blood from their feet, and almost as often without provisions as with them, marching through the frost and snow, and at Christmas taking up their winter quarters within a day's march of the enemy, without a house or hut to cover them, 'till they could be built, and submitting to it without a

[1] Burnaby to Washington, April 9, 1788; *Cor. Rev.*: Sparks, ii, 100–02. Washington sent no written answer to Burnaby.
[2] See *infra*.

murmur, is proof of patience and obedience which, in my opinion can scarce be paralleled."[1]

Further shaming Congress into action, Washington says that "with us ... the officer ... must break in upon his private fortune for present support, without a prospect of future relief"; while, with the British, company commands "are esteemed so honorable and so valuable that they have sold of late from fifteen to twenty-two hundred pounds sterling and ... four thousand guineas have been given for a troop of dragoons." [2]

Finally came the spring of 1778. The spirits of the men rose with the budding of the trees. Games and sport alternated with drill and policing of the camp. The officers made matches for quoits, running, and jumping. Captain-Lieutenant Marshall was the best athlete in his regiment. He could vault over a pole "laid on the heads of two men as high as himself." A supply from home had reached him at last, it appears, and in it were socks. So sometimes Marshall ran races in his stocking feet. In knitting this foot apparel, his mother had made the heels of white yarn, which showed as he ran. Thus came his soldier nickname of "Silver Heels." [3]

As spring advanced, the troops recovered their

[1] Washington to Banister, April 21, 1778; *Writings:* Ford, vi, 477–87. In thus trying to arouse Congress to a sense of duty, Washington exaggerates the patience of his troops. They complained bitterly; many officers resigned and privates deserted in large numbers. (See *supra*.)

[2] *Ib.*

[3] Thayer, 12. For camp sports, see Waldo's poem, *Hist. Mag.*, vii, 272–74.

strength and, finally, were ready and eager again to meet the enemy. Washington had persuaded General Greene to accept the vital office of Quartermaster-General; and food, clothing, and munitions had somewhat relieved the situation.[1] Baron von Steuben had wrought wonders in the drill and discipline of the men and in the officers' knowledge of their technical duties.[2] "I should do injustice if I were to be longer silent with regard to the merits of the Baron de [von] Steuben" Washington told Congress, in hearty appreciation of the Prussian general's services.[3]

Another event of immense importance cheered the patriot forces and raised patriot hopes throughout America. The surrender of Burgoyne had encouraged the French statesmen to attempt the injury of England by helping the revolting colonies. On May 6, 1778, the treaty of alliance with Louis XVI was laid before Congress.[4] The miseries of the past winter were forgotten by the army at Valley Forge in the joy over the French Monarch's open championship of the American cause and his attack upon the British.[5] For it meant trained troops, ships of war, munitions, and money. It meant more — it signified, in the end, war by France upon England.

[1] Lossing, ii, 595, *et seq.*
[2] Marshall, i, 230. And see Hatch's clear account of the training given by this officer (63). To the work of Von Steuben was due the excellent discipline under fire at Monmouth. And see Kapp, already cited; and Bolton, 132. Even Belcher says that our debt to Von Steuben is as great as that to Lafayette. (Belcher, ii, 14.)
[3] Washington to President of Congress, April 30, 1778; *Writings:* Ford, vi, 507, and footnote to 505–06. And see Channing, iii, 292.
[4] See Channing, iii, 286, 288; and Marshall, i, 235, 236.
[5] Marshall, i, 237.

The hills of Valley Forge were vocal with huzzas and the roar of cannon. Songs filled the air. The army paraded. Sermons were preached. The rebound went to heights of enthusiasm equaling the former depths of despair.[1] Marshall, we may be sure, joined with his characteristic zest in the patriots' revel of happiness. Washington alone had misgivings. He feared that, because of the French alliance, Congress and the States would conclude that "we have nothing more to do" and so "relapse into a state of supineness and perfect security."[2] Precisely this occurred.

Soon, however, other inspiring tidings came — the British, it was said, were about to quit Philadelphia. The gayety in that city had continued throughout the winter, and just before the evacuation, reached its climax in a festival of almost unbelievable opulence and splendor. Processions of flower-decked boats, choruses, spectacles, and parades crowded the day; dancing and music came with sunset, and at midnight, lighted by hundreds of wax candles, twelve hundred people sat down to a dinner of Oriental luxury served by negroes clad in the rich costumes of the East "with silver collars and bracelets."[3]

When, on June 18, the Royal forces abandoned the city, the Americans were quick in pursuit.

---

[1] Sparks, 267; and Moore's *Diary*, i, 48–50.

[2] Washington to McDougall, May 5, 1778; *Writings:* Ford, vii, 6. Washington was advised of the treaty with the French King before it was formally presented to Congress.

[3] Description by Major André, who took part in this amazing performance, reprinted in *American Historical and Literary Curiosities,* following plate 26. And see Moore's *Diary*, ii, 52–56.

VALLEY FORGE AND AFTER

On June 28, a day of blistering heat, the battle of Monmouth was fought. That scorching Sunday "was long remembered all over the United States as the most sultry day which had ever been endured since mankind learned to read the thermometer." [1]

It must have been very hot indeed, for Marshall himself speaks of "the intense heat"; [2] and he disliked extreme terms. Marshall was one of the advance guard [3] under Wayne, with Lee in command of the division. In a previous council of war most of the higher officers were decidedly against risking the action; but Washington overruled them and ordered Lee to attack the British force "the moment it should move from its ground." [4]

The Commander-in-Chief, with the main body of American troops, was to come to Lee's support. It is unnecessary to go over the details of Lee's unhappy blunder, his retreat, Washington's Berserker rage and stinging rebuke on the battlefield in sight and hearing of officer and private, the turning of the rout into attack, and attack into victory by the sheer masterfulness of the mighty Virginian. From ten o'clock until nightfall the conflict raged, the Americans generally successful.

The overpowering sun made the action all but insufferable. Many died from the effects of the furnace-like heat. The fighting was heavy and often

---

[1] Trevelyan, iv, 376. [2] Marshall, i, 252.
[3] Marshall speaks of "one thousand select men" under Wayne; Maxwell's division was with Wayne under Lee; Marshall was in the battle, and it seems certain that he was among Wayne's "select men" as on former and later occasions.
[4] Marshall, i, 252.

hand to hand. Throughout the day Washington was the very soul of battle. His wrath at Lee's retreat unleashed the lion in him. He rode among the troops inspiring, calming, strengthening, steadying. Perhaps at no time in his life, except at Braddock's defeat, was his peculiar combination of cool-headed generalship and hot-blooded love of combat so manifest in a personal way as on this blazing June day at Monmouth.

"Never," testifies Lafayette, who commanded part of the advance and fought through the whole battle, "was General Washington greater in war than in this action. His presence stopped the retreat. His dispositions fixed the victory. His fine appearance on horseback, his calm courage, roused by the animation produced by the vexation of the morning, gave him the air best calculated to excite enthusiasm." [1]

When Washington was preparing the final stroke, darkness fell. The exhausted Americans, their clothing drenched with sweat, slept on their arms upon the field of battle, their General-in-Chief himself lying on the ground among the living, the wounded, and the dead. Somewhere on that hard-fought ground, Captain-Lieutenant John Marshall stretched himself by his comrades. Washington was determined to press the attack at break of day. But at midnight the British stole away so silently that the Americans did not hear a sound from their retreat.[2] The Americans lost eight officers and sixty-one privates killed,

---

[1] Lafayette to Marshall; Marshall, i, footnote to 255.
[2] Marshall, i, 254–59.

VALLEY FORGE AND AFTER 137

one hundred and sixty wounded, and one hundred and thirty missing. The British left more than two hundred and fifty dead upon the field.[1]

Upon Charles Lee most accounts of the battle of Monmouth have placed the brand of infamy. But John Marshall did not condemn Lee utterly. There were, it appears, two sides of the business — the difficulty of the ground, the mistake made by Scott, a reinforcement of the British rear, and other incidents.[2] These appealed even to Washington when the calm of judgment returned to him after the battle was fought and his blazing wrath had cooled; and had Lee not sent insulting letters to the Commander-in-Chief, it is probable that no further action would have been taken.[3]

Marshall had been in the fight from first to last; he had retreated unwillingly with the other five thousand men whom Lee commanded; he was a fighting man, always eager for the shock of arms; he cherished a devotion to Washington which was the ruling attachment of his life — nevertheless, Marshall felt that more was made of Lee's misconduct than the original offense deserved. Writing as the chosen biographer of Washington, Marshall gives both sides of this controversy.[4]

This incident throws light upon Marshall's temperament. Other historians in their eulogy of Wash-

---

[1] For descriptions of the battle of Monmouth see Washington to President of Congress, July 1, 1778; *Writings:* Ford, vii, 76–86; and to John Augustine Washington, July 4, 1778; *ib.*, 89–92. Also Marshall, i, 251–56; Trevelyan, iv, 376–80; Irving, iii, 423–34; Sparks, 272–78; Lossing, ii, 354–65.

[2] Marshall, i, 251–56.   [3] *Ib.*, 257.   [4] *Ib.*, 257–58.

ington, have lashed the memory of Lee naked through the streets of public scorn. Marshall refuses to join the chorus of denunciation. Instead, he states the whole case with fairness.[1]

Three days after Monmouth, he was promoted to a full captaincy;[2] and, as we have seen, he had been made Deputy Judge Advocate at Valley Forge. Holding these two offices, Marshall continued his military service.

The alliance with the French King, followed by the American success at Monmouth, lulled the patriots into an unwarranted feeling of security. Everybody seemed to think the war was over. Congress became more lethargic than ever, the States more torpid and indifferent. The British had seized the two points commanding King's Ferry on the North River, thus cutting the communication between the small American forces on opposite sides of the Hudson.[3] To restore this severed connection was important; and it was essential to arouse once more the declining interest of the people. Washington resolved to take Stony Point, the then wellnigh impregnable position dominating King's Ferry from the New Jersey side.

A body of light infantry was carefully selected from all ranks. It was the flower of Washington's troops in health, stability, courage, and discipline.

[1] Girardin follows Marshall in his fair treatment of Lee. (Burk, iv, 290.)

[2] He was promoted July 1, 1778. (Heitman, 285.)

[3] The whole patriot army everywhere, except in the extreme south and west, now numbered only sixteen thousand men. (Marshall, i, 306–07.)

VALLEY FORGE AND AFTER

Upon this "*élite* of the army," says Dawson, "the safety of the Highlands and, indirectly, that of the cause of America, were dependent." [1] This corps of picked soldiers was intended for quick and desperate enterprises of extra hazard. John Marshall was one of those selected.[2] Their first notable task was to take Stony Point by assault. Anthony Wayne was placed in command. "I have much at heart," Washington told Wayne, in the capture of this position, "the importance of which . . . is too obvious to need explanation." [3]

Yet even to these men on missions of such moment, supplies came tardily and in scant quantities. Wayne's "men were almost naked." [4]

---

[1] The fullest and most accurate account of the capture of Stony Point, and conditions immediately preceding, is given by Dawson in his *Assault on Stony Point*.

[2] Binney, in Dillon, iii, 315–16. The care in the selection of the various commands of "light infantry," so often used by Washington after the first year of the war, is well illustrated by his orders in this case. "The officers commanding regiments," runs Washington's orders, "will be particularly careful in the choice of the men. . . . The Adjutant General is desired to pass the men . . . under critical inspection, and return all who on any account shall appear unfit for this kind of service to their regiments, to be replaced by others whom he shall approve." (Washington's Order Book, iii, 110–11; MS., Lib. Cong.)

[3] Washington to Wayne (Private and Confidential), July 1, 1779; Dawson, 18–19.

[4] Dawson, 20. Wayne's demand for sustenance and clothing, however, is amusing. "The Light Corps under my Command," writes Wayne, ". . . have had but two days fresh Provision . . . nor more than three days allowance of Rum *in twelve days*, which article I borrowed from Genl McDougall with a Promise to Replace it. I owe him Seventy five Gallons — must therefore desire you to forward three Hod^{ds} [hogsheads] of Rum to this place with all possible Dispatch together with a few fat sheep & ten Head of good Cattle." (Wayne to Issuing Commissary, July 9, 1779; *ib.*, 20–21.)

Wayne wrote to Washington concerning clothing: "I have an

Finally, on June 15, 1779, the time came for the storming of the fort. It was washed on three sides by the waters of the Hudson and a marsh separated it from the solid land on the west. Heavy guns were on the great hill of rock; lighter batteries were placed on its slope; two rows of abatis were farther down; and the British ships in the river commanded almost every point of attack.[1]

A party of Wayne's men was detailed to remove obstructions, capture the sentries, and, in general, prepare the way for the assault by the first detachment of the Light Infantry, which was to advance with unloaded muskets, depending exclusively on the bayonet.[2] The fort was taken by those assigned to make the initial attempt, Colonel Fleury being the first to enter the stronghold. Below at the edge of the marsh waited the major part of Wayne's little force, among whom was the future Chief Justice of the United States.

[word illegible] Prejudice in favor of an Elegant Uniform & Soldierly Appearance — ... I would much rathar risque my life and Reputation at the Head of the same men in an Attack Clothed & Appointed as I could wish — with a Single Charge of Ammunition — than to take them as they appear in Common with Sixty Rounds of Cartridges." (Dawson, 20-21.)

Washington wrote in reply: "I agree perfectly with you." (*Ib.*, 21.)

[1] Marshall, i, 310.

[2] Wayne's order of battle was as picturesque as it was specific. Officer and private were directed "to fix a Piece of White paper in the most Conspicuous part of his Hat or Cap ... their Arms unloaded placing their whole Dependence on the Bay^t ... If any Soldier presumes to take his Musket from his Shoulder or Attempt to fire or begin the battle until Ordered by his proper Officer he shall be Instantly put to death by the Officer next him. ... Should any Soldier ... attempt to Retreat one Single foot or Sculk in the face of danger, the Officer next to him is Immediately to put him to death." (*Ib.*, 35-38.)

VALLEY FORGE AND AFTER

If the state of Wayne's nerves is an indication, we know how the young Virginia captain felt, there in the midnight, holding himself in readiness for the order to advance. For early in the evening Wayne thus wrote to his brother-in-law: "This will not reach your eye until the Writer is no mor^e — the Enclosed papers . . . [will] enable [you] to defend the Character and Support the Honor of the man who . . . fell in defense of his Country. . . . Attend to the Education of my Little *Son & Daughter* — I fear that their tender Mother will not Survive this Stroke."[1] But the British were overcome more easily than anybody had thought possible,[2] and, though wounded, Wayne survived to give more displays of his genuine heroism, while Providence spared John Marshall for a no less gallant and immeasurably greater part in the making of the American Nation.[3]

But the brilliant exploit went for nothing. The Americans failed to take Verplanck's Point on the eastern bank of the river and the patriot forces were still separated. Unable to spare enough men to garrison Stony Point permanently and since the Ferry remained under the British guns, Washington moved his army to the Highlands. The British at

[1] Wayne to Delaney, July 15, 1779; Dawson, 46–47.
[2] The generous and even kindly treatment which the Americans accorded the vanquished British is in striking contrast with the latter's treatment of Americans under similar circumstances. When the fort was taken, the British cried, "*Mercy, mercy, dear, dear Americans,*" and not a man was injured by the victors after he ceased to resist. (Dawson, 53; and Marshall, i, 311.)
[3] The fort was captured so quickly that the detachment to which Marshall was assigned had no opportunity to advance.

once reoccupied the abandoned fort which Wayne's men had just captured.

A detail from the Light Infantry was placed under Major Henry Lee of Virginia, who was instructed to watch the main forces of the enemy. Among Lee's flying detachment was Captain John Marshall. For three weeks this scouting expedition kept moving among the ravines, hills, and marshes, always in close touch with the British. "At Powles Hook, a point of land on the west side of the Hudson, immediately opposite the town of New York, penetrating deep into the river,"[1] the enemy had erected works and garrisoned them with several hundred men. The British had made the Hook an island by digging a deep ditch through which the waters of the river flowed; and otherwise had rendered their position secure.

The daring Lee resolved to surprise and capture the defending force, and Washington, making sure of lines of retreat, approved the adventure. All night of August 18, 1779, Lee's men marched stealthily among the steep hills, passed the main body of the British army who were sleeping soundly; and at three o'clock in the morning crossed the ditch, entered the works, and carried away one hundred and fifty-nine prisoners, losing in the swift, silent effort only two killed and three wounded.[2] This audacious feat fired the spirits of the patriot forces and covered the British with humiliation and chagrin.

Here, except for a small incident in Arnold's invasion of Virginia, John Marshall's active participa-

[1] Marshall, i, 314.   [2] *Ib.*, 314–16.

tion in actual warfare ended. He was sent home [1] because of the expiration of the term of enlistments of the regiments in which he had commanded and the excess of officers which this created.[2] The Revolution dragged along; misfortune and discouragement continued to beat upon the granite Washington. The support of Louis XVI was a staff upon which, substantial as it was, the people of the States leaned too heavily. Their exertions relaxed, as we have seen; Jefferson, patriot and reformer, but not efficient as an executive, was Governor of Virginia; and John Marshall waited in vain for the new command which never appeared.

On December 30, 1780, Jefferson received positive news of Arnold's invasion.[3] He had been warned by Washington that just this event was likely to occur; [4] but he had not summoned to the colors a single man of the militia, probably fifty thousand of whom were available,[5] nor taken any measures to prepare for it. Not until the hostile vessels entered Virginia waters to disembark the invading force was General Nelson sent to watch the enemy and call out the local militia of the adjacent vicinity; and not until news came that the British were on their way up the James River did the Governor summon the militia of the neighboring counties. The Royal soldiers reached

---

[1] The rolls show Marshall in active service as captain until December 9, 1779. (Records, War Dept.) He retired from the service February 12, 1781. (Heitman, 285.)

[2] Binney, in Dillon, iii, 290. There often were more officers of a State line than there were men to be officered; this caused by expiring enlistments of regiments.

[3] Tucker, i, 136.   [4] Marshall, i, 418.

[5] *Ib.*, 139.

Richmond on January 4, 1781, without opposition; there Arnold burned some military factories and munitions, and returned down the river. John Marshall hastened to the point of danger, and was one of the small American force that ambushed the British some distance below Westover, but that scattered in panic at the first fire of the invaders.[1]

Jefferson's conduct at this time and especially during the subsequent invasion of the State has given an unhappy and undeserved coloring to his personal character.[2] It all but led to his impeachment by the Virginia Legislature;[3] and to this day his biographers are needlessly explanatory and apol-

[1] Marshall, i, 419; Binney, in Dillon, iii, 290.

[2] Even the frightened Virginia women were ashamed. "Such terror and confusion you have no idea of. Governor, Council, everybody scampering. . . . How dreadful the idea of an enemy passing through such a country as ours committing enormities that fill the mind with horror and returning exultantly without meeting one impediment to discourage them." (Eliza Ambler to Mildred Smith, 1781 MS. Also *Atlantic Monthly*, lxxxiv, 538–39.) Miss Ambler was amused, too, it seems. She humorously describes a boastful man's precipitate flight and adds: "But this is not more laughable than the accounts we have of our illustrious G–[overno]–r [Jefferson] who, they say, took neither rest nor food for man or horse till he reached C–[arte]–r's mountain." (*Ib.*) This letter, as it appears in the *Atlantic Monthly*, differs slightly from the manuscript, which has been followed in this note.

These letters were written while the laughing young Tarleton was riding after the flying Virginia Government, of which Eliza Ambler's father was a part. They throw peculiar light on the opinions of Marshall, who at that time was in love with this lady's sister, whom he married two years later. (See *infra*, chap. v.)

[3] An inquiry into Jefferson's conduct was formally moved in the Virginia Legislature. But the matter was not pressed and the next year the Legislature passed a resolution of thanks for Jefferson's "impartial, upright, and attentive Administration." (See Eckenrode's thorough treatment of the subject in his *Revolution in Virginia*, chap. vii. And see Tucker, i, 149–56, for able defense of Jefferson; and Dodd, 63–64; also Ambler, 37.)

ogetic in regard to this phase of his career. These incidents confirmed the unfortunate impressions of Jefferson which Marshall and nearly all the Virginia officers and soldiers had formed at Valley Forge. Very few of them afterward changed their unfavorable opinion.[1]

It was his experience, then, on the march, in camp, and on the battlefield, that taught John Marshall the primary lesson of the necessity of efficient government. Also his military life developed his real temperament, which was essentially conservative. He had gone into the army, as he himself declared, with "wild and enthusiastic notions,"[2] unlike those of the true Marshall. It did not occur to this fighting Virginia youth when, responding to Patrick Henry's call, he marched southward under the coiled-rattlesnake flag inscribed "Don't tread on me," that anything was needed except to drive the oppressor into the sea. A glorious, vague "liberty" would do the rest, thought the stripling backwoods "shirtman," as indeed almost all of those who favored the patriot cause seemed to think.[3]

[1] Monroe, Bland, and Grayson are the only conspicuous exceptions.
[2] Story, in Dillon, iii, 338.
[3] This prevalent idea is well stated in one of Mrs. Carrington's unpublished letters. "What sacrifice would not an American, or Virginian (even) at the earliest age have made for so desireable an end — young as I was [twelve years old when the war began] the Word Liberty so *continually* sounding in my ears seemed to convey an idea of everything that was desirable on earth — true that in attaining it, I was to see every present comfort abandoned; a charming home where peace and prosperous fortune afforded all the elegancies of life, where nature and art united to render our residence delightful, where my ancestors had acquired wealth, and where my parents looked forward to days of ease and comfort, all this was to be given up; but in infancy the love of change is so predominant that we lose sight of con-

And when in blue and buff, as an officer of the Continental army, he joined Washington, the boyish Virginia lieutenant was still a frontier individualist, though of the moderate type. But four years of fighting and suffering showed him that, without a strong and practical government, democracy cannot solve its giant problems and orderly liberty cannot live. The ramshackle Revolutionary establishment was, he found, no government at all. Hundreds of instances of its incredible dissensions and criminal inefficiency faced him throughout these four terrible years; and Marshall has recorded many of them.

Not only did each State do as it pleased, as we have seen, but these pompous sovereignties actually interfered in direct and fatal fashion with the Continental army itself. For example, when the soldiers of the line from one State happened to be in another State, the civil power of the latter often "attempted to interfere and to discharge them, notwithstanding the fact that they were not even citizens of that State."[1] The mutiny of underfed, poorly clothed, unpaid troops, even in the State lines; the yielding of Congress to their demands, which, though just in themselves, it was perilous to grant on compulsion;[2] the discontent of the people caused by the forcible State seizure of supplies, — a seizure which a strong National Government could not have surpassed in harshness,[3] — were still other

sequences and are willing to relinquish present good for the sake of novelty, this was particularly the case with me." (Mrs. Carrington to her sister Nancy, March, 1809; MS.; and see *infra*, chap. viii.)

[1] Marshall, i, 355-65.   [2] *Ib.*, 422-24.   [3] *Ib.*, 425.

illustrations of the absolute need of an efficient central power. A few "judicious patriots" did urge the strengthening of National authority, but, writes Marshall, they were helpless to "correct that fatal disposition of power [by States and Congress] which had been made by enthusiasm uninstructed by experience." [1] Time and again Marshall describes the utter absence of civil and military correlations and the fearful results he had felt and witnessed while a Revolutionary officer.

Thus it is that, in his service as a soldier in the War for our Independence, we find the fountain-head of John Marshall's National thinking. And every succeeding circumstance of his swift-moving and dramatic life made plainer and clearer the lesson taught him on red battlefield and in fetid camp. No one can really understand Marshall's part in the building of the American Nation without going back to these sources. For, like all living things, Marshall's constructive opinions were not made; they grew. They were not the exclusive result of reasoning; they were the fruit of an intense and vivid human experience working upon a mind and character naturally cautious, constructive, and inclined to order and authority.

[1] Marshall, i, 425.

CHAPTER V

MARRIAGE AND LAW BEGINNINGS

He was always and under all circumstances an enthusiast in love. (Mrs. Carrington, of Marshall's devotion to his wife.)

IT was upon a night of gentle gayety in the late winter or early spring of 1779-80 that Captain John Marshall first met Mary Ambler. When he went back to Virginia to take charge of troops yet to be raised, he visited his father, then commanding at the village of Yorktown.[1] More than a year had gone by since Colonel Marshall had left his son at Valley Forge. On this visit befell the most important circumstance of John Marshall's private life. While he was waiting for his new command, an event came to pass which relieved his impatience to prolong still further his four years of active warfare and inspired him to improve this period of enforced absence from

[1] Mrs. Carrington to her sister Nancy, 1810; *Atlantic Monthly*, lxxxiv, 546; and same to same, March, 1809; MS. Thomas Marshall was now Colonel of the Virginia State Regiment of Artillery and continued as such until February 26, 1781, when his men were discharged and he became "a reduced officer." (Memorial of Thomas Marshall, *supra*. See Appendix IV.) This valuable historical document is the only accurate account of Thomas Marshall's military services. It disproves the statement frequently made that he was captured when under Lincoln at Charleston, South Carolina, May 12, 1780. Not only was he commanding the State Artillery in Virginia at that time, but on March 28 he executed a deed in Fauquier County, Virginia, and in June he was assisting the Ambler family in removing to Richmond. (See *infra*.) If a Thomas Marshall was captured at Charleston, it must have been one of the many others of that name. There was a South Carolina officer named Thomas Marshall and it is probably he to whom Heitman refers. Heitman (ed. 1914), 381. For account of the surrender of Charleston, see McCrady, iii, 507-09.

the front, by preparing himself for his chosen profession.

Jacquelin Ambler had been one of Yorktown's wealthiest men, and his house was called a "mansion." But the war had ruined him financially;[1] and the year 1780 found the Ambler family dwelling in humble quarters. "The small retired tenement" to which reduced circumstances forced him to take his invalid wife and young children stood next door to the headquarters of Colonel Thomas Marshall. The Ambler family was under Colonel Marshall's protection, for the father's duties as State Councillor kept him at Williamsburg.[2] But the reverse of Jacquelin Ambler's fortunes did not make this little house less attractive than his "mansion" had been.

The unusual charm of his daughters rendered that modest abode very popular. Indeed, this quality of pleasing seems to have been a common possession of the Ambler family, and has become historic. It was this very Jacquelin Ambler for whom Rebecca Burwell threw over Thomas Jefferson. This Virginia belle was the love of Jefferson's youth. She was the "Campana in die,"[3] "Belinda," "Adnileb," and "R. B." of Jefferson's letters.[4] But Rebecca Bur-

[1] "Certain it is that another Revolutionary War can never happen to affect and ruin a family so completely as ours has been!" It "involved our immediate family in poverty and perplexity of every kind." (Mrs. Carrington to her sister Nancy; *Atlantic Monthly*, lxxxiv, 545–47.)

[2] *Ib.*   [3] Dog Latin and crude pun for "bell in day."

[4] Jefferson to Page and to Fleming, from Dec. 25, 1762, to March 20, 1764; *Works:* Ford, i, 434–52. In these delightful letters Jefferson tells of his infatuation, sometimes writing "Adnileb" in Greek.

"He is a boy and is indisputably in love in this good year 1763, and

well preferred Jacquelin Ambler and became his wife.[1] The Ambler daughters inherited from both mother and father that beauty, grace, and goodness which gave them their extraordinary personal appeal.

During John Marshall's visit to his father the young ladies of Yorktown saw to it that a "ball" was given. All the officers had been invited, of course; but none of them aroused such interest as did Captain John Marshall of the Eleventh Virginia Regiment of the line.

The fame of this young soldier, fresh from the war, was very bright in Virginia. His name was on the lips of all the fair attendants of the dance. They were in a quiver of expectancy at the prospect of meeting the gallant captain who had fought under the great Washington and who had proved himself a hero at Brandywine and Germantown, at Valley Forge and Monmouth.

Years afterwards, Eliza, the eldest of the Ambler daughters, described the event in a letter full of color written to her sister. "We had been accustomed to hear him [Marshall] spoken of by all as a very *paragon*," writes Mrs. Carrington, "we had often seen

---

he courts and sighs and tries to capture his pretty little sweetheart, but like his friend George Washington, fails. The young lady will not be captured!" (Susan Randolph's account of Jefferson's wooing Rebecca Burwell; *Green Bag*, viii, 481.)

[1] Tradition says that George Washington met a like fate at the hands of Edward Ambler, Jacquelin's brother, who won Mary Cary from the young Virginia soldier. While this legend has been exploded, it serves to bring to light the personal attractiveness of the Amblers; for Miss Cary was very beautiful, heiress of a moderate fortune, and much sought after. It was Mary Cary's sister by whom Washington was captivated. (Colonel Wilson Miles Cary, in Pecquet du Bellet, i, 24-25.)

letters from him fraught with filial and paternal affection. The eldest of fifteen children, devoted from his earliest years to his younger brothers and sisters, he was almost idolized by them, and every line received from him was read with rapture." [1]

"Our expectations were raised to the highest pitch," writes the elder sister, "and the little circle of York was on tiptoe on his arrival. Our girls particularly were emulous who should be first introduced"; but Mary Ambler, then only fourteen years old, and very diffident and retiring, astonished her sister and friends by telling them that "we were giving ourselves useless trouble; for that she, for the first time, had made up her mind to go to the ball, though she had not even been at dancing school, and was resolved to set her cap at him and eclipse us all." [2]

Great was their disappointment when finally Captain Marshall arrived. His ungainly dress, slouch hat, and rustic bearing instantly quenched their enthusiasm.[3] They had looked forward to seeing a handsome, romantic figure, brilliantly appareled, and a master of all the pleasing graces; instead they beheld a tall, loose-jointed young man, thin to gauntness, whose clothes were hanging about him as if upon a rack, and whose manners were awkward and timid to the point of embarrassment. No game was he for Cupid's bow, thought these belles of old Yorktown.

[1] Mrs. Carrington to her sister Nancy; *Atlantic Monthly*, lxxxiv, 547. Of the letters which John Marshall wrote home while in the army, not one has been preserved.
[2] *Ib.*   [3] *Ib.*

"I, expecting an Adonis, lost all desire of becoming agreeable in his eyes when I beheld his awkward figure, unpolished manners, and total negligence of person"; [1] thus writes Eliza Ambler of the impression made upon her by the young soldier's disheveled aspect and unimpressive deportment. But Mary Ambler stuck to her purpose, and when John Marshall was presented to her, both fell in love at first sight. Thus began a lifelong romance which, in tenderness, exaltation, and constancy is unsurpassed in the chronicle of historic affections.

It was no longer alone the veneration for a father that kept the son in Yorktown. Day followed day, and still the gallant captain tarried. The unfavorable first judgment gave way to appreciation. He soon became a favorite at every house in the village.[2] His gift of popularity was as great, it seems, among women as among men; and at the domestic fireside as well as in the armed camp. Everybody liked John Marshall. There was a quality in him that inspired confidence. Those who at first had been so disappointed in his dress and manners soon forgot both in his wholesome charm. They found him delightfully companionable.[3] Here was preëminently a social being, they discovered. He liked people, and wanted people to like him. He was full of fun and hearty laughter; and his rare good sense and sheer manliness furnished solid foundation to his lighter qualities.

[1] Mrs. Carrington to her sister Nancy; *Atlantic Monthly*, lxxxiv, 547.
[2] *Hist. Mag.*, iii, 165. While this article is erroneous as to dates, it is otherwise accurate. [3] *Ib.*, 167.

without waiting to be asked. You must know then that I begin with the ball at York, and with the dinner on the first at your house the next day; I then trace my visit to York, our splendid assembly at the place in Williamsburg, my visit to Richmond where I asked Pa for a fortnight, my return ... and the very welcome reception you gave me ... your arrival from Dover, our little tiffs & ma... ups, my feelings while Major Dick was courting ..., my trip to the cottage, the lock of hair, my visit again to Rich... and the ensuing fall, and all the thousand inde... ble but deeply affecting instances of your ... oldness which constituted for a time the ... ... of my life and will always ... ted with a degree of interest which can never be ... while recollection remains.

Thus it is that I find amusement for ... hours which I pass without company or books.

Farewell my dearest Polly. I beg you believe ... confined I am free from pain & shall soon be free ... confinement. Yours very
J Marshall

AGE OF A LETTER FROM JOHN MARSHALL TO HIS WIFE DESCRIBING THEIR COURTSHIP
DATED AT WASHINGTON, FEBRUARY 23, 1824
(Facsimile)

So every door in Yorktown was thrown open to Captain John Marshall. But in Jacquelin Ambler's house was the lodestone which drew him. April had come and the time of blossoming. On mellow afternoons, or by candlelight when the sun had set, the young lover spent as much time as the proprieties would permit with Mary Ambler, telling her of the war, no doubt; and, as her sister informs us, reading poetry by the hour.[1] Through it all he made love as hard as he could. He wooed as ardently and steadily as he had fought.[2]

The young lover fascinated the entire Ambler family. "Under the slouched hat," testifies Mary Ambler's sister, "there beamed an eye that penetrated at one glance the inmost recesses of the human character; and beneath the slovenly garb there dwelt a heart complete with every virtue. From the moment he loved my sister he became truly a brother to me.... Our whole family became attached to him, and though there was then no certainty of his becoming allied to us, we felt a love for him that can never cease.... There was no circumstance, however trivial, in which we were concerned, that was not his care."

He would "read to us from the best authors, particularly the Poets, with so much taste and feeling, and pathos too, as to give me an idea of their sublimity, which I should never have had an idea of. Thus did he lose no opportunity of blending improvement with our amusements, and thereby gave

---

[1] Mrs. Carrington to her sister Nancy; *Atlantic Monthly*, lxxxiv, 547.
[2] *Hist. Mag.*, iii, 167.

us a taste for books which probably we might never otherwise have had." [1]

The time had come when John Marshall must acquire a definite station in civil life. This was especially necessary if he was to take a wife; and married he would be, he had decided, whenever Mary Ambler should be old enough and would consent. He followed his parents' wishes [2] and began his preparation for the bar. He told his sweetheart of his purpose, of course, and her family "learned [of it] with pleasure." [3] William and Mary College, "the only public seminary of learning in the State," [4] was only twelve miles from Yorktown; and there the young officer attended the law lectures of George Wythe for perhaps six weeks [5] — a time so short that, in the opinion of the students, "those who finish this Study [law] in a few months, either have strong natural parts or else they know little about it." [6] Recalling a criticism of one of Marshall's "envious contemporaries" some years later, Mrs. Carrington says: "Allusion was made to his short stay at William and Mary, and that he could have gained little there." [7]

---

[1] Mrs. Carrington to her sister Nancy; *Atlantic Monthly*, lxxxiv, 547.
[2] *Supra*, chap. ii.
[3] Mrs. Carrington to her sister Nancy; *Atlantic Monthly*, lxxxiv, 547.
[4] "Notes on Virginia": Jefferson; *Works:* Ford, iv, 65.
[5] Mrs. Carrington to her sister Nancy; *supra*. William and Mary was the first American institution of learning to adopt the modern lecture system. (Tyler: *Williamsburg*, 153.) The lecture method was inaugurated Dec. 29, 1779 (*ib.*, 174-75), only four months before Marshall entered.
[6] John Brown to Wm. Preston, Feb. 15, 1780; *W. and M. C. Q.*, ix, 76.
[7] Mrs. Carrington to her sister Nancy; MS.

MARRIAGE AND LAW BEGINNINGS 155

It is said also that Marshall took a course in philosophy under President Madison, then the head of the little college and afterwards Bishop of Virginia; but this is unlikely, for while the soldier-student took careful notes of Wythe's lectures, there is not a word in his notebook [1] concerning any other college activity. The faculty consisted of five professors.[2] The college was all but deserted at that time and closed entirely the year after John Marshall's flying attendance.[3]

Although before the Revolution "the Necessary Expence of each Scholar *yearly* . . . [was] only 15 £ Currency," [4] one of Marshall's fellow students testifies that: "The amazing depreciation of our Currency has raised the price of Every Article so enormously that I despair'd of my Father's ability to support me here another year. . . . Board & entring under two Professors amounts to 4000^{wt} of Tobacco." [5]

---

[1] See *infra*.

[2] The Reverend James Madison, Professor of Natural Philosophy and Mathematics; James McClung, Professor of Anatomy and Medicine; Charles Bellini, Professor of Modern Languages; George Wythe, Professor of Law; and Robert Andrews, Professor of Moral and Intellectual Philosophy. (*History of William and Mary College*, Baltimore, 1870, 70–71.) There was also a fencing school. (John Brown to Wm. Preston, Feb. 15, 1780; *W. and M. C. Q.*, ix, 76.)

[3] *History of William and Mary College*, Baltimore, 1870, 45. "Thirty Students and three professors joined the army at the beginning of the Revolutionary War." (*Ib.*, 41.) Cornwallis occupied Williamsburg, June, 1781, and made the president's house his headquarters. (Tyler: *Williamsburg*, 168.)

[4] Fithian, 107.

[5] John Brown to Wm. Preston, Jan. 26, 1780; *W. and M. C. Q.*, ix, 75. Seventeen years later the total cost to a student for a year at the college was one hundred and fifty to one hundred and seventy dollars. (La Rochefoucauld, iii, 49–56.) The annual salary of the

The intercourse of students and faculty was extremely democratic. There was a "college table" at which the students took their meals. According to the college laws of that time, beer, toddy, and spirits and water might be served, if desired.[1] The students were not required to wear either coats or shoes if the weather was warm.[2]

At a later period the students boarded at private houses in the town.[3] Jefferson, who, several years professors was four hundred dollars and that of the president was six hundred dollars.

[1] In Marshall's time the college laws provided that "No liquors shall be furnished or used at [the college students'] table except beer, cider, toddy or spirits and water." (*History of William and Mary College* (Baltimore, 1870), 44; and see Fithian, Feb. 12, 1774, 106–07.)

Twelve years after Marshall took his hasty law course at William and Mary College, a college law was published prohibiting "the drinking of spirituous liquors (except in that moderation which becomes the prudent and industrious student)." (*History of William and Mary College*, 44.)

In 1769 the Board of Visitors formally resolved that for professors to marry was "contrary to the principles on which the College was founded, and their duty as Professors"; and that if any professor took a wife "his Professorship be immediately vacated." (Resolution of Visitors, Sept. 1, 1769; *ib.*, 45.) This law was disregarded; for, at the time when Marshall attended William and Mary, four out of the five professors were married men.

The college laws on drinking were merely a reflection of the customs of that period. (See chaps. VII and VIII.) This historic institution of learning turned out some of the ablest and best-educated men of the whole country. Wythe, Bland, Peyton and Edmund Randolph, Taylor of Caroline, Nicholas, Pendleton, Madison, and Jefferson are a few of the William and Mary's remarkable products. Every one of the most distinguished families of Virginia is found among her alumni. (See Catalogue of Alumni, *History of William and Mary College*, 73–147. An error in this list puts John Marshall in the class of 1775 instead of that of 1780; also, he did not graduate.)

[2] *Infra*, chap. VII.

[3] La Rochefoucauld, iii, 49; and see Schoepf, ii, 79–80.

William Wirt, writing twenty-three years after Marshall's short attendance, thus describes the college: "They [Virginians] have only one publick seminary of learning.... This college ... in the nig-

MARRIAGE AND LAW BEGINNINGS 157

before Marshall's short attendance, was a student at William and Mary, describes the college and another public building as "rude, mis-shapen piles, which, but that they have roofs, would be taken for brick-kilns."[1] Chastellux, however, declares that "the beauty of the edifice is surpassed [only] by the richness of its library and that still farther, by the distinguished merit of several of the professors," and he describes the college as "a noble establishment ... which does honour to Virginia."[2]

The youths attending William and Mary during Marshall's brief sojourn were disgusted by the indifference of the people of the vicinity toward the patriot cause. "The want of Men, Money, Provisions, & still more of Public Virtue & Patriotism is universal — a melancholy Lethargick disposition pervades all Ranks in this part of the Country, they appear as if determined to struggle no more, but to 'stand still & see what the Lord will do for them,'" wrote John Brown in July, 1780.[3]

Mr. Wythe, the professor of law, was the life of

gardly spirit of parsimony which they dignify with the name of economy, these democrats have endowed with a few despicable fragments of surveyors' fees &c. thus converting their national academy into a mere *lazaretto* and feeding its ... highly respectable professors, like a band of beggars, on the scraps and crumbs that fall from the financial table. And, then, instead of aiding and energizing the police of the college, by a few civil regulations, they permit their youth to run riot in all the wildness of dissipation." (Wirt: *The British Spy*, 131, 132.)

[1] "Notes on Virginia": Jefferson; *Works:* Ford, iv, 69.
[2] Chastellux, 299. It is difficult to reconcile Jefferson's description of the college building with that of the French traveler. Possibly the latter was influenced by the French professor, Bellini.
[3] John Brown to Col. Wm. Preston, July 6, 1780; *W. and M. C. Q.*, ix, 80.

the little institution in this ebbing period of wartime. He established "a Moot Court, held monthly or oftener ... Mr. Wythe & the other professors sit as Judges. Our Audience consists of the most respectable of the Citizens, before whom we plead our Causes, given out by Mr. Wythe Lawyer like I assure you." The law professor also "form'd us into a Legislative Body, Consisting of about 40 members." Wythe constituted himself Speaker of these seedling lawmakers and took "all possible pains to instruct us in the Rules of Parliament." These nascent Solons of old William and Mary drew original bills, revised existing laws, debated, amended, and went through all the performances of a legislative body.[1]

The parent chapter of the Phi Beta Kappa Society had been instituted at the college; and to this Marshall was immediately elected. "At a meeting of the Society the 18 of May, 1780, Capt. John Marshall being recommended as a gentleman who would make a worthy member of this Society was balloted for & received."[2] This is an important date; for it fixes with reasonable certainty the time of Marshall's entrance at William and Mary. He was probably the oldest of all the students; his army service made him, by far, the most interesting and notable; his extraordinary social qualities never failed to render him popular. It is, therefore, certain that he was made a member of Phi Beta Kappa

[1] John Brown to Col. Wm. Preston, July 6, 1780; *W. and M. C. Q.*, ix, 80.

[2] Records, Phi Beta Kappa Society of William and Mary College, printed in *W. and M. C. Q.*, iv, 236.

MARRIAGE AND LAW BEGINNINGS 159

without much delay. He probably entered college about May 1.[1]

At once we find the new member appointed on the society's debating team. Two students were selected to "declaim" the question and two to "argue" it.

"Mr. Cabell & Mr. Peyton Short appointed to declaim the Question whether any form of government is more favorable to our new virtue than the Commonwealth.

"Mr. Joseph Cabell and Mr. Marshall to argue the same. An adjournment. William Short President.

"At a meeting in course Saturday June ye 3rd, 1780, Mr. President leaving ye chair with Mr. Fitzhugh to ye same. Mr. Wm Cabell according to order delivered his declamation on ye question given out. Mr. Peyton Short, being unprepared, was silent on ye occasion. Mr. Marshall, a gentleman not immediately interested, argued ye Question." [2]

But it was not debating on which John Marshall was intent, nor any other college duties. He had hard work, it appears, to keep his mind on the learned words that fell from the lips of Mr. Wythe; for on the inside cover and opposite page of the book in which he made notes of Wythe's law lectures,[3] we find in John Marshall's handwriting the words, "Miss Maria Ambler"; and again "Miss M. Ambler"; and still again, this time upside down,

---

[1] Dr. Lyon G. Tyler, now President of William and Mary College, thinks that this date is approximately correct.
[2] Records, Phi Beta Kappa Society of William and Mary College; printed in *W. and M. C. Q.*, iv, 236.
[3] See *infra*.

"Miss M. Ambler — J. Marshall"; and "John Marshall, Miss Polly Am."; and "John, Maria"; and "John Marshall, Miss Maria"; and "Molly Ambler"; and below this once more, "Miss M. Ambler"; on the corner of the page where the notes of the first lecture are recorded is again inscribed in large, bold letters the magic word, "Ambler." [1]

Jacquelin Ambler had been made Treasurer of State, and, early in June, 1780, the family removed from Yorktown to Richmond, stopping for a day or two in Williamsburg. While there "a ball was ... given ... by certain gentlemen in compliment ... 'to the Misses Amblers.'" Eliza Ambler describes the incidents of this social event. The affair was "simple and frugal as to its viands," she writes, "but of the brilliancy of the company too much cannot be said; it consisted of more Beauty and Elegance than I had ever witnessed before. ... I was transported with delight." Yet she could not "treat ... the prime mover in this civility with common good manners. ... His more successful friend Marshall, was devoted to my sister." [2]

This "ball" ended John Marshall's college studies; the lure of Mary Ambler was greater than that of learning to the none too studious captain. The abrupt ending [3] of the notes he was making of Mr. Wythe's lectures, in the midst of the course, otherwise so inexplicable, was caused by her two days' sojourn in the college town. Forthwith he followed to Rich-

[1] Marshall's Notebook; MS. See *infra*.
[2] Betsy Ambler to Mildred Smith, 1780; *Atlantic Monthly*, lxxxiv, 536.
[3] See *infra*.

mond, where, for two weeks he gayly played the part of the head of the family (acted "Pa," as Marshall quaintly expresses it), apparently in Jacquelin Ambler's absence.[1]

Although he had scarcely begun his studies at William and Mary; although his previous instruction by professional teachers was meager and fragmentary; and although his father could well afford the small expense of maintaining him at Williamsburg long enough for him to secure at least a moderate education, John Marshall never returned to college.[2] No more lectures of Professor Wythe for the young lover. He would begin his professional career at once and make ready for the supreme event that filled all his thoughts. So while in Richmond he secured a license to practice law. Jefferson was then Governor, and it was he who signed the license to the youth who was to become his greatest antagonist. Marshall then went to Fauquier County, and there, on August 28, 1780, was admitted to the bar. "John Marshall, Gent., produced a license from his Excellency the Governor to practice law and took the oaths prescribed by act of Assembly," runs the entry in the record.[3]

He waited for the recruiting of the new troops he was to command, and held himself in readiness to

[1] Marshall to his wife, *infra*.
[2] Marshall could have had at least one year at William and Mary, for the college did not close until June, 1781. Also he could have continued to attend for several weeks after he left in June, 1780; for student John Brown's letters show that the college was still open on July 20 of that year.
[3] County Court Minutes of Fauquier County, Virginia, 1773–80, 473.

take the field, as indeed he rushed to do without
orders when Arnold's invasion came. But the new
troops never were raised and Marshall finally left
the service. "I continued in the army until the year
1781," he tells us, "when, being without a command,
I resigned my commission in the interval between
the invasion of Virginia by Arnold and Phillips."[1]

During this season of inaction he resolved to be
inoculated against the smallpox. This was another
effect which falling in love had on the young soldier;
for he could, had he wished, have had this done
more than once while with Washington's army.[2] He
would now risk his health no longer. But the laws of
Virginia made the new method of treating smallpox
almost impossible.[3] So away on foot[4] went John
Marshall to Philadelphia to be made proof against
this disfiguring malady.

According to Marshall's own account, he covered
the ground at an amazing pace, averaging thirty-
five miles a day; but when he arrived, so disreputa-
ble did he appear that the tavern refused to take

[1] *Autobiography.*

[2] Marshall, with other officers, did go to Philadelphia in January or
February of 1777 to be inoculated for smallpox (Marshall to Colonel
Stark, June 12, 1832, supporting latter's pension claim; MSS. Rev. War,
S. F. no. 7592, Pension Bureau); but evidently he was not treated or
the treatment was not effective.

[3] First, the written permission to be inoculated had to be secured
from all the justices of the county; next, all the neighbors for two
miles around must consent — if only one of them refused, the treatment could not be given. Any physician was fined ten thousand dollars, if he inoculated without these restrictions. (Hening, ix, 371.)
If any one was stricken with smallpox, he was carried to a remote
cabin in the woods where a doctor occasionally called upon him. (La
Rochefoucauld, iii, 79–80; also De Warville, 433.)

[4] Horses were very scarce in Virginia at this time. It was almost
impossible to get them even for military service.

MARRIAGE AND LAW BEGINNINGS 163

him in.[1] Long-bearded and slovenly clothed, with battered hat and uncouth manners, he gave the unfavorable first impression which the same causes so often produced throughout his life. This is not to be wondered at, for, writing twenty years afterward, when Marshall as Chief Justice was at the height of his career, his sister-in-law testifies that his "total negligence of person . . . often produced a blush on her [Marshall's wife's] cheek."[2] But he finally secured lodgings, was inoculated, and, made secure from the attacks of the dreaded scourge, back he fared to Virginia and Mary Ambler.

And Marshall made love as he made war, with all his might. A very hurricane of a lover he must have been; for many years afterward he declared to his wife's sister that "he looked with astonishment at the present race of lovers, so totally unlike what he had been himself."[3] In a touching letter to his wife, written almost half a century later, Marshall thus recalls the incidents of his courtship: —

"I begin with the ball at York, and with the dinner on the fish at your house the next day: I then retrace my visit to York, our splendid assembly at the Palace [4] in Williamsburg, my visit to Richmond

---

[1] *Southern Literary Messenger* (quoting from a statement by Marshall), ii, 183.

[2] Mrs. Carrington to her sister Nancy; *Atlantic Monthly*, lxxxiv, 547.

[3] *Ib.*, 548. A story handed down through generations of lawyers confirms Mrs. Carrington. "I would have had my wife if I had had to climb Alleghanys of skulls and swim Atlantics of blood" the legend makes Marshall say in one of his convivial outbursts. (The late Senator Joseph E. McDonald to the author.)

[4] "The Palace" was a public building "not handsome without but

where I acted Pa for a fortnight, my return the ensuing fall and the very welcome reception you gave me on your arrival from Dover, our little tiffs & makings up, my feelings while Major Dick [1] was courting you, my trip to the cottage,[2] the lock of hair, my visit again to Richmond the ensuing fall, and all the thousand indescribable but deeply affecting instances of your affection or coldness which constituted for a time the happiness or misery of my life and will always be recollected with a degree of interest which can never be lost while recollection remains." [3]

When he left the army in 1781, Marshall, although a member of the bar, found no legal business to do.[4] He probably alternated between the Oak Hill plantation in Fauquier County, where his help was sadly needed, and Richmond, where the supreme attraction drew him. Thus another year wore on. In this interval John Marshall engaged in politics, as was the custom of young gentlemen of standing and ambition; and in the fall of 1782 was elected to the House of Delegates from Fauquier County.[5] This

... spacious and commodious within and prettily situated." ("Notes on Virginia": Jefferson; *Works:* Ford, iv, 69.)

[1] Richard Anderson, the father of the defender of Fort Sumter. (Terhune: *Colonial Homesteads*, 97.)

[2] A country place of Edward Ambler's family in Hanover County. (See Pecquet du Bellet, i, 35.) Edward Ambler was now dead. His wife lived at "The Cottage" from the outbreak of the war until her death in 1781. (*Ib.*, 26; and Mrs. Carrington to Mrs. Dudley, Oct. 10, 1796; MS.)

[3] Marshall to his wife, Feb. 23, 1826; MS.

[4] Most of the courts were closed because of the British invasion. (Flanders, ii, 301.)

[5] *Infra*, chap. VI.

MARRIAGE AND LAW BEGINNINGS 165

honor was a material help, not only in his career, but in his suit for the hand of Mary Ambler.

Also, membership in the Legislature required him to be, where his heart was, in Richmond, and not two months had John Marshall been in the Capital as a member of Virginia's Legislature when he was married. "In January [3d] 1783," writes Marshall, "I intermarried with Mary Willis Ambler, the second daughter of Mr. Jacquelin Ambler, then Treasurer of Virginia, who was the third son of Mr. Richard Ambler, a gentleman who had migrated from England, and settled at York Town, in Virginia." [1]

The Ambler abode in Richmond was not a romantic place for the wedding. The primitive town was so small that when the Ambler family reached it Eliza exclaimed, "*where* we are to lay our weary heads Heaven knows!" And she describes the house her father rented as "a little dwelling" so small that "our whole family can scarcely stand up altogether in it"; but Jacquelin Ambler took it because, poor as it was, it was "the only decent tenement on the hill."[2]

The elder Ambler sister thus pictures the Richmond of 1780: "This little town is made up of Scotch factors who inhabit small tenements scattered here and there from the river to the hill. Some of them look, as Colonel [Thomas] Marshall has observed, as if the poor Caledonians had brought them over on their backs, the weakest of whom being glad enough to stop at the bottom of the hill, others

---

[1] *Autobiography.*
[2] Betsy Ambler to Mildred Smith, 1780; *Atlantic Monthly*, lxxxiv, 537.

a little stronger proceeding higher, whilst a few of the stoutest and the boldest reached the summit."[1] Eight years after the Amblers moved to Richmond, Jefferson wrote: "The town below Shockoe creek is so deserted you cannot get a person to live in a house there rent free."[2]

But Mary's cousin, John Ambler, who, at twenty-one years of age, found himself "one of the richest men in the State of Virginia,"[3] solved the difficulty by offering his country seat for the wedding.[4] Mary Ambler was only seventeen when she became the young lawyer's bride,[5] and John Marshall was a little more than ten years older. After the bridegroom had paid the minister his fee, "he had but one solitary guinea left."[6]

This does not mean that John Marshall was without resources, but it indicates the scarcity of ready money in Virginia at the close of the war. Indeed, Marshall's father, while not yet the wealthy man he afterwards became,[7] had, as we have seen, already

[1] Betsy Ambler to Mildred Smith, 1780; *Atlantic Monthly*, lxxxiv, 537.

[2] Jefferson to Short, Dec. 14, 1788; *Works:* Ford, vi, 24. Twelve years after Marshall's marriage, there were but seven hundred houses in Richmond. (Weld, i, 188.)

[3] Pecquet du Bellet, i, 35–37. He was very rich. (See inventory of John Ambler's holdings, *ib.*) This opulent John Ambler married John Marshall's sister Lucy in 1792 (*ib.*, 40–41); a circumstance of some interest when we come to trace Marshall's views as influenced by his connections and sympathies.

[4] Mrs. Carrington to her sister Nancy; *Atlantic Monthly*, lxxxiv, 548.

[5] She was born March 18, 1766, and married January 3, 1783. (Paxton, 37.) Marshall's mother was married at the same age.

[6] Mrs. Carrington to her sister Nancy; *Atlantic Monthly*, lxxxiv, 548.

[7] Thomas Marshall's will shows that he owned, when he died, several years later, an immense quantity of land.

MARRIAGE AND LAW BEGINNINGS 167

acquired very considerable property. He owned at this time at least two thousand acres in Fauquier County;[1] and twenty-two negroes, nine of them tithable (sixteen years old), twelve horses, and twenty-two head of cattle.[2]

When John Marshall married Miss Ambler, his father gave him one negro and three horses.[3] The following year (1784) the Tithable Book shows but five tithable negroes, eight young negroes, eight horses, and eighteen head of cattle in Thomas Marshall's name. He evidently sold his other slaves and personal property or took them with him to Kentucky. So it is likely that the slaves, horses, and cattle left behind were given to his son, together with a part of Thomas Marshall's Fauquier County farm.[4]

During the Revolution Thomas Marshall was, like most other Continental officers, in sore need of money. He tried to sell his land to Washington for cash. Washington was anxious to buy "Lands in my own Neck at (almost) any price . . . in ye way of Barter . . . for Negroes . . . or . . . for any thing else (except Breeding Mares and Stock)." But he could not pay money. He estimated, by memory, Thomas Marshall's land at £3000, at a time when, because of depreciated money and inflated prices, "a Barrl. of Corn which used to sell for 10/ will now fetch 40 — when a Barl. of Porke that formerly could be had for £3 sells for £15." So

[1] *Supra*, chap. II.
[2] Fauquier County Tithable Book, 1783-84; MS., Va. St. Lib.
[3] *Ib.* [4] See *infra*.

Washington in 1778 thought that "Marshall is not a necessitous man." When it came to trading, the father of his country was keen and suspicious, and he feared, it would seem, that his boyhood friend and comrade in arms would "practice every deception in his power in order to work me . . . up to his price." [1]

Soon after John Marshall met Mary Ambler at the "ball" at Yorktown, and just before he went to William and Mary College, his father sold this very land that Washington had refused to purchase. On March 28, 1780, Thomas Marshall conveyed to Major Thomas Massey [Massie] one thousand acres in Fauquier County for "thirty thousand pounds Currency." [2] This was a part of the seventeen hundred acres for which the elder Marshall had paid "nine hundred and twelve pounds ten shillings" seven years before.[3] The change shows the startling depreciation of Virginia currency as well as Continental paper, both of which in 1780 had reached a very low point and were rapidly going down.[4]

It reveals, too, the Marshall family's extreme need of cash, a want sorely felt by nearly everybody at this period; and the familiar fact that ownership of land did not mean the ready command of money. The year after John Marshall's marriage he wrote to James Monroe: "I do not know what to say to your scheme of selling out. If you can execute it you will have made a very capital sum, if you can

---

[1] Washington to Lund Washington, Aug. 15, 1778; *Writings:* Ford, vii, 151–52.
[2] Records of Fauquier County (Va.), Deed Book, vii, 533.
[3] *Supra,* chap. II.   [4] See *infra,* chap. VIII.

Mary Ambler Marshall

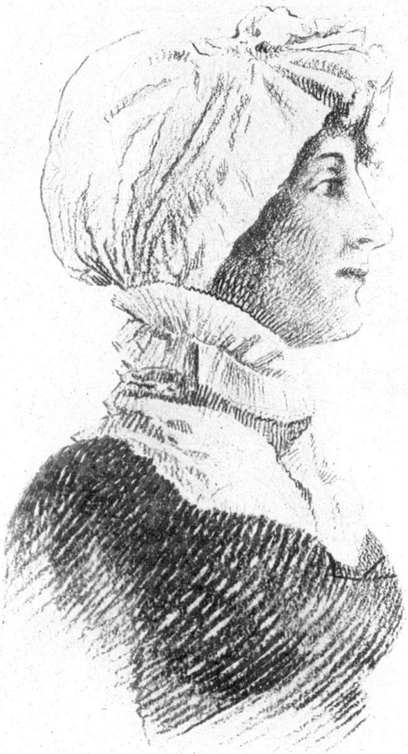

MARRIAGE AND LAW BEGINNINGS 169

retain your lands you will be poor during life unless you remove to the western country, but you have secured for posterity an immense fortune"; and Marshall tells Monroe that the latter can avail himself of the knowledge of Kentucky lands possessed by the members of the Marshall family who were on the ground.[1]

Writing twenty years later of economic conditions during the period now under review, Marshall says: "Real property was scarcely vendible; and sales of any article for ready money could be made only at a ruinous loss.... In every quarter were found those who asserted it to be impossible for the people to pay their public or private debts." [2]

So, although his father was a very well-to-do man when John Marshall began married life, he had little or no ready money, and the son could not expect much immediate paternal assistance. Thomas Marshall had to look out for the bringing-up of a large number of other children and to consider their future; and it is this fact which probably induced him to seek fortune anew in the Kentucky wilderness after he was fifty years of age. Legend has it that Thomas Marshall made his venture on Washington's advice. At any rate, he settled, permanently, in Kentucky in the fall of 1783.[3]

---

[1] Marshall to Monroe, Dec. 28, 1784; Monroe MSS., vii, 832; Lib. Cong.

[2] Marshall, ii, 104.

[3] Marshall to Monroe, Dec. 12, 1783; Draper Collection, Wis. Hist. Soc. Thomas Marshall first went to Kentucky in 1780 by special permission of the Governor of Virginia and while he was still Colonel of the State Artillery Regiment. (Humphrey Marshall, i, 104, 120.) During his absence his regiment apparently became somewhat de-

The fledgling lawyer evidently expected to start upon a legal career in the county of his birth; but immediately after marrying Miss Ambler, he established himself at Richmond, where her family lived, and there began the practice of the law. While his marriage into the Ambler family was inspired exclusively by an all-absorbing love, the alliance was a fortunate one for John Marshall from the practical point of view. It gave him the support of a powerful State official and one of the best-liked men in all Virginia. A favor asked by Jacquelin Ambler was always granted if possible; and his recommendation of any one was final. The Ambler household soon became the most attractive in Richmond, as it had been in Yorktown; and Marshall's marriage to Mary Ambler gave him a social standing which, in the Virginia of that day, was a very great asset in business and politics.

The house to which he took his bride was a tiny

moralized. (Thomas Marshall to Colonel George Muter, Feb. 1781; MS. Archives, Va. St. Lib. and partly printed in *Cal. Va. St. Prs.*, i, 549.) Upon his return to Virginia, he was appointed Surveyor of a part of Kentucky, November 1, 1780. (Collins: *History of Kentucky*, i, 20.) The following year he was appointed on the commission "to examine and settle the Public Accts in the Western Country" and expected to go to Kentucky before the close of the year, but did not, because his military certificates were not given him in time. (Thomas Marshall to Governor Harrison, March 17, 1781; *Cal. Va. St. Prs.*, i, 578; and to Lieutenant-Governor Jameson, Oct. 14, 1781; *ib.*, 549.) He opened his surveyor's office in Kentucky in November, 1782. (Butler: *History of Kentucky*, 138.) In 1783 he returned to Virginia to take his family to their new home, where he remained until his death in 1802. (Paxton, 19.) Thomas Marshall was immediately recognized as one of the leading men in this western Virginia district, and was elected to the Legislature and became "Surveyor [Collector] of Revenue for the District of Ohio." (See *infra*, chaps. III and v.)

one-story affair of wood, with only two rooms; the best house the Amblers themselves could secure, as we have seen, was so small that the "whole family" could scarcely crowd into it. Three years before John Marshall and his young wife set up housekeeping, Richmond could "scarce afford one comfort in life."[1] According to Mrs. Carrington the dwelling-houses had no curtains for the windows.[2] The streets were open spaces of earth, unpaved and without sidewalks. Many years after Marshall established himself at the new and raw Virginia Capital, Main Street was still unpaved, deep with dust when dry and so muddy during a rainy season that wagons sank up to the axles. Footways had been laid only at intervals along the town's chief thoroughfare; and piles of ashes and cinders were made to serve as street-crossings, from which, if one misstepped on a dark and rainy night, he found himself deep in the mire. A small stream flowed diagonally across Main Street, flooding the surface; and the street itself ended in gullies and swamps.[3] In 1783 the little town was, of course, still more primitive.

There were no brick or stone buildings in Richmond when Marshall was married. The Capitol, itself, was an ugly structure — "a mere wooden barn" — on an unlovely site at the foot of a hill.[4] The private dwellings, scattered about, were the poor, mean, little wooden houses already described by Eliza Ambler.

[1] Betsy Ambler to Mildred Smith; *Atlantic Monthly*, lxxxiv, 537.
[2] Mrs. Carrington to Mildred Smith, Jan. 10, 1786; MS.
[3] Mordecai, 45–47.   [4] *Ib.*, 40.

Trade was in the hands of British merchants who managed to retain their commercial hold in spite of the Revolution.[1] Rough, heavy wagons drawn by four or six horses brought in the produce of the country, which included "deer and bear skins, furs, ginseng, snake-root," and even "dried rattlesnakes ... used to make a viper broth for consumptive patients."[2] These clumsy vehicles were sometimes a month in covering less than two hundred miles.[3] Specie was the money chiefly used in the back country and the frontier tradesmen made remittances to Richmond by placing a "bag of gold or silver in the centre of a cask of melted wax or tallow ... or [in a] bale of hemp."[4]

There was but one church building and attendance was scanty and infrequent.[5] The principal amusement was card-playing, in which everybody indulged,[6] and drinking was the common practice.[7] The town sustained but one tavern which was kept by a Neapolitan named Farmicola. This hostelry had two large rooms downstairs and two above. The beds were under the roof, packed closely together and unseparated by partitions. When the Legislature met, the inn was crowded; and "Generals, Colonels, Captains, Senators, Assembly-men, Judges, Doctors, Clerks, and crowds of Gentlemen of every weight and calibre and every hue of dress, sat alto-

---

[1] Mordecai, chap. ii.
[2] *Ib.*, 51–52. This was more than twenty years after Marshall and his young wife started housekeeping in Richmond.
[3] *Ib.*, 53. [4] *Ib.*
[5] Meade, i, 140; Schoepf, ii, 62.
[6] Mordecai, chap. xxi; Schoepf, ii, 63 *et seq.*
[7] See *supra*, chaps. I and VII.

MARRIAGE AND LAW BEGINNINGS 173

gether about the fire, drinking, smoking, singing, and talking ribaldry." [1]

Such were conditions in the town of Richmond when John Marshall hazarded his adventure into the legal profession there in 1783. But it was the seat of the State Government, and the place where the General Court of Appeals and the High Court of Chancery were located. Yet small, poor, and mean as was the Virginia Capital of that day, not even Philadelphia, New York, or Boston could boast of a more brilliant bar.

Randolph and Wickham, Innes and Ronald, Campbell and Call, and others whose distinction has made the bar of the Old Dominion historic, practiced at Richmond. And the court around which this extraordinary constellation gathered was equally eminent. Pendleton, whose intellect and industry more than supplied early defects in education, was president of the Court of Appeals; Wythe was one of the judges of the High Court of Chancery, of which he afterwards became sole chancellor; Paul Carrington and others of almost equal stature sat with Pendleton on the Supreme Bench. Later on appeared the erudite, able, and commanding Roane, who, long afterwards, when Marshall came into his own, was to be his most formidable antagonist in the clash of courts.

Among such lawyers and before a court of this high quality the young attorney from the backwoods of Fauquier County began his struggle for a share

[1] Schoepf, ii, 64. Marshall frequented this place and belonged to a club which met there. (See entries from Marshall's Account Book, *infra*.)

of legal business. He had practically no equipment except his intellect, his integrity, and his gift for inspiring confidence and friendship. Of learning in the law, he had almost none at all. He had read Blackstone, although not thoroughly;[1] but the only legal training that Marshall had received was acquired during his few weeks at William and Mary College. And in this romantic interval, as we have seen, he was thinking a good deal more about Mary Ambler than about preparing himself for his career.

We know exactly to which of Wythe's lectures Marshall had listened; for he took notes of them. He procured a thick, blank book strongly bound in calf. In this he wrote in a large, firm hand, at the top of the page, the topics of lectures which Wythe had announced he would give, leaving after each headline several pages for notes.[2] Since these notes are a full record of Marshall's only formal instruction in the law, a complete list of the subjects, together with the space allotted to each, is as important as it is interesting.

On the subject of Abatement he wrote three pages; on Accounts, two pages; on Accord and Satisfaction, one page; Actions in General, one and a half pages; Actions Local and Transitory, one fourth page; Actions Qui Tam, one and one fourth pages; Actions on the Case, three and one half pages; Agree-

---

[1] *Supra*, chap. II.

[2] This invaluable Marshall source is not a law student's commonplace book alphabetically arranged, but merely a large volume of blank leaves. It is six inches wide by eight in length and more than one in thickness. The book also contains Marshall's accounts for twelve years after his marriage. All reference hereafter to his receipts and expenses are from this source.

ments, three pages; Annuity and Rent Charge, two pages; Arbitrament and Award, one and one half pages; Assault and Battery, two thirds of a page; Assignment, one half page; Assumpsit, one and a half pages; Attachment, one half page; Audita Querela, one fourth page; Authority, one fourth page; Bail in Civil Causes, one half page; Bail in Criminal Causes, one and two thirds pages; Bailment, two pages; Bargain and Sale, one half page; Baron and Feme, four pages; Bastardy, three quarters page; Bills of Sale, one half page; Bills of Exceptions, one half page; Burglary, one page; Carriers, one page; Certiorari, one half page; Commitments, one half page; Condition, five and one half pages; Coparceners, one and one half pages; Costs, one and one fourth pages; Covenant, three pages; Curtesy of England, one half page; Damages, one and one half pages; Debt, one and one half pages; Descent, one and one half pages; Detinue, one half page; Devises, six and one half pages; Disseisin, two lines; Distress, one and two thirds pages; Dower, two pages; Duress, one third page; Ejectment, two and two thirds pages; Election, two thirds page; Error, two and one third pages; Escape in Civil Cases, one and one fifth pages; Estates in Fee Simple, three fourths page; Estate for Life and Occupancy, one and four fifths pages; Evidence, four pages, two lines; Execution, one and five sixths pages; Executors and Administrators, eleven pages; Extinguishment, two thirds page; Extortion, one half page; Felony, three and one sixth pages; Forcible Entry and Detainer, three fourths page; Forgery, three pages; Forfeiture, two and four fifths pages; Fraud, three pages, one line; Grants, three and three fourths pages; Guardian, two and five sixths pages; Heir and Ancestor, five pages, two lines; Idiots and Lunatics, three pages; Indictments, four pages, three lines; Infancy and Age, nine and one half pages; Information, one and one fifth pages; Injunction, one and two thirds pages; Inns and Innkeepers, two and two thirds pages; Joint Tenants and Tenants in Common, nine and one sixth pages; Jointure, three pages.

We find six pages he had reserved for notes on the subject of Juries left blank, and two blank pages follow the caption, "Justice of the Peace." But he made seventeen and two thirds pages of notes on the subjects of Leases and Terms for Years, and twelve and one half pages on the subject of Legacies. This ended his formal legal studies; for he made no notes under the remaining lecture subjects.[1]

Not an ideal preparation to attract clients, we must admit, nor to serve them well when he got them. But slender and elementary as was his store of learning, his apparel, manners, and habits were even less likely to bring business to this meagerly equipped young advocate.

Marshall made practically no money as a lawyer during his first year in Richmond. Most of his slender income seems to have been from his salary as a member of the Legislature.[2] He enters in his Account Book in 1783 (where it begins) several

[1] The notes are not only of lectures actually delivered by Wythe, but of Marshall's reading on topics assigned for study. It is probable that many of these notes were made after Marshall left college.

[2] See *infra*, chap. VI.

receipts "by my civil list warrants," and several others, "Rec.ᵈ from Treasury." Only four fees are entered for the whole year — one for three pounds, another for two pounds, eleven shillings, one for two pounds, ten shillings, and a fourth for two pounds, eight shillings.

On the contrary, he paid one pound, two shillings, sixpence for "advice fee given the attorney for opinion on surveyors fees." He bought "one pair Spectacles" for three shillings and ninepence. His sociable nature is revealed at the beginning of his career by entries, "won at Whist 24–1–4" and "won at Whist 22/"; and again "At Backgammon 30/–1–10." Also the reverse entry, "Lost at Whist £3 14/." [1]

The cost of living in Richmond at the close of the Revolution is shown by numerous entries. Thirty-six bushels of oats cost Marshall three pounds, ten shillings, sixpence. He paid one pound for "one pair stockings"; and one pound, eighteen shillings, sixpence for a hat. In 1783 a tailor charged him one pound, eight shillings, sixpence for "making a Coat." He enters "stockings for P.[olly] [2] 6 dollars." A stove "Dutch Oven" cost fourteen shillings and eightpence; and "150 bushels coal for self 7–10" (seven pounds, ten shillings).

[1] Such entries as these denote only Marshall's social and friendly spirit. At that period and for many years afterward card-playing for money was universal in Virginia (La Rochefoucauld, iii, 77; and Mordecai, ed. 1856, chap. xxi), particularly at Richmond, where the women enjoyed this pastime quite as much as the men. (*Ib.*) This, indeed, was the case everywhere among women of the best society who habitually played cards for money. (Also see Chastellux, 333–34.)

[2] Marshall's wife.

In October of the year of his marriage he paid six shillings for wine and "For rum £9–15." His entries for household expenditures for these months give an idea of the housekeeping: "Given Polly 6 dollars £4–10–6; . . . a coffe pot 4/; 1 yd. Gauze 3/6; 2 Sugar boxes £1–7–6; Candlestick &c. 3/6 1 y^d Linnen for P. 2/6; 2 pieces of bobbin 1/6; Tea pot 3/; Edging 3/6; Sugar pot 1/6; Milk 1/; Thimble 4/2; Irons 9/, . . . Tea 20/." [1]

The entries in Marshall's Account Book for the first year and a half of his married life are indiscriminately and poorly made, without dates of receipts and expenditures. Then follows a period up to June, 1785, where the days of the month are stated. Then come entries without dates; and later, the dates sometimes are given and sometimes not. Marshall was as negligent in his bookkeeping as he was in his dress. Entries in the notebook show on their face his distaste for such details. The Account Book covers a period of twelve years, from 1783 to 1795.

He was exceedingly miscellaneous in his expenses. On January 14, 1784, he enters as items of outlay: "Whist 30/" and "Whist 12/," "cow £3–12–8"

[1] The references are to pounds, shillings, and pence. Thus "3 14/" means three pounds and fourteen shillings. "30–5–10" means thirty pounds, five shillings, and tenpence; or "3/6" means three shillings, sixpence. Where the Account Book indicates the amount without the signs of denomination, I have stated the amount indicated by the relative positions of the figures in the Account Book. Computation should be by Virginia currency (which was then about three and one half dollars to the Virginia pound) and not by the English pound sterling. This is not very helpful, however, because there is no standard of comparison between the Virginia dollar of that period and the United States dollar of to-day. It is certain only that the latter has greater purchasing power than the former. All paper money had greatly depreciated at the time, however.

MARRIAGE AND LAW BEGINNINGS 179

and "poker 6/," "To Parson 30/." This date is jammed in, plainly an afterthought, and no more dates are specified until June 7. Other characteristic entries at this time are, on one day, "Turkeys 12/ Wood 24/ Whist £18"; and on another day, "Beef 26/8 — Backgammon £6." An important entry, undated, is, "Paid the University in the hands of Mr. Tazewell for Col° Marshall as Surveyor of Fayette County 100" (pounds).[1]

On July 5, 1784, he enters among receipts "to my service in the Assembly 34-4" (pounds and shillings); and among his expenses for June 22 of that year, he enters "lost at Whist £19" and on the 26th, "Col° [James] Monroe & self at the Play 1-10"[2] (one pound, ten shillings). A week later the theater again cost him twelve shillings; and on the third he enters an outlay "to one Quarter cask wine 14" (pounds, or about fifty dollars Virginia currency). On the same day appears a curious entry of "to the play 13/" and "Pd for Col° Monroe £16-16." He was lucky at whist this month, for there are two entries during July, "won at whist £10"; and again, "won at whist 4-6" (four pounds, six shillings). He contributes to St. John's Church one pound, eight shillings. During this month their first child was born to the young couple;[3] and there are various

---

[1] The "University" was William and Mary College, then partly supported by a portion of the fees of official surveyors. Thomas Marshall was now Surveyor of Fayette County, Kentucky. (See *supra*.) This entry occurs several times.

[2] Such entries are frequent throughout his Account Book. During his entire life, Marshall was very fond of the theater. (See *infra*, II, chap. v; also vol. III of this work.)

[3] Thomas Marshall, born July 21, 1784. (Paxton, 90.)

entries for the immediate expenses of the event amounting to thirteen pounds, four shillings, and threepence. The child was christened August 31 and Marshall enters, "To house for christening 12/ do. 2/6."

The Account Book discloses his diversified generosity. Preacher, horse-race, church, festival, card-game, or "ball" found John Marshall equally sympathetic in his contributions. He was looking for business from all classes in exactly the same way that young lawyers of our own day pursue that object. Also, he was, by nature, extremely sociable and generous. In Marshall's time the preachers bet on horses and were pleasant persons at balls. So it was entirely appropriate that the young Richmond attorney should enter, almost at the same time, "to Mr. Buchanan 5" (pounds)[1] and "to my subscription for race £4–4";[2] "Saint Taminy 11 Dollars — 3–6"[3] (three pounds, six shillings); and still again, "paid my subscription to the ball 20/–1"; and later, "expenses at St. John's [church] 2–3" (pounds and shillings).

Marshall bought several slaves. On July 1, 1784, he enters, "Paid for Ben 90–4"[4] (ninety pounds, four shillings). And in August of that year, "paid for two Negroes £30" and "In part for two servants

[1] Buchanan was the Episcopal clergyman in Richmond at the time. (Meade, i, 29, 140.)

[2] The races at Richmond, held bi-annually, were the great social events of Virginia. (Mordecai, 178 *et seq.*)

[3] This fixes the equivalent in State dollars for Virginia pounds and shillings.

[4] He already owned one tithable negro in Fauquier County in 1783. (Fauquier County Tithable Book, 1783–84; MS., Va. St. Lib. See *supra*.)

£20." And in September, "Paid for servants £25," and on November 23, "Kate & Evan £63." His next purchase of a slave was three years later, when he enters, May 18, 1787, "Paid for a woman bought in Gloster £55."

Shoeing two horses in 1784 cost Marshall eight shillings; and a hat for his wife cost three pounds. For a bed-tick he paid two pounds, nine shillings. We can get some idea of the price of labor by the following entry: "Pd. Mr. Anderson for plaistering the house £10–2." Since he was still living in his little rented cottage, this entry would signify that it cost him a little more than thirty-five dollars, Virginia currency, to plaster two rooms in Richmond, in 1784. Possibly this might equal from seven to ten dollars in present-day money. He bought his first furniture on credit, it appears, for in the second year of his married life he enters, December "31st P⁴ M⁺ Mason in part for furniture 10" (pounds).

At the end of the year, "Pd balance of my rent 43–13" (pounds and shillings). During 1784, his third year as a lawyer, his fees steadily increased, most of them being about two pounds, though he received an occasional fee of from five to nine pounds. His largest single fee during this year was "From Mr. Stead 1 fee 24" (pounds).

He mixed fun with his business and politics. On February 24, 1784, he writes to James Monroe that public money due the latter could not be secured. "The exertions of the Treasurer & of your other friends have been ineffectual. There is not one shilling in the Treasury & the keeper of it could not borrow one on the faith of the government." Marshall confides to Monroe that he himself is "pressed for money," and adds that Monroe's "old Land Lady Mrs. Shera begins now to be a little clamorous. . . . I shall be obliged I apprehend to negotiate your warrants at last at a discount. I have kept them up this long in hopes of drawing Money for them from the Treasury."

But despite financial embarrassment and the dull season, Marshall was full of the gossip of a convivial young man.

"The excessive cold weather," writes Marshall, "has operated like magic on our youth. They feel the necessity of artificial heat & quite wearied with lying alone, are all treading the broad road to Matrimony. Little Steward (could you believe it?) will be married on Thursday to Kitty Haie & Mr. Dunn will bear off your old acquaintance Miss Shera.

"Tabby Eppes has grown quite fat and buxom, her charms are renovated & to see her & to love her are now synonimous terms. She has within these six weeks seen in her train at least a score of Military & Civil characters. Carrington, Young, Selden, Wright (a merchant), & Foster Webb have alternately bow'd before her & been discarded.

"Carrington 'tis said has drawn off his forces in order to refresh them & has march'd up to Cumberland where he will in all human probability be reinforced with the dignified character of Legislator. Webb has returned to the charge & the many think from their similitude of manners & appetites that they were certainly designed for each other.

"The other Tabby is in high spirits over the success of her antique sister & firmly thinks her time will come next, she looks quite spruce & speaks of Matrimony as of a good which she yet means to experience. Lomax is in his county. Smith is said to be electioneering. Nelson has not yet come to the board. Randolph is here and well. . . . Farewell, I am your J. Marshall."[1]

Small as were the comforts of the Richmond of that time, the charm, gayety, and hospitality of its inhabitants made life delightful. A young foreigner from Switzerland found it so. Albert Gallatin, who one day was to be so large a factor in American public life, came to Richmond in 1784, when he was twenty-two years old. He found the hospitality of the town with "no parallel anywhere within the circle of my travels. . . . Every one with whom I became acquainted," says Gallatin, "appeared to take an interest in the young stranger. I was only the interpreter of a gentleman, the agent of a foreign house that had a large claim for advances to the State. . . . Every one encouraged me and was disposed to promote my success in life. . . . John Marshall, who, though but a young lawyer in 1783, was almost at the head of the bar in 1786, offered to take

[1] Marshall to Monroe, Feb. 24, 1784; MS., N.Y. Pub. Lib. Compare with Jefferson's sentimental letters at the same age. Very few of Marshall's letters during this period are extant. This one to Monroe is conspicuously noticeable for unrestraint and joyousness. As unreserved as he always was in verbal conversation, Marshall's correspondence soon began to show great caution, unlike that of Jefferson, which increased, with time, in spontaneity. Thus Marshall's letters became more guarded and less engaging; while Jefferson's pen used ever more highly colored ink and progressively wrote more entertaining if less trustworthy matter.

me in his office without a fee, and assured me that I would become a distinguished lawyer." [1]

During his second year in Richmond, Marshall's practice showed a reasonable increase. He did not confine his legal activities to the Capital, for in February we find thirteen fees aggregating thirty-three pounds, twelve shillings, "Rec^d in Fauquier" County. The accounts during this year were fairly well kept, considering that happy-go-lucky John Marshall was the bookkeeper. Even the days of the month for receipts and expenditures are often given. He starts out with active social and public contributions. On January 18, 1785, he enters, "my subscription to Assemblies [balls] 4–4" (pounds and shillings), and "Jan. 29 Annual subscription for Library 1–8" (pound, shillings).

On January 25, 1785, he enters, "laid out in purchasing Certificates 35–4–10." And again, July 4, "Military Certificates pd for self £13–10–2 at 4 for one £3–7–7. Interest for 3 years £2–8 9." A similar entry is made of purchases made for his father; on the margin is written, "pd commissioners."

He made his first purchase of books in January, 1785, to the amount of "£4–12/." He was seized with an uncommon impulse for books this year, it appears. On February 10 he enters, "laid out in books £9–10–6." He bought eight shillings' worth of pamphlets in April. On May 5, Marshall paid "For Mason's Poems" nine shillings. On May 14, "books 17/–8" and May 19, "book 5/6"

---

[1] Gallatin to Maxwell, Feb. 15, 1848; Gallatin's *Writings: Adams*, ii, 659. Also see Mordecai, 94–95.

Richmond in 1800

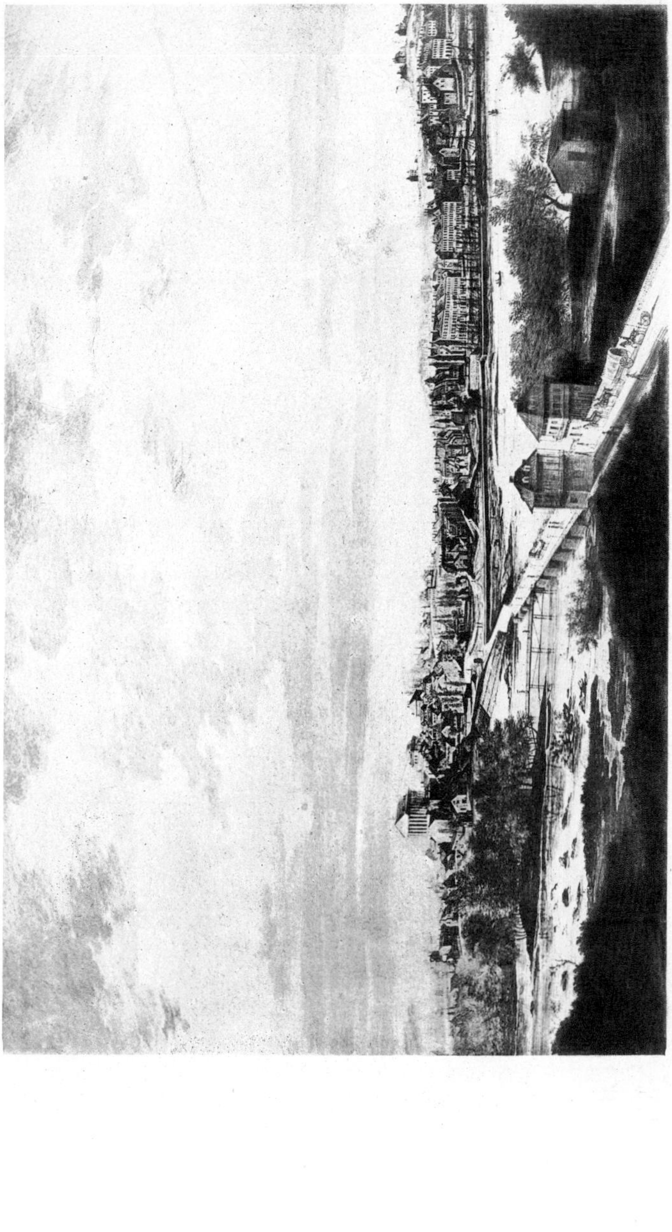

MARRIAGE AND LAW BEGINNINGS 185

and "Blackstones Commentaries [1] 36/," and May 20, "Books 6/." On May 25, there is a curious entry for "Bringing books in stage 25/." On June 24, he purchased "Blair's Lectures" for one pound, ten shillings; and on the 2d of August, a "Book case" cost him six pounds, twelve shillings. Again, on September 8, Marshall's entries show, "books £1–6," and on October 8, "Kaim's Principles of Equity 1–4" (one pound, four shillings). Again in the same month he enters, "books £6–12," and "Spirit of Law" (undoubtedly Montesquieu's essay), twelve shillings.

But, in general, his book-buying was moderate during these formative years as a lawyer. While it is difficult to learn exactly what literature Marshall indulged in, besides novels and poetry, we know that he had "Dionysius Longinus on the Sublime"; the "Works of Nicholas Machiavel," in four volumes; "The History and Proceedings of the House of Lords from the Restoration," in six volumes; the "Life of the Earl of Clarendon, Lord High Chancellor of England"; the "Works of C. Churchill — Poems and Sermons on Lord's Prayer"; and the "Letters of Lord Chesterfield to his son." A curious and entertaining book was a condensed cyclopædia of law and business entitled "Lex Mercatoria Rediviva or The Merchant's Directory," on the title-page of which is written in his early handwriting, "John Marshall Richmond." [2] Marshall also

[1] His father must have kept, for the time being, the Blackstone purchased in 1772, although the volume later turned up in Marshall's possession.
[2] This book, with the others named, bears the signature of Mar-

had an English translation of "The Orations of Æschines and Demosthenes on the Crown."[1]

Marshall's wine bills were very moderate for those days, although as heavy as a young lawyer's resources could bear. On January 31, 1785, he bought fourteen shillings' worth of wine; and two and a half months later he paid twenty-six pounds and ten shillings "For Wine"; and the same day, "beer 4d," and the next day, "Gin 30/." On June 14 of the same year he enters, "punch 2/6," the next day, "punch 3/," and on the next day, "punch 6/."[2]

Early in this year Marshall's father, now in Kentucky and with opulent prospects before him, gave his favorite son eight hundred and twenty-four acres

shall at this period of his life. They are the only books in existence which certainly were bought by Marshall at that time, all other volumes he is positively known to have had in his library being published at a later date. All except one of those named, with others hereafter mentioned, are in the possession of Judge J. K. M. Norton, Alexandria, Virginia. The *Lex Mercatoria* is, of course, in English. It is a large book containing seven hundred seventy-five pages, seven by eight inches, firmly bound in calf. It is "compiled from many standard authorities." While it is an encyclopædia of law and business containing items such as a comparison of the values of money of all lands, it is very readable and entertaining. It is just the kind of book from which Marshall could have derived information without being wearied by research. John Adams also had a copy of Malynes's *Lex Mercatoria*, which seems to have been a common possession of commercial lawyers throughout the country.

[1] This book is now in the possession of Hon. William Marshall Bullitt, of Louisville, Kentucky.

[2] The numerous entries of this kind occurring throughout Marshall's Account Book must not be misunderstood. At that time and for many decades afterward, the habitual use of whiskey, wine, rum, brandy, etc., was the universal custom. They were bought in quantities and consumed much as ordinary table waters now are. The common people, especially those in the South, distilled their own stimulants. The people of New England relied on the great distilleries of Boston and vicinity for rum, of which they consumed enormous quantities. (See *infra*, chap. VII; also chap. II, vol. II, of this work.)

of the best land in Fauquier County.[1] So the rising Richmond attorney was in comfortable circumstances. He was becoming a man of substance and property; and this condition was reflected in his contributions to various Richmond social and religious enterprises.

He again contributed two pounds to "S.t Taminy's" on May 9, 1785, and the same day paid six pounds, six shillings to "My club at Farmicolas."[2] On May 16 he paid thirty shillings for a "Ball" and nine shillings for "music"; and May 25 he enters, "Jockie Club 4-4" (pounds and shillings). On July 5 he spent six shillings more at the "Club"; and the next month he again enters a contribution to "S.t Johns [Episcopal Church] £1-16." He was an enthusiastic Mason, as we shall see; and on September 13, 1785, he enters, "p.d Mason's Ball subscription for 10" (pounds). October 15 he gives eight pounds and four shillings for an "Episcopal Meeting"; and the next month (November 2, 1785) subscribes eighteen shillings "to a ball." And at the end of the year (December 23, 1785) he enters his "Subscription to Richmond Assem. 3" (pounds).

Marshall's practice during his third year at the Richmond bar grew normally. The largest single fee received during this year (1785) was thirty-five pounds, while another fee of twenty pounds, and still another of fourteen pounds, mark the nearest approaches to this high-water mark. He had by now

[1] Records of Fauquier County (Va.), Deed Book, viii, 241, March 16, 1785.

[2] The tavern kept by Farmicola, where Marshall's club met. (See *supra*.)

in Richmond two negroes (tithable), two horses, and twelve head of cattle.[1]

He was elected City Recorder during this year; and it was to the efforts of Marshall, in promoting a lottery for the purpose, that the Masonic Hall was built in the ambitious town.[2]

The young lawyer had deepened the affection of his wife's family which he had won in Yorktown. Two years after his marriage the first husband of his wife's sister, Eliza, died; and, records the sorrowing young widow, "my Father . . . dispatched . . . my darling Brother Marshall to bring me." Again the bereaved Eliza tells of how she was "conducted by my good brother Marshall who lost no time" about this errand of comfort and sympathy.[3]

February 15, 1786, he enters an expense of twelve pounds "for moving my office" which he had painted in April at a cost of two pounds and seventeen shillings. This year he contributed to festivities and social events as usual. In addition to his subscriptions to balls, assemblies, and clubs, we find that on May 22, 1786, he paid nine shillings for a "Barbecue," and during the next month, "barbecue 7/" and still again, "barbecue 6/." On June 15, he "paid for Wine 7-7-6," and on the 26th, "corporation dinner 2-2-6." In September, 1786, his doctor's bills were very high. On the 22d of that month he

---

[1] Henrico County Tithable Book; Va. St. Lib. He had, of course, other slaves, horses, and cattle on his Fauquier County plantation.

[2] Christian, 28.

[3] Eliza Ambler to Mildred Smith, July 10, 1785; MS.; also printed in *Atlantic Monthly*, lxxxiv, 540-41.

MARRIAGE AND LAW BEGINNINGS 189

paid nearly forty-five pounds for the services of three physicians.[1]

Among the books purchased was "Blair's sermons" which cost him one pound and four shillings.[2] In July he again "P^d for St Taminy's feast 2" (pounds). The expense of traveling is shown by several entries, such as, "Expenses up & down to & from Fauquier 4–12" (four pounds, twelve shillings); and "Expenses going to Gloster &c 5" (pounds); "expenses going to W^{m}sburg 7" (pounds); and again, "expenses going to and returning from Winchester 15" (pounds); and still again, "expenses going to W^{m}sburg 7" (pounds). On November 19, Marshall enters, "For quarter cask of wine 12–10" (twelve pounds and ten shillings). On this date we find, "To Barber 18" (shillings) — an entry which is as rare as the expenses to the theater are frequent.

He appears to have bought a house during this year (1786) and enters on October 7, 1786, "P^d Mr. B. Lewis in part for his house £70 cash & 5£ in an order in favor of James Taylor ——75"; and November 19, 1786, "Paid Mr. B. Lewis in part for house 50" (pounds); and in December he again "P^d Mr. Lewis in part for house 27–4" (twenty-seven pounds, four shillings); and (November 19) "P^d Mr. Lewis 16" (pounds); and on the 28th, "Paid Mr. Lewis in full 26–17–1 1/4."

In 1786, the Legislature elected Edmund Ran-

[1] Drs. McClurg, Foushee, and Mackie.
[2] This book was purchased for his wife, who was extremely religious. The volume is in the possession of Judge J. K. M. Norton, Alexandria, Virginia. On the fly-leaf appears, "Mrs. Mary W. Marshall," in Marshall's handwriting. The book was also useful to Marshall for his own study of rhetoric, since Blair's sermons stood very high, at this time, as examples of style.

dolph Governor; and, on November 10, 1786, Randolph advertised that "The General Assembly having appointed me to an office incompatible with the further pursuit of my profession, I beg leave to inform my clients that John Marshall Esq. will succeed to my business in General &c." [1]

At the end of this year, for the first time, Marshall adds up his receipts and expenditures, as follows: "Received in the Year 1786 according to the foregoing accounts 508–4–10." And on the opposite page he enters [2] —

To my expenses	432		
	1		8
	433	—	8

In 1787 Marshall kept his accounts in better fashion. He employed a housekeeper in April, Mrs. Marshall being unable to attend to domestic duties; and from February, 1787, until May of the following year he enters during each month, "Betsy Mumkins 16/." The usual expenditures were made during this year, and while Marshall neglects to summarize his income and outlay, his practice was still growing, although slowly. On December 3, 1787, his second child was born.[3]

In January of 1787 occurred the devastating Richmond fire which destroyed much of the little city; [4] and on February 7, Marshall enters among his expenses, "To my subscription to the sufferers by fire 21" (pounds).

[1] Christian, 29, 30.
[2] This unbusinesslike balancing is characteristic of Marshall.
[3] Jacquelin Ambler Marshall, Dec. 3, 1787. (Paxton, 99.) [4] *Ib.*

MARRIAGE AND LAW BEGINNINGS 191

Marshall's name first appears in the reports of the cases decided by the Virginia Court of Appeals in 1786. In May of that year the court handed down its opinion in Hite *et al. vs.* Fairfax *et al.*[1] It involved not only the lands directly in controversy, but also the validity of the entire Fairfax title and indirectly that of a great deal of other land in Virginia. Baker, who appears to have been the principal attorney for the Fairfax claimants, declared that one of the contentions of the appellants "would destroy every title in the Commonwealth." The case was argued for the State by Edmund Randolph, Attorney-General, and by John Taylor (probably of Caroline). Marshall, supporting Baker, acted as attorney for "such of the tenants as were citizens of Virginia." The argument consumed three days, May 3 to 5 inclusive.[2]

Marshall made an elaborate argument, and since it is the first of his recorded utterances, it is important as showing his quality of mind and legal methods at that early period of his career. Marshall was a little more than thirty years old and had been practicing law in Richmond for about three years.

The most striking features of his argument are his vision and foresight. It is plain that he was acutely conscious, too, that it was more important to the settlers who derived their holdings from Lord Fairfax to have the long-disputed title settled than it was to win as to the particular lands directly in controversy. Indeed, upon a close study of the complicated records in the case, it would

[1] Call, i, 42.   [2] Records of the Court of Appeals.

seem that Joist Hite's claim could not, by any possibility, have been defeated. For, although the lands claimed by him, and others after him, clearly were within the proprietary of Lord Fairfax, yet they had been granted to Hite by the King in Council, and confirmed by the Crown; Lord Fairfax had agreed with the Crown to confirm them on his part; he or his agents had promised Hite that, if the latter would remain on the land with his settlers, Fairfax would execute the proper conveyances to him, and Fairfax also made other guarantees to Hite.

But it was just as clear that, outside of the lands immediately in controversy, Lord Fairfax's title, from a strictly legal point of view, was beyond dispute except as to the effect of the sequestration laws.[1] It was assailed, however, through suggestion at least, both by Attorney-General Randolph and by Mr. Taylor. There was, at this time, a strong popular movement on foot in Virginia to devise some means for destroying the whole Fairfax title to the Northern Neck. Indeed, the reckless royal bounty from which this enormous estate sprang had been resented bitterly by the Virginia settlers from the very beginning;[2] the people never admitted the justice and morality of the Fairfax grant. Also, at this particular period, there was an epidemic of debt repudiation, evasion of contracts and other obligations, and assailing of titles.[3]

[1] The estate had been sequestered during the Revolution.
[2] Wertenbaker: *V. U. S.*, 123-26. For history of these grants, see chap. IV, vol. II, of this work.
[3] See *infra*, chap. VI.

MARRIAGE AND LAW BEGINNINGS 193

So, while Baker, the senior Fairfax lawyer, referred but briefly to the validity of the Fairfax title and devoted practically the whole of his argument to the lands involved in the case then before the court, Marshall, on the other hand, made the central question of the validity of the whole Fairfax title the dominant note of his argument. Thus he showed, in his first reported legal address, his most striking characteristic of going directly to the heart of any subject.

Briefly reported as is his argument in Hite *vs.* Fairfax, the qualities of far-sightedness and simple reasoning, are almost as plain as in the work of his riper years: —

"From a bare perusal of the papers in the cause," said Marshall, "I should never have apprehended that it would be necessary to defend the title of Lord *Fairfax* to the Northern Neck. The long and quiet possession of himself and his predecessors; the acquiescence of the country; the several grants of the crown, together with the various acts of assembly recognizing, and in the most explicit terms admitting his right, seemed to have fixed it on a foundation, not only not to be shaken, but even not to be attempted to be shaken.

"I had conceived that it was not more certain, that there was such a tract of country as the Northern Neck, than that Lord *Fairfax* was the proprietor of it. And if his title be really unimpeachable, to what purpose are his predecessors criminated, and the patents they obtained attacked? What object is to be effected by it? Not, surely, the destruction of the grant; for gentlemen cannot suppose, that a grant made by the crown to the ancestor for services rendered, or even for affection, can be invalidated in the hands of the heir because those services and affection are forgotten; or because the thing granted has, from causes which must have been foreseen, become more valuable than when it was given. And if it could not be invalidated in the hands of the heir, much less can it be in the hands of a purchaser.

"Lord *Fairfax* either was, or was not, entitled to the territory; if he was, then it matters not whether the gentlemen themselves, or any others, would or would not have made the grant, or may now think proper to denounce it as a wise, or impolitic, measure; for still the title must prevail; if he was not entitled, then why was the present bill filed; or what can the court decree upon it? For if he had no title, he could convey none, and the court would never have directed him to make the attempt.

"In short, if the title was not in him, it must have been in the crown; and, from that quarter, relief must have been sought. The very filing of the bill, therefore, was an admission of the title, and the appellants, by prosecuting it, still continue to admit it. . . .

"It [the boundary] is, however, no longer a question; for it has been decided, and decided by that tribunal which has the power of determining it. That decision did not create or extend Lord *Fairfax's* right, but determined what the right originally was. The bounds of many patents are doubtful; the extent of many titles uncertain; but when a decision is once made on them, it removes the doubt, and ascertains what the original boundaries were. If this be a principle universally acknowledged, what can destroy its application to the case before the court?"

The remainder of Marshall's argument concerns the particular dispute between the parties. This, of course, is technical; but two paragraphs may be quoted illustrating what, even in the day of Henry and Campbell, Wickham and Randolph, men called "Marshall's eloquence."

"They dilate," exclaimed Marshall, "upon their hardships as first settlers; their merit in promoting the population of the country; and their claims as purchasers without notice. Let each of these be examined.

"Those who explore and settle new countries are generally bold, hardy, and adventurous men, whose minds, as well as bodies, are fitted to encounter danger and fatigue; their object is the acquisition of property, and they generally succeed.

"None will say that the complainants have failed; and, if their hardships and danger have any weight in the cause, the defendants shared in them, and have equal claim to countenance; for they, too, with humbler views and less extensive prospects, 'have explored, bled for and settled a, 'till then, uncultivated desert.'"[1]

Hite won in this particular case; but, thanks to Marshall's argument, the court's decision did not attack the general Fairfax title. So it was that Marshall's earliest effort at the bar, in a case of any

[1] Call, iv, 69–72.

magnitude, was in defense of the title to that estate of which, a few years later, he was to become a principal owner.[1] Indeed, both he and his father were interested even then; for their lands in Fauquier County were derived from or through Fairfax.

Of Marshall's other arguments at this period, no record exists. We know, however, from his Account Book, that his business increased steadily; and, from tradition, that he was coming to be considered the ablest of the younger members of the distinguished Richmond bar. For his services in this, his first notable case, Marshall received one hundred and nine pounds, four shillings, paid by fifty-seven clients. Among those employing the young attorney was George Washington. In the account of fees paid him in Hite *vs.* Fairfax, he enters: "Gen$^{l.}$ G. Washington 1–4" (pounds and shillings) and "A. Washington 1–4." Marshall's record of this transaction is headed: "List of fees rec'd from Ten$^{ts.}$ Fairfax Ad^{s} Hite," referring to the title of the case in the lower court.

An evidence of his growing prosperity is the purchase from Aquella and Lucy Dayson of two hundred and sixty acres of land in Fauquier County, for "one hundred and sixty pounds current money of Virginia." [2] This purchase, added to the land already given him by his father,[3] made John Marshall, at thirty-one years of age, the owner of nearly one thousand acres of land in Fauquier.

Marshall's Account Book shows his generosity

[1] *Infra*, vol. II, chap. IV.
[2] Records Fauquier County (Va.), Deed Book, x, 29.
[3] See *supra*.

toward his brothers and sisters, who remained in Virginia when Thomas Marshall went to Kentucky to establish himself. There are frequent entries of money advanced to his brothers, particularly James M., as, "Given my brother James £3–9"; or, "To my brother James £36–18," etc. Marshall's sister Lucy lived in his house until her marriage to the wealthy John Ambler.[1] The young lawyer was particularly attentive to the wants of his sister Lucy and saw to it that she had all the advantages of the Virginia Capital. In his Account Book we find many entries of expenses in her behalf; as, for example, "for Lucy £5–8–3"; and again, a few days later, "given Eliza[2] for Lucy" four pounds, sixteen shillings; and still later, "for Lucy 10–6" (ten pounds, six shillings); and, "P^d for Lucy entering into dancing school 2–2" (two pounds, two shillings).

Throughout Marshall's Account Book the entries that most frequently occur are for some expense for his wife. There is hardly a page without the entry, "given Polly" so much, or "for Polly" so much, and the entries are for liberal amounts. For instance, on January 15, 1785, he enters, "Sundries for Polly £8–6–8 1/2"; on the 18th, "Given Polly 6/"; on the 25th, "for Polly 11/ 7 1/2"; and on the 29th, "Given Polly for a hat 36/." And later, "Given Polly 56/" and "Given Polly 2–16" (pounds and shillings); and "for Polly £3." "For Polly 5–7–5"; "Sundries for Polly, 12–6" and "Left with Polly 10–4" (pounds and shillings). "Given Polly

---

[1] See *supra*, 166, footnote 3.
[2] Mrs. Carrington.

£1-8"; "Gloves for Polly 7/6." Such entries are very numerous.

The young wife, who had become an invalid soon after her marriage, received from her husband a devotion and care, which realized poetic idealism. "His exemplary tenderness to our unfortunate sister is without parallel," testifies Mrs. Carrington. "With a delicacy of frame and feeling that baffles all description, she became, early after her marriage, a prey to an extreme nervous affliction which more or less has embittered her comfort thro' life; but this only served to increase his care and tenderness. . . . He is always and under every circumstance an enthusiast in love." [1]

Marshall's affection for his wife grew with the years and was nourished by her increasing infirmities. It is the most marked characteristic of his entire private life and is the one thing which differentiates him sharply from most of the eminent men of that heroic but, socially, free-and-easy period. Indeed, it is in John Marshall's worship of his delicate and nerve-racked wife that we find the beginnings of that exaltation of womankind, which his life, as it unrolls, will disclose.

John Marshall's respect, admiration, reverence, for woman became so notable that it was remarked by all who knew him, and remains to this day a living tradition in Richmond. It resembled the sentiment of the age of chivalry. While the touching incidents, glowing testimonials, and most of the letters that

[1] Mrs. Carrington to her sister Nancy; MS. The mother and sister of Mrs. Marshall were similarly afflicted. Mrs. Carrington frequently mentions this fact in her correspondence.

May

31	To Betsy Munkus	16
	Saddle & bridle for Polly	5
2	for water cask 9/- market 4/	-13
	punch ladle 22/6 knee buckles postage	1-9-6
9th	to Polly expended about home	2.10-0
12	My expenses going to Gloucester	5
	expenses in country ℔ 4-4-	4.4
15	razor &c.	6-6
16	Tea 10/6 woods 3/- for Polly 10/ market 16/4	1-19-10
18	Paid for a Woman bought in Gloucester	55
	market 13.9 — gauze 3/ candles 2/	1-8-9
	Subscription Jocky club	2.2
	Shrub 6/ capers 2/6 nuts 1/3	9-9
	plants 3/3 market 2/6	5-9
	market 20/ do 10/4 expenses 8/	1-18-4
23	shoeing my horse 3/	3
	lost at cards 34/ wood 9/	2-3
	market 3/ worsted 4/7	7
		37.19.2
	the negroe	55
30	market 11/6	92.19-2

[115]

PAGE OF MARSHALL'S ACCOUNT BOOK, MAY, 1787
(Facsimile)

reveal this feature of Marshall's character occur more vividly after he ascended the bench,[1] the heart of the man cannot be understood as we go along without noting the circumstance in his earlier married life.

[1] See vol. III of this work.

CHAPTER VI

IN THE LEGISLATURE AND COUNCIL OF STATE

The proceedings of the Assembly are, as usual, rapidly degenerating with the progress of the session. (Madison.)

Our Assembly has been employed chiefly in rectifying the mistakes of the last and committing new ones for emendation at the next. (Washington.)

It is surprising that gentlemen cannot dismiss their private animosities but will bring them in the Assembly. (Marshall.)

IN 1783, a small wooden building stood among the two or three hundred little frame houses [1] which, scattered irregularly from the river to the top of the hill, made up the town of Richmond at the close of the Revolution. It was used for "balls," public banquets, and other functions which the merriment or inclination of the miniature Capital required. But its chief use was to house the legislative majesty of Virginia. In this building the General Assembly of the State held its bi-yearly sessions. Here met the representatives of the people after their slow and toilsome journey on horseback through the dense forests and all but impassable roads from every county of the Commonwealth.[2]

The twenty years that had passed since Marshall's father entered the House of Burgesses had brought changes in the appearance and deportment of Virginia's legislative body corresponding to those in the government of the newly established State. But few elegancies of velvet coat, fine lace, silk stock-

[1] Richmond grew rapidly thereafter. The number of houses was trebled within a decade.
[2] Schoepf, ii, 55-56.

ing, and silver buckle were to be seen in the Virginia Legislature of 1783. Later these were to reappear to some extent; but at the close of the Revolution democracy was rampant, and manifested itself in clothing and manners as well as in curious legislation and strange civil convulsions.

The visitor at a session of the Old Dominion's lawmakers beheld a variegated array — one member in homespun trousers thrust into high boots; still another with the fringed Indian leggings and hunting-shirt of the frontier. Some wore greatcoats, some jackets, and, in general, an ostentatious disregard of fashionable apparel prevailed, which occasional silk knee-breeches and stockings emphasized.

The looker-on would have thought this gathering of Virginia lawmakers to be anything but a deliberative body enacting statutes for the welfare of over four hundred thousand people. An eye-witness records that movement, talk, laughter went on continuously; these Solons were not quiet five minutes at a time.[1] All debating was done by a very few men.[2] The others "for most part ... without clear ... ideas, with little education or knowledge ... merely ... give their votes."[3]

Adjoining the big room where this august assembly sat, was an anteroom; and at the entrance between these two rooms stood a burly doorkeeper, who added to the quiet and gravity of the proceedings by frequently calling out in a loud voice the names of members whom constituents or visitors

---

[1] Schoepf, ii, 55–56.   [2] *Ib.*; and see Journals.   [3] *Ib.*, ii, 57.

wanted to see; and there was a constant running back and forth. The anteroom itself was a scene of conversational tumult. Horse-racing, runaway slaves, politics, and other picturesque matters were the subjects discussed.[1] Outsiders stood in no awe of these lawgivers of the people and voiced their contempt, ridicule, or dislike quite as freely as their approval or admiration.[2]

Into this assembly came John Marshall in the fall of 1782. Undoubtedly his father had much to do with his son's election as one of Fauquier County's representatives. His predominant influence, which had made Thomas Marshall Burgess, Sheriff, and Vestryman before the Revolution, had been increased by his admirable war record; his mere suggestion that his son should be sent to the House of Delegates would have been weighty. And the embryo attorney wanted to go, not so much as a step in his career, but because the Legislature met in the town where Mary Ambler lived. In addition to his father's powerful support, his late comrades, their terms of enlistment having expired, had returned to their homes and were hotly enthusiastic for their captain.[3] He was elected almost as a matter of course.

No one in that motley gathering called the House of Delegates was dressed more negligently than this young soldier-lawyer and politician from the backwoods of Fauquier County. He probably wore the short "round about" jacket, which was his favorite

[1] Schoepf, 55-56.   [2] *Ib.*, 58.
[3] Story, in Dillon, iii, 337. Marshall was a prime favorite of his old comrades all his life. (*Ib.*)

costume. And among all that free-and-easy crowd no one was less constrained, less formal or more sociable and "hail-fellow, well-met" than this black-eyed, laughter-loving representative from the up country.

But no one had a sounder judgment, a more engaging personality, or a broader view of the drift of things than John Marshall. And notable men were there for him to observe; vast forces moving for him to study. Thomas Jefferson had again become a member of the House after his vindication from threatened impeachment. Patrick Henry was a member, too, and William Cabell, Richard Henry Lee, Benjamin Harrison, and other men whose names have become historic. During Marshall's later years in the Legislature, James Madison, George Mason, William Grayson, Edmund Randolph, George Nicholas, and others of like stature became Marshall's colleagues.

It took eighteen days to organize the House at the first session John Marshall attended.[1] The distance that members had to come was so great, traveling so hard and slow, that not until November 9 had enough members arrived to make a quorum.[2] Thomas Jefferson and Patrick Henry were two of the absent and several times were ordered to be taken into the custody of the sergeant-at-arms.[3] The Journal for Friday, November 8, gravely announces that "it was ordered that Mr. Thomas

[1] Journal, H.D. (Oct. Sess., 1782), 3–10.
[2] The roads were so bad and few that traveling even on horseback was not only toilsome but dangerous. (See *infra*, chap. VII.)
[3] Journal, H.D. (Oct. Sess., 1782), 4–8.

Jefferson, one of the members for Albemarle county who was taken into the custody of a special messenger by Mr. Speaker's warrant, agreeable to an order of the 28th ult., be discharged out of custody; it appearing to the House that he has good cause for his present non-attendance." [1]

Marshall must have favorably impressed the Speaker; for he was immediately appointed a member of the important Committee for Courts of Justice; [2] and two days later a member of a special committee "To form a plan of national defense against invasions"; to examine into the state of public arms, accouterments, and ammunition, and to consult with the Executive "on what assistance they may want from the Legislature for carrying the plan into execution." [3] Two days afterwards Marshall was appointed on a special committee to frame a bill to amend the ordinance of Convention. [4]

His first vote was for a bill to permit John M'Lean, who, because of illness, went to England before the outbreak of the war, and who had returned, to remain in Virginia and live with his family. [5] Marshall's next two votes before taking his place as a member of the Council of State are of no moment except as indicating the bent of his mind for honest business legislation and for a strong and effi-

[1] Journal, H.D. (Oct. Sess., 1782.), 9–10. [2] Ib., 10.
[3] Ib., 13–15.   [4] Ib., 15.
[5] Ib., 22; Hening, xi, 111. The "ayes" and "noes" were taken on this bill and Marshall's vote is, of course, without any importance except that it was his first and that it was a little straw showing his kindly and tolerant disposition. Also the fact that the "ayes" and "noes" were called for — something that was very rarely done — shows the popular feeling against Englishmen.

cient militia.[1] During November, Marshall was appointed on several other committees.[2] Of these, the most important was the select committee to bring in a bill for the reorganization of the militia,[3] which reported a comprehensive and well-drawn measure that became a law.[4] He was also on the Standing Committee of Privileges and Elections.[5]

The Virginia Legislature, during these years, was not a body to inspire respect.[6] Madison had a great contempt for it and spoke with disgust of the "temper of the Legislature & the wayward course of its proceedings."[7] Indeed, the entire government of the State was an absurd medley of changing purposes and inefficiency. "Nothing," wrote Madison to Jefferson, "can exceed the confusion which reigns throughout our Revenue department.... This confusion indeed runs through all of our public affairs, and must continue as long as the present mode of legislating continues"; the method of drawing bills "must soon bring our laws and our Legislature into contempt among all orders of Citizens."[8]

[1] Journal, H.D. (Oct. Sess., 1782), 27–28. Marshall voted in favor of bringing in a bill for strengthening the credit account; and against postponing the consideration of the militia bill. (*Ib.*, 45.)
[2] *Ib.*, 23, 25, 27, 36, 42, 45. [3] *Ib.*, 23.
[4] Hening, xi, 173–75. [5] Journal, H.D., 36.
[6] "It greatly behoves the Assembly to revise several of our laws, and to abolish all such as are contrary to the fundamental principles of justice; and by a strict adherence to the distinctions between Right and Wrong for the future, to restore that confidence and reverence ... which has been so greatly impaired by a contrary conduct; and without which our laws can never be much more than a dead letter." (Mason to Henry, May 6, 1783, as quoted in Henry, ii, 185.)
[7] *Writings:* Hunt, ii, 397. This notable fact is worthy of repetition if we are to get an accurate view of the Virginia Legislature of that day. Yet that body contained many men of great ability.
[8] Madison to Jefferson, July 3, 1784; *Writings:* Hunt, ii, 62.

Nor did Virginia's lawmakers improve for several years. Madison in 1787 advised Washington that "The proceedings of the Assembly are, as usual, rapidly degenerating with the progress of the session." [1] And the irritated soldier at Mount Vernon responded with characteristic heat that "Our Assembly has been ... employed ... chiefly in rectifying some of the mistakes of the last, and committing new ones for emendations at the next." [2] Washington, writing to Lafayette of American affairs in 1788, said, with disgust, that "Virginia in the very last session ... was about to pass some of the most extravagant and preposterous edicts ... that ever stained the leaves of a legislative code." [3]

Popular as he was with the members of the Legislature, Marshall shared Madison's opinion of their temper and conduct. Of the fall session of the Assembly of 1783, he writes to Colonel Levin Powell: "This long session has not produced a single bill of Public importance except that for the readmission of Commutables.[4] ... It ought to be perfect as it has

[1] Madison to Washington, Dec. 14, 1787; *ib.*, v, 69–70.
[2] Washington to Madison, Jan. 10, 1788; *Writings:* Ford, xi, 208.
[3] Washington to Lafayette, April 28, 1788; *ib.*, 254. Washington wrote bitterly of State antagonism. "One State passes a prohibitory law respecting some article, another State opens wide the avenue for its admission. One Assembly makes a system, another Assembly unmakes it." (*Ib.*)
[4] Hening, xi, 299–306. This statement of Marshall's was grossly incorrect. This session of the Legislature passed several laws of the very greatest public consequence, such as the act to authorize Congress to pass retaliatory trade laws against Great Britain (*ib.*, 313); an immigration and citizenship act (*ib.*, 322–24); an act prohibiting British refugees from coming to Virginia; and a quarantine act (*ib.*, 29–31). It was this session that passed the famous act to authorize

twice passed the House. It fell the first time (after an immensity of labor and debate) a sacrifice to the difference of opinion subsisting in the House of Delegates and the Senate with respect to a money bill. A bill for the regulation of elections and inforcing the attendance of members is now on the Carpet and will probably pass.[1] ... It is surprising that Gentlemen of character cannot dismiss their private animosities, but will bring them in the Assembly."[2]

Early in the session Marshall in a letter to Monroe describes the leading members and the work of the House.

"The Commutable bill,"[3] writes he, "has at Virginia's delegates in Congress to convey to the United States the Northwest Territory (*ib.*, 326–28).

This remarkable oversight of Marshall is hard to account for. An explanation is that this was the year of his marriage; and the year also in which he became a resident of Richmond, started in the practice of the law there, and set up his own home. In addition to these absorbing things, his duty as a member of the Council of State took his attention. Also, of course, it was the year when peace with Great Britain was declared. Still, these things do not excuse Marshall's strange misstatement. Perhaps he underestimated the importance of the work done at this particular session.

[1] Hening, xi, 387–88. This bill became a law at the spring session of the following year. The impracticable part enforcing attendance of members was dropped. The bill as passed imposes a penalty of fifty pounds on any sheriff or other officer for failure to return certificates of elections; a forfeit of two hundred pounds upon any sheriff interfering in any election or showing any partiality toward candidates.

[2] Marshall to Powell, Dec. 9, 1783; *Branch Historical Papers*, i, 130–31.

[3] An act allowing one half of the taxes to be paid in tobacco, hemp, flour, or deerskins, and suspending distress for taxes until January, 1784. (Hening, xi, 289.) The scarcity of specie was so great and the people so poor that the collection of taxes was extremely difficult. In 1782 the partial payment of taxes in commutables — tobacco, hemp, flour, or deerskins — was introduced. This occasioned such loss to the

length pass'd and with it a suspension of the collections of taxes till the first of January next. . . . Colo. Harry Lee of the Legionary corps" is to take the place of "Col? R. H. Lee" whose "services are lost to the Assembly forever"; and Marshall does not know "whether the public will be injur'd by the change." Since the passage of the "Commutable bill . . . the attention of the house has been so fix'd on the Citizen bill that they have scarcely thought on any other subject. . . . Col. [George] Nicholas (politician not fam'd for hitting a medium) introduced one admitting into this country every species of Men except Natives who had borne arms against the state. . . . Mr. Jones introduc'd by way of amendment, one totally new and totally opposite to that which was the subject of deliberation. He spoke with his usual sound sense and solid reason. Mr. Henry opposed him.

"The Speaker replied with some degree of acrimony and Henry retorted with a good deal of tartness but with much temper; 'tis his peculiar excellence when he altercates to appear to be drawn unwillingly into the contest and to throw in the eyes of others the whole blame on his adversary. His influence is immense." [1]

Marshall's strange power of personality which,

treasury that in May, 1783, the Commutable Acts were repealed; but within five months the Legislature reversed itself again and passed the Commutable Bill which so disgusted Marshall.

[1] Marshall to Monroe, Dec. 12, 1783; MS., Draper Collection, Wisconsin Historical Society; also printed in *Amer. Hist. Rev.*, iii, 673. This letter is not addressed, but it has been assumed that it was written to Thomas Jefferson. This is incorrect; it was written to James Monroe.

in after years, was so determining an influence on the destiny of the country, together with the combined influence of his father and of the State Treasurer, Jacquelin Ambler, Marshall's father-in-law, now secured for the youthful legislator an unusual honor. Eleven days after the House of Delegates had organized, Marshall was elected by joint ballot of the Senate and the House a member of the Council of State,[1] commonly called the Executive Council. The Journal of the Council for November 20, 1782, records: "John Marshall esquire having been elected a Member of the Privy Council or Council of State in the room of John Bannister esquire who hath resigned and producing a Certificate from under the hand of Jaq. Ambler esq^r of his having qualified according to law; he took his seat at the board." [2]

Marshall had just turned his twenty-seventh year, and the Council of State was supposed to be made up of men of riper years and experience. Older men, and especially the judges of the courts, resented the bestowal of this distinction upon so youthful a member serving his first term. Edmund Pendleton, Judge of the High Court of Chancery and President of the Court of Appeals, wrote to Madison that: "Young Mr. Marshall is elected a Councillor. . . .

[1] Journal, H.D. (Oct. Sess., 1782), 27. It is almost certain that his father and Jacquelin Ambler were pushing him. The Speaker and other prominent members of the House had been colleagues of Thomas Marshall in the House of Burgesses and Ambler was popular with everybody. Still, Marshall's personality must have had much to do with this notable advancement. His membership in the Council cannot be overestimated in considering his great conflict with the Virginia political "machine" after he became Chief Justice. See volume III of this work.

[2] Journal of the Council of State, Nov. 20, 1782; MS., Va. St. Lib.

He is clever, but I think too young for that department, which he should rather have earned as a retirement and reward, by ten or twelve years hard service in the Assembly." [1]

The Council consisted of eight members elected by the Legislature either from the delegates or from the people at large. It was the Governor's official cabinet and a constitutional part of the executive power. The Governor consulted the Council on all important matters coming before him; and he appointed various important officers only upon its advice.[2]

The Constitution of Virginia of 1776 was the basis upon which was built one of the most perfect political machines ever constructed; and this machine in later years came to be Marshall's great antagonist. As a member of the Council of State, Marshall learned by actual experience the possible workings of this mechanism, first run by Patrick Henry, perfected by Thomas Jefferson, and finally developed to its ultimate efficiency by Spencer Roane and Thomas Ritchie.[3] Thus Marshall took part in the appointment of surveyors, justices of the peace, tobacco inspectors, and other officers;[4] and passed on requisitions from other States for the delivery of fugitive criminals.[5]

Marshall's signature to the minutes of the Coun-

---

[1] Pendleton to Madison, Nov. 25, 1782; quoted in Rives, i, 182.
[2] Constitution of Virginia, 1776.
[3] Dodd, in *Amer. Hist. Rev.*, xii, 776.
[4] Marshall participated in the appointment of General George Rogers Clark to the office of Surveyor of Officers' and Soldiers' lands. (Journal, Ex. Council, 1784, 57; MS., Va. St. Lib.) [5] *Ib.*

MARSHALL'S SIGNATURE AS A MEMBER OF THE COUNCIL OF STATE, 1784

MARSHALL'S SIGNATURE IN 1797

SIGNATURE OF THOMAS MARSHALL AS COLONEL
OF THE 3D VIRGINIA REGIMENT

cil is totally unlike that of his more mature years, as, indeed, is the chirography of his letters of that period. He signed the Council records in large and dashing hand with flourishes — it is the handwriting of a confident, care-free, rollicking young man with a tinge of the dare-devil in him. These signatures are so strangely dissimilar to his later ones that they deserve particular attention. They denote Marshall's sense of his own importance and his certainty of his present position and future prospects.

The criticisms from the judges — first expressed by Pendleton, before whom Marshall was trying to practice law — of his membership of the Executive Council continued. Because of these objections, Marshall finally resigned and at once sought another election from his native county to the House of Delegates. The accepted version of this incident is that Marshall resigned from the Executive Council because the duties of that position took too much time from his profession; and that, without his request or desire, his old neighbors in Fauquier, from "their natural pride in connecting his rising name with their county, spontaneously elected him to the Legislature." [1]

Thus does greatness, once achieved, throw upon a past career a glory that dazzles the historian's eye; and the early steps of advancement are seen and described as unasked and unwished honors paid by a discerning public to modest and retiring merit. Thus, too, research and fact are ever in collision

[1] Binney, in Dillon, iii, 291-92. This story is repeated in almost all of the sketches of Marshall's life.

with fancy and legend. The cherished story about Marshall's resignation from the Council and "spontaneous" election to the Legislature from his home county is a myth. The discontent of the judges practically forced him out of the Council and he personally sought another election from Fauquier County to the House of Delegates. Marshall himself gives the true account of these important incidents.

"I am no longer a member of the Executive [Council]," Marshall informs his friend James Monroe, "the opinion of the Judges with regard to a Councillor's standing at the bar determined me to retire from the Council board. Every person is now busied about the ensuing election." Certainly Marshall was thus occupied; for he writes Monroe that "I had made a small excursion into Fauquier to enquire into the probability of my being chosen by the people, should I offer as a candidate at the next election." Marshall tells the political news, in which he shows minute information, and finally advises Monroe that "I have been maneuvering amazingly to turn your warrants into cash if I succeed I shall think myself a first rate speculator." [1]

Marshall's personal attention [2] to his candidacy bore fruit; and for the second time he was chosen as Delegate from Fauquier, although he now lived in Henrico County.[3]

When the Legislature convened, nine days again

[1] Marshall to Monroe, April 17, 1784; MS., N.Y. Pub. Lib.
[2] His father, now in Kentucky, could no longer personally aid his son in his old home. Thus Marshall himself had to attend to his own political affairs.
[3] Marshall did not try for the Legislature again until 1787 when he sought and secured election from Henrico. (See *infra*.)

Richmond April 17th 84

Dear sir

Yours of the 12th of March I did not till yesterday receive. — I had made a small excursion into Fauquier to enquire into the probability of my being chosen by the people s'd I offer as a Candidate at the next election. — I am no longer a member of the Executive, the opinion of the Judges with respect to a Counsellors standing at the bar determind me to retire from the Council board. Every person is now busied about the ensuing election. Your friend Wilson Ni-cholas is the first Representative

FIRST PAGE OF A LETTER FROM MARSHALL TO JAMES MONROE
(Facsimile)

LEGISLATURE AND COUNCIL OF STATE 213

passed before enough members were in Richmond to make up a House.[1] Marshall was among the tardy. On May 13, the sergeant-at-arms was ordered to take him and other members into custody; and later in the day he and four others were brought in by that officer and "admitted to their seats on paying fees."[2]

He was at once appointed to his old place on the Committee for Courts of Justice and upon the immensely important Standing Committee on Propositions and Grievances, to which was referred the flood of petitions of soldiers and officers, the shower of applications of counties and towns for various laws and other matters of pressing local and personal concern in every part of Virginia.[3] To the cases of his old comrades in arms who applied to the Legislature for relief, Marshall was particularly attentive.[4] He became the champion of the Revolutionary veterans, most of whom were very poor men.[5]

Upon Washington's suggestion a bill was brought in for the relief of Thomas Paine by vesting in him a moderate tract of public lands. Upon the third reading it was "committed to a committee of the whole house" and there debated. Marshall, who apparently led the fight for Paine, "read in his place" several amendments. But notwithstanding Washington's plea, the immense services of Paine

---

[1] Journal, H.D. (Spring Sess., 1784), 5. A Robert Marshall was also a member of the House during 1784 as one of the representatives for Isle of Wight County. He was not related in any way to John Marshall.
[2] Ib. [3] Ib. [4] Story, in Dillon, iii, 335-36.
[5] As an example of the number and nature of these soldier petitions see Journal, H.D. (Spring Sess., 1784), 7, 9, 11, 16, 18, 44.

to the American cause during the Revolution, and the amendments which, obviously, met all objections, the bill was defeated.[1]

Numerous things of human interest happened during this session which show the character of the Legislature and the state of the people. An Englishman named Williamson[2] had gone to Essex County a year before by permission of the Governor, but in violation of the law against British refugees. When he refused to leave, the people tarred and feathered him and drove him out of the country in this condition.[3] The Attorney-General began prosecutions against the leaders of the mob; and the offending ones petitioned the Legislature to interfere. The petition was referred to the Committee on Propositions and Grievances[4] of which Marshall was a member. This committee reported that the petition ought to be granted "and that all irregularities committed by any citizen of this state on the person or properties of refugees previous to the ratification of the definitive treaty of peace . . . should be indemnified by law and buried in utter obliv-

---

[1] See chap. VIII and footnote to p. 288.

[2] Williamson was a Tory of the offensive type. He had committed hostile acts which embittered the people against him. (See *Cal. Va. St. Prs.*, ii. And see Eckenrode: *R. V.*, chap. xi, for full account of this and similar cases.)

[3] The gentle pastime of tarring and feathering unpopular persons and riding them on sharp rails appears to have been quite common in all parts of the country, for a long time before the Revolution. Men even burned their political opponents at the stake. (See instances in Belcher, i, 40–45.) Savage, however, as were the atrocities committed upon the Loyalists by the patriots, even more brutal treatment was dealt out to the latter by British officers and soldiers during the Revolution. (See *supra*, chap. IV, footnote to p. 116.)

[4] Journal, H.D. (Spring Sess., 1784), 19.

LEGISLATURE AND COUNCIL OF STATE 215

ion." [1] But when the bill came to a vote, it was defeated.[2]

It was reported to the House that a certain John Warden had insulted its dignity by saying publicly that if the House had voted against paying the British debts, some of its members had voted against paying for the coats on their backs — a charge which was offensively true. The Committee on Privileges and Elections was instructed to take this serious matter up and order the offender before it. He admitted the indiscretion and apologized for it. The committee read Warden's written acknowledgment and apology before the House and thus he was purged of the contempt of that sensitive body.[3]

A William Finnie, who had been deputy quartermaster in the military service, had purchased, at the request of the Board of War, a large quantity of boots for a corps of cavalry in active service and then on the march. Although the seller of the boots knew that they were bought for the public service, he sued Finnie and secured judgment against him, which was on the point of being executed. Finnie petitioned the Legislature that the debt be paid by the State. The Committee on Propositions and Grievances took charge of this petition, reported the facts to be as Finnie had stated them, and recommended that the debt "ought to be paid him by the public and charged to the United States." [4] But the House rejected the resolution. Incidents

[1] Journal, H.D. (Spring Sess., 1784), 23, 27.
[2] *Ib.*, 45. For thorough examination of this incident see Eckenrode: *R. V.*, chap. xi.
[3] Journal, H.D. (Spring Sess., 1784), 57.   [4] *Ib.*, 14.

like these, as well as the action of the Legislature and the conduct of the people themselves, had their influence on the radical change which occurred in Marshall's opinions and point of view during the decade after the war.

Marshall was appointed on many special committees to prepare sundry bills during this session. Among these was a committee to frame a bill to compel payment by those counties that had failed to furnish their part of the money for recruiting Virginia's quota of troops to serve in the Continental army. This bill was passed.[1]

A vote which gives us the first sight of Marshall's idea about changing a constitution was taken during this session. Augusta County had petitioned the Legislature to alter Virginia's fundamental law. The committee reported a resolution against it, "such a measure not being within the province of the House of Delegates to assume; but on the contrary, it is the express duty of the representatives of the people at all times, and on all occasions, to preserve the same [the Constitution] inviolable, until a majority of all the people shall direct a reform thereof." [2]

Marshall voted to amend this resolution by striking out the words quoted. Thus, as far as this vote indicates, we see him standing for the proposition that a form of government could be changed by convention, which was the easiest, and, indeed, at that time the only practicable, method of altering the constitution of the State. Madison also favored

[1] Hening, xi, 390.   [2] Journal, H.D., 70–71.

this plan, but did nothing because of Patrick Henry's violent opposition. The subject was debated for two days and the project of a convention with full powers to make a new Constitution was overwhelmingly defeated, although nearly all of the "young men of education & talents" were for it.[1]

A few of the bills that Marshall voted for or reported from committee are worthy of note, in addition to those which had to do with those serious questions of general and permanent historic consequence to the country presently to be considered. They are important in studying the development of Marshall's economic and governmental views.

In 1784, Washington brought vividly before the Virginia Legislature the necessity of improving the means of transportation.[2] At the same time this subject was also taken up by the Legislature of Maryland. A law was passed by the Virginia Legislature for "opening and extending the navigation of the Potowmack river from tidewater to the highest place practicable on the north branch"; and Maryland took similar action. These identical laws authorized the forming of a corporation called the "Potowmack

[1] Madison to Jefferson, July 3, 1794; *Writings:* Hunt, ii, 56-57. The Constitution of 1776 never was satisfactory to the western part of Virginia, which was under-represented. Representation was by counties and not population. Also suffrage was limited to white freeholders; and this restriction was made more onerous by the fact that county representation was based on slave as well as free population. Also, the Constitution made possible the perpetuation of the Virginia political machine, previously mentioned, which afterward played a part of such vast importance in National affairs. Yet extreme liberals like the accomplished and patriotic Mason were against the Legislature turning itself into a convention to make a new one. (Mason to Henry, May 6, 1783; Henry, ii, 185.)

[2] Madison to Jefferson, Jan. 9, 1785; *Writings:* Hunt, ii, 104.

Company" with a quarter of a million dollars capital. It was given the power of eminent domain; was authorized to charge tolls "at all times forever hereafter"; and the property and profits were vested in the shareholders, "their heirs and assigns forever."[1]

John Marshall voted for this bill, which passed without opposition.[2] He became a stockholder in the corporation and paid several assessments on his stock.[3] Thus early did Marshall's ideas on the nature of a legislative franchise to a corporation acquire the vitality of property interest and personal experience.

Marshall was on the Committee for Courts of Justice during every session when he was a member of the House and worked upon several bills concerning the courts. On November 2, 1787, he was appointed upon a special committee to bring in a bill "to amend the act establishing the High Court of Chancery."[4] Three weeks later he reported this

[1] Hening, xi, 510–18. This law shows the chief articles of commerce at that time and the kind of money which might be received as tolls. The scale of equivalents in pounds sterling vividly displays the confused currency situation of the period. The table names Spanish milled pieces of eight, English milled crowns, French silver crowns, johannes, half johannes, moidores, English guineas, French guineas, doubloons, Spanish pistoles, French milled pistoles, Arabian sequins; the weight of each kind of money except Spanish pieces of eight and English and French milled crowns being carefully set out; and "other gold coin (German excepted) by the pennyweight." If any of this money should be reduced in value by lessening its weight or increasing its alloy it should be received at "its reduced value only." (*Ib.*)

[2] Madison to Jefferson, Jan. 9, 1785; *Writings:* Hunt, ii, 102. Madison gives a very full history and description of this legislation.

[3] Marshall's Account Book contains entries of many of these payments.

[4] Journal, H.D. (Nov. 1787), 27–127.

bill to the House;[1] and when the bill passed that body it was "ordered that Mr. Marshall do carry the bill to the Senate and desire their concurrence." The committee which drew this bill was made up from among the ablest men in the House: Henry, Mason, Nicholas, Matthews, Stuart, and Monroe being the other members,[2] with Marshall who was chairman.

The act simplified and expedited proceedings in equity.[3] The High Court of Chancery had been established by an act of the Virginia Legislature of 1777.[4] This law was the work of Thomas Jefferson. It contained one of the reforms so dear to his heart during that period — the right of trial by jury to ascertain the facts in equity causes. But six years' experience proved that the reform was not practical. In 1783 the jury trial in equity was abolished, and the old method that prevailed in the courts of chancery before the Revolution was reinstated.[5] With this exception the original act stood in Virginia as a model of Jeffersonian reforms in legal procedure; but under its provisions, insufferable delays had grown up which defeated the ends of justice.[6] It was to remedy this practical defect of Jefferson's

[1] Journal, H.D. (Nov. 1787), 70.   [2] *Ib.*, 27.

[3] Hening, xii, 464-67. The preamble of the act recites that it is passed because under the existing law "justice is greatly delayed by the tedious forms of proceedings, suitors are therefore obliged to waste much time and expense to the impoverishment of themselves and the state, and decrees when obtained are with difficulty carried into execution." (*Ib.*)

[4] *Ib.*, ix, 389-99.   [5] *Ib.*, xi, 342-44.

[6] See Jefferson's letter to Mazzei, explaining the difference between law and equity and the necessity for courts of chancery as well as courts of law. This is one of the best examples of Jefferson's calm, clear, simple style when writing on non-political subjects. (Jefferson to Mazzei, Nov., 1785; *Works:* Ford, iv, 473-80.)

monumental law that Marshall brought in the bill of 1787.

But the great matters which came before the Legislature during this period, between the ending of the war and the adoption of the Constitution, were: The vexed question of the debts owed by Virginia planters to British subjects; the utter impotence of the so-called Federal Government and the difficulty of getting the States to give it any means or authority to discharge the National debts and uphold the National honor; and the religious controversy involving, at bottom, the question of equal rights for all sects.[1]

The religious warfare [2] did not greatly appeal to Marshall, it would seem, although it was of the gravest importance. Bad as the state of religion was at the beginning of the Revolution, it was worse after that struggle had ended. "We are now to rank among the nations of the world," wrote Mason to Henry in 1783; "but whether our independence shall prove a blessing or a curse must depend upon our wisdom or folly, virtue or wickedness. . . . The prospect is not promising. . . . A depravity of manners and morals prevails among us, to the destruction of all confidence between man and man." [3] The want of public worship "increases daily; nor have

[1] For the best contemporaneous description of Virginia legislation during this period see Madison's letters to Jefferson when the latter was in Paris. (*Writings:* Hunt, i and ii.)

[2] For a thorough account of the religious struggle in Virginia from the beginning see Eckenrode: *S. of C. and S.* On the particular phase of this subject dealt with while Marshall was a member of the Virginia Legislature see *ib.*, chap. v.

[3] Mason to Henry, May 6, 1783, as quoted in Rowland, ii, 44.

we left in our extensive State three churches that are decently supported," wrote Mrs. Carrington, the sister of John Marshall's wife, a few years later.[1]

Travelers through Virginia during this period note that church buildings of all denominations were poor and mean and that most of these were falling into ruins; while ministers barely managed to keep body and soul together by such scanty mites as the few pious happened to give them or by the miserable wages they earned from physical labor.[2] These scattered and decaying little church houses, the preachers toiling with axe or hoe, formed, it appears, an accurate index of the religious indifference of the people.[3]

There were gross inequalities of religious privileges. Episcopal clergymen could perform marriage ceremonies anywhere, but ministers of the other denominations could do so only in the county where they lived. The property of the Episcopal Church came from the pockets of all the people; and the vestries could tax members of other churches as well as their own for the relief of the poor.[3] It was a curious swirl of conflicting currents. Out of it came

[1] Meade, i, footnote to 142. And see *Atlantic Monthly, supra.*

[2] Eckenrode: *S. of C. and S.*, 75. On this general subject see Meade, i, chaps. i and ii. "Infidelity became rife, in Virginia, perhaps, beyond any other portion of land. The Clergy, for the most part, were a laughing stock or objects of disgust." (*Ib.*, 52.) Even several years later Bishop Meade says that "I was then taking part in the labours of the field, which in Virginia was emphatically *servile labour.*" (*Ib.*, 27.)

"One sees not only a smaller number of houses of worship [in Virginia] than in other provinces, but what there are in a ruinous or ruined condition, and the clergy for the most part dead or driven away and their places unfilled." (Schoepf, ii, 62-63.)

[3] Henry, ii, 199-206.   [4] Eckenrode: *S. of C. and S.*, 77.

the proposition to levy an assessment on everybody for the support of religion; a bill to incorporate the Episcopal Church which took away its general powers of vestry taxation, but confirmed the title to the property already held; and the marriage law which gave ministers of all denominations equal authority.[1]

Although these propositions were debated at great length and with much spirit and many votes were taken at various stages of the contest, Marshall recorded his vote but twice. He did not vote on the resolution to incorporate the Episcopal Church;[2] or to sell the glebe lands;[3] nor did he vote on the marriage bill.[4] He voted against Madison's motion to postpone consideration of the bill for a general assessment to support religion, which carried,[5] thus killing the bill. When the bill to incorporate the Episcopal Church came to a final vote, Marshall voted "aye," as, indeed, did Madison.[6]

But if Marshall took only a languid interest in the religious struggle, he was keen-eyed and active on the other two vital matters — the payment of debts, both public and private, and the arming of the Fed-

---

[1] Journal, H.D. (2d Sess., 1784), 19.   [2] Ib., 27.
[3] Ib., 82.   [4] Ib.   [5] Ib.
[6] Ib., 97. For the incorporation law see Hening, xi, 532-37; for marriage law see ib., 532-35. Madison describes this law to Jefferson and excuses his vote for it by saying that "the necessity of some sort of incorporation for the purpose of holding & managing the property of the Church could not well be denied, nor a more harmless modification of it now be obtained. A negative of the bill, too, would have doubled the eagerness and the pretexts for a much greater evil, a general Assessment, which, there is good ground to believe, was parried by this partial gratification of its warmest votaries." (Madison to Jefferson, Jan. 9, 1785; *Writings:* Hunt, ii, 113.)

LEGISLATURE AND COUNCIL OF STATE 223

eral Government with powers necessary to its existence. Throughout this whole period we see the rapid and solid growth of the idea of Nationality, the seeds of which had been planted in John Marshall's soul by the fingers of military necessity and danger. Here, too, may be found the beginning of those ideas of contract which developed throughout his life and hardened as they developed until finally they became as flint. And here also one detects the first signs of the change in what Marshall himself called "the wild and enthusiastic notions" [1] with which, only a few years earlier, he had marched forth from the backwoods, to fight for independence and popular government.

Virginia planters owed an immense amount of money to British merchants. It had been the free-and-easy habit of Virginians to order whatever they wanted from England and pay for it in the produce of their fields, chiefly tobacco. The English merchants gave long credit and were always willing to extend it when the debt fell due. The Virginians, on their part, found the giving of new notes a convenient way of canceling old obligations and thus piled up mountains of debt which they found hard to remove. After the war was over, they had little means with which to discharge their long overdue accounts.[2]

[1] Story, in Dillon, iii, 338.
[2] "Virginia certainly owed two millions sterling [$10,000,000] to Great Britain at the conclusion of the war. Some have conjectured the debt as high as three millions [$15,000,000]. . . . These debts had become hereditary from father to son for many generations, so that the planters were a species of property annexed to certain mercantile houses in London. . . . I think that state owed near as much as all the rest put together." Jefferson's explanation of these obligations is ex-

During the Revolution stringent and radical laws were passed, preventing the recovery of these debts in the courts, sequestering the property and even forfeiting the estates owned by British subjects in Virginia; and a maze of acts, repealing and then reviving the statutes that prevented payment, were passed after the war had ended.[1] The Treaty between the United States and Great Britain provided as one of the conditions of peace that all these legal impediments to the recovery of British debts should be removed.[2] Failure to repeal the anti-debt legislation passed during the war was, of course, a plain infraction of this contract between the two countries; while the enactment of similar laws after the Treaty had become binding, openly and aggressively violated it.

Within two weeks after Marshall took his seat in the House in 1784, this sorely vexed question came up. A resolution was brought in "that so much of all and every act or acts of the Assembly, now in force in this commonwealth as prevents a due compliance with the stipulation contained in the definitive Treaty of Peace entered into between Great

---

tremely partial to the debtors, of whom he was one. (Jefferson to Meusnier, Jan. 24, 1786; *Works:* Ford, v, 28.)

Most of Jefferson's earlier debts were contracted in the purchase of slaves. "I cannot decide to sell my lands. . . . nor would I willingly sell the slaves as long as there remains any prospect of paying my debts with their labor." This will "enable me to put them ultimately on an easier footing, which I will do the moment they have paid the [my] debts, . . . two thirds of which have been contracted by purchasing them." (Jefferson to Lewis, July 29, 1787; *ib.*, 311.)

[1] For Virginia legislation on this subject see Hening, ix, x, and xi, under index caption "British Debts."

[2] Definitive Treaty of Peace, 1783, art. 4.

Britain and America ought to be repealed"; but a motion to put the question to agree with this resolution was defeated by a majority of twenty. John Marshall voted to put the question.[1]

Those resisting the effort to carry out the Treaty of Peace declared that Great Britain itself had not complied with it, because the British had not surrendered the American posts retained by them at the close of the war and had not returned or paid for the slaves carried away by the British forces.[2] A fortnight after the first defeat of the movement against the anti-debt law, a resolution was laid before the House instructing Virginia's Representatives in Congress to request that body to protest to the British Government against this infraction of the Treaty and to secure reparation therefor, and stating that the Virginia Legislature would not coöperate "in the complete fulfillment of said treaty" until this was done. The intent of the resolution was that no British debts should be paid for a long time to come.

But the resolution did provide that, when this reparation was made, or when "Congress shall adjudge it indispensably necessary," the anti-debt laws "ought to be repealed and payment made to all [creditors] in such time and manner as shall consist with the exhausted situation of this Commonwealth"; and that "the further operation of all and every act or acts of the Assembly concerning escheats and forfeitures from British subjects ought to be

---

[1] Journal, H.D. (1st Sess.), 1784, 41.
[2] Ib., 54; 72–73. The Treaty required both.

prevented."[1] An amendment was offered containing the idea that the debtors might deduct their losses from their debts, thus taking a little step toward payment. Another amendment to strengthen this was also proposed.

Had these amendments carried, the policy of an early payment of the British debts would have prevailed. Marshall voted for both as did Madison. The amendments, however, were overwhelmingly defeated.[2] The situation and point of view of the British merchants to whom these debts were due and who, depending upon the faithful performance of the Treaty, had come to Virginia to collect the money owing them, is illustrated by a petition which George F. Norton presented to the House. He was a member of the mercantile firm of Norton and Sons, of London, from whom Virginians had made purchases on credit for a generation before the war. He declared that his firm had "been compelled to pay many debts due from the said company, but he has been unable to collect any due to them, in consequence of the laws prohibiting recovery of British debts, by which he has been reduced to the greatest extremes."[3]

After the summer adjournment the irrepressible conflict between keeping or breaking the National faith once more arose. Henry, who was the champion of the debtors, had been elected Governor and

[1] Journal, H.D. (1st Sess., 1784), 74.
[2] *Ib.*, 74–75. Henry led the fight against repealing the anti-debt laws or, as he contended, against Great Britain's infraction of the Treaty.
[3] Journal, H.D. (1st Sess., 1784), 25.

was "*out of the way.*" [1] Several British merchants had proposed to accept payments of their debts in installments. Ratifications of the Treaty had been exchanged. The friends of National honor and private good faith had gathered headway. Finally a bill passed the House repealing the anti-debt laws. The Senate and the House came to an agreement.

Here arose a situation which pictures the danger and difficulty of travel in that day. Before the bill had been sent back to the House, enrolled, examined, and signed by both presiding officers, several members went across the river to spend the night at the neighboring hamlet of Manchester. It was the day before adjournment and they expected to return the next morning. But that night the river froze [2] and they could not get back. So this important measure fell through for the session.[3]

No "ayes" and "noes" were called for during this final battle, but Marshall probably took part in the debate and it is certain that he used the influence which his popularity among members gave him for the passage of this law.

"I wish with you," wrote Marshall to Monroe, in early December, "that our Assembly had never passed those resolutions respecting the British Debts which have been so much the subject of reprehension throughout the States. I wish it because it affords a pretext to the British to retain possession of the posts on the lakes but much more because I ever considered

[1] Madison to Jefferson, Jan. 9, 1785; *Writings:* Hunt, ii, 114.
[2] See Madison's vivid description of this incident; *ib.*, 116; also Henry, ii, 233.
[3] *Ib.*

it as a measure tending to weaken the federal bands which in my conception are too weak already. We are about, tho reluctantly, to correct the error."

Marshall despondently summed up the work of the session: "We have as yet done nothing finally. Not a bill of public importance, in which an individual was not particularly interested, has passed." [1]

Marshall was not a candidate for the Legislature in 1785–86, but sought and secured election in 1787, when he was sent from Henrico County, where Richmond was situated. During this hiatus in Marshall's public life another effort was made to repeal the anti-debt laws, but so bitter was the resistance that nothing was accomplished. Madison was distressed.[2] When Marshall again became a member of the General Assembly the question of the British debts was brought forward once more. This time the long-delayed bill was passed, though not until its foes had made their point about the runaway slaves and the unevacuated posts.[3]

[1] Marshall to Monroe, Dec. 2, 1784; MS., Monroe Papers, Lib. Cong.

[2] Madison to Monroe, Dec. 24, 1785; *Writings:* Hunt, ii, 205.

"Being convinced myself that nothing can be now done that will not extremely dishonor us, and embarass Cong? my wish is that the report may not be called for at all. In the course of the debates no pains were spared to disparage the Treaty by insinuations agst Cong?, the Eastern States, and the negociators of the Treaty, particularly J. Adams. These insinuations & artifices explain perhaps one of the motives from which the augmention of the foederal powers & respectability has been opposed." (Madison to Monroe, Dec. 30, 1785; *ib.*, 211.)

[3] Curiously enough, it fell to Jefferson as Secretary of State to report upon, explain, and defend the measures of Virginia and other States which violated the Treaty of Peace. (See Jefferson to the British Minister, May 29, 1792; *Works:* Ford, vii, 3–99.) This masterful statement is one of the finest argumentative products of Jefferson's brilliant mind.

LEGISLATURE AND COUNCIL OF STATE

A resolution was brought in that the anti-debt laws "ought to be repealed," but that any act for this purpose should be suspended until the other States had passed similar laws. An amendment was defeated for making the suspension until Great Britain complied with the Treaty. John Marshall voted against it, as did his father Thomas Marshall, who was now a member of the Virginia Legislature from the District of Kentucky.[1] Another amendment to pay the British debts "in such time and manner as shall consist with the exhausted situation of this Commonwealth" met a similar fate, both Marshalls, father and son, voting against it.[2] The resolution was then passed, the two Marshalls voting for it.[3]

Marshall was then appointed a member of the special committee to prepare and bring in a bill to carry out the resolution.[4] In a few days this bill was laid before the House. Except the extension clause, this bill was probably drawn by Marshall. It was short and to the point. It repealed everything on the statute books repugnant to the Treaty of Peace. It specifically "directed and required" the courts to decide all cases "arising from or touching said treaty" "according to the tenor, true intent, and

[1] Journal, H.D. (1787), 51.   [2] *Ib.*, 52.
[3] *Ib.* James Monroe was a member of the House at this session and voted against the first amendment and for the second. On the contrary, Patrick Henry voted for the first and against the second amendment. George Mason voted against both amendments. So did Daniel Boone, who was, with Thomas Marshall, then a member of the Virginia Legislature from the District of Kentucky. On the passage of the resolution, James Monroe and Patrick Henry again swerved around, the former voting for and the latter against it.
[4] Journal, H.D. (1787), 52.

meaning of same" regardless of the repealed laws. But the operation of the law was suspended until Congress informed the Governor "that the other states in the Union have passed laws enabling British creditors to recover their debts agreeably to the terms of the treaty." [1] The bill was emphasized by a brief preamble which stated that "it is agreed by the fourth article of the treaty of peace with Great Britain that creditors on either side shall meet with no lawful impediment to the recovery of the full value in sterling money, of all bona fide debts heretofore contracted."

The opponents of the bill tried to emasculate it by an amendment that the law should not go into effect until the Governor of Virginia made public proclamation "that Great Britain hath delivered up to the United States the posts therein now occupied by British troops" and was taking measures to return the runaway slaves or to pay for them. They succeeded. Whether from agitation outside the legislative hall [2] or from the oratory of Patrick Henry, or from a greater power of the leaders in lobbying among their fellow members, a quick and radical transformation of sentiment took place. Probably all these causes joined to produce it. By a crushing

[1] Journal, H.D. (1787), 79.
[2] "If we are now to pay the debts due to the British merchants, what have we been fighting for all this while?" was the question the people "sometimes" asked, testifies George Mason. (Henry, ii, 187.) But the fact is that this question generally was asked by the people. Nothing explains the struggle over this subject except that the people found it a bitter hardship to pay the debts, as, indeed, was the case; and the idea of not paying them at all grew into a hope and then a policy.

LEGISLATURE AND COUNCIL OF STATE 231

majority of forty-nine the amendment was adopted and the bill denatured. Both John Marshall and his father voted against the amendment, as did George Mason, Benjamin Harrison, and James Monroe.[1]

Thus, in two weeks, a majority of thirty-three against this very scheme for breaking the force of the bill was changed to a majority of forty-nine in favor of it. The bill as amended passed the next day.[2] Such were the instability of the Virginia Legislature at this period and the people's bitter opposition to the payment of the debts owed to British subjects.

The effect on Marshall's mind was very great. The popular readiness to escape, if not to repudiate, contracted obligations, together with the whimsical capriciousness of the General Assembly, created grave misgivings in his mind. His youthful sympathy with the people was beginning to disappear. Just as the roots of his Nationalist views run back to Valley Forge, so do the roots of his economic-political opinions penetrate to the room in the small frame building where sat the Legislature of Virginia in the first years that followed the close of the war.

But the mockery of government exhibited by the Federal establishment at this period of chaos impressed Marshall even more than the spirit of repudiation of debts and breaking of contracts which was back of the anti-debt legislation.[3] The want of

[1] Journal, H.D. (1787), 80.
[2] Hening, xii, 528. Richard Henry Lee thought that both countries were to blame. (Lee to Henry, Feb. 14, 1785; quoted in Henry, iii, 279.)
[3] For an excellent statement regarding payment of British debts, see letter of George Mason to Patrick Henry, May 6, 1783, as quoted

the National power during the Revolution, which Marshall had seen from the "lights . . . which glanced from the point of his sword,"[1] he now saw through the tobacco smoke which filled the grimy room where the Legislature of Virginia passed laws and repealed them almost at the same time.[2] The so-called Federal Government was worse than no government at all; it was a form and a name without life or power. It could not provide a shilling for the payment of the National debt nor even for its own support. It must humbly ask the States for every dollar needed to uphold the National honor, every penny necessary for the very existence of the masquerade "Government" itself. This money the States were slow and loath to give and doled it out in miserable pittances.

Even worse, there was as yet little conception of Nationality among the people — the spirit of unity was far weaker than when resistance to Great Britain compelled some kind of solidarity; the idea of coöperation was even less robust than it was when fear of French and Indian depredations forced the colonists to a sort of common action. Also, as we shall see, a general dislike if not hostility toward all government whether State or National was prevalent.[3]

As to the National Government, it would appear that, even before the war was over, the first impulse

in Henry, ii, 186–87. But Mason came to put it on the ground that Great Britain would renew the war if these debts were not paid.

[1] Story, in Dillon, iii, 338.
[2] Hening, x, chaps. ii and ix, 409–51.
[3] For a general review of the state of the country see *infra*, chaps. VII and VIII.

LEGISLATURE AND COUNCIL OF STATE 233

of the people was to stop entirely the feeble heart that, once in a while, trembled within its frail bosom: in 1782, for instance, Virginia's Legislature repealed the law passed in May of the preceding year authorizing Congress to levy a duty on imports to carry on the war, because "the permitting any power other than the general assembly of this commonwealth, to levy duties or taxes upon the citizens of this state within the same, is injurious to its sovereignty" and "may prove destructive of the rights and liberty of the people." [1]

A year later the Legislature was persuaded again to authorize Congress to levy this duty; [2] but once more suspended the act until the other States had passed "laws" of the same kind and with a proviso which would practically have nullified the working of the statute, even if the latter ever did go into effect. [3] At the time this misshapen dwarf of a Nationalist law was begotten by the Virginia Legislature, Marshall was a member of the Council of State; but the violent struggle required to get the Assembly to pass even so puny an act as this went on under his personal observation.

When Marshall entered the Legislature for the second time, the general subject of the debts of the Confederation arose. Congress thought that the money to pay the loans from foreign Governments by which the war had been carried on, might be secured more easily by a new mode of apportioning their quotas among the thirteen States. The Articles of

[1] Hening, xi, chap. xlii, 171.   [2] *Ib.*, chap. xxxi, 350.
[3] Journal, H.D., 52.

Confederation provided that the States should pay on the basis of the value of lands. This worked badly, and Congress asked the States to alter the eighth Article of Confederation so as to make the States contribute to the general treasury on a basis of population. For fear that the States would not make this change, Congress also humbly petitioned the thirteen "sovereignties" to ascertain the quantity and value of land as well as the number of people in each State.

On May 19, 1784,[1] after the usual debating, a strong set of Nationalist resolutions was laid before the Virginia House of Delegates. They agreed to the request of Congress to change the basis of apportioning the debt among the States; favored providing for the payment of a part of what each State owed Congress on the requisition of three years before; and even went so far as to admit that if the States did not act, Congress itself might be justified in proceeding. The last resolution proposed to give Congress the power to pass retaliatory trade laws.[2] These resolutions were adopted with the exception of one providing for the two years' overdue payment of the Virginia share of the requisition of Congress made in 1781.

Marshall was appointed a member of a special committee to "prepare and bring in bills" to carry out the two resolutions for changing the basis of apportionment from land to population, and for

[1] In order to group subjects such as British debts, extradition, and so forth, it is, unfortunately, essential to bring widely separated dates under one head.

[2] Journal, H.D. (1st Sess., 1784), 11-12.

authorizing Congress to pass retaliatory trade laws. George Mason and Patrick Henry also were members of this committee on which the enemies of the National idea had a good representation. Two weeks later the bills were reported.[1] Three weeks afterwards the retaliatory trade bill was passed.[2] But all the skill and ability of Madison, all the influence of Marshall with his fellow members, could not overcome the sentiment against paying the debts; and, as usual, the law was neutralized by a provision that it should be suspended until all the other States had enacted the same kind of legislation.

The second contest waged by the friends of the Nationalist idea in which Marshall took part was over the extradition bill which the Legislature enacted in the winter of 1784. The circumstances making such a law so necessary that the Virginia Legislature actually passed it, draw back for a moment the curtain and give us a view of the character of our frontiersmen. Daring, fearless, strong, and resourceful, they struck without the sanction of the law. The object immediately before their eyes, the purpose of the present, the impulse or passion of the moment — these made up the practical code which governed their actions.

Treaties of the American "Government" with the Governments of other countries were, to these wilderness subduers, vague and far-away engagements which surely never were meant to affect those on the outskirts of civilization; and most certainly could

---

[1] Journal, H.D. (1st Sess., 1784), 37.
[2] *Ib.*, 81; also, Hening, xi, 388.

not reach the scattered dwellers in the depths of the distant forests, even if such international compacts were intended to include them. As for the Government's treaties or agreements of any kind with the Indian tribes, they, of course, amounted to nothing in the opinion of the frontiersmen. Who were the Indians, anyway, except a kind of wild animal very much in the frontiersman's way and to be exterminated like other savage beasts? Were not the Indians the natural foes of these white Lords of the earth?[1]

Indeed, it is more than likely that most of this advance guard of the westward-marching American people never had heard of such treaties until the Government's puny attempt to enforce them. At any rate, the settlers fell afoul of all who stood in their way; and, in the falling, spared not their hand. Madison declared that there was "danger of our being speedily embroiled with the nations contiguous to the U. States, particularly the Spaniards, by the licentious & predatory spirit of some of our Western people. In several instances, gross outrages are said to have been already practiced." [2] Jay, then Secretary of State, mournfully wrote to Jefferson in Paris, that "Indians have been murdered by our

[1] "The white people who inhabited the frontier, from the constant state of warfare in which they lived with the Indians, had imbibed much of their character; and learned to delight so highly in scenes of crafty, bloody, and desperate conflict, that they as often gave as they received the provocation to hostilities. Hunting, which was their occupation, became dull and tiresome, unless diversified occasionally by the more animated and piquant amusement of an Indian skirmish." (Wirt, 257.)

[2] Madison to Jefferson, Jan. 9, 1785; *Writings:* Hunt, ii, 110–11.

people in cold blood, and no satisfaction given; nor are they pleased with the avidity with which we seek to acquire their lands."

Expressing the common opinion of the wisest and best men of the country, who, with Madison, were horrified by the ruthless and unprovoked violence of the frontiersmen, Jay feared that "to pitch our tents through the wilderness in a great variety of places, far distant from each other," might "fill the wilderness with white savages . . . more formidable to us than the tawny ones which now inhabit it." No wonder those who were striving to found a civilized nation had "reason . . . to apprehend an Indian war." [1]

To correct this state of things and to bring home to these sons of individualism the law of nations and our treaties with other countries, Madison, in the autumn of 1784, brought in a bill which provided that Virginia should deliver up to foreign Governments such offenders as had come within the borders of the Commonwealth. The bill also provided for the trial and punishment by Virginia courts of any Virginia citizen who should commit certain crimes in "the territory of any Christian nation or Indian tribe in amity with the United States." The law is of general historic importance because it was among the first, if not indeed the very first, ever passed by any legislative body against filibustering.[2]

The feebleness of the National idea at this time; the grotesque notions of individual "rights"; the weak-

[1] Jay to Jefferson, Dec. 14, 1786; *Jay:* Johnston, iii, 224.
[2] Hening, xi, 471; and Henry, ii, 217.

ness or absence of the sense of civic duty; the general feeling that everybody should do as he pleased; the scorn for the principle that other nations and especially Indian tribes had any rights which the rough-and-ready settlers were bound to respect, are shown in the hot fight made against Madison's wise and moderate bill. Viewed as a matter of the welfare and safety of the frontiersmen themselves, Madison's measure was prudent and desirable; for, if either the Indians or the Spaniards had been goaded into striking back by formal war, the blows would have fallen first and heaviest on these very settlers.

Yet the bill was stoutly resisted. It was said that the measure, instead of carrying out international law, violated it because "such surrenders were unknown to the law of nations."[1] And what became of Virginia's sacred Bill of Rights, if such a law as Madison proposed should be placed on the statute books, exclaimed the friends of the predatory backwoodsmen? Did not the Bill of Rights guarantee to every person "speedy trial by an impartial jury of twelve men of his vicinage," where he must "be confronted with the accusers and witnesses," said they?

But what did this Nationalist extradition bill do? It actually provided that men on Virginia soil should be delivered up for punishment to a foreign nation which knew not the divine right of trial by jury. As for trying men in Virginia courts and before Virginia juries for something they had done in the fastnesses of the far-away forests of the West and

[1] Madison to Jefferson, Jan. 9, 1785; *Writings:* Hunt, ii, 111.

South, as Madison's bill required, how could the accused "call for evidence in his favor"? And was not this "sacred right" one of the foundation stones, quarried from Magna Charta, on which Virginia's "liberties" had been built?[1] To be sure it was! Yet here was James Madison trying to blast it to fragments with his Nationalism!

So ran the arguments of those early American advocates of *laissez-faire*. Madison answered, as to the law of nations, by quoting Vattel, Grotius, and Puffendorf. As to the Bill of Rights, he pointed out that the individualist idealism by which the champions of the settlers interpreted this instrument "would amount to a license for every aggression, and would sacrifice the peace of the whole community to the impunity of the worst members of it."[2] Such were the conservative opinions of James Madison three years before he helped to frame the National Constitution.

Madison saw, too, — shocking treason to "liberty," — "the necessity of a qualified interpretation of the bill of rights,"[3] if we were to maintain the slightest pretense of a National Government of any kind. The debate lasted several days.[4] With all the weight of argument, justice, and even common prudence on the side of the measure, it certainly would have failed had not Patrick Henry come to the rescue of it with all the strength of his influence and oratory.[5]

[1] Article VIII, Constitution of Virginia, 1776.
[2] Madison to Jefferson, Jan. 9, 1785; *Writings:* Hunt, ii, 111.
[3] *Ib.*   [4] Journal, H.D. (2d Sess., 1784), 34–41.
[5] "The measure was warmly patronized by Mr. Henry." (Madison

The bill was so mangled in committee that it was made useless and it was restored only by amendment. Yet such was the opposition to it that even with Henry's powerful aid this was done only by the dangerous margin of four votes out of a total of seventy-eight.[1] The enemies of the bill mustered their strength overnight and, when the final vote came upon its passage the next morning, came so near defeating it that it passed by a majority of only one vote out of a total of eighty-seven.[2]

John Marshall, of course, voted for it. While there is no record that he took part in the debate, yet it is plain that the contest strengthened his fast-growing Nationalist views. The extravagance of those who saw in the Bill of Rights only a hazy "liberty"

to Jefferson, Jan. 9, 1785; *Writings:* Hunt, ii, 111.) The reason of Henry's support of this extradition bill was not its Nationalist spirit, but his friendship for the Indians and his pet plan to insure peace between the white man and the red and to produce a better race of human beings; all of which Henry thought could be done by intermarriages between the whites and the Indians. He presented this scheme to the House at this same session and actually carried it by the "irresistible earnestness and eloquence" with which he supported it. (Wirt, 258.)

The bill provided that every white man who married an Indian woman should be paid ten pounds and five pounds more for each child born of such marriage; and that if any white woman marry an Indian they should be entitled to ten pounds with which the County Court should buy live stock for them; that once each year the Indian husband to this white woman should be entitled to three pounds with which the County Court should buy clothes for him; that every child born of this Indian man and white woman should be educated by the State between the age of ten and twenty-one years, etc., etc. (*Ib.*)

This amazing bill actually passed the House on its first and second reading and there seems to be no doubt that it would have become a law had not Henry at that time been elected Governor, which took him "*out of the way*," to use Madison's curt phrase. John Marshall favored this bill.

[1] Journal, H.D. (2d Sess., 1784), 41. [2] *Ib.*

LEGISLATURE AND COUNCIL OF STATE 241

which hid evil-doers from the law, and which caused even the cautious Madison to favor a "qualified interpretation" of that instrument, made a lasting impression on Marshall's mind.

But Marshall's support was not wholly influenced by the prudence and Nationalism of the measure. He wished to protect the Indians from the frontiersmen. He believed, with Henry, in encouraging friendly relations with them, even by white and red amalgamation. He earnestly supported Henry's bill for subsidizing marriages of natives and whites [1] and was disappointed by its defeat.

"We have rejected some bills," writes Marshall, "which in my conception would have been advantageous to the country. Among these, I rank the bill for encouraging intermarriages with the Indians. Our prejudices however, oppose themselves to our interests, and operate too powerfully for them." [2]

During the period between 1784 and 1787 when Marshall was out of the Legislature, the absolute need of a central Government that would enable the American people to act as a Nation became ever more urgent; but the dislike for such a Government also crystallized. The framing of the Constitution by the Federal Convention at Philadelphia in 1787 never could have been brought about by any abstract notions of National honor and National power, nor by any of those high and rational ideas of government which it has become traditional to

---

[1] See note 5, p. 239, *ante*.
[2] Marshall to Monroe, Dec., 1784; MS. Monroe Papers, Lib. Cong.; also partly quoted in Henry, ii, 219.

ascribe as the only source and cause of our fundamental law.

The people at large were in no frame of mind for any kind of government that meant power, taxes, and the restrictions which accompany orderly society. The determination of commercial and financial interests to get some plan adopted under which business could be transacted, was the most effective force that brought about the historic Convention at Philadelphia in 1787. Indeed, when that body met it was authorized only to amend the Articles of Confederation and chiefly as concerned the National regulation of commerce.[1]

Virginia delayed acting upon the Constitution until most of the other States had ratified it. The Old Dominion, which had led in the Revolution, was one of the last Commonwealths to call her Convention to consider the "new plan" of a National Government. The opposition to the proposed fundamental law was, as we shall see, general and determined; and the foes of the Constitution, fiercely resisting its ratification, were striving to call a second general Convention to frame another scheme of government or merely to amend the Articles of Confederation.

To help to put Virginia in line for the Constitution, John Marshall, for the third time, sought election to the Legislature. His views about government had now developed maturely into a broad, well-defined Nationalism; and he did not need the spur of the wrathful words which Washington had been

[1] See *infra*, chap. IX.

flinging as far as he could against the existing chaos and against everybody who opposed a strong National Government.

If Marshall had required such counsel and action from his old commander, both were at hand; for in all his volcanic life that Vesuvius of a man never poured forth such lava of appeal and denunciation as during the period of his retirement at Mount Vernon after the war was over and before the Constitution was adopted.[1]

But Marshall was as hot a Nationalist as Washington himself. He was calmer in temperament, more moderate in language and method, than his great leader; but he was just as determined, steady, and fearless. And so, when he was elected to the Legislature in the early fall of 1787, he had at heart and in mind but one great purpose. Army life, legislative experience, and general observation had modified his youthful democratic ideals, while strengthening and confirming that Nationalism taught him from childhood. Marshall himself afterwards described his state of mind at this period and the causes that produced it.

"When I recollect," said he, "the wild and enthusiastic notions with which my political opinions of that day were tinctured, I am disposed to ascribe my devotion to the Union and to a government competent to its preservation, at least as much to casual

[1] One of the curious popular errors concerning our public men is that which pictures Washington as a calm person. On the contrary, he was hot-tempered and, at times, violent in speech and action. It was with the greatest difficulty that he trained himself to an appearance of calmness and reserve.

circumstances as to judgment. I had grown up at a time when the love of the Union, and the resistance to the claims of Great Britain were the inseparable inmates of the same bosom; when patriotism and a strong fellow-feeling with our suffering fellow-citizens of Boston were identical; when the maxim, 'United we stand, divided we fall,' was the maxim of every orthodox American.

"And I had imbibed these sentiments so thoroughly that they constituted a part of my being. I carried them with me into the army, where I found myself associated with brave men from different States, who were risking life and everything valuable in a common cause, believed by all to be most precious; and where I was confirmed in the habit of considering America as my country, and Congress as my government.... My immediate entrance into the State Legislature opened to my view the causes which had been chiefly instrumental in augmenting those sufferings [of the army]; and the general tendency of State politics convinced me that no safe and permanent remedy could be found but in a more efficient and better organized General Government." [1]

On the third day of the fall session of the Virginia Legislature of 1787, the debate began on the question of calling a State Convention to ratify the proposed National Constitution.[2] On October 25 the debate came to a head and a resolution for calling a State Convention passed the House.[3] The debate

[1] Story, in Dillon, iii, 338, 343.
[2] Journal, H.D. (Oct. Sess., 1787), 7.   [3] *Ib.*, 11, 15.

was over the question as to whether the proposed Convention should have authority either to ratify or reject the proposed scheme of government entirely; or to accept it upon the condition that it be altered and amended.

Francis Corbin, a youthful member from Middlesex, proposed a flat-footed resolution that the State Convention be called either to accept or reject the "new plan." He then opened the debate with a forthright speech for a Convention to ratify the new Constitution as it stood. Patrick Henry instantly was on his feet. He was for the Convention, he said: "No man was more truly federal than himself." But, under Corbin's resolution, the Convention could not propose amendments to the Constitution. There were "errors and defects" in that paper, said Henry. He proposed that Corbin's resolution should be changed so that the State Convention might propose amendments [1] as a condition of ratification.

The debate waxed hot. George Nicholas, one of the ablest men in the country, warmly attacked Henry's idea. It would, declared Nicholas, "give the impression" that Virginia was not for the Constitution, whereas "there was, he believed, a decided majority in its favor." Henry's plan, said Nicholas, would throw cold water on the movement to ratify the Constitution in States that had not yet acted.

George Mason made a fervid and effective speech for Henry's resolution. This eminent, wealthy, and cultivated man had been a member of the Philadel-

[1] *Pennsylvania Packet*, Nov. 10, 1787; Pa. Hist. Soc.

phia Convention that had framed the Constitution; but he had refused to sign it. He was against it for the reasons which he afterwards gave at great length in the Virginia Convention of 1788.[1] He had "deeply and maturely weighed every article of the new Constitution," avowed Mason, and if he had signed it, he "might have been justly regarded as a traitor to my country. I would have lost this hand before it should have marked my name to the new government." [2]

At this juncture, Marshall intervened with a compromise. The Constitutionalists were uncertain whether they could carry through Corbin's resolution. They feared that Henry's plan of proposing amendments to the Constitution might pass the House. The effect of such an Anti-Constitutional victory in Virginia, which was the largest and most populous State in the Union, would be a blow to the cause of the Constitution from which it surely could not recover. For the movement was making headway in various States for a second Federal Convention that should devise another sytsem of government to take the place of the one which the first Federal Convention, after much quarreling and dissension, finally patched up in Philadelphia.[3]

So Marshall was against both Corbin's resolution and Henry's amendment to it; and also he was for the ideas of each of these gentlemen. It was plain, said Marshall, that Mr. Corbin's resolution was open to the criticism made by Mr. Henry. To be sure, the

[1] *Infra*, chaps. xi and xii.
[2] *Pennsylvania Packet*, Nov. 10, 1787; also see in Rowland, ii, 176.
[3] *Infra*, chaps. ix, xii; and also Washington to Lafayette, Feb. 7, 1788; *Writings:* Ford, xi, 220.

Virginia Convention should not be confined to a straight-out acceptance or rejection of the new Constitution; but, on the other hand, it would never do for the word to go out to the other States that Virginia in no event would accept the Constitution unless she could propose amendments to it. He agreed with Nicholas entirely on that point.

Marshall also pointed out that the people of Virginia ought not to be given to understand that their own Legislature was against the proposed Constitution before the people themselves had even elected a Convention to pass upon that instrument. The whole question ought to go to the people without prejudice; and so Marshall proposed a resolution of his own "that a Convention should be called and that the new Constitution should be laid before them for their free and ample discussion." [1]

Marshall's idea captured the House. It placated Henry, it pleased Mason; and, of course, it was more than acceptable to Corbin and Nicholas, with whom Marshall was working hand in glove, as, indeed, was the case with all the Constitutionalists. In fact, Marshall's tactics appeared to let every man have his own way and succeeded in getting the Convention definitely called. And it did let the contending factions have their own way for the time being; for, at that juncture, the friends of the new National Constitution had no doubt that they would be able to carry it through the State Convention unmarred by amendments, and its enemies were equally certain that they would be able to defeat or alter it.

[1] *Pennsylvania Packet*, Nov. 10, 1787; Pa. Hist. Soc.

Marshall's resolution, therefore, passed the House "unanimously." [1] Other resolutions to carry Marshall's resolution into effect also passed without opposition, and it was "ordered that two hundred copies of these resolutions be printed and dispersed by members of the general assembly among their constituents; and that the Executive should send a copy of them to Congress and to the Legislature and Executive of the respective states." [2] But the third month of the session was half spent before the Senate passed the bill.[3] Not until January 8 of the following year did it become a law.[4]

In addition, however, to defining the privileges of the members and providing money for its expenses, the bill also authorized the Convention to send representatives "to any of the sister states or the conventions thereof which may be then met," in order to gather the views of the country "concerning the great and important change of government which hath been proposed by the federal convention." [5] Thus the advocates of a second general Convention to amend the Articles of Confederation or frame another Constitution scored their point.

So ended the first skirmish of the historic battle soon to be fought out in Virginia, which would determine whether the American people should begin their career as a Nation. Just as John Marshall was among the first in the field with rifle,

---

[1] Journal, H.D. (Oct. Sess., 1787), 15. [2] Ib.
[3] Ib., 95. [4] Ib. (Dec., 1787), 143, 177.
[5] Hening, xii, 462–63.

tomahawk, and scalping-knife, to fight for Independence, so, now, he was among those first in the field with arguments, influence, and political activities, fighting for Nationalism.

CHAPTER VII

LIFE OF THE PEOPLE: COMMUNITY ISOLATION

An infant people, spreading themselves through a wilderness occupied only by savages and wild beasts. (Marshall.)

Of the affairs of Georgia, I know as little as of those of Kamskatska. (James Madison, 1786.)

"LEAN to the right," shouted the driver of a lumbering coach to his passengers; and all the jostled and bethumped travelers crowded to that side of the clumsy vehicle. "Left," roared the coachman a little later, and his fares threw themselves to the opposite side. The ruts and gullies, now on one side and now on the other, of the highway were so deep that only by acting as a shifting ballast could the voyagers maintain the stage's center of gravity and keep it from an upset.[1]

This passageway through the forest, called a "road," was the thoroughfare between Philadelphia and Baltimore and a part of the trunk line of communication which connected the little cities of that period. If the "road" became so bad that the coach could not be pulled through the sloughs of mud, a new way was opened in the forest; so that, in some places, there were a dozen of such cuttings all leading to the same spot and all full of stumps, rocks, and trees.[2]

The passengers often had to abandon this four-wheeled contraption altogether and walk in the mud;

[1] Weld, i, 37–38; also, Morris, ii, 393–94.   [2] Weld, i, 38.

and were now and again called upon to put their shoulders to the wheels of the stage when the horses, unaided, were unable to rescue it.[1] Sometimes the combined efforts of horses and men could not bring the conveyance out of the mire and it would have to be left all night in the bog until more help could be secured.[2] Such was a main traveled road at the close of the Revolutionary War and for a long time after the Constitution was adopted.

The difficulty and danger of communication thus illustrated had a direct and vital bearing upon the politics and statesmanship of the times. The conditions of travel were an index to the state of the country which we are now to examine. Without such a survey we shall find ourselves floating aimlessly among the clouds of fancy instead of treading, with sure foothold, the solid ground of fact. At this point, more perhaps than at any other of our history, a definite, accurate, and comprehensive inventory of conditions is essential. For not only is this phase of American development more obscure than any other, but the want of light upon it has led to vague consideration and sometimes to erroneous conclusions.

We are about to witness the fierce and dramatic struggle from which emerged the feeble beginnings of a Nation that, even to-day, is still in the making; to behold the welter of plan and counterplot, of scheming and violence, of deal and trade, which finally resulted in the formal acceptance of the Constitution with a certainty that it would be modified, and, to some extent, mutilated, by later

[1] Baily's *Journal* (1796-97), 108.   [2] *Ib.*, 109-10.

amendments. We are to listen to those "debates" which, alone, are supposed to have secured ratification, but which had no more, and indeed perhaps less effect than the familiar devices of "practical politics" in bringing about the adoption of our fundamental law.

Since the victory at Yorktown a serious alteration had taken place in the views of many who had fought hardest for Independence and popular government. These men were as strong as ever for the building of a separate and distinct National entity; but they no longer believed in the wisdom or virtue of democracy without extensive restrictions. They had come to think that, at the very best, the crude ore of popular judgment could be made to enrich sound counsels only when passed through many screens that would rid it of the crudities of passion, whimsicality, interest, ignorance, and dishonesty which, they believed, inhered in it. Such men esteemed less and less a people's government and valued more and more a good government And the idea grew that this meant a government the principal purpose of which was to enforce order, facilitate business, and safeguard property.

During his early years in the Legislature, as has appeared, Marshall's opinions were changing. Washington, as we shall see, soon after peace was declared, lost much of his faith in the people; Madison arrived at the opinion that the majority were unequal to the weightier tasks of popular rule; and Marshall also finally came to entertain the melancholy fear that the people were not capable of self-government. Indeed, almost all of the foremost men of the period now under review were brought to doubt the good sense or sound heart of the multitude. The fires of Jefferson's faith still burned, and, indeed, burned more brightly; for that great reformer was in France and neither experienced nor witnessed any of those popular phenomena which fell like a drenching rain upon the enthusiasm of American statesmen at home for democratic government.

This revolution in the views of men like Washington, Madison, and Marshall was caused largely by the conduct of the masses, which, to such men, seemed to be selfish, violent, capricious, vindictive, and dangerous. The state of the country explains much of this popular attitude and disposition. The development of Marshall's public ideas cannot be entirely understood by considering merely his altered circumstances and business and social connections. More important is a review of the people, their environment and condition.

The extreme isolation of communities caused by want of roads and the difficulties and dangers of communication; the general ignorance of the masses; their childish credulity, and yet their quick and acute suspicion springing, largely, from isolation and lack of knowledge; their savage and narrow individualism, which resisted the establishment of a central authority and was antagonistic to any but the loosest local control; their envy and distrust of the prosperous and successful which their own economic condition strengthened, if, indeed, this circumstance did not create that sullen and dangerous state of mind — an understanding of all these elements of American life at that time is vital if we are to trace the development of Marshall's thinking and explore the origins of the questions that confronted our early statesmen.

The majority of the people everywhere were poor; most of them owed debts; and they were readily influenced against any man who favored payment, and against any plan of government that might compel it. Also, the redemption of State and Continental debts, which was a hard and ever-present problem, was abhorrent to them. Much of the scrip had passed into the hands of wealthy purchasers. Why, exclaimed the popular voice, should this expedient of war be recognized? Discharge of such public obligations meant very definite individual taxes. It was as easy to inflame a people so situated and inclined as it was hard to get accurate information to them or to induce them to accept any reasoning that made for personal inconvenience or for public burdens.

Marshall could not foresee the age of railway and telegraph and universal education. He had no vision of a period when speedy and accurate information would reach the great body of our population and the common hearthstone thus become the place of purest and soundest judgment. So it is impossible to comprehend or even apprehend his intellectual metamorphosis during this period unless we survey the physical, mental, and spiritual state of the country. How the people lived, their habits,

COMMUNITY ISOLATION

the extent of their education, their tendency of thought, and, underlying all and vitally affecting all, the means or rather want of means of communication — a knowledge of these things is essential to an understanding of the times.[1] The absence of roads and the condition of the few that did exist were thoroughly characteristic of the general situation and, indeed, important causes of it. It becomes indispensable, then, to visualize the highways of the period and to picture the elements that produced the thinking and acting of the larger part of the people. Many examples are necessary to bring all this, adequately and in just proportion, before the eye of the present.

When Washington, as President, was on his way to meet Congress, his carriage stuck in the mud, and only after it had been pried up with poles and pulled out by ropes could the Father of his Country proceed on his journey;[2] and this, too, over the principal highway of Maryland. "My nerves have not yet quite recovered the shock of the *wagon*," wrote Samuel Johnston of a stage trip from Baltimore to New York two years after our present Government

---

[1] Professor Beard, in his exposition of the economic origins of the Constitution, shows that nearly all of the men who framed it were wealthy or allied with property interests and that many of them turned up as holders of Government securities. (Beard: *Econ. I. C.*, chap. v.) As a matter of fact, none but such men could have gone to the Federal Convention at Philadelphia, so great were the difficulties and so heavy the expenses of travel, even if the people had been minded to choose poorer and humbler persons to represent them; at any rate, they did not elect representatives of their own class until the Constitution was to be ratified and then, of course, only to State Conventions which were accessible.

[2] Weld, i, 47-48.

was established.[1] Richard Henry Lee objected to the Constitution, because, among other things, "many citizens will be more than three hundred miles from the seat of this [National] government";[2] and "as many assessors and collectors of federal taxes will be above three hundred miles from the seat of the federal government as will be less."[3]

The best road throughout its course, in the entire country, was the one between Boston and New York; yet the public conveyance which made regular trips with relays of horses in the most favorable season of the year usually took an entire week for the journey.[4] The stage was "shackling"; the horses' harness "made of ropes"; one team hauled the stage only eighteen miles; the stop for the night was made at ten o'clock, the start next morning at half-past two; the passengers often had to "help the coachman lift the coach out of the quagmire."[5]

Over parts even of this, the finest long highway in the United States, the stage had to struggle against rocks and to escape precipices. "I knew not which to admire the most in the driver, his intrepidity or dexterity. I cannot conceive how he avoided twenty times dashing the carriage to pieces,"[6] testifies a traveler. In central Massachusetts, the roads "were intolerable" even to a New Englander; and "the

[1] Johnston to Iredell, Jan. 30, 1790; McRee, ii, 279.
[2] "Letters of a Federal Farmer," no. 2; Ford: *P. on C.*, 292.
[3] *Ib.*, no. 3, 302.
[4] De Warville made a record trip from Boston to New York in less than five days. (De Warville, 122.) But such speed was infrequent.
[5] Josiah Quincy's description of his journey from Boston to New York in 1794. (Quincy: *Figures of the Past*, 47-48.)
[6] De Warville, 138-39.

COMMUNITY ISOLATION

country was sparsely inhabited by a rude population."[1] In Rhode Island not far from Providence the traveler was forced to keep mounting and dismounting from his horse in order to get along at all.[2] Dr. Taylor, in the Massachusetts Convention of 1788, arguing for frequent elections, said that it would take less than three weeks for Massachusetts members of Congress to go from Boston to Philadelphia.[3]

Farmers only a short distance from New York could not bring their produce to the city in the winter because the roads were impassable.[4] Up State, in Cooper's Otsego settlement, "not one in twenty of the settlers had a horse and the way lay through rapid streams, across swamps or over bogs. . . . If the father of a family went abroad to labour for bread, it cost him three times its value before he could bring it home."[5] As late as 1790, after forty thousand acres in this region had been taken up "by the poorest order of men . . . there were neither roads nor bridges"; and about Otsego itself there was not even "any trace of a road."[6] Where Utica now stands, the opening through the wilderness, which went by the name of a road, was so nearly impassable that a horseback traveler could make no

---

[1] Watson, 266.

[2] "The road is execrable; one is perpetually mounting and descending and always on the most rugged roads." (Chastellux, 20.)

[3] Elliott, ii, 21–22.

[4] "In December last, the roads were so intollerably bad that the country people could not bring their forage to market, though *actually offered the cash on delivery*." (Pickering to Hodgdon; *Pickering:* Pickering, i, 392.)

[5] Cooper, 1875–86, as quoted in Hart, iii, 98.   [6] *Ib.*

more than two miles an hour over it. Rocks, stumps, and muddy holes in which the horse sank, made progress not only slow and toilsome, but dangerous.[1]

Twenty days was not an unusual time for ordinary wagons, carrying adventurous settlers to the wilderness west of the Alleghanies, to cross Pennsylvania from Philadelphia to Pittsburg;[2] and it cost a hundred and twenty dollars a ton to haul freight between these points.[3] Three years after our present Government was established, twenty out of twenty-six lawsuits pending in Philadelphia were settled out of court "rather than go ninety miles from Phil$^{\underline{a}}$ for trial."[4]

Talleyrand, journeying inland from the Quaker City about 1795, was "struck with astonishment" at what he beheld: "At less than a hundred and fifty miles distance from the Capital," he writes, "all trace of men's presence disappeared; nature in all her primeval vigor confronted us. Forests old as the world itself; decayed plants and trees covering the very ground where they once grew in luxuriance." And Talleyrand testifies that the fields, only a few miles' walk out of the "cities," had been "mere wildernesses of forest" at the time the Constitution was adopted.[5]

[1] Watson, 270. Along one of the principal roads of New York, as late as 1804, President Dwight discovered only "a few lonely plantations" and he "occasionally found a cottage and heard a distant sound of an axe and of a human voice. All else was grandeur, gloom, and solitude." (Halsey: *Old New York Frontier*, 384.)

[2] Hart, iii, 116.

[3] *Mag. Western Hist.*, i, 530.

[4] Justice Cushing to Chief Justice Jay, Oct. 23, 1792; *Jay:* Johnston, iii, 450.

[5] *Memoirs of Talleyrand:* Broglie's ed., i, 176–77.

COMMUNITY ISOLATION

"The length and badness of the roads from hence [Mount Vernon] to Philadelphia" made Washington grumble with vexation and disgust;[1] and Jefferson wrote of the President's Southern tour in 1791: "I shall be happy to hear that no accident has happened to you in the bad roads . . . that you are better prepared for those to come by lowering the hang [body] of your carriage and exchanging the coachman for two postilions . . . which [are] . . . essential to your safety."[2]

No more comfortable or expeditious, if less dangerous, was travel by boat on the rivers. "Having lain all night in my Great Coat and Boots in a berth not long enough for me," chronicles Washington of this same Presidential journey, "we found ourselves in the morning still fast aground."[3]

So difficult were the New Jersey roads that the stout and well-kept harness with which Washington always equipped his horses was badly broken going through New Jersey in 1789.[4] "The roads [from Richmond to New York] thro' the whole were so bad that we could never go more than three miles an hour, some times not more than two, and in the night, but one," wrote Jefferson[5] in March, 1790.

A traveler starting from Alexandria, Virginia, to visit Mount Vernon, nine miles distant, was all day on the road, having become lost, in the "very thick

[1] Washington to Jay, Nov. 19, 1790; *Jay:* Johnston, iii, 409.
[2] Jefferson to Washington, March 27, 1791; *Cor. Rev.*: Sparks, iv, 366.
[3] Washington's *Diary:* Lossing, Feb. 25, 1791.
[4] Washington to Jay, Dec. 13, 1789; *Jay:* Johnston, iii, 381.
[5] Jefferson to T. M. Randolph, March 28, 1790; *Works:* Ford, vi, 36.

woods." So confusing was the way through this forest that part of this time he was within three miles of his destination.[1] Twelve years after our present Government was established James A. Bayard records of his journey to the Capital: "Tho' traveling in the mail stage . . . we were unable to move at more than the rate of two or three miles an hour." [2]

Throughout Virginia the roads were execrable and scarcely deserved the name. The few bridges usually were broken.[3] The best road in the State was from Williamsburg, the old Capital, to Richmond, the new, a distance of only sixty-three miles; yet, going at highest speed, it required two days to make the trip.[4] Traveling in Virginia was almost exclusively by horseback; only negroes walked.[5] According to Grigsby, the familiar vision in our minds of the picturesque coach comfortably rolling over attractive highways, with postilions and outriders, which we now picture when we think of traveling in old Virginia, is mostly an historical mirage; for, says Grigsby, "coaches were rarely seen. There were thousands of respectable men in the Commonwealth who had never seen any other four-wheeled vehicle than a wagon and there were thousands who had never seen a wagon" at the time when the Constitution was ratified.[6]

If horseback journeys were sore trials to the rider, they were desperately hard and sometimes fatal to

[1] Weld, i, 91.
[2] Bayard to Rodney, Jan. 5, 1801; *Bayard Papers:* Donnan, ii, 118.
[3] Schoepf, ii, 46.   [4] *Ib.*, 78.   [5] *Ib.*, 45.   [6] Grigsby, i, 26.

COMMUNITY ISOLATION

the poor brute that carried him. In crossing unfordable rivers on the rude ferryboats, the horses' legs frequently were broken or the animals themselves often killed or drowned.[1] From Fredericksburg to Alexandria the roads were "frightfully bad."[2] As late as 1801 the wilderness was so dense just above where the City of Washington now stands that Davis called it "the wilds of the Potomac." In most parts of Virginia a person unacquainted with the locality often became lost in the forests.[3] South of Jamestown the crude and hazardous highways led through "eternal woods."[4]

A short time before the Revolution, General Wilkinson's father bought five hundred acres on the present site of the National Capital, including the spot where the White House now stands; but his wife refused to go there from a little hamlet near Baltimore where her family then lived, because it was so far away from the settlements in the backwoods of Maryland.[5] A valuable horse was stolen from a Virginia planter who lived one hundred and forty miles from Richmond; but, although the thief was known, the expense of going to the Capital with witnesses was double the value of the horse, and so the planter pocketed his loss.[6] It cost more to transport tobacco from Augusta County, Virginia, to market than the tobacco was worth, so difficult and expensive was the carriage.[7]

A sergeant in a Virginia regiment during the Rev-

[1] Weld, i, 170. [2] Watson, 60. [3] Davis, 372. [4] Schoepf, ii, 95.
[5] Wilkinson: *Memoirs*, i, 9–10. The distance which General Wilkinson's mother thought "so far away" was only forty miles.
[6] Schoepf, ii, 53. [7] Zachariah Johnson, in Elliott, iii, 647.

olutionary War, living in a part of the State which at present is not two hours' ride from the Capital, petitioned the House of Delegates in 1790 for payment of his arrears because he lived so far away from Richmond that he had found it impossible to apply within the time allowed for the settlement of his accounts in the regular way.[1] In 1785 the price of tobacco on the James River or the Rappahannock, and in Philadelphia varied from twenty to ninety-five per cent, although each of these places was "the same distance from its ultimate market,"[2] so seriously did want of transportation affect commerce. "The trade of this Country is in a deplorable Condition ... the loss direct on our produce & indirect on our imports is not less than 50 per ct.," testifies Madison.[3]

Only in the immediate neighborhood of Philadelphia, Boston,[4] or New York, neither of which "cities" was as large as a moderate-sized inland town of to-day, were highways good, even from the point of view of the eighteenth century. In all other parts of America the roads in the present-day sense did not exist at all. Very often such trails as had been made were hard to find and harder to keep after they had been found. Near the close of the Revolution, Chastellux became tangled up in the woods on his way to visit Jefferson at Monticello "and travelled a long time without seeing any habitation."[5]

[1] Journal, H.D. (1790), 13.
[2] Madison to Lee, July 7, 1785; *Writings:* Hunt, ii, 149–51.
[3] *Ib.*
[4] Boston was not a "city" in the legal interpretation until 1822.
[5] Chastellux, 225. "The difficulty of finding the road in many parts of America is not to be conceived except by those strangers who

COMMUNITY ISOLATION

Whoever dared to take in North Carolina what, at present, would be a brief and pleasant jaunt, then had to go through scores of miles of "dreary pines" in which the traveler often lost his way and became bewildered in the maze of the forest.[1] Again, the wanderer would find himself in a desolation of swamp and wood without the hint of a highway to follow out of it; and sleeping on the ground beneath the trees of this wilderness, with only wild animals about him, was, for the ordinary traveler, not an uncommon experience.[2]

Even when the road could be traced, bears would follow it, so much was it still a part of their savage domain.[3] The little traveling possible when the weather was good was sometimes entirely suspended for days after a rain or snowfall, even out of a "city" like Baltimore.[4] Six years after the Constitution

have travelled in that country. The roads, which are through the woods, not being kept in repair, as soon as one is in bad order, another is made in the same manner, that is, merely by felling trees, and the whole interior parts are so covered that without a compass it is impossible to have the least idea of the course you are steering. The distances, too, are so uncertain as in every county where they are not measured, that no two accounts resemble each other. In the back parts of Pennsylvania, Maryland, and Virginia, I have frequently travelled thirty miles for ten, though frequently set right by passengers and negroes." (*Ib.* Translator's note.)

[1] Smyth, *Tour of the United States*, i, 102–103.

[2] Watson, 40. "Towards the close of the day I found myself entangled among swamps amid an utter wilderness, and my horse almost exhausted in my efforts to overtake Harwood. As night closed upon me I was totally bewildered and without a vestige of a road to guide me. Knowing the impossibility of retracing my steps in the dark, through the mazes I had traversed, I felt the necessity of passing the night in this solitary desert ... in no trifling apprehension of falling a prey to wild beasts before morning." (*Ib.*)

[3] *Ib.*

[4] "I waited at Baltimore near a week before I could proceed on my

was adopted, Talleyrand found the buildings of that ambitious town "disput[ing] the ground with trees whose stumps have not yet been removed." [1]

Such were the means of communication of a people scattered over a territory of almost half a million square miles. The total population of the United States was about three and a quarter millions; the same part of the country to-day has a population of not far from fifty-five millions. Including cities, and adding to these the more thickly settled portions adjoining them, there were not in the original States seven men, women, and children, all told, to the square mile. If we add Kentucky, Tennessee, Ohio, Illinois, and Indiana, into which the restless settlers already were moving, the people then living in the United States were fewer than five persons to the square mile.

The various little clusters of this scanty and widely separated population were almost entirely out of touch one with another. Inhabitants were scattered through those far-flung stretches called the United States, but they were not a people. Scarcely any communication existed between them; while such a thing as mail service was unknown to all but a comparatively few thousands. It required six days and sometimes nine to carry mail between Boston and New York. As late as 1794 a letter of Jefferson, then in Charlottesville, Virginia, to Madison at Philadelphia, reached the latter nine days after it

journey the roads being rendered impassable." (Baily's *Journal* (1796–97), 107.)

[1] *Memoirs of Talleyrand:* Broglie's ed., i, 177.

COMMUNITY ISOLATION

was sent; and another letter between the same correspondents was eight days on the journey.[1]

Yet this was unusually expeditious. One month later, on January 26, 1795, Madison wrote Jefferson that "I have received your favor of Dec. 28, but [not] till three weeks after the date of it."[2] Summer, when the post-riders made better time, seemed not greatly to increase the dispatch of mail; for it took more than a month for a letter posted in New York in that season of the year to reach an accessible Virginia county seat.[3] Letters from Richmond, Virginia, to New York often did not arrive until two months after they were sent.[4] But better time was frequently made and a letter between these points was, commonly, hurried through in a month.[5]

Many weeks would go by before one could send a letter from an interior town in Pennsylvania. "This Uniontown is the most obscure spot on the face of the globe.... I have been here seven or eight weeks without one opportunity of writing to the land of the living," complains a disgusted visitor.[6] A letter posted by Rufus King in Boston, February 6, 1788, to Madison in New York was received February 15;[7] and although anxiously awaiting news, Madison

[1] Madison to Jefferson, Dec. 21, 1794; *Writings:* Hunt, vi, 227.

[2] Madison to Jefferson, Jan. 26, 1795; *ib.*, 230.

[3] "Your favor of July 6 having been address^d to Williamsburg, instead of *Orange C. Ho[u]se*, did not come to hand till two days ago." (Madison to Livingston, Aug. 10, 1795; *ib.*, vi, 234.)

[4] Lee to Henry, May 28, 1789; Henry, iii, 387.

[5] Lee to Henry, Sept. 27, 1789; Henry, iii, 402.

[6] Ephraim Douglass to Gen. James Irvine, 1784; *Pa. Mag. Hist. and Biog.*, i, 50.

[7] Madison to Washington, Feb. 15, 1788; and King to Madison, Feb. 6, 1788; *Writings:* Hunt, v, footnote to p. 100.

had not, on February 11, heard that Massachusetts had ratified the Constitution, although that momentous event had occurred five days before.[1] New York first learned of that historic action eight days after it was taken.[2] But for the snail-like slowness of the post, the Constitution would certainly have been defeated in the Virginia Convention of 1788.[3]

Transatlantic mail service was far more expeditious considering the distance; a letter from Jay in London reached Wolcott at Philadelphia in less than eight weeks.[4] But it sometimes required five months to carry mail across the ocean;[5] even this was very much faster than one could travel by land in America. Four weeks from Cowes, England, to Lynnhaven Bay, Virginia, was a record-breaking voyage.[6]

Such letters as went through the post-offices were opened by the postmasters as a matter of course, if these officials imagined that the missives contained information, or especially if they revealed the secret or familiar correspondence of well-known public men.[7] "By passing through the post-office they [letters] should become known to all" men, Wash-

[1] Madison to Washington, Feb. 11, 1788; *Writings:* Hunt, v, 99.
[2] Madison to Washington, Feb. 15, 1788; *ib.*, 100.
[3] The Randolph-Clinton Correspondence; see *infra*, chap. x.
[4] Jay to Wolcott, mailed June 23, and received by Wolcott Aug. 16, 1794; Gibbs, i, 157.
[5] *Ib.*, 160.
[6] Jefferson to Short, Nov. 21, 1789; *Works:* Ford, vi, 20.
[7] So notorious was this practice that important parts of the correspondence of the more prominent politicians and statesmen of the day always were written in cipher. Jefferson, Madison, and Monroe appear to have been especially careful to take this precaution. (See Washington's complaint of this tampering with the mails in a letter

ington cautioned Lafayette in 1788.[1] In 1791, the first year of the Post-Office under our present Government, there were only eighty-nine post-offices in the entire country.[2] "As late as 1791 there were only six post-offices in New Jersey and none south of Trenton."[3]

Yet letters were the principal means by which accounts of what was happening in one part of the country were made known to the people who lived in other sections; and this personal correspondence was by far the most trustworthy source of information, although tinctured as it naturally was by the prejudice of the writer and often nothing but report of mere rumor.

Newspapers were few in number and scanty in news. When the Constitution was adopted, not many regularly issued newspapers were printed in the whole country. Most of these were published in Philadelphia, Boston, New York, and in two or three of the other larger towns. Only ten papers were printed in Connecticut, one of the best informed and best served of all the States, and of these several soon expired;[4] in Ridgefield, with twelve hundred inhabitants, there were but four newspaper subscribers.[5] In 1784, Virginia had only one newspaper, published at Richmond twice a week.[6]

to Fairfax, June 25, 1786; *Writings:* Sparks, ix, 175.) Habitual violation of the mails by postmasters continued into the first decades of the nineteenth century.

[1] Washington to Lafayette, Feb. 7, 1788; *Writings:* Ford, xi, 218.
[2] Kettell, in *Eighty Years' Progress*, ii, 174.
[3] *Pa. Mag. Hist. and Biog.*, ix, 444.
[4] *Am. Ant. Soc. Pubs.*, xxiii, Part ii, 254–330.   [5] Goodrich, i, 61.
[6] Schoepf, ii, 61; see note, *ib.* Even this journal died for want of subscribers.

These papers carried scarcely any news and the little they published was often weeks and sometimes months old, and as uncertain as it was stale. "It is but seldom that I have an opportunity of peeping into a newspaper," wrote "Agricola" to the Salem (Massachusetts) "Gazette," September 13, 1791, "and when it happens it is commonly a stale one of 2 or 3 weeks back; but I lately met with your fresh Gazette of August 30th — may be I shan't see another for months to come." [1] "Newspaper paragraphs, unsupported by other testimony, are often contradictory and bewildering," wrote Washington of so big, important, and exciting news as the progress of Shays's Rebellion.[2] On the same day Washington complained to General Knox that he was "bewildered with those vague and contradictory reports which are presented in the newspapers." [3]

But what this pygmy press lacked in information it made up in personal abuse. Denunciation of public men was the rule, scandal the fashion. Even the mild and patient Franklin was driven to bitter though witty protest. He called the press "THE SUPREMEST COURT OF JUDICATURE," which "may judge, sentence, and condemn to infamy, not only private individuals, but public bodies, &c. with or without inquiry or hearing, *at the court's discretion.*" This "Spanish Court of Inquisition," asserts Frank-

[1] Salem *Gazette*, Sept. 13, 1791; Hist. Col., Topsfield (Mass.) Hist. Soc., iii, 10.
[2] Washington to Humphreys, Dec. 26, 1786; *Writings:* Ford, xi, 98–103.
[3] Washington to General Knox, Dec. 26, 1786; *ib.*, 103–05.

lin, works "in the dark" and so rapidly that "an honest, good Citizen may find himself suddenly and unexpectedly accus'd, and in the same Morning judg'd and condemn'd, and sentence pronounced against him, that he is a *Rogue* and a *Villian.*"

"The liberty of the press," writes Franklin, operates on citizens "somewhat like the *Liberty of the Press* that Felons have, by the Common Law of England, before Conviction, that is, to be *press'd* to death or hanged." "Any Man," says he, "who can procure Pen, Ink, and Paper, with a Press, and a huge pair of BLACKING BALLS, may commissionate himself" as a court over everybody else, and nobody has any redress. "For, if you make the least complaint of the *judge's* [editor's] conduct, he daubs his blacking balls in your face wherever he meets you; and, besides tearing your private character to flitters marks you out for the odium of the public, as an *enemy to the liberty of the press.*" Franklin declared that the press of that day was supported by human depravity.

Searching for a remedy which would destroy the abuse but preserve the true liberty of the press, Franklin finally concludes that he has found it in what he calls "the *liberty of the cudgel.*" The great philosopher advised the insulted citizen to give the editor "a good drubbing"; but if the public should feel itself outraged, it should restrain itself and, says Franklin, "in moderation content ourselves with tarring and feathering, and tossing them [editors] in a blanket." [1]

---

[1] *Writings:* Smyth, x, 36 *et seq.* This arraignment of the press by

Even Jefferson was sometimes disgusted with the press. "What do the foolish printers of America mean by retailing all this stuff in our papers? — As if it were not enough to be slandered by one's enemies without circulating the slanders among his friends also."[1] An examination of the newspapers of that period shows that most of the "news" published were accounts of foreign events; and these, of course, had happened weeks and even months before.

Poor, small, and bad as the newspapers of the time were, however, they had no general circulation many miles from the place where they were published. Yet, tiny driblets trickled through by the belated posts to the larger towns and were hastily read at villages where the post-riders stopped along the way. By 1790 an occasional country newspaper appeared, whose only source of news from the outside world was a fugitive copy of some journal published in the city and such tales as the country editor could get travelers to tell him: whether these were true or false made not the slightest difference — everything was fish that came to his net.[2]

America's first journalist was written when Franklin was eighty-three years old and when he was the most honored and beloved man in America, Washington only excepted. It serves not only to illuminate the period of the beginning of our Government, but to measure the vast progress during the century and a quarter since that time.

[1] Jefferson to Mrs. Adams, Paris, Sept. 25, 1785; *Works:* Ford, iv, 465.

[2] "Country Printer," in Freneau, iii, 60. Freneau thus describes the country editor of that day: —

"Three times a week, by nimble geldings drawn,
A stage arrives; but scarcely deigns to stop,
Unless the driver, far in liquor gone,
Has made some business for the black-smith-shop;

Common schools in the present-day understanding of the term did not exist. "There was not a grammar, a geography, or a history of any kind in the school," testifies Samuel G. Goodrich[1] (Peter Parley) of Ridgefield, Connecticut; and this at a time when the Constitution had been adopted and our present Government was in operation. "Slates & pencils were unknown, paper was imported, scarce and costly"; most pupils in New England "cyphered

> Then comes this printer's harvest-time of news,
> Welcome alike from Christians, Turks, or Jews.
>
> "Each passenger he eyes with curious glance,
> And, if his phiz be mark'd of courteous kind,
> To conversation, straight, he makes advance,
> Hoping, from thence, some paragraph to find,
> Some odd adventure, something new and rare,
> To set the town a-gape, and make it stare.
>
> "All is not Truth ('tis said) that travellers tell —
> So much the better for this man of news;
> For hence the country round, that know him well,
> Will, if he prints some lies, his lies excuse.
> Earthquakes, and battles, shipwrecks, myriads slain —
> If false or true — alike to him are gain.
> . . . . . .
> "Ask you what matter fills his various page?
> A mere farrago 'tis, of mingled things;
> Whate'er is done on Madam Terra's stage
> He to the knowledge of his townsmen brings:
> One while, he tells of monarchs run away;
> And now, of witches drown'd in Buzzard's bay.
>
> "Some miracles he makes, and some he steals;
> Half Nature's works are giants in his eyes;
> Much, very much, in wonderment he deals, —
> New-Hampshire apples grown to pumpkin size,
> Pumpkins almost as large as country inns,
> And ladies bearing, each, — three lovely twins."

Freneau was himself a country printer in New Jersey, after editing the *National Gazette* in Philadelphia. Thus the above description was from his personal experience and in a town in a thickly settled part, on the main road between New York and Philadelphia.

[1] Goodrich, i, 38.

on birch bark"; and a teacher who could compute interest was considered "great in figures."[1] "The teacher was not infrequently a person with barely education enough to satisfy the critical requirements of some illiterate committeemen. ... The pay was only from three to five dollars a month, and two months during the winter season was the usual term."[2] The half-dozen small but excellent colleges and the few embryonic academies surrounded by forests, where educated and devout men strove to plant the seeds of institutions of learning, could not, altogether, reach more than a few hundred pupils.

"*Anthony McDonald* teaches boys and girls their grammar tongue; also Geography terrestrial and celestial — Old hats made as good as new." So read the sign above the door of McDonald's "school" in Virginia, a dozen years after Washington was elected President.[3] For the most part children went untaught, except in "the three R's," which, in some mysterious manner, had been handed down from father to son. Yet in the back settlements it was common to find men of considerable property who could not read or write; and some of those who could make out to read did not know whether the earth was round or flat.[4] There were but thirty students at Virginia's historic college in 1795. Weld dined

[1] A letter from Salem Town about 1786-87; in *American Journal of Education*, xiii, 738.
[2] Van Santvoord: *Memoirs of Eliphalet Nott*, 19.   [3] Davis, 333.
[4] "Many cannot read or write, and many that can, know nothing of geography and other branches. The country is too thinly settled to carry out a system of common schools." (Howe, 153, speaking of western Virginia about 1830.)

with President Madison, of William and Mary's, and several of the students were at the table. Some of these young seekers after culture were without shoes, some without coats; and each of them rose and helped himself to the food whenever he liked.[1]

Parts of the country, like the Mohawk Valley in New York, were fairly settled and well cultivated.[2] In the more thickly inhabited parts of New England there were order, thrift, and industry.[3] The houses of the most prosperous farmers in Massachusetts, though "frequently but one story and a garret," had "their walls papered"; tea and coffee were on their tables when guests appeared; the women were clad in calicoes and the men were both farmers and artisans.[4] Yet on the road from Boston to Providence houses were seen already falling into decay; "women and children covered with rags."[5] In Newport, Rhode Island, idle men loafed on the street corners, houses were tumbling down from negligence, grass grew in the public square, and rags were stuffed into the windows.[6]

In Connecticut the people were unusually prosperous; and one enthusiastic Frenchman, judging that State from the appearance of the country around Hartford, exclaimed: "It is really the Paradise of

---

[1] Weld, i, 168. But President Tyler says that the boys Weld saw were grammar-school pupils.

[2] Watson, 269. [3] Chastellux, 319–20.
[4] De Warville, 126–27. [5] Ib., 145 and 450.
[6] Ib., 145. All travelers agree as to the wretched condition of Rhode Island; and that State appears to have acted as badly as it looked. "The ... infamous [scenes] in Rhode Island have done inexpressable injury to the Republican character," etc. (Madison to Pendleton, Feb. 24, 1787; *Writings: Hunt*, ii, 319.)

the United States." [1] Weld found that, while the "southeast part of ... Pennsylvania is better cultivated than any other part of America, yet the style of farming is ... very slovenly.... The farmer ... in England ... who rents fifty acres ... lives far more comfortably in every respect than the farmer in Pennsylvania, or any other of the middle states, who owns two hundred acres." [2]

In the homes of Quaker farmers near Philadelphia, however, the furniture was of black walnut, the beds and linen white and clean, the food varied and excellent.[3] Yet a settler's house in the interior of Pennsylvania was precisely the reverse, as the settler himself was the opposite of the industrious and methodical Quaker husbandman. A log cabin lighted only by the open door, and with the bare earth for a floor, housed this pioneer and his numerous family. Often he was a man who had lost both fortune and credit and therefore sought regions where neither was necessary. When neighbors began to come in such numbers that society (which to him meant government, order, and taxes) was formed, he moved on to a newer, more desolate, and more congenial spot. Mostly hunter and very little of a farmer, he with his nomad brood lived "in the filth of his little cabin," the rifle or rod, and corn from the meager clearing, supplying all his wants except that of whiskey, which he always made shift to get.

One idea and one alone possessed this type — the idea of independence, freedom from restraint. He

[1] De Warville, 132.
[2] Weld, i, 113.   [3] De Warville, 186–87.

was the high priest of the religion of do-as-you-like. He was the supreme individualist, the ultimate democrat whose non-social doctrine has so cursed modern America. "He will not consent to sacrifice a single natural right for all the benefits of government,"[1] chronicles a sympathetic observer of these men.

Freneau, a fervent admirer of this shiftless and dissolute type, thus describes him and his home: —

> "Far in the west, a paltry spot of land,
> That no man envied, and that no man owned,
> A woody hill, beside a dismal bog —
> This was your choice; nor were you much to blame;
> And here, responsive to the croaking frog,
> You grubbed, and stubbed,
> And feared no landlord's claim."[2]

Nor was hostility to orderly society confined to this class. Knox wrote Washington that, in Massachusetts, those who opposed the Constitution acted "from deadly principle levelled at the existence of all government whatever."[3]

The better class of settlers who took up the "farms" abandoned by the first shunners of civilization, while a decided improvement, were, nevertheless, also improvident and dissipated. In a poor and

---

[1] De Warville, 186 and 332. See La Rochefoucauld's description of this same type of settler as it was several years after De Warville wrote. "The Dwellings of the new settlers . . . consist of huts, with roofs and walls which are made of bark and in which the husband, wife and children pass the winter wrapped up in blankets. . . . Salt pork and beef are the usual food of the new settlers; their drink is water and whiskey." (La Rochefoucauld, i, 293–96.)

[2] Freneau, iii, 74.

[3] Knox to Washington, Feb. 10, 1788; *Writings:* Ford, xi, footnote to 229. And see *infra*, chap. VIII.

slip-shod fashion, they ploughed the clearings which had now grown to fields, never fertilizing them and gathering but beggarly crops. Of these a part was always rye or corn, from which whiskey was made. The favorite occupation of this type was drinking to excess, arguing politics, denouncing government, and contracting debts.[1] Not until debts and taxes had forced onward this second line of pioneer advance did the third appear with better notions of industry and order and less hatred of government and its obligations.[2]

In New England the out-push of the needy to make homes in the forests differed from the class just described only in that the settler remained on his clearing until it grew to a farm. After a few years his ground would be entirely cleared and by the aid of distant neighbors, cheered to their work by plenty of rum, he would build a larger house.[3] But meanwhile there was little time for reading, small opportunity for information, scanty means of getting it;

---

[1] De Warville, 187. In 1797, La Rochefoucauld speaks of "the credulity and ignorance of the half-savage sort of people who inhabit the back settlements." (La Rochefoucauld, i, 293.)

[2] "A relaxation is observable among all orders of society. Drunkenness is the prevailing vice, and with few exceptions, the source of all other evils. A spirit, or rather a habit, of equality is diffused among this people as far as it possibly can go. . . . The inhabitants exhibit to strangers striking instances both of the utmost cleanliness and excessive nastiness." (La Rochefoucauld, i, 125.)

During Washington's second term as President, La Rochefoucauld thus describes manners in western Pennsylvania: "They are much surprised at a refusal to sleep with one, two, or more men, in the same bed, or between dirty sheets, or to drink after ten other persons out of the same dirty glass. . . . Whiskey mixed with water is the common drink in the country." (*Ib.*)

[3] *Ib.*, i, 293-96. See *infra*, note 4, pp. 281-82.

COMMUNITY ISOLATION 277

and mouth-to-mouth rumor was the settler's chief informant of what was happening in the outside world. In the part of Massachusetts west of the Connecticut Valley, at the time the Constitution was adopted, a rough and primitive people were scattered in lonesome families along the thick woods.[1]

In Virginia the contrast between the well-to-do and the masses of the people was still greater.[2] The social and economic distinctions of colonial Virginia persisted in spite of the vociferousness of democracy which the Revolution had released. The small group of Virginia gentry were, as has been said, well educated, some of them highly so, instructed in the ways of the world, and distinguished in manners.[3] Their houses were large; their table service was of plate; they kept their studs of racing and carriage horses.[4] Sometimes, however, they displayed a grotesque luxury. The windows of the mansions, when broken, were occasionally replaced with rags; servants sometimes appeared in livery with silk stockings thrust into boots;[5] and again dinner would be served by naked negroes.[6]

---

[1] Watson, 266.

[2] "You see [in Maryland and Virginia] real misery and apparent luxury insulting each other." (De Warville, 159.)

[3] Chastellux, 279, and translator's note.

[4] Anburey, ii, 331–32.   [5] De Warville, 242.

[6] "Soon after entering Virginia, and at a highly respectable house, I was shocked ... at seeing for the first time, young negroes of both sexes, from twelve even to fifteen years old, not only running about the house but absolutely tending table, as naked as they came into the world.... Several young women were at the table, who appeared totally unmoved." (Watson, 33.) Watson's statement may perhaps be questionable; a livelier description, however, was given with embellishments, some years later. (See translator's note to Chastellux, 245; and see Schoepf, ii, 47.)

The second class of Virginia people were not so well educated, and the observer found them "rude, ferocious, and haughty; much attached to gaming and dissipation, particularly horse-racing and cock-fighting"; and yet, "hospitable, generous, and friendly." These people, although by nature of excellent minds, mingled in their characters some of the finest qualities of the first estate, and some of the worst habits of the lower social stratum. They "possessed elegant accomplishments and savage brutality." [1] The third class of Virginia people were lazy, hard-drinking, and savage; yet kind and generous.[2] "Whenever these people come to blows," Weld testifies, "they fight just like wild beasts, biting, kicking, and endeavoring to tear each other's eyes out with their nails"; and he says that men with eyes thus gouged out were a common sight.[3]

The generation between the birth of Marshall and the adoption of the Constitution had not modified the several strata of Virginia society except as to apparel and manners, both of which had become worse than in colonial times.

Schoepf found shiftlessness[4] a common characteristic; and described the gentry as displaying the baronial qualities of haughtiness, vanity, and idleness.[5] Jefferson divides the people into two sections as regards characteristics, which were not entirely creditable to either. But in his comparative estimate Jefferson is far harsher to the Southern population

---

[1] Anburey, ii, 331-32.   [2] *Ib.*, 332-33.
[3] Weld, i, 192. See Weld's description of "gouging." And see Fithian's interesting account; Fithian, 242-43.
[4] Schoepf, ii, 89.   [5] *Ib.*, 91-95.

of that time than he is to the inhabitants of other States; and he emphasizes his discrimination by putting his summary in parallel columns.

"While I am on this subject," writes Jefferson to Chastellux, "I will give you my idea of the characters of the several States.

In the North they are	In the South they are
cool	fiery
sober	voluptuary
laborious	indolent
persevering	unsteady
independent	independent
jealous of their own liberties, and just to those of others	zealous for their own liberties, but trampling on those of others
interested	generous
chicaning	candid
superstitious and hypocritical in their religion	without attachment or pretensions to any religion but that of the heart.

"These characteristics," continues Jefferson, "grow weaker and weaker by graduation from North to South and South to North, insomuch that an observing traveller, without the aid of the quadrant may always know his latitude by the character of the people among whom he finds himself."

"It is in Pennsylvania," Jefferson proceeds in his careful analysis, "that the two characters seem to meet and blend, and form a people free from the extremes both of vice and virtue. Peculiar circumstances have given to New York the character which climate would have given had she been placed on the South instead of the north side of Pennsylvania. Perhaps too other circumstances may have occasioned in Virginia a transplantation of a particular vice foreign to its climate." Jefferson finally concludes: "I think it for their good that the vices of their character should be pointed out to them that they may amend them; for a malady of either body or mind once known is half cured."[1]

A plantation house northwest of Richmond grumblingly admitted a lost traveler, who found his sleeping-room with "filthy beds, swarming with bugs" and cracks in the walls through which the sun shone.[2] The most bizarre contrasts startled the observer — mean cabins, broken windows, no bread, and yet women clad in silk with plumes in their hair.[3] Eight years after our present National Government was established, the food of the people living in the Shenandoah Valley was salt fish, pork, and greens; and the wayfarer could not get fresh meat except at Staunton or Lynchburg,[4] notwithstanding the surrounding forests filled with game or the domestic animals which fed on the fields where the forests had been cleared away.

Most of the houses in which the majority of Virginians then lived were wretched;[5] Jefferson tells us,

[1] Jefferson to Chastellux, Sept. 2, 1785; *Thomas Jefferson Correspondence,* Bixby Collection: Ford, 12; and see Jefferson to Donald, July 28, 1787; Jefferson's *Writings:* Washington, ii, 193, where Jefferson says that the qualities of Virginians are "indolence, extravagance, and infidelity to their engagements."

[2] Weld, i, 199.

[3] Schoepf, ii, 34. This strange phenomenon was witnessed everywhere, even in a place then so far remote as Maine. "Elegant women come out of log or deal huts [in Maine] all wearing fashionable hats and head dresses with feathers, handsome cloaks and the rest of their dress suitable to this." (La Rochefoucauld, ii, 314.)

[4] *Ib.,* 89; and Weld, i, 199, 236. The reports of all travelers as to the want of fresh meat in the Valley are most curious. That region was noted, even in those early days, for its abundance of cattle.

[5] *Ib.,* 144.

speaking of the better class of dwellings, that "it is impossible to devise things more ugly, uncomfortable, and happily more perishable." "The poorest people," continues Jefferson, "build huts of logs, laid horizontally in pens, stopping the interstices with mud. ... The wealthy are attentive to the raising of vegetables, but very little so to fruits. ... The poorer people attend to neither, living principally on ... animal diet." [1]

In general the population subsisted on worse fare than that of the inhabitants of the Valley.[2] Even in that favored region, where religion and morals were more vital than elsewhere in the Commonwealth, each house had a peach brandy still of its own; and it was a man of notable abstemiousness who did not consume daily a large quantity of this spirit. "It is scarcely possible," writes Weld, "to meet with a man who does not begin the day with taking one, two, or more drams as soon as he rises." [3]

Indeed, at this period, heavy drinking appears to have been universal and continuous among all classes throughout the whole country [4] quite as much

---

[1] "Notes on Virginia": Jefferson; *Works:* Ford, iv, 69; and see Weld, i, 114, for similar diet in Pennsylvania.   [2] *Ib.*, 183–84.

[3] Weld, i, 206. "Sigars and whiskey satisfy these good people who thus spend in a quarter of an hour in the evening, the earnings of a whole day. The landlord of the Inn has also a distillery of whiskey," writes La Rochefoucauld, in 1797, of the mountain people of Virginia. He thus describes the houses and people living in the valley towards Staunton: "The habitations are in this district more numerous than on the other side of the Blue Mountains, but the houses are miserable; mean, small log houses, inhabited by families which swarm with children. There exists here the same appearance of misery as in the back parts of Pennsylvania." (La Rochefoucauld, iii, 173–76.)

[4] "It took a good deal of New England rum to launch a 75 ton

as in Virginia. It was a habit that had come down from their forefathers and was so conspicuous, ever-present and peculiar, that every traveler through America, whether native or foreign, mentions it time and again. "The most common vice of the inferior class of the American people is drunkenness," writes La Rochefoucauld in 1797.[1] And Washington eight years earlier denounced "drink which is the source of all evil — and the ruin of half the workmen in this country."[2] Talleyrand, at a farmer's house in the heart of Connecticut, found the daily food to consist of "smoked fish, ham, potatoes, strong beer and brandy."[3]

Court-houses built in the center of a county and often standing entirely alone, without other buildings near them, nevertheless always had attached to them a shanty where liquor was sold.[4] At country taverns which, with a few exceptions, were poor

schooner ... to raise a barn ... or to ordain a regular minister. ... Workingmen in the fields, in the woods, in the mills and handling logs and lumber on the river were supplied with regular rations of spirits." (Maine Hist. Soc. Col. (2d Series), vi, 367-68.)

The rich people of Boston loved picnic parties in the near-by country, at which was served "Punch, warm and cold, before dinner; excellent beef, Spanish and Bordeaux wines, cover their tables ... Spruce beer, excellent cyder, and Philadelphia porter precede the wines." (De Warville, 58.) This inquiring Frenchman called on Hancock, but found that he had a "marvelous gout which dispenses him from all attentions and forbids the access to his house." (*Ib.*, 66.) As to New England country stores, "you find in the same shop, hats, nails, liquors." (*Ib.*, 127.)

[1] La Rochefoucauld, iv, 577.

[2] Washington to Green (an employee) March 31, 1789; *Writings:* Ford, xi, 377.

[3] *Memoirs of Talleyrand:* Broglie's ed., i, footnote to 181; and see Talleyrand's description of a brandy-drinking bout at this house in which he participated.

[4] Schoepf, ii, 47.

and sometimes vile,[1] whiskey mixed with water was the common drink.[2] About Germantown, Pennsylvania, workingmen received from employers a pint of rum each day as a part of their fare;[3] and in good society men drank an astonishing number of "full bumpers" after dinner, where, already, they had imbibed generously.[4] The incredible quantity of liquor, wine, and beer consumed everywhere and by all classes is the most striking and conspicuous feature of early American life. In addition to the very heavy domestic productions of spirits,[5] there were imported in 1787, according to De Warville, four million gallons of rum, brandy, and other spirits; one million gallons of wine; three million gallons of molasses (principally for the manufacture of rum); as against only one hundred and twenty-five thousand pounds of tea.[6]

Everybody, it appears, was more interested in sport and spending than in work and saving. As in colonial days, the popular amusements continued to be horse-racing and cock-fighting; the first the peculiar diversion of the quality; the second that of the baser sort, although men of all conditions of society attended and delighted in both.[7] But the horse-

---

[1] Watson, 252. [2] Chastellux, 224; see also 243.
[3] La Rochefoucauld, iv, 119. [4] Ib., 590.
[5] See *infra*, II, chap. II. [6] De Warville, 262.
[7] Watson, 261-62. "The indolence and dissipation of the middling and lower classes of white inhabitants in Virginia are such as to give pain. . . . Horse-racing, cock-fighting, and boxing-matches are standing amusements, for which they neglect all business." (*Ib.*; and see Chastellux, 292, translator's note. Also see Chastellux's comments on the economic conditions of the Virginians, 291-93.) For habits of Virginians nearly twenty years after Watson wrote, see La Rochefoucauld, iii, 75-79.

racing and the cock-fighting served the good purpose of bringing the people together; for these and the court days were the only occasions on which they met and exchanged views. The holding of court was an event never neglected by the people; but they assembled then to learn what gossip said and to drink together rather than separately, far more than they came to listen to the oracles from the bench or even the oratory at the bar; and seldom did the care-free company break up without fights, sometimes with the most serious results.[1]

Thus, scattered from Maine to Florida and from the Atlantic to the Alleghanies, with a skirmish line thrown forward almost to the Mississippi, these three and a quarter millions of men, women, and children, did not, for the most part, take kindly to government of any kind. Indeed, only a fraction of them had anything to do with government, for there were no more than seven hundred thousand adult males among them,[2] and of these, in most States, only property-holders had the ballot. The great majority of the people seldom saw a letter or even a newspaper; and the best informed did not know what was going on in a neighboring State, although anxious for the information.

"Of the affairs of Georgia, I know as little as of

[1] "The session assembles here, besides the neighboring judges, lawyers, and parties whose causes are to be tried, numbers of idle people who come less from desire to learn what is going forward than to drink together," says La Rochefoucauld; and see his picturesque description of his arrival at the close of court day at Goochland Court-House. (La Rochefoucauld, iii, 126–29.)

[2] One man to every five men, women, and children, which is a high estimate.

those of Kamskatska," wrote Madison to Jefferson in 1786.[1] But everybody did know that government meant law and regulation, order and mutual obligation, the fulfillment of contracts and the payment of debts. Above all, everybody knew that government meant taxes. And none of these things aroused what one would call frantic enthusiasm when brought home to the individual. Bloated and monstrous individualism grew out of the dank soil of these conditions. The social ideal had hardly begun to sprout; and nourishment for its feeble and languishing seed was sucked by its overgrown rival.

Community consciousness showed itself only in the more thickly peopled districts, and even there it was feeble. Generally speaking and aside from statesmen, merchants, and the veterans of the Revolution, the idea of a National Government had not penetrated the minds of the people. They managed to tolerate State Governments, because they always had lived under some such thing; but a National Government was too far away and fearsome, too alien and forbidding for them to view it with friendliness or understanding. The common man saw little difference between such an enthroned central power and the Royal British Government which had been driven from American shores.

To be sure, not a large part of the half-million men able for the field[2] had taken much of any militant part in expelling British tyranny; but these

[1] Madison to Jefferson, Aug. 12, 1786; *Writings:* Hunt, ii, 261.
[2] Randolph in the Virginia Constitutional Convention estimated that the colonies could have put four hundred thousand soldiers in the field. (Elliott, iii, 76–77.)

"chimney-corner patriots," as Washington stingingly described them, were the hottest foes of British despotism — after it had been overthrown. And they were the most savage opponents to setting up any strong government, even though it should be exclusively American.

Such were the economic, social, and educational conditions of the masses and such were their physical surroundings, conveniences, and opportunities between the close of the War for Independence and the setting-up of the present Government. All these facts profoundly affected the thought, conduct, and character of the people; and what the people thought, said, and did, decisively influenced John Marshall's opinion of them and of the government and laws which were best for the country.

During these critical years, Jefferson was in France witnessing government by a decaying, inefficient, and corrupt monarchy and nobility, and considering the state of a people who were without that political liberty enjoyed in America.[1] But the vagaries, the changeableness, the turbulence, the envy toward those who had property, the tendency to repudiate debts, the readiness to credit the grossest slander or to respond to the most fantastic promises, which the newly liberated people in America were then displaying, did not come within Jefferson's vision or experience.

[1] It is a curious fact, however, that in his journey through France Jefferson observed no bad conditions, but, on the whole, his careful diary states that he found the people "well clothed and well fed," as Professor Hazen expresses it. For impartial treatment of this subject see Hazen, 1-21.

Thus, Marshall and Jefferson, at a time destined to be so important in determining the settled opinions of both, were looking upon opposite sides of the shield. It was a curious and fateful circumstance and it was repeated later under reversed conditions.

CHAPTER VIII

POPULAR ANTAGONISM TO GOVERNMENT

Mankind, when left to themselves, are unfit for their own government. (George Washington, 1786.)

There are subjects to which the capacities of the bulk of mankind are unequal and on which they must and will be governed by those with whom they happen to have acquaintance and confidence. (James Madison, 1788.)

I fear, and there is no opinion more degrading to the dignity of man, that these have truth on their side who say that man is incapable of governing himself. (John Marshall, 1787.)

"GOVERNMENT, even in its best state," said Mr. Thomas Paine during the Revolution, "is but a necessary evil."[1] Little as the people in general had read books of any kind, there was one work which most had absorbed either by perusal or by listening to the reading of it; and those who had not, nevertheless, had learned of its contents with applause.

Thomas Paine's "Common Sense," which Washington and Franklin truly said did so much for the patriot cause,[2] had sown dragon's teeth which the

[1] *Writings:* Conway, i, 69 *et seq.*

[2] "*Common Sense* had a prodigious effect." (Franklin to Le Veillard, April 15, 1787; *Writings:* Smyth, ix, 558.) "Its popularity was unexampled.... The author was hailed as our angel sent from Heaven to save all from the horrors of Slavery.... His pen was an appendage [to the army] almost as necessary and formidable as its cannon." (Cheetenham, 46–47, 55.) In America alone 125,000 copies of *Common Sense* were sold within three months after the pamphlet appeared. (Belcher, i, 235.)

"Can nothing be done in our Assembly for poor Paine? Must the merits of *Common Sense* continue to glide down the stream of time unrewarded by this country? His writings certainly have had a powerful effect upon the public mind. Ought they not, then, to meet an adequate return?" (Washington to Madison, June 12, 1784; *Writings:* Ford, x, 393; and see Tyler, i, 458–62.) In the Virginia Legislature Marshall introduced a bill for Paine's relief. (*Supra*, chap. VI.)

ANTAGONISM TO GOVERNMENT 289

author possibly did not intend to conceal in his brilliant lines. Scores of thousands interpreted the meaning and philosophy of this immortal paper by the light of a few flashing sentences with which it began. Long after the British flag disappeared from American soil, this expatriated Englishman continued to be the voice of the people;[1] and it is far within the truth to affirm that Thomas Paine prepared the ground and sowed the seed for the harvest which Thomas Jefferson gathered.

"Government, like dress, is the badge of lost innocence; the palaces of kings are built on the ruins of the bowers of paradise." And again, "Society is produced by our wants, and government by our wickedness."[2] So ran the flaming maxims of the great iconoclast; and these found combustible material.

Indeed, there was, even while the patriots were fighting for our independence, a considerable part of the people who considered "all government as dissolved, and themselves in a state of absolute liberty, where they wish always to remain"; and they were strong enough in many places "to prevent any courts being opened, and to render every attempt to administer justice abortive."[3] Zealous bearers, these, of the torches of anarchy which Paine's burn-

---

[1] Graydon, 358.

[2] *Common Sense:* Paine; *Writings:* Conway, i, 61. Paine's genius for phrase is illustrated in the *Crisis*, which next appeared. "These are the times that try men's souls"; "Tyranny like hell, is not easily conquered"; "The summer soldier and the sunshine patriot," are examples of Paine's brilliant gift.

[3] Moore's *Diary*, ii, 143-44. Although this was a British opinion, yet it was entirely accurate.

ing words had lighted. Was it not the favored of the earth that government protected? What did the poor and needy get from government except oppression and the privilege of dying for the boon? Was not government a fortress built around property? What need, therefore, had the lowly for its embattled walls?

Here was excellent ammunition for the demagogue. A person of little ability and less character always could inflame a portion of the people when they could be assembled. It was not necessary for him to have property; indeed, that was a distinct disadvantage to the Jack Cades of the period.[1] A lie traveled like a snake under the leaves and could not be overtaken;[2] bad roads, scattered communities, long distances, and resultant isolation leadened and

[1] "They will *rise* and for lack of argument, say, M! Speaker, this measure will never do, the *People* Sir, will never bear it.... These small Politicians, returned home, ... tell their Constituents such & such measures are taking place altho' I did my utmost to prevent it — The People must take care of themselves or they are undone. Stir up a County Convention and by Trumpeting lies from Town to Town get one [a convention] collected and Consisting of Persons of small Abilities — of little or no property — embarrass'd in their Circumstances — and of no great Integrity — and these Geniouses vainly conceiving they are competent to regulate the affairs of State — make some hasty incoherent Resolves, and these end in Sedition, Riot, & Rebellion." (Sewell to Thatcher, Dec., 1787; *Hist. Mag.* (2d Series), vi, 257.)

[2] More than a decade after the slander was set afoot against Colonel Levin Powell of Loudoun County, Virginia, one of the patriot soldiers of the Revolution and an officer of Washington, that he favored establishing a monarchy, one of his constituents wrote that "detraction & defamation are generally resorted to promote views injurious to you. ... Can you believe it, but it is really true that the old & often refuted story of your predilection for Monarchy is again revived." (Thomas Sims to Colonel Levin Powell, Leesburg, Virginia, Feb. 5 and 20, 1801; *Branch Historical Papers*, i, 58, 61.)

delayed the feet of truth. Nothing was too ridiculous for belief; nothing too absurd to be credited.

A Baptist preacher in North Carolina was a candidate for the State Convention to pass upon the new National Constitution, which he bitterly opposed. At a meeting of backwoodsmen in a log house used for a church, he told them in a lurid speech that the proposed "Federal City" (now the District of Columbia) would be the armed and fortified fortress of despotism. "'This, my friends,' said the preacher, 'will be walled in or fortified. Here an army of 50,000, or, perhaps 100,000 men, will be finally embodied and will sally forth, and enslave the people who will be gradually disarmed.'" A spectator, who attempted to dispute this statement, narrowly escaped being mobbed by the crowd. Everything possible was done to defeat this ecclesiastical politician; but the people believed what he said and he was elected.[1]

So bizarre an invention as the following was widely circulated and generally believed as late as 1800: John Adams, it was said, had arranged, by intermarriage, to unite his family with the Royal House of Great Britain, the bridegroom to be King of America. Washington, attired in white clothing as a sign of conciliation, called on Adams and objected; Adams rebuffed him. Washington returned, this time dressed in black, to indicate the solemnity of

[1] Watson, 262-64. This comic prophecy that the National Capital was to be the fortified home of a standing army was seriously believed by the people. Patrick Henry urged the same objection with all his dramatic power in the Virginia Convention of 1788. So did the scholarly Mason. (See *infra*, chaps. XI and XII.)

his protest. Adams was obdurate. Again the Father of his Country visited the stubborn seeker after monarchical relationship, this time arrayed in full regimentals to show his earnestness; Adams was deaf to his pleas. Thereupon the aged warrior drew his sword, avowing that he would never sheathe it until Adams gave up his treasonable purpose; Adams remained adamant and the two parted determined enemies.[1]

Such are examples of the strange tales fed to the voracious credulity of the multitude. The attacks on personal character, made by setting loose against public men slanders which flew and took root like thistle seed, were often too base and vile for repetition at the present day, even as a matter of history; and so monstrous and palpably untruthful that it is difficult to believe they ever could have been circulated much less credited by the most gossip-loving.

Things, praiseworthy in themselves, were magnified into stupendous and impending menaces. Revolutionary officers formed "The Society of the Cincinnati" in order to keep in touch with one another, preserve the memories of their battles and their campfires, and to support the principles for which they had fought.[2] Yet this patriotic and fraternal order was, shouted the patriots of peace, a plain attempt to establish an hereditary nobility on which a new tyranny was to be builded. Jefferson, in Paris, declared that "the day . . . will certainly come, when a single fibre of this institution will produce an

[1] Graydon, 392–93.
[2] *Memorials of the Society of the Cincinnati*, 1790, 3–24.

ANTAGONISM TO GOVERNMENT

hereditary aristocracy which will change the form of our governments [Articles of Confederation] from the best to the worst in the world."[1]

Ædanus Burke,[2] one of the Justices of the Supreme Court of South Carolina, wrote that the Society of the Cincinnati was "deeply planned"; it was "an hereditary peerage"; it was "planted in a fiery hot ambition, and thirst for power"; "its branches will end in Tyranny ... the country will be composed only of two ranks of men, the patricians, or nobles, and the rabble."[3] In France, Mirabeau was so aroused by Burke's pamphlet that the French orator wrote one of his own. Mirabeau called the Cincinnati "that nobility of barbarians, the price of blood, the off-spring of the sword, the fruit of conquest." "The distinction of Celts and Ostrogoths," exclaimed the extravagant Frenchman, "are what they claim for their inheritance."[4]

The "Independent Chronicle" of Boston was so excited that it called on "legislators, Governors, and magistrates *and their* ELECTORS" to suppress the Cincinnati because it "is concerted to establish a

[1] Jefferson to Washington, Nov. 14, 1786; *Works:* Ford, v, 222-23; and see Jefferson's denunciation of the Cincinnati in Jefferson to Madison, Dec. 28, 1794; *ib.*, viii, 156-57. But see Jefferson's fair and moderate account of the Cincinnati before he had learned of its unpopularity in America. (Jefferson to Meusnier, June 22, 1786; *ib.*, v, 50-56.)

[2] The same who broke the quorum in the Continental Congress. (*Supra*, chap. IV.)

[3] Burke: *Considerations on the Society of the Order of Cincinnati;* 1784.

[4] Mirabeau: *Considerations on the Order of Cincinnati;* 1786. Mirabeau here refers to the rule of the Cincinnati that the officer's eldest son might become a member of the order, as in the Military Order of the Loyal Legion of the present time.

complete and perpetual *personal* discrimination between" its members "and the whole remaining body of the people who will be styled Plebeians."[1]

John Marshall was a member of this absurdly traduced patriotic fraternity. So were his father and fellow officers of our War for Independence. Washington was its commander. Were the grotesque charges against these men the laurels with which democracy crowned those who had drawn the sword for freedom? Was this the justice of liberty? Was this the intelligence of the masses? Such must have been the queries that sprang up in the minds of men like Marshall. And, indeed, there was sound reason for doubt and misgiving. For the nightmares of men like Burke and Mirabeau were pleasant dreams compared with the horrid visions that the people conjured.

Nor did this popular tendency to credit the most extraordinary tale, believe the most impossible and outrageous scandal, or accept the most impracticable and misshapen theory, end only in wholesome hatred of rank and distinction. Among large numbers there was the feeling that equality should be made real by a general division of property. Three years after peace had been established, Madison said he "strongly suspected" that many of the people contemplated "an abolition of debts public & private, and a new division of property."[2] And Jay thought that "a reluctance to taxes, an

---

[1] As quoted in Hudson: *Journalism in the United States*, 158.
[2] Madison to James Madison, Nov. 1, 1786; *Writings:* Hunt, ii, 278.

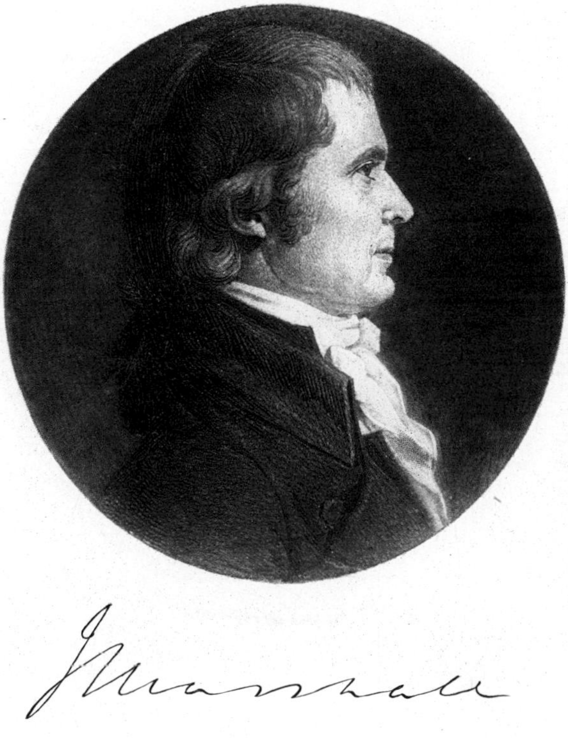
J Marshall

ANTAGONISM TO GOVERNMENT 295

impatience of government, a rage for property, and little regard to the means of acquiring it, together with a desire for equality in all things, seem to actuate the mass of those who are uneasy in their circumstances." [1] The greed and covetousness of the people is also noted by all travelers.[2]

Very considerable were the obligations "public and private" which Madison wrote his father that he "strongly suspected" a part of the country intended to repudiate. The public debt, foreign and domestic, of the Confederation and the States, at the close of the Revolutionary War, appeared to the people to be a staggering sum.[3] The private debt aggregated a large amount.[4] The financial situation was chaos. Paper money had played such havoc with specie that, in Virginia in 1786, as we have seen, there was not enough gold and silver to pay current taxes.[5] The country had had bitter experience with a fictitious medium of exchange. In Virginia by 1781 the notes issued by Congress "fell to 1000 for 1," records Jefferson, "and then expired, as it had done in other States, without a single groan." [6]

Later on, foreigners bought five thousand dollars

[1] Jay to Jefferson, Oct. 27, 1786; *Jay:* Johnston, iii, 212.
[2] See Weld, i, 114–15, as a fair example of foreign estimate of this American characteristic at that period.
[3] See chap. II, vol. II, of this work.
[4] Private debts which Virginia planters alone owed British merchants were "20 or 30 times the amount of all money in circulation in that state." (Jefferson to Meusnier, Jan. 24, 1786; *Works:* Ford, v, 17–18; and see Jefferson to McCaul, April 19, 1786; *ib.*, 88.)
[5] "It cannot perhaps be affirmed that there is gold & silver en^o in the Country to pay the next tax." (Madison to Monroe, June 4, 1786; *Writings:* Hunt, ii, 245.)
[6] Jefferson to Meusnier, Jan. 24, 1786; *Works:* Ford, v, 27.

of this Continental scrip for a single dollar of gold or silver.[1] In Philadelphia, toward the end of the Revolution, the people paraded the streets wearing this make-believe currency in their hats, with a dog tarred and covered with paper dollars instead of feathers.[2] For land sold by Jefferson before paper currency was issued he "did not receive the money till it was not worth Oak leaves." [3]

Most of the States had uttered this fiat medium, which not only depreciated and fluctuated within the State issuing it, but made trade between citizens of neighboring States almost impossible. Livingston found it a "loss to shop it in New York with [New] Jersey Money at the unconscionable discount which your [New York] brokers and merchants exact; and it is as damnifying to deal with our merchants here [New Jersey] in that currency, since they proportionably advance the price of their commodities." [4] Fithian in Virginia records that: "In the evening I borrowed of *Ben Carter* 15/ — I have plenty of money with me but it is in Bills of Philadelphia Currency and will not pass at all here." [5]

Virginia had gone through her trial of financial fiction-for-fact, ending in a law fixing the scale of depreciation at forty to one, and in other unique

[1] Jefferson to Meusnier, Jan. 24, 1786: *Works:* Ford, v, 27.

[2] Moore's *Diary*, ii, 425–26. The merchants of Philadelphia shut their shops; and it was agreed that if Congress did not substitute "solid money" for paper, "all further resistance to" Great Britain "must be given up." (*Ib.*)

[3] Jefferson to McCaul, April 19, 1786; *Works:* Ford, v, 90; also to Wm. Jones, Jan. 5, 1787; *ib.*, 247. — "Paiment was made me in this money when it was but a shadow."

[4] Livingston to Jay, July 30, 1789; *Jay:* Johnston, iii, 373–74.

[5] Fithian, 91.

ANTAGONISM TO GOVERNMENT

and bizarre devices;[1] and finally took a determined stand against paper currency.[2] Although Virginia had burned her fingers, so great was the scarcity of money that there was a formidable agitation to try inflation again.[3] Throughout the country there once more was a "general rage for paper money."[4] Bad as this currency was, it was counterfeited freely.[5] Such coin as existed was cut and clipped until Washington feared that "a man must travel with a pair of money scales in his pocket, or run the risk of receiving gold of one fourth less by weight than it counts."[6]

If there was not money enough, let the Government make more — what was a government for if not for that? And if government could not make good money, what was the good of government? Courts were fine examples of what government meant — they were always against the common people. Away with them! So ran the arguments and appeals of the demagogues and they found an answer in the breasts of the thoughtless, the ignorant, and the uneasy. This answer was broader than the

---

[1] Virginia's paper money experiment was the source of many lawsuits in which Marshall was counsel. See, for example, Pickett *vs.* Claiborne (Call, iv, 99–106); Taliaferro *vs.* Minor (Call, i, 456–62).

[2] The House of Delegates toward the end of 1786 voted 84 to 17 against the paper money resolution. (Madison to James Madison, Nov. 1, 1786; *Writings:* Hunt, ii, 277.)

[3] "The advocates for paper money are making the most of this handle. I begin to fear exceedingly that no efforts will be sufficient to parry this evil." (Madison to Monroe, June 4, 1786; *ib.*, 245.)

[4] Madison to Jefferson, Aug. 12, 1786; *ib.*, 259.

[5] "Enclosed are one hundred Dollars of new Emmission Money which Col. Steward desires me to have exchanged for Specie. Pray, inform him they are all counterfeit." (Gerry to King, April 7, 1785; King, i, 87.)

[6] Washington to Grayson, Aug. 22, 1785; *Writings:* Ford, x, 493–94.

demand for paper money, wider than the protest against particular laws and specific acts of administration. This answer also was, declared General Knox, "that the property of the United States . . . ought to be the common property of all. And he that attempts opposition to this creed is an enemy to equity and justice, and ought to be swept from off the face of the earth." Knox was convinced that the discontented were "determined to annihilate all debts, public and private." [1]

Ideas and purposes such as these swayed the sixteen thousand men who, in 1787, followed Daniel Shays in the popular uprising in Massachusetts against taxes, courts, and government itself.[2] "The restlessness produced by the uneasy situation of individuals, connected with lax notions concerning public and private faith, and erroneous[3] opinions which confound liberty with an exemption from legal control, produced . . . unlicensed conventions, which, after voting on their own constitutionality, and assuming the name of the people, arrayed themselves against the legislature," was John Marshall's summary of the forces that brought about the New England rebellion.

The "army" of lawlessness, led by Shays, took the field, says Marshall, "against taxes, and against the administration of justice; and the circulation of

[1] Knox to Washington, Oct. 28, 1786; *Writings:* Hunt, ii, footnote to p. 407-08.
[2] Minot: *History of the Insurrections in Massachusetts in 1786* (2d ed.), 1810.
[3] Printed in the first edition (1807) "enormous" — a good example of the haste of the first printing of Marshall's *Life of Washington.* (See vol. III of this work.)

a depreciated currency was required, as a relief from the pressure of public and private burdens, which had become, it was alleged, too heavy to be borne. Against lawyers and courts the strongest resentments were manifested; and to such a dangerous extent were these dispositions indulged, that, in many instances, tumultuous assemblages of people arrested the course of law, and restrained the judges from proceeding in the execution of their duty."

"The ordinary recourse to the power of the country was found insufficient protection," records Marshall, "and the appeals made to reason were attended with no beneficial effect. The forbearance of the government was attributed to timidity rather than moderation, and the spirit of insurrection appeared to be organized into a regular system for the suppression of courts." [1] Such was Marshall's analysis of the Northern convulsion; and thus was strengthened in him that tendency of thought started at Valley Forge, and quickened in the Virginia House of Delegates.

"It rather appears to me," wrote David Humphries to Washington, in an attempt to explain the root of the trouble, "that there is a licentious spirit prevailing among many of the people; a levelling principle; and a desire of change; with a wish to annihilate all debts, public and private." [2] Unjust taxes were given as the cause of the general dislike of government, yet those who composed the mobs erupting from this crater of anarchy, now located in New England, paid few or no taxes.

[1] Marshall, ii, 117. [2] *Ib.*, 118.

"High taxes are the ostensible cause of the commotions, but that they are the real cause is as far remote from truth as light from darkness," asserts Knox. "The people who are the insurgents have never paid any, or but very little taxes," testifies this stanch Revolutionary officer. "But," continues Knox, "they see the weakness of the government. They feel at once their own poverty, compared with the opulent, and their own force, and they are determined to make use of the latter, in order to remedy the former." [1]

This condition brought to a head a distrust of the good sense, justice, and moderation of the people, which had been forming in the minds of many of the best and ablest men of the time.[2] "The knaves and fools of this world are forever in alliance," was the conclusion reached in 1786 [3] by Jay, who thought that the people considered "liberty and licentiousness" as the same thing.[4] The patient but bilious Secretary of State felt that "the wise and the good never form the majority of any large society, and it seldom happens that their measures are uniformly adopted, or that they can always prevent being overborne themselves by the strong and almost never-ceasing union of the wicked and the weak." [5] The cautious Madison was equally doubtful of the peo-

[1] Knox to Washington, Oct. 28, 1786; *Writings:* Hunt, ii, footnote to 408.

[2] Shays's Rebellion was only a local outburst of a general feeling throughout the United States. Marshall says, "those causes of discontent . . . existed in every part of the union." (Marshall, ii, 117.)

[3] Jay to Jefferson, Oct. 27, 1786; *Jay:* Johnston, iii, 213.

[4] Jay to Reed, Dec. 12, 1786; *ib.*, 222.

[5] Jay to Price, Sept. 27, 1786; *ib.*, 168.

ple: "There are subjects to which the capacities of the bulk of mankind are unequal and on which they must and will be governed by those with whom they happen to have acquaintance and confidence" was Madison's judgment.[1]

Washington, black with depression, decided and bluntly said "that mankind, when left to themselves, are unfit for their own government." Lee had suggested that Washington use his "influence" to quiet the disorders in New England; but, flung back Washington, "*Influence* is no *government*. Let us have one by which our lives, liberties, and properties will be secured, or let us know the worst at once. . . . To be more exposed in the eyes of the world, and more contemptible than we already are, is hardly possible."[2]

"No morn ever dawned more favorably than ours did; and no day was ever more clouded than the present. . . . We are fast verging to anarchy,"[3] cried the great captain of our war for liberty. The wings of Washington's wrath carried him far. "Good God!" cried he, "Who, besides a Tory, could have foreseen, or a Briton predicted" the things that were going on! "The disorders which have arisen in these States, the present prospect of our affairs . . . seems to me to be like the vision of a dream. My mind can scarcely realize it as a thing in actual existence. . . . There are combustibles in every State, which a spark might set fire to."[4]

[1] Madison to Randolph, Jan. 10, 1788; *Writings:* Hunt, v, 81.
[2] Washington to Lee, Oct. 31, 1786; *Writings:* Ford, xi, 76-77.
[3] Washington to Madison, Nov. 5, 1786; *ib.*, 81.
[4] Washington to Knox, Dec. 26, 1786; *ib.*, 103-04. And Washing-

Marshall echoed his old commander's views. The dreams of his youth were fading, his confidence in the people declining. He records for us his altered sentiments: "These violent, I fear bloody, dissensions in a state [Massachusetts] I had thought inferior in wisdom and virtue to no one in the union, added to the strong tendency which the politics of many eminent characters among ourselves have to promote private and public dishonesty, cast a deep shade over the bright prospect which the revolution in America and the establishment of our free governments had opened to the votaries of liberty throughout the globe. I fear, and there is no opinion more degrading to the dignity of man, that these have truth on their side who say that man is incapable of governing himself." [1] Thus wrote Marshall in 1787, when he was not yet thirty-two years old.

But Jefferson in Paris was beholding a different picture that strengthened the views which he and Marshall held in common when America, in arms, challenged Great Britain. "The Spirit of resistance to government is so valuable on certain occasions that I wish it to be always kept alive. It will often be exercised when wrong, but better so than not to be exercised at all. I like a little rebellion now & then. It is like a storm in the atmosphere." So wrote Jefferson after the Massachusetts insurrection had been quelled.[2]

ton wrote to Lafayette that "There are seeds of discontent in every part of the Union." (*Writings:* Sparks, ix, 263.)

[1] Marshall to James Wilkinson, Jan. 5, 1787; *Amer. Hist. Rev.*, xii, 347-48.

[2] Jefferson to Mrs. Adams, Feb. 22, 1787; *Works:* Ford, v, 263.

ANTAGONISM TO GOVERNMENT

The author of our Declaration of Independence was tasting the delights of the charming French Capital at this time, but he also was witnessing the shallowness and stupidity of the peculiarly weak royalty and nobility; and although it was this same Royal Government that had aided us with men and money in our struggle to throw off the yoke of England, Jefferson's heart grew wrathful against it and hot for popular rule in France. Yet in the same apostrophe to rebellion, Jefferson declares that the French people were too shallow for self-rule. "This [French] nation," writes Jefferson, "is incapable of any serious effort but under the word of command." [1]

After having had months to think about it, this enraptured enthusiast of popular upheaval spread his wings and was carried far into crimson skies. "Can history produce an instance of rebellion so honourably conducted?" exclaimed Jefferson, of the Massachusetts anarchical outburst, nearly a year after it had ended; and continued thus: —

"God forbid! we should ever be 20 years without such a rebellion. . . . What country can preserve its liberties if their rulers are not warned from time to time that their people preserve the spirit of resistance? Let them take arms! . . . What signify a few lives lost in a century or two? The tree of liberty must be refreshed from time to time with the blood of patriots & tyrants. It is its natural manure." [2]

Thus did his contact with a decadent monarchy on the one hand and an enchanting philosophy on

---

[1] Jefferson to Mrs. Adams, Feb. 22, 1787; *Works:* Ford, v, 263.
[2] Jefferson to Smith, Nov. 13, 1787; *ib.*, 362.

the other hand, help to fit him for the leadership of American radicalism. No better training for that mission could have been afforded. French thought was already challenging all forms of existing public control; it was a spirit Gamaliel which found in Jefferson an eager Saul at its feet; and American opinion was prepared for its doctrines. In the United States general dislike and denunciation of the established governments had uncovered the feeling against government itself which lay at the root of opposition to any stronger one.

The existing American system was a very masterpiece of weakness. The so-called Federal Government was like a horse with thirteen bridle reins, each held in the hands of separate drivers who usually pulled the confused and powerless beast in different directions. Congress could make treaties with foreign nations; but each of the States could and often did violate them at will. It could borrow money, but could not levy taxes or impose duties to pay the debt. Congress could get money only by making humble requests, called "requisitions," on the "sovereign" Commonwealths. It had to depend upon the whims of the various States for funds to discharge principal and interest of public obligations; and these springs of revenue, when not entirely dry, yielded so little that the Federal establishment was like to die of financial thirst.[1]

[1] "The payments from the States under the calls of Congress have in no year borne any proportion to the public wants. During the last year . . . the aggregate payments . . . fell short of 400,000 doll[rs], a sum neither equal to the interest due on the foreign debts, nor even to the current expenses of the federal Government. The greatest part of

ANTAGONISM TO GOVERNMENT

The requisitions of Congress upon the various States for money to pay the National obligations to foreign creditors were usually treated with neglect and often with contempt by those jealous and pompous "Sovereignties." "Requisitions are a perfect nullity where thirteen sovereign, independent, disunited States are in the habit of discussing and refusing compliance with them at their option. Requisitions are actually little better than a jest and a by-word throughout the land. If you tell the legislatures they have violated the treaty of peace, and invaded the prerogatives of the confederacy, they will laugh in your face." [1] Thus raged Washington. "Congress cannot command money" even to redeem Americans held in slavery in Algiers,[2] testified the powerless and despondent Secretary of State. Indeed, Congress amounted to so little that the delegates from many States often refused to attend.[3]

Though debts were great and financial confusion

this sum too went from Virg^a, which will not supply a single shilling the present year." (Madison to Jefferson, March 18, 1786; *Writings:* Hunt, ii, 228.)

[1] Washington to Jay, Aug. 1, 1786; *Writings:* Ford, xi, 54–55.

[2] Jay (Secretary of State under the Confederation) to Jefferson, Dec. 14, 1786; *Jay:* Johnston, iii, 223.

[3] "We are wasting our time & labour in vain efforts to do business" (because of State delegates not attending), wrote Jefferson in 1784. (Jefferson to Washington, March 15, 1784; *Works:* Ford, iv, 266.) And at the very climax of our difficulties "a sufficient number of States to do business have not been represented in Congress." (Jay to Wm. Carmichael, Jan. 4, 1786; *Jay:* Johnston, iii, 225.) During half of September and all of October, November, December, January, and February, nine States "have not been represented in congress"; and this even after the Constitution had been adopted. (Jay to Jefferson, March 9, 1789; *Jay:* Johnston, iii, 365.)

maddening, they furnished no solid excuse for the failure of the States to enable Congress to preserve American honor by the payment of our admitted National debt. Jay reviewed the situation and showed that "the resources of the country ... notwithstanding all appearances to the contrary, are abundant.... Our country is fertile, abounding in useful productions, and those productions in demand and bearing a good price."[1] The general opinion appears to have been that the people did not want to support the Government.

"The treasury is empty, though the country abounds in resources, and our people are far more unwilling than unable to pay taxes," wrote Jay, early in 1787.[2] Madison excused his support of the bill authorizing tobacco to be taken for specie in payment of taxes, upon the ground that it "could not be rejected without ... exciting some worse project of

[1] Jay to Jefferson, Dec. 14, 1786; *Jay:* Johnston, iii, 223–24. And Melancton Smith declared that "the farmer cultivates his land and reaps the fruit.... The merchant drives his commerce and none can deprive him of the gain he honestly acquires.... The mechanic is exercised in his art, and receives the reward of his labour." (1797–98; Ford: *P. on C.*, 94.) Of the prosperity of Virginia, Grigsby says, "our agriculture was most prosperous, and our harbors and rivers were filled with ships. The shipping interest ... was really advancing most rapidly to a degree of success never known in the colony." (Grigsby, i, footnote to p. 82; and see his brilliant account of Virginia's prosperity at this time; *ib.*, 9–19.) "The spirit of industry throughout the country was never greater. The productions of the earth abound," wrote Jay to B. Vaughan, Sept. 2, 1784. (*Jay:* Johnston, iii, 132.)

[2] Jay to John Adams, Feb. 21, 1787; *Jay:* Johnston, iii, 235. Jay thought that the bottom of the trouble was that "relaxation in government and extravagance in individuals create much public and private distress, and much public and private want of good faith." (*Ib.*, 224.)

a popular cast"; [1] and "by a fear that some greater evil under the name of relief to the people would be substituted." [2] Debt "made it extremely inconvenient to most people to submit to a regular government," was the conclusion Rutledge finally reached.[3]

But, whatever the cause, the States did not act. Washington thought it a combination of the scheming of demagogues and the ignorance and dishonesty of the people. "I think there is more wickedness than ignorance mixed in our councils. . . . Ignorance and design are difficult to combat. . . . To be so fallen! so lost! . . . Virtue, I fear has in a great degree taken its departure from our land and the want of a disposition to do justice is the source of the national embarrassments; for, whatever guise or colorings are given to them, this I apprehend is the origin of the evils we now feel." [4] Such was Washington's cry of despair four years after he had wrested American liberty from Great Britain.

Look where one will among the class of men of whom Washington was the highest representative, one finds that they believed the fountain head of the country's desperate conditions to be in the people

[1] Madison to Jefferson, Dec. 4, 1786; *Writings:* Hunt, ii, 293. "This indulgence to the people as it is called & considered was so warmly wished for out of doors, and so strenuously pressed within that it could not be rejected without danger of exciting some worse project of a popular cast." (*Ib.*)

[2] Madison to Washington, Dec. 24, 1786; *ib.*, 301. "My acquiescence in the measure was against every general principle which I have embraced, and was extorted by a fear that some greater evil under the name of relief to the people would be substituted." (*Ib.*)

[3] Rutledge to Jay, May 2, 1789; *Jay:* Johnston, iii, 368.

[4] Washington to Jay, May 18, 1786; *Writings:* Ford, xi, 31-32.

themselves. Jay put this opinion in a nutshell when he said, "The mass of men are neither wise nor good."[1] Not that these leaders despaired that an American People would finally be evolved who should realize the exalted expectations of the patriot leaders of the Revolution; not that out of the flux of popular heedlessness and dishonor, indifference and disorder, idleness and avarice, the nobler qualities of human nature would not, in the end, bring forth a nation and rule it for the happiness and well-being of its people. But they thought that only a strong government could fashion the clay and breathe into its nostrils the breath of life. "Virtue, like the other resources of a country, can only be drawn to a point and exerted by strong circumstances ably managed, or a strong government ably administered," said Jay.[2]

The shield of all this turmoil and baseness was the State Governments. "Their unreasonable jealousy of that body [Congress] and of one another ... will, if there is not a change in the system, be our downfall as a nation," exclaimed Washington only a few months after peace had been established.[3] It was the States, he declared, which made the Federal establishment "a half-starved, limping government, that appears to be always moving upon crutches and tottering at every step."[4]

It was the States which always were thwarting every plan for the general welfare; the States which

[1] Jay to Washington, June 27, 1786; *Jay:* Johnston, iii, 204.
[2] *Ib.*, 205.
[3] Washington to Harrison, Jan. 18, 1784; *Writings:* Ford, x, 345.
[4] *Ib.*

were forever impairing the National obligations; the States which bound hand and foot the straw man of the central power, clothed it in rags and made it a mere scarecrow of government. And it was State pride, prejudice, and ignorance which gave provincial demagogues their advantage and opportunity. The State Governments were the "people's" Governments; to yield State "sovereignty" was to yield the "people's" power over their own affairs, shouted the man who wished to win local prominence, power, and office.

Those who did not want to pay taxes and who disliked much government of any kind felt that they could make shift with mere State establishments.[1] "A thirst for power, and the bantling, I had liked to have said monster for sovereignty, which have taken such fast hold of the States individually, will, when joined by the many whose personal consequence in the control of State politics will in a manner be annihilated, form a strong phalanx against"[2] the National Constitution, prophesied the leader of the Revolution.

But it was not alone the powerlessness of the Federal Government to keep the National faith, plighted by solemn treaties with foreign Governments; or to uphold the National honor by paying debts made to win American independence, that wrought that bloodless revolution[3] which produced the Constitution. Nor was it the proud and far-

[1] See Madison's masterful summary of the wickedness, weakness, and folly of the State Governments in *Writings:* Hunt, ii, 361–69.
[2] Washington to Jay, March 10, 1787; *Writings:* Ford, xi, 125.
[3] See *supra*, chap. VI.

seeing plans of a few great minds whose heart's desire was to make the American People a Nation.

Finance, commerce, and business assembled the historic Philadelphia Convention; although it must be said that statesmanship guided its turbulent councils. The senseless and selfish nagging at trade in which the States indulged, after peace was declared, produced a brood of civil abuses as noisome as the military dangers which State control of troops had brought forth during the Revolution. Madison truly said that "most of our political evils may be traced up to our commercial ones." [1] The States passed tariff laws against one another as well as against foreign nations; and, indeed, as far as commerce was concerned, each State treated the others as foreign nations.[2] There were retaliations, dis-

[1] Madison to Jefferson, March 18, 1786; *Writings:* Hunt, ii, 228. "Another unhappy effect of a continuance of the present anarchy of our commerces will be a continuance of the unfavorable balance on it, which by draining us of our metals, furnishes pretexts for the pernicious substitution of paper money, for indulgencies to debtors, for postponements of taxes." (*Ib.*)

[2] Virginia carefully defined her revenue boundaries as against Pennsylvania and Maryland; and provided that any vessel failing to enter and pay duties as provided by the Virginia tariff laws might be seized by any person and prosecuted "one half to the use of the informer, and the other half to the use of the commonwealth." (Va. Statutes at Large (1785), chap. 14, 46.)

Virginia strengthened her tariff laws against importations by land. "If any such importer or owner shall unload any such wagon or other carriage containing any of the above goods, wares, or merchandise brought into this state by land without first having entered the same as directed above, every such wagon or other carriage, together with the horses thereto belonging and all such goods wares and merchandise as shall be brought therein, shall be forfeited and recovered by information in the court of the county; two-thirds to the informer and one-third toward lessening the levy of the county where such conviction shall be made." (*Ib.*)

Even Pennsylvania, already the principal workshop of the country,

criminations, and every manner of trade restrictions and impediments which local ingenuity and selfishness could devise.

The idea of each State was to keep money from going outside its borders into other States and to build up its own business and prosperity at the expense of its neighbors.[1] States having no seaports were in a particularly hard case. Madison picturesquely describes their unhappy plight: "New Jersey placed between Phil^a & N. York, was likened to a cask tapped at both ends; And N. Carolina, between Virg^a & S. Carolina to a patient bleeding at both Arms."[2] Merchants and commercial bodies were at their wits' end to carry on business and petitioned for a general power over commerce.[3]

The commercial view, as stated by Madison, was

while enacting an avowedly protective tariff on "Manufactures of Europe and Other foreign parts," included "cider, malted barley or grain, fish, salted or dried, cheese, butter, beef, pork, barley, peas, mustard, manufactured tobacco" which came, mostly, from sister States. The preamble declares that the duties are imposed to protect "the artisans and mechanics of this state" without whose products "the war could not have been carried on."

In addition to agricultural articles named above, the law includes "playing cards, hair powder, wrought gold or silver utensils, polished or cut stones, musical instruments, walking canes, testaments, psalters, spelling books or primers, romances, novels and plays, and horn or tortoise shell combs," none of which could be called absolutely indispensable to the conduct of the war. The preamble gives the usual arguments for protective tariffs. It is the first protective tariff law, in the present-day sense, ever passed. (Pa. Statutes at Large (1785), 99.)

[1] Even at the present time the various States have not recovered from this anti-National and uneconomic practice, as witness the tax laws and other statutes in almost every State designed to prevent investments by the citizens of that State in industries located in other States. Worse, still, are the multitude of State laws providing variable control over railways that are essentially National.

[2] *Writings:* Hunt, ii, 395.   [3] Marshall (1st ed.), v, 76–79.

that "the National Government should be armed with positive and compleat authority in all cases which require uniformity; such as the regulation of trade, including the right of taxing both exports & imports, the fixing the terms and forms of naturalization, &c., &c."

Madison then lays down this extreme Nationalist principle as the central article of his political faith: "Over and above this positive power, a negative *in all cases whatsoever* on the legislative acts of the States, as heretofore exercised by the Kingly prerogative, appears to me to be absolutely necessary, and to be the least possible encroachment on the State jurisdictions. Without this defensive power, every positive power that can be given on paper will be evaded & defeated. The States will continue to invade the National jurisdiction, to violate treaties and the law of nations & to harass each other with rival and spiteful measures dictated by mistaken views of interest." [1]

Too much emphasis cannot be put upon the fact that the mercantile and financial interests were the weightiest of all the influences for the Constitution; the debtors and agricultural interests the strongest groups against it. It deserves repetition, for a proper understanding of the craft and force practiced by both sides in the battle over ratification, that those who owed debts were generally against the Constitution and practically all to whom debts were due

[1] Madison to Washington, April 16, 1787; *Writings:* Hunt, ii, 345–46. This ultra-Nationalist opinion is an interesting contrast to Madison's States' Rights views a few years later. (See *infra*, vol. II, chaps. II, III, and IV.)

were for the new Government. "I have little prospect of bringing Banks [a debtor] to terms as the Law of this State now stands," wrote a Virginia agent of a creditor, "but I hope when the New Federal constitution is adopted that the Laws will be put upon a better footing. . . . Three fourths of the people that oppose it [the Constitution] are those that are deeply in debt & do not wish to pay." [1]

London merchants were very anxious for a new order of things. "I hope ere long your Federal Government will be established, and that honest Men will again have the Assendency in your Country, for without such a change it must ever remain a poor place to live in," was the opinion of a business man living in the British Capital.[2]

A few weeks after Virginia ratified the Constitution, Minton Collins reported to his principal about a person named Banks, who, says Collins, "begins to be a little alarmed from the adoption of the Federal Constitution. I hope it will alarm every such R[asca]l. He had run his rig long enough for he boasts of being worth from 150,000£ to 200,000 pounds; this is not bad for a man that six years ago could scarcely raise a suit of clothes to his back." [3]

Marshall was becoming a prosperous lawyer and his best clients were from the mercantile interests. His family relationships were coming to be more and more with the property classes. He had no ambition

[1] Minton Collins at Richmond to Stephen Collins at Philadelphia, May 8, 1788; MS., Lib. Cong.
[2] Sam Smith in London to Stephen Collins in Philadelphia, July 21, 1788; *ib.*
[3] Minton Collins to Stephen Collins, Aug. 9, 1788; *ib.*

for a political career, which might have given to his thinking and conclusions a "more popular cast," to use Madison's contemptuous phrase. Thus Marshall's economic and political convictions resulting from experience and reasoning were in harmony with his business connections and social environment.

Undoubtedly he would have taken the same stand had none of these circumstances developed; his constructive mind, his conservative temperament, his stern sense of honor, his abhorrence of disorder and loose government, his army experience, his legislative schooling, his fidelity to and indeed adoration of Washington, would have surely placed him on the side of the Constitution. Still, the professional and social side of his life should not be ignored, if we are to consider fully all the forces which then surrounded him, and which, with ever-growing strength, worked out the ultimate Marshall.

Jefferson, in France, experienced only the foreign results of the sharp and painful predicament which John Marshall was sadly witnessing in America. While not busy with the scholars and society of the French Capital, Jefferson had been engaged in the unhappy official task of staving off our French creditors and quieting, as well as he could, complaints of our trade regulations and other practices which made it hard and hazardous for the French to do business with us.[1] He found that "the nonpaiment of our

[1] "Vergennes complained, and with a good deal of stress, that they did not find a sufficient dependence on arrangements taken with us. This was the third time, too, he had done it.... He observed too, that the administration of justice with us was tardy, insomuch that their merchants, when they had money due to them within our States,

ANTAGONISM TO GOVERNMENT 315

debts and the want of energy in our government . . . discourage a connection with us"; [1] and "want of punctuality & a habitual protection of the debtor" prevented him from getting a loan in France to aid the opening of the Potomac.[2] All this caused even Jefferson to respond to the demand for unifying the American Government as to foreign nations; but he would not go further. "Make the States one as to every thing connected with foreign nations, & several as to everything purely domestic," counseled Jefferson while the Constitutional Convention was quarreling at Philadelphia.[3]

But he did not think badly of the weakness of the Articles of Confederation which so aroused the disgust, anger, and despair of Washington, Madison, Jay, and other men of their way of thinking, who were on the ground. "With all the imperfections of our present government [Articles of Confederation]," wrote Jefferson in Paris, in 1787, "it is without comparison the best existing or that ever did exist"; [4] and he declared to one of his French friends that "the confederation is a wonderfully perfect instrument." [5] Jefferson found but three serious defects in the Articles of Confederation: no general rule for admitting States; the apportionment of the State's

considered it as desperate; and that our commercial regulations, in general, were disgusting to them." (Jefferson's Report; *Works:* Ford, iv, 487.)

[1] Jefferson to Stuart, Jan. 25, 1786; *ib.*, v, 74.
[2] Jefferson to Madison, Dec. 16, 1786; *ib.*, v, 230.
[3] Jefferson to Carrington, Paris, Aug. 4, 1787; *ib.*, 318; also 332; and Jefferson to Wythe, Sept. 16, 1787; *ib.*, 340.
[4] Jefferson to Carrington, Paris, Aug. 4, 1787; *ib.*, 318.
[5] Jefferson to Meusnier, Jan. 24, 1786; *ib.*, 8.

quota of money upon a land instead of a population basis; and the imperfect power over treaties, import duties, and commerce.[1]

He frankly said: "I am not a friend to a very energetic government"; and he thought that "our governments will remain virtuous for many centuries" — but added with seer-like vision: "as long as ... there shall be vacant lands in America."[2] Jefferson wished the United States "to practice neither commerce nor navigation, but to stand with respect to Europe precisely on the footing of China."[3] Far from thinking that the low state of our credit was a bad thing for us, he believed that its destruction would work an actual benefit to America. "Good will arise from the destruction of our credit," he asserted in a letter to Stuart written from Paris in 1786. "I see nothing else which can restrain our disposition to luxury, and the loss of those manners which alone can preserve republican government."[4]

We have now seen the state of the country and the condition of the people, their situation and habits, their manner of life and trend of feeling. We have witnessed the change thus wrought in the leading men during this period, so destructive of confidence in the wisdom or virtue of majorities, at least on first impulse and without abundant time for reflection and second thought. Thus we have measured,

[1] Jefferson to Meusnier, Jan. 24, 1786; *Works:* Ford, v, 8.
[2] Jefferson to Madison, Dec. 20, 1787; *ib.*, 373-74. Jefferson concluded, prophetically, that when the people "get piled upon one another, in large cities, as in Europe, they will become as corrupt as Europe." (*Ib.*)
[3] Jefferson to Hogendorp, Oct. 13, 1785; *ib.*, iv, 469.
[4] Jefferson to Stuart, Jan. 25, 1786; *ib.*, v, 74.

ANTAGONISM TO GOVERNMENT 317

with some degree of accuracy, the broad and well-marked space that separated the hostile forces which were to meet in what was for the moment a decisive conflict when Virginia's Constitutional Convention should assemble at Richmond.

In one camp the uninformed and credulous, those who owed debts and abhorred government, with a sprinkling among them of eminent, educated, and well-meaning men who were philosophic apostles of theoretical liberty; and in the other camp men of property and lovers of order, the trading and moneyed interests whose first thought was business; the veterans of the Revolution who had learned on the battlefield the need of a strong central Government; and, here and there, a prophetic and constructive mind who sought to build a Nation. John Marshall was one of the latter; and so he promptly took his place by the side of his old general and leader in the camp of the builders.

At last the supreme hour is striking. The Virginians, about to assemble in State Convention, will determine the fate of that unauthorized and revolutionary plan for a National Government,[1] the National Constitution. The movement for a second general Convention to have another try at framing a Constitution has made distinct progress by the time the Virginia representatives gather at the State Capital.[2] There is widespread, positive, and growing resentment at the proposed new form of government;

[1] See *infra*, chap. IX.
[2] For a careful study of this important but neglected subject see Professor Edward Payson Smith's paper in Jameson, 46–115.

and if Virginia, the largest and most populous of the States, rejects it, the flames of opposition are certain to break out in every part of the country. As Washington asserts, there is, indeed, "combustible material" everywhere.

Thus it is that the room where Virginia's Convention is about to meet in June, 1788, will become the "bloody angle" in the first great battle for Nationalism. And Marshall will be there, a combatant as he had been at Great Bridge and Brandywine. Not for John Marshall the pallid rôle of the trimmer, but the red-blooded part of the man of conviction.

CHAPTER IX

THE STRUGGLE FOR RATIFICATION

The plot thickens fast. A few short weeks will determine the political fate of America. (Washington.)

On Sunday, June 1, 1788, the dust lay deep in the streets of the little town of Richmond. Multitudes of horses were tethered here and there or stabled as best the Virginia Capital's meager accommodations permitted. Cavalcades of mounted men could be seen from Shockoe Hill, wending their way over the imperfect earthen roads from every direction to the center of interest.[1] Some of these had come hundreds of miles and arrived in the garb of the frontier, pistol and hanger at belt.[2] Patrick Henry, prematurely old at fifty-two, came in a one-horse, uncovered gig; Pendleton, aged, infirm, and a cripple, arrived in a phaeton.[3]

As we have seen, it was very hard for members of Virginia's Legislature to get to the seat of the State Government even from counties not far distant; and a rainy season, or even one week's downpour during the latter part of May, would have kept large numbers of the members of the Virginia Convention from reaching their destination in time and perhaps have decided the impending struggle[4] before it

---

[1] Grigsby, i, 25.
[2] Travelers from the District of Kentucky or from the back settlements of Virginia always journeyed fully armed, in readiness to defend themselves from attack by Indians or others in their journey through the wilderness.
[3] Grigsby, i, 27-28.   [4] *Ib.*, 25.

began. The year's great social and sporting event added to the throng and colored the dark background of political anxiety and apprehension with a faint tinge of gayety.[1]

Although seven months had elapsed since the Federal Convention had finished its work, there was, nevertheless, practically no accurate knowledge among the people of the various parts of the " New Plan " of government. Even some members of the Virginia State Convention had never seen a copy of the Constitution until they arrived in Richmond to deliberate upon it and decide its fate.[2] Some of the most inquiring men of this historic body had not read a serious or convincing argument for it or against it.[3] "The greater part of the members of the [Virginia] convention will go to the meeting without information on the subject," wrote Nicholas to Madison immediately after the election of delegates.[4]

One general idea, however, had percolated through the distances and difficulties of communication to the uninformed minds of the people — the idea that the new Constitution would form a strong, consolidated National Government, superior to and dominant over the State Governments; a National Sovereignty overawing State Sovereignties, dangerous to

[1] The Jockey Club was holding its annual races at Richmond when the Constitutional Convention of 1788 convened. (Christian, 31.)

[2] Grigsby, i, 31.

[3] Humphrey Marshall, from the District of Kentucky, saw for the first time one number of the *Federalist*, only after he had reached the more thickly peopled districts of Virginia while on his way to the Convention. (*Ib.*, footnote to 31.)

[4] George Nicholas to Madison, April 5, 1788; *Writings:* Hunt, v, footnote to p. 115.

if not entirely destructive of the latter; a general and powerful authority beyond the people's reach, which would enforce contracts, collect debts, impose taxes; above all, a bayonet-enforced rule from a distant point, that would imperil and perhaps abolish "liberty." [1]

So a decided majority of the people of Virginia were against the proposed fundamental law; [2] for, as in other parts of the country, few of Virginia's masses wanted anything stronger than the weak and ineffective Government of the State and as little even of that as possible. Some were "opposed to any system, was it even sent from heaven, which tends to confirm the union of the States." [3] Madison's father reported the Baptists to be "generally opposed to it"; and the planters who went to Richmond to sell their tobacco had returned foes of the "new plan" and had spread the uprising against it among others "who are no better acquainted with the necessity of adopting it than they themselves." [4] At first the friends of the Constitution deceived themselves into thinking that the work of the Philadelphia Convention met with approval in Virginia; but they soon found that "the tide next took a sudden and strong turn in the opposite direction." [5] Henry wrote to

---

[1] "The most common and ostensible objection was that it [the Constitution] would endanger state rights and personal liberty — that it was too strong." (Humphrey Marshall, i, 285.)

[2] Tyler, i, 142. Grigsby estimates that three fourths of the people of Virginia were opposed to the Constitution. (Grigsby, i, footnote to 160.)

[3] Lee to Madison, Dec. 1787; *Writings:* Hunt, v, footnote to p. 88.

[4] Madison's father to Madison, Jan. 30, 1788; *Writings:* Hunt, v, footnote to p. 105.

[5] Madison to Jefferson, Feb. 19, 1788; *ib.*, 103.

Lamb that "Four-fifths of our inhabitants are opposed to the new scheme of government"; and he added that south of the James River "I am confident nine-tenths are opposed to it." [1]

That keen and ever-watchful merchant, Minton Collins, thus reported to the head of his commercial house in Philadelphia: "The New Federal Constitution will meet with much opposition in this State [Virginia] for many pretended patriots has taken a great deal of pains to poison the minds of the people against it. . . . There are two Classes here who oppose it, the one is those who have power & are unwilling to part with an atom of it, & the others are the people who owe a great deal of money, and are very unwilling to pay, as they are afraid this Constitution will make them *Honest Men* in spite of their teeth." [2]

And now the hostile forces are to meet in final and decisive conflict. Now, at last, the new Constitution is to be really *debated;* and debated openly before the people and the world. For the first time, too, it is to be opposed in argument by men of the highest order in ability, character, and standing — men who cannot be hurried, or bullied, or shaken, or bought. The debates in the Virginia Convention of 1788 are the only masterful discussions on *both* sides of the controversy that ever took place.

While the defense of the Constitution had been very able in Pennsylvania and Massachusetts (and

[1] Henry to Lamb, June 9, 1788; Henry, ii, 342.
[2] Minton Collins to Stephen Collins, March 16, 1788; Collins MSS., Lib. Cong.

later in New York was to be most brilliant), the attack upon it in the Virginia Convention was nowhere equaled or approached in power, learning, and dignity. Extravagant as the assertion appears, it nevertheless is true that the Virginia contest was the only real *debate* over the whole Constitution. It far surpassed, especially in presenting the reasons against the Constitution, the discussion in the Federal Convention itself, in weight of argument and attractiveness of presentation, as well as in the ability and distinction of the debaters.

The general Federal Convention that framed the Constitution at Philadelphia was a secret body; and the greatest pains were taken that no part of its proceedings should get to the public until the Constitution itself was reported to Congress. The Journals were confided to the care of Washington and were not made public until many years after our present Government was established. The framers of the Constitution ignored the purposes for which they were delegated; they acted without any authority whatever; and the document, which the warring factions finally evolved from their quarrels and dissensions, was revolutionary.[1] This capital fact

[1] Even Hamilton admitted this. "The framers of it [the Constitution] will have to encounter the disrepute of having brought about a revolution in government, without substituting anything that was worthy of the effort; they pulled down one Utopia, it will be said, to build up another." (Hamilton to Washington, Sept., 1788; Hamilton's *Works*: Lodge, ix, 444; and also in Jefferson, *Writings*: Ford, xi, footnote to 330.) Martin Van Buren describes the action of the Federal Convention that framed the Constitution, in "having . . . set aside the instructions of Congress by making a new Constitution . . . an heroic but lawless act." (Van Buren, 49–50.)

Professor Burgess does not overstate the case when he declares:

requires iteration, for it is essential to an understanding of the desperate struggle to secure the ratification of that then unpopular instrument.

"Not one legislature in the United States had the most distant idea when they first appointed members for a [Federal] convention, entirely commercial . . . that they would without any warrant from their constituents, presume on so bold and daring a stride," truthfully writes the excitable Gerry of Massachusetts in his bombastic denunciation of "the fraudulent usurpation at Philadelphia." [1] The more reliable Melancton Smith of New York testifies that "previous to the meeting of the Convention the subject of a new form of government had been little thought of and scarcely written upon at all. . . . The idea of a government similar to" the Constitution "never entered the minds of the legislatures who appointed the Convention and of but very few of the members who composed it, until they had assembled and heard it proposed in that body." [2]

"Had the idea of a total change [from the Confederation] been started," asserts the trustworthy Richard Henry Lee of Virginia, "probably no state would have appointed members to the Convention. . . . Probably not one man in ten thousand in the United States . . . had an idea that the old ship [Confederation] was to be destroyed. Pennsylvania

---

"Had Julius or Napoleon committed these acts [of the Federal Convention in framing and submitting the Constitution], they would have been pronounced *coups d'état*." (Burgess, i, 105.)

Also see Beard: *Econ. I. C.*, 217–18.

[1] Ford: *P. on C.*, 14. [2] *Ib.*, 100–01.

appointed principally those men who are esteemed aristocratical. . . . Other States . . . chose men principally connected with commerce and the judicial department." Even so, says Lee, "the non-attendance of eight or nine men" made the Constitution possible. "We must recollect, how disproportionately the democratic and aristocratic parts of the community were represented" in this body.[1]

This "child of fortune,"[2] as Washington called the Constitution, had been ratified with haste and little or no discussion by Delaware, New Jersey, Connecticut, and Georgia. The principal men in the first three Commonwealths felt that the Constitution gave those States large commercial advantages and even greater political consequence;[3] and Georgia, with so small a population as to be almost negligible, felt the need of some strong Government to defend her settlers against the Indians. It is doubtful whether many of the people of these four States had read the Constitution or had heard much about it, except that, in a general way, they were to be better off under the new than under the old arrangement.

[1] Ford: *P. on C.*, 284–85. And see Jameson, 40–49.

[2] Washington to Lafayette, Sept. 18, 1788; *Writings:* Sparks, ix, 265.

[3] Connecticut, New Jersey, and Delaware had practically no ports and, under the Confederation, were at the mercy of Massachusetts, New York, and Pennsylvania in all matters of trade. The Constitution, of course, remedied this serious defect. Also, these smaller States had forced the compromise by which they, with their comparatively small populations, were to have an equal voice in the Senate with New York, Pennsylvania, and Virginia, with their comparatively great populations. And therefore they would have practically equal weight in the law- and treaty-making power of the Government. This was the most formidable of the many rocks on which the Federal Convention all but broke up.

Their ratification carried no weight other than to make up four of the nine States necessary to set the new system in motion.

In other States its friends had whipped up all possible speed. Not a week had passed after the Federal Convention had laid the proposed Constitution before Congress when a resolution was introduced in the Legislature of Pennsylvania for the election, within five weeks,[1] of delegates to a State Convention to ratify the "New Plan." When its opponents, failing in every other device to delay or defeat it, refused to attend the sessions, thus breaking a quorum, a band of Constitutionalists "broke into their lodgings, seized them, dragged them though the streets to the State House and thrust them into the Assembly room with clothes torn and faces white with rage." And there the objecting members were forcibly kept until the vote was taken. Thus was the quorum made and the majority of the Legislature enabled to "pass" the ordinance for calling the Pennsylvania State Convention to ratify the National Constitution.[2] And this action was taken before the Legislature had even received from Congress a copy of that document.

[1] One proposition was to call the State Convention "within *ten days*." (See "Address of the Minority of the Pennsylvania Convention," in McMaster and Stone, 458.)

[2] *Ib.*, 3–4; and see *ib.*, 75. An excuse for these mob methods was that the Legislature previously had resolved to adjourn *sine die* on that very day. This would put off action until the next session. The Anti-Constitutionalists urged — with entire truthfulness — that even this delay would give the people too little time to inform themselves upon the "New Plan" of government, as it was called, which the Convention was to pass upon in the people's name. "Not one in twenty know anything about it." (Mr. Whitehall in debate in the Legislature; *ib.*, 32.)

THE STRUGGLE FOR RATIFICATION

The enemies in Pennsylvania of the proposed National Government were very bitter. They said that the Legislature had been under the yoke of Philadelphia — a charge which, indeed, appears to be true. Loud were the protests of the minority against the feverish haste. When the members of the Pennsylvania Convention, thus called, had been chosen and had finished their work, the Anti-Constitutionalists asserted that no fair election had really taken place because it "was held at so early a period and want of information was so great" that the people did not know that such an election was to be held; and they proved this to their own satisfaction by showing that, although seventy thousand Pennsylvanians were entitled to vote, only thirteen thousand of them really had voted and that the forty-six members of the Pennsylvania Convention who ratified the Constitution had been chosen by only sixty-eight hundred voters. Thus, they pointed out, when the State Convention was over, that the Federal Constitution had been ratified in Pennsylvania by men who represented less than one tenth of the voting population of the State.[1]

[1] McMaster and Stone, 459-60. This charge was wholly accurate. Both sides exerted themselves to carry the "election." The Anti-Constitutionalists declared that they stood for "the principles of the Revolution"; yet, asserts Graydon, who was at Reading at the time, they sought the support of the Tories; the country lawyers were opposed to the "New Plan" and agreed not "to practice or accept any office under the Constitution"; but the Constitutionalists promised "prothonotaryships, attorney generalships, chief justiceships, and what not," and the hostile attorneys "were tempted and did eat." Describing the spirit of the times, Graydon testifies that "pelf was a better goal than liberty and at no period in my recollection was the worship of Mammon more widely spread, more sordid and disgusting."

Everybody who wanted it had a military title, that of major being

Indeed, a supporter of the Constitution admitted that only a small fraction of the people did vote for members of the Pennsylvania State Convention; but he excused this on the ground that Pennsylvanians seldom voted in great numbers except in contested elections; and he pointed out that in the election of the Convention which framed the State's Constitution itself, only about six thousand had exercised their right of suffrage and that only a little more than fifteen hundred votes had been cast in the whole Commonwealth to elect Pennsylvania's first Legislature.[1]

The enemies of the proposed plan for a National Government took the ground that it was being rushed through by the "aristocrats"; and the "Independent Gazetteer" published "The humble address of the *low born* of the United States of America, to their fellow slaves scattered throughout the world," which sarcastically pledged that "we, the *low born*, that is,

"the very lowest that a dasher of any figure would accept." To "clap on a uniform and a pair of epaulettes, and scamper about with some militia general for a day or two" was enough to acquire the coveted rank. Thus, those who had never been in the army, but "had played a safe and calculating game" at home and "attended to their interests," were not only "the men of mark and consideration," but majors, colonels, and generals as well. (Graydon, 331-33.)

Noting, at a later time, this passion for military titles Weld says: "In every part of America a European is surprised at finding so many men with military titles . . . but no where . . . is there such a superfluity of these military personages as in the little town of Staunton; there is hardly a decent person in it . . . but what is a colonel, a major, or a captain." (Weld, i, 236-37.)

Such were the conditions in the larger towns when the members of the Pennsylvania Convention were chosen. The small vote cast seems to justify the charge that the country districts and inaccessible parts of the State did not even know of the election.

[1] McMaster and Stone, 503-04.

all the people of the United States, except 600 or thereabouts, *well born*," would "allow and admit the said 600 *well born* immediately to establish and confirm this most noble, most excellent, and truly divine constitution." [1]

James Wilson, they said, had been all but mobbed by the patriots during the Revolution; he never had been for the people, but always "strongly tainted with the spirit of *high aristocracy*." [2] Yet such a man, they declared, was the ablest and best person the Constitutionalists could secure to defend "that political monster, the proposed Constitution"; "a monster" which had emerged from "the thick veil of secrecy." [3]

When the Pennsylvania State Convention had assembled, the opponents of the Constitution at once charged that the whole business was being speeded by a "system of precipitancy." [4] They rang the changes on the secret gestation and birth of the Nation's proposed fundamental law, which, said Mr. Whitehill, "originates in mystery and must terminate in despotism," and, in the end, surely would annihilate the States.[5] Hardly a day passed that the minority did not protest against the forcing tactics of the majority.[6] While much ability was displayed on both sides, yet the debate lacked dignity, courtesy, judgment, and even information. So scholarly a man as Wilson said that "Virginia has

---
[1] McMaster and Stone, 173–74.
[2] *Independent Gazetteer; ib.*, 183–84.   [3] *Ib.*, 184–85.
[4] Pennsylvania Debates, in McMaster and Stone, 231. Elliott prints only a small part of these debates.
[5] *Ib.*, 283–85.   [6] *Ib.*, 219.

no bill of rights"; [1] and Chief Justice McKean, supported by Wilson, actually declared that none but English-speaking peoples ever had known trial by jury.[2]

"Lack of veracity," "indecent," "trifling," "contempt for arguments and person," were a few of the more moderate, polite, and soothing epithets that filled Pennsylvania's Convention hall throughout this so-called debate. More than once the members almost came to blows.[3] The galleries, filled with city people, were hot for the Constitution and heartened its defenders with cheers. "This is not the voice of the people of Pennsylvania," shouted Smilie, denouncing the partisan spectators. The enemies of the Constitution would not be "intimidated," he dramatically exclaimed, "were the galleries filled with bayonets."[4] The sarcastic McKean observed in reply that Smilie seemed "mighty angry, merely because somebody was pleased."[5]

Persons not members of the Convention managed to get on the floor and laughed at the arguments of those who were against the Constitution. Findley was outraged at this "want of sense of decency and order."[6] Justice McKean treated the minority with contempt and their arguments with derision. "*If the sky falls, we shall catch larks; if the rivers run dry, we shall catch eels,*" was all, said this conciliatory

[1] McMaster and Stone, 253.
[2] Findley covered them with confusion in this statement by citing authority. Wilson irritably quoted in retort the words of Maynard to a student: "Young Man! I have forgotten more law than ever you learned." (*Ib.*, 352-64.)
[3] *Ib.*, 361-63.   [4] *Ib.*, 365.   [5] *Ib.*
[6] *Ib.*, 419.

advocate of the Constitution, that its enemies' arguments amounted to; they made nothing more than a sound "like *the working of small beer*."[1]

The language, manners, and methods of the supporters of the Constitution in the Pennsylvania Convention were resented outside the hall. "If anything could induce me to oppose the New Constitution," wrote a citizen signing himself "Federalist," "it would be the indecent, supercilious carriage of its advocates towards its opponents."[2]

While the Pennsylvania State Convention was sitting, the Philadelphia papers were full of attacks and counter-attacks by the partisans of either side, some of them moderate and reasonable, but most of

[1] McMaster and Stone, 365.
[2] *Ib.*, 453. The conduct of the Pennsylvania supporters of the Constitution aroused indignation in other States, and caused some who had favored the new plan of government to change their views. "On reception of the Report of the [Federal] Convention, I perused, and admir'd it; — Or rather, like many who still *think* they admire it, I loved Geo. Washington — I venerated Benj. Franklin — and therefore concluded that I must love and venerate all the works of their hands; — . . . . The honest and uninformed *freemen* of America entertain the same opinion of those two gentlemen as do European *slaves* of their Princes, — '*that they can do no wrong.*'"

But, continues Wait, "on the unprecedented Conduct of the Pennsylvania Legislature [and Convention] I found myself Disposed to lend an ear to the arguments of the opposition — not with an expectation of being convinced that the new Constitution was defective; but because I thought the minority had been ill used; and I felt a little curious to hear the particulars," with the result that "I am dissatisfied with the proposed Constitution." (Wait to Thatcher, Jan. 8, 1788; *Hist. Mag.* (2d Series), vi, 262; and see *infra*.)

Others did not, even then, entertain Mr. Wait's reverence for Washington, when it came to accepting the Constitution because of his support. When Hamilton asked General Lamb how he could oppose the Constitution when it was certain that his "good friend Genl. Washington would . . . be the first President under it," Lamb "reply'd that . . . after him Genl. Slushington might be the next or second president." (Ledlie to Lamb; MS., N.Y. Hist. Soc.)

them irritating, inflammatory, and absurd. A well-written petition of citizens was sent to the Convention begging it to adjourn until April or May, so that the people might have time to inform themselves on the subject: "The people of Pennsylvania have not yet had sufficient time and opportunity afforded them for this purpose. The great bulk of the people, from the want of leisure from other avocations; their remoteness from information, their scattered situation, and the consequent difficulty of conferring with each other" did not understand the Constitution, declared this memorial.

"The unaccountable zeal and precipitation used to hurry the people into premature decision" had excited and alarmed the masses, "and the election of delegates was rushed into before the greater part of the people . . . knew what part to take in it." So ran the cleverly drawn indictment of the methods of those who were striving for ratification in Pennsylvania.[1] In the State Convention, the foes of the Constitution scathingly denounced to the very last the jamming-through conduct of its friends; and just before the final vote, Smilie dared them to adjourn that the sense of the people might be taken.[2]

Even such of the people as could be reached by the newspapers were not permitted to be enlightened by the Convention "debates"; for reports of them were suppressed.[3] Only the speeches of James Wilson and Chief Justice McKean, both ardent advocates of the Constitution, were allowed to be published.[4]

[1] McMaster and Stone, 432-35.
[2] Ib., 424.   [3] Ib., 14-15.   [4] Ib.

But although outnumbered two to one, cuffed and buffeted without mercy in debate, scoffed at and jeered at by the people of the Quaker City, the minority was stiff-necked and defiant. Their heads were "bloody but unbowed." Three days after the vote for ratification, forty-six "ayes" to twenty-three "nays," had been taken, the minority issued an address to their constituents.[1] It relates the causes which led to the Federal Convention, describes its members, sets forth its usurpation of power, details the efforts to get popular support for the Constitution even "whilst the gilded chains were forging in the secret conclave."

The address recounts the violence by which the State Convention was called, "not many hours" after the "New Plan" had "issued forth from the womb of suspicious secrecy"; and reaffirms the people's ignorance of the Constitution, the trifling vote, the indecorous, hasty, "insulting" debate. It gives the amendments asked for by the minority, and finally presents most if not all the arguments which before had been or since have been advanced against the Constitution, and especially the National principle which pervades it.

The powers given Congress would produce "one consolidated government, which, from the nature of things, will be an *iron handed despotism*"; the State Governments would be annihilated; the general welfare clause would justify anything which "*the will and pleasure* of congress" dictated; that National body, "with complete and unlimited power over

[1] "Address of the Minority"; McMaster and Stone, 454–83.

the *purse* and the *sword*," could [1] by taxation "command the whole or any part of the property of the people" — imposts, land taxes, poll taxes, excises, duties — every kind of tax on every possible species of property and written instrument could be laid by the "monster" of National power. By the Judiciary provided in the Constitution "the rich and wealthy suitors would eagerly lay hold of the infinite mazes, perplexities and delays ... and the poor man being plunged in the bottomless pit of legal discussion" could not get justice.[2]

Two coördinate "sovereignties," State and National, "would be contrary to the nature of things"; the Constitution without a bill of rights "would of itself necessarily produce a despotism"; a standing army might be used to collect the most burdensome taxes and with it "an ambitious man ... may step up into the throne and seize upon absolute power"[3] — such are the broad outlines of the document with which the undismayed enemies of the Constitution began their campaign against it among the people of Pennsylvania after the Convention had ratified it.

The wrath of the Pennsylvania foes of the Constitution fed and grew upon its own extravagance. The friends of the "New Plan" tried to hold a meeting in Carlisle to rejoice over its ratification; but the crowd broke up their meeting, wrecked their cannon, and burned the Constitution in the very bonfire which the Constitutionalists had prepared to celebrate its victory. Blows were struck and violence

[1] "Address of the Minority"; McMaster and Stone, 466.
[2] *Ib.*, 469-70.   [3] *Ib.*, 480.

done.[1] For almost a year, an Anti-Constitutionalist paper in Philadelphia kept up the bombardment of the Constitution and its advocates, its gunner being a writer signing himself "Centinel." [2] His ammunition was a mixture of argument, statement, charge, and abuse, wrapped up in cartridge paper of blistering rhetoric. The Constitution was, wrote "Centinel," a "spurious brat"; "the evil genius of darkness presided at its birth" and "it came forth under the veil of mystery." [3]

Should the small fraction of the people who had voted for the members of the Pennsylvania State Convention bind the overwhelming majority who had not voted, asked "Centinel." No, indeed! The people, wrote he with pen of gall, had nothing but contempt for the "solemn mummery" that had been acted in their name.[4] As to the citizens of Philadelphia, everybody understood, asserted "Centinel," that the "spirit of independency" was dead within *their* breasts; Philadelphia merchants, as was well known, were mere vassals to a commercial "colossus" (Robert Morris) who held the city in "thraldom." [5]

"Mankind in the darkest ages, have never been so insulted," cried "Centinel," as the men of Pennsylvania had been by this "flagrant . . . audacious . . .

[1] See various contemporary accounts of this riot reprinted in McMaster and Stone, 486–94.
[2] The authorship of the "Letters of Centinel" remains unsettled. It seems probable that they were the work of Eleazer Oswald, printer of the *Independent Gazetteer*, and one George Bryan, both of Philadelphia. (See *ib.*, 6–7, and footnote.)
[3] "Letters of Centinel," no. 4, *ib.*, 606.
[4] *Ib.*, 620. [5] *Ib.*, 625.

conspiracy [the Constitution] against the liberties of a free people."[1] The whole thing, he declared, was a dastardly plot. The conspirators had disarmed the militia, kept out of the mails such newspapers as had dared to voice the "people's rights";[2] and "all intercourse between the patriots of America is as far as possible cut off; whilst on the other hand the conspirators have the most exact information, a common concert is everywhere evident; they move in unison."[3]

The Constitutionalists were not content with their vile work in thrusting upon Pennsylvania "the empire of delusion," charged "Centinel,"[4] but their agents were off for Virginia to do the like there.[5] The whole world knew, said he, that the Constitutionalists had rushed the Constitution through in Pennsylvania;[6] and that the "immaculate convention [that framed the Constitution] . . . contained a number of the principal public defaulters,"[7] chief of whom was Robert Morris, who, though a bankrupt in the beginning of the Revolution, had, by "peculation and embezzlement of the public property," accumulated "the immense wealth he has dazzled the world with since."[8]

If only the address of Pennsylvania's heroic minority, "Centinel" lamented, had reached Boston in time, it would "have enabled patriotism to triumph" there; but, of course, the *"high born"* Constitutionalist managers of post-offices kept it back.[9] Was not

[1] McMaster and Stone, 624.
[2] *Ib.*, 630, 637, 639, 642, 653, 655.
[3] *Ib.*, 629.   [4] *Ib.*, 641.   [5] *Ib.*, 631; and see *infra*, chap. xi.
[6] *Ib.*, 639.   [7] *Ib.*, 658.   [8] *Ib.*, 661.   [9] *Ib.*, 667.

THE STRUGGLE FOR RATIFICATION 337

the scandal so foul, asked "Centinel," that, on the petition of Philadelphia printers, Pennsylvania's Legislature appealed to Congress against the suppression of the mails? [1] Of course Philadelphia was for "this system of tyranny"; but three fourths of the people in the eastern counties and nineteen twentieths of those in the middle, northern, and western counties were against it. [2]

The grape and canister which its enemies poured upon the Constitution and its friends in Pennsylvania brought an answering fire. The attacks, said the Constitutionalists, had been written by "hireling writers" and "sowers of sedition"; their slanders showed "what falsehoods disappointed ambition is capable of using to impose upon the public." According to the Constitutionalists, their opponents were "incendiaries" with "infamous designs." [3] "If every lie was to be punished by clipping, as in the case of other forgeries, not an ear would be left amongst the whole party," wrote a Constitutionalist of the conduct of the opposition. [4]

But the Constitutionalists were no match for their enemies in the language of abuse, recklessness in making charges, or plausibility in presenting their case. Mostly they vented their wrath in private correspondence, which availed nothing. Yet the letters of business men were effective in consolidating the commercial interests. Also they illuminate the situation.

[1] McMaster and Stone, 667.   [2] *Ib.*, 668.
[3] "A Real Patriot," in *Independent Gazetteer*, reprinted in McMaster and Stone, 524.
[4] "Gomes," in *ib.*, 527.

"That restless firebrand, the Printer of your city [Oswald, editor of the "Independent Gazetteer"], is running about as if driven by the Devil," wrote a New York merchant to a Philadelphia business correspondent, "seemingly determined to do all the mischief he can; indeed, in my opinion he is an actual incendiary & ought to be the object of legal restraint. He is in his own person a strong argument of the necessity of speedily adopting the new System & putting it into immediate motion." [1]

And "firebrands," indeed, the Anti-Constitutionalists prove themselves in every possible way.

Madison was alarmed. He writes to Jefferson that the "minority ... of Pennsylvania has been extremely intemperate and continues to use very bold and menacing language." [2] Little did Madison then foresee that the very men and forces he now was fighting were laying the foundation for a political party which was to make him President. Far from his thought, at this time, was the possibility of that antipodal change which public sentiment and Jefferson's influence wrought in him two years later. When the fight over the Constitution was being waged, there was no more extreme Nationalist in the whole country than James Madison.

So boiled the stormy Pennsylvania waters through which the Constitution was hastened to port and such was the tempest that strained its moorings after it was anchored in the harbor of ratification.

In Massachusetts, "all the men of abilities, of

[1] H. Chapman to Stephen Collins, June 20, 1788; MS., Lib. Cong. Oswald, like Thomas Paine, was an Englishman.
[2] Madison to Jefferson, Feb. 19, 1788; *Writings:* Hunt, v, 102.

THE STRUGGLE FOR RATIFICATION

property and of influence," [1] were quite as strong for the Constitution as the same class in Pennsylvania; but, impressed by the revolt against the tactics of hurry and force which the latter had employed, the Constitutionalists of the Bay State took an opposite course. Craft, not arrogance, was their policy. They were "wise as serpents," but appeared to be "as harmless as doves." Unlike the methods of the Pennsylvania Constitutionalists, they were moderate, patient, conciliatory, and skillful. They put up Hancock for President of the Convention, in order, as they said, "that we might have advantage of [his] ... name — whether capable of attending or not." [2]

The Massachusetts adversaries of the Constitution were without a leader. Among them "there was not a single character capable of uniting their wills or directing their measures." [3] Their inferiority greatly impressed Madison, who wrote to Pendleton that "there was scarce a man of respectability" among them.[4] They were not able even to state their own case.

[1] Madison to Jefferson, Feb. 19, 1788; *Writings:* Hunt, v, 101.
[2] Gore to Thatcher, June 9, 1788; *Hist. Mag.* (2d Series), vi, 263. This was a very shrewd move; for Hancock had not yet been won over to the Constitution; he was popular with the protesting delegates, and perhaps could not have been defeated had they made him their candidate for presiding officer; the preferment flattered Hancock's abnormal vanity and insured the Constitutionalists against his active opposition; and, most of all, this mark of their favor prepared the way for the decisive use the Constitutionalist leaders finally were able to make of him. Madison describes Hancock as being "weak, ambitious, a courtier of popularity, given to low intrigue." (Madison to Jefferson, Oct. 17, 1788; *Writings:* Hunt, v, 270.)
[3] Madison to Jefferson, Feb. 19, 1788; *Writings:* Hunt, v, 101.
[4] Madison to Pendleton, Feb. 21, 1788; *ib.*, 108.

"The friends of the Constitution, who in addition to their own weight . . . represent a very large proportion of the good sense and property of this State, have the task not only of answering, but also of stating and bringing forward the objections of their opponents," wrote King to Madison.[1] The opponents admitted this themselves. Of course, said they, lawyers, judges, clergymen, merchants, and educated men, all of whom were in favor of the Constitution, could make black look white; but "if we had men of this description on our side" we could run these foxes to earth.[2] Mr. Randall hoped "that these great men of eloquence and learning will not try to *make* arguments to make this Constitution go down, right or wrong. . . . It takes the best men in this state to gloss this Constitution. . . . Suppose . . . these great men would speak half as much against it, we might complete our business and go home in forty-eight hours."[3]

The election of members to the Massachusetts Convention had shown widespread opposition to the proposed establishment of a National Government. Although the Constitutionalists planned well and worked hard, some towns did not want to send delegates at all; forty-six towns finally refused to do so and were unrepresented in the Convention.[4] "Bidde-

[1] King to Madison, Jan. 27, 1788; King, i, 316.
[2] *Ib.*, 317.   [3] Elliott, ii, 40.
[4] Harding, 48. These towns were bitterly opposed to the Constitution. Had they sent delegates, Massachusetts surely would have rejected the Constitution; for even by the aid of the deal hereafter described, there was a very small majority for the Constitution. And if Massachusetts had refused to ratify it, Virginia would, beyond the possibility of a doubt, have rejected it also. (See *infra*, chaps. x,

THE STRUGGLE FOR RATIFICATION 341

ford has backsliden & fallen from a state of Grace to a state of nature, met yesterday & a dumb Devil seized a Majority & they voted not to send, & when called on for a Reason they were dumb, *mirabile dictu!*" [1] King Lovejoy was chosen for Vassalborough; but when the people learned that he would support the Constitution they "called another Meeting, turned him out, & chose another in his room who was desidedly against it." [2]

The division among the people in one county was: "The most reputable characters . . . on . . . *the right* side [for the Constitution] . . . but the middling & common sort . . . on the opposite"; [3] and in another county "the Majority of the Common people" were opposed,[4] which seems to have been generally true throughout the State. Of the sentiment in Worcester, a certain E. Bangs wrote: "I could give you but a very disagreeable account: The most of them entertain such a dread of arbitrary power, that they are afraid even of limited authority. . . . Of upwards of 50 members from this county not more than 7 or 8 delegates are" for the Constitution, "& yet some of them are good men — Not all [Shays's] insurgents I assure you." [5]

Judge Sewall reported from York that the dele-

xi, and xii.) And such action by Massachusetts and Virginia would, with absolute certainty, have doomed the fundamental law by which the Nation to-day exists. Thus it is that the refusal of forty-six Massachusetts towns to send representatives to the State Convention changed the destiny of the Republic.

[1] Hill to Thatcher, Dec. 12, 1787; *Hist. Mag.* (2d Series), vi, 259.
[2] Lee to Thatcher, Jan. 23, 1788; *ib.*, 266–67.
[3] *Ib.*, 267.   [4] *Ib.*
[5] Bangs to Thatcher, Jan. 1, 1788; *Hist. Mag.* (2d Series), vi, 260.

gates there had been chosen "to Oppose the Business. . . . Sanford had one meeting and Voted not to Send any — But M^r. S. come down full charged with Gass and Stirred up a 2nd Meeting and procured himself Elected, and I presume will go up charged like a Baloon."[1] Nathaniel Barrell of York, a successful candidate for the Massachusetts Convention, "behaved so indecently before the Choice, as extorted a severe Reprimand from Judge Sewall, and when chosen modestly told his Constituents, he would sooner loose his Arm than put his Assent to the new proposed Constitution, it is to be feared many of his Brethern are of his mind."[2]

Barrell explained to Thatcher: "I see it [the Constitution] pregnant with the fate of our libertys . . . I see it entails wretchedness on my posterity — Slavery on my children; . . . twill not be so much for our advantage to have our taxes imposed & levied at the pleasure of Congress as [by] the method now pursued. . . . a Continental Collector at the head of a standing army will not be so likely to do us justice in collecting the taxes . . . I think such a Government impracticable among men with such high notions of liberty as we americans."[3]

The "Address of the Minority" of Pennsylvania's Convention had reached a few men in Massachusetts, notwithstanding the alleged refusal of the post-office to transmit it; and it did some execution. To Thomas B. Wait it "was like the Thunder of Sinai —

---

[1] Sewall to Thatcher, Jan. 5, 1788; *Hist. Mag.* (2d Series), vi, 260–61.
[2] Savage to Thatcher, Jan. 11, 1788; *ib.*, 264.
[3] Barrell to Thatcher, Jan. 15, 1788; *ib.*, 265.

its lightenings were irresistible" to him. He deplored the "darkness, duplicity and studied ambiguity ... running thro' the whole Constitution," which, to his mind, made it certain that "as it now stands but very few individuals do or ever will understand it. ... The vast Continent of America cannot long be subjected to a Democracy if consolidated into one Government — you might as well attempt to rule Hell by Prayer." [1]

Christopher Gore condensed into one sentence the motives of those who favored the Constitution as the desire for "an honorable & efficient Govt. equal to the support of our national dignity — & capable of protecting the property of our citizens." [2]

The spirit of Shays's Rebellion inspired the opponents of the Constitution in Massachusetts. "Many of the [Shays's] insurgents are in the Convention," Lincoln informed Washington; "even some of Shays's officers. A great proportion of these men are high in the opposition. We could hardly expect any thing else; nor could we ... justly suppose that those men, who were so lately intoxicated with large draughts of liberty, and who were thirsting for more would ... submit to a Constitution which would further take up the reins of Government, which, in their opinion, were too straight before." [3]

Out of three hundred and fifty-five members of

---

[1] Wait to Thatcher, Jan. 8, 1788; *Hist. Mag.* (2d Series), vi, 261. Wait was an unusually intelligent and forceful editor of a New England newspaper, the *Cumberland Gazette*. (*Ib.*, 258.)
[2] Gore to Thatcher, Dec. 30, 1787; *ib.*, 260.
[3] Lincoln to Washington, Feb. 3, 1788; *Cor. Rev.*: Sparks, iv, 206.

the Massachusetts Convention, one hundred and sixty-eight held out against the Constitution to the very last, uninfluenced by the careful, able, and convincing arguments of its friends, unmoved by their persuasion, unbought by their promises and deals.[1] They believed "that some injury is plotted against them — that the system is the production of the rich and ambitious," and that the Constitution would result in "the establishment of two orders in Society, one comprehending the opulent and great, the other the poor and illiterate." [2] At no time until they won over Hancock, who presided over the Massachusetts Convention, were the Constitutionalists sure that a majority was not against the new plan.

The struggle of these rude and unlearned Massachusetts men against the cultured, disciplined, powerful, and ably led friends of the Constitution in that State was pathetic. "Who, sir, is to pay the debts of the yeomanry and others?" exclaimed William Widgery. "Sir, when oil will quench fire, I will believe all this [the high-colored prophesies of the Constitutionalists] and not till then . . . I cannot see why we need, for the sake of a little meat, swallow a great bone, which, if it should happen to stick in our throats, can never be got out." [3]

Amos Singletary "wished they [the Constitutionalists] would not play round the subject with their fine stories like a fox round a trap, but come to it." [4] "These lawyers," said he, "and men of learning and moneyed men, that talk so finely, and gloss over

---

[1] See *infra*. [2] King to Madison, Jan. 27, 1788; King, i, 317.
[3] Elliott, ii, 105–06. [4] *Ib.*, 101.

matters so smoothly, to make us poor illiterate people swallow down the pill, expect to get into Congress themselves; they expect to be the managers of this Constitution, and get all the power and all the money, into their own hands, and then they will swallow up all us little folks like the great *Leviathan;* ... yes, just as the whale swallowed up *Jonah*." [1] Replying to the Constitutionalist argument that the people's representatives in Congress would be true to their constituents, Abraham White said that he "would not trust a 'flock of Moseses.'" [2]

The opposition complained that the people knew little or nothing about the Constitution — and this, indeed, was quite true. "It is strange," said General Thompson, "that a system which its planners say is so plain, *that he that runs may read it*, should want so much explanation." [3] "Necessity compelled them to hurry," [4] declared Widgery of the friends of the Constitution. "Don't let us go too fast. ... Why all this racket?" asked the redoubtable Thompson.[5] Dr. John Taylor was sure that Senators "once chosen ... are chosen forever."[6]

Time and again the idea cropped out of a National Government as a kind of foreign rule. "I beg the indulgence of this honorable body," implored Samuel Nason, "to permit me to make a short apostrophe to Liberty. O Liberty! thou greatest good! thou fairest property! with thee I wish to live — with thee I wish to die! Pardon me if I drop a tear on the peril to which she is exposed: I cannot, sir, see this

[1] Elliott, ii, 102. [2] *Ib.*, 28. [3] *Ib.*, 96.
[4] *Ib.*, 94. [5] *Ib.*, 80. [6] *Ib.*, 48.

brightest of jewels tarnished — a jewel worth ten thousand worlds; and shall we part with it so soon? O no." [1] And Mr. Nason was sure that the people would part with this brightest of jewels if the Constitution was adopted. As to a standing army, let the Constitutionalists recall Boston on March 5, 1770. "Had I a voice like Jove," cried Nason, "I would proclaim it throughout the world; and had I an arm like Jove, I would hurl from the globe those villains that would dare attempt to establish in our country a standing army." [2]

These "poor, ignorant men," as they avowed themselves to be, were rich in apostrophes. The reporter thus records one of General Thompson's efforts: "Here the general broke out in the following pathetic apostrophe: 'O my country, never give up your annual elections! Young men, never give up your jewel.'" [3] John Holmes showed that the Constitution gave Congress power to "institute judicatories" like "that diabolical institution, the *Inquisition*." "*Racks*," cried he, "and *gibbets*, may be amongst the most mild instruments of their [Congress's] discipline." [4] Because there was no religious test, Major Thomas Lusk "shuddered at the idea that Roman Catholics, Papists, and Pagans might be introduced into office, and that Popery and the Inquisition may be established in America"; [5] and Singletary pointed out that under the Constitution a "Papist, or an Infidel, was as eligible as ... a Christian." [6]

[1] Elliot, ii, 133.   [2] *Ib.*, 136–37.   [3] *Ib.*, 16.
[4] *Ib.*, 111.   [5] *Ib.*, 148.   [6] *Ib.*, 44.

THE STRUGGLE FOR RATIFICATION 347

Thus the proceedings dragged along. The overwhelming arguments of the advocates of the Constitution were unanswered and, apparently, not even understood by its stubborn foes. One Constitutionalist, indeed, did speak their language, a farmer named Jonathan Smith, whom the Constitutionalist managers put forward for that purpose. "I am a plain man," said Mr. Smith, "and get my living by the plough. I am not used to speak in public, but I beg leave to say a few words to my brother ploughjoggers in this house"; and Mr. Smith proceeded to make one of the most effective speeches of the Convention.[1] But all to no purpose. Indeed, the pleadings and arguments for the Constitution seemed only to harden the feeling of those opposed to it. They were obsessed by an immovable belief that a National Government would destroy their liberties; "and," testifies King, "a distrust of men of property or education has a more powerful effect upon the minds of our opponents than any specific objections against the Constitution."[2]

Finally, in their desperation, the Constitutionalist managers won Hancock,[3] whose courting of the insurgents in Shays's Rebellion had elected him Gov-

[1] Elliott, ii, 102–04. Mr. Thatcher made the best summary of the unhappy state of the country under the Confederation. (*Ib.*, 141–48.)

[2] King to Madison, Jan. 20, 1788; King, i, 314.

[3] Rives, ii, 524–25. "To manage the cause against them (the jealous opponents of the Constitution) are the present and late governor, three judges of the supreme court, fifteen members of the Senate, twenty-four among the most respectable of the clergy, ten or twelve of the first characters at the bar, judges of probate, high sheriffs of counties, and many other respectable people, merchants, &c., Generals Heath, Lincoln, Brooks, and others of the late army." (Nathaniel Gorham to Madison, quoted in *ib.*)

ernor. He had more influence with the opposition than any other man in New England. For the same reason, Governor Bowdoin's friends, who included most of the men of weight and substance, had been against Hancock. By promising the latter their support and by telling him that he would be made President if Washington was not,[1] the Constitutionalist leaders induced Hancock to offer certain amendments which the Massachusetts Convention should recommend to Congress along with its ratification of the Constitution. Hancock offered these proposals as his own, although they were drawn by the learned and scholarly Parsons.[2] Samuel Adams, hitherto silent, joined in this plan.

Thus the trick was turned and the Massachusetts Convention ratified the Constitution a few days later by a slender majority of nineteen out of a vote of three hundred and fifty-five.[3] But not without bitter protest. General Thompson remarked that "he could not say amen to them [the amendments], but they might be voted for by some men — he did not say Judases."[4] The deal by which the Constitutionalists won Hancock was suspected, it appears, for Dr. Charles Jarvis denied that "these amendments have been artfully introduced to lead to a decision

---

[1] "Hancock has committed himself in our favor.... You will be astonished, when you see the list of names that such an union of men has taken place on this question. Hancock will, hereafter, receive the universal support of Bowdoin's friends; *and we told him, that, if Virginia does not unite, which is problematical, he is considered as the only fair candidate for President.*" (King to Knox, Feb. 1, 1788; King, i, 319. The italics are those of King.)

[2] *Ib.*, ii, 525.   [3] Elliott, ii, 178-81.

[4] *Ib.*, 140.

which would not otherwise be had." [1] Madison in New York, watching the struggle with nervous solicitude, thought that the amendments influenced very few members of the Massachusetts opposition because of "their objections being levelled against the very essence of the proposed Government." [2] Certainly, those who changed their votes for ratification had hard work to explain their conversion.

Nathaniel Barrell, who had pledged his constituents that he would part with his arm rather than vote for the "Slavery of my children," had abandoned his vow of amputation and decided to risk the future bondage of his offspring by voting for the Constitution. In trying to justify his softened heroism, he said that he was "awed in the presence of this august assembly"; he knew "how little he must appear in the eyes of those giants of rhetoric, who have exhibited such a pompous display of declamation"; but although he did not have the "eloquence of Cicero, or the blaze of Demosthenian oratory," yet he would try to explain. He summarized his objections, ending with his wish that "this Constitution had not been, in some parts of the continent, hurried on, like the driving of Jehu, very furiously." So he hoped the Convention would adjourn, but if it would not — well, in that case, Mr. Barrell would brave the wrath of his constituents and vote for ratification with amendments offered by Hancock.[3]

[1] Elliott, ii, 153.
[2] Madison to Randolph, April 10, 1788; *Writings:* Hunt, v, 117.
[3] Elliott, ii, 159-61.

Just as the bargain with Hancock secured the necessary votes for the Constitution in the Massachusetts Convention, so did the personal behavior of the Constitutionalists forestall any outbreak of protest after ratification. "I am at Last overcome," wrote Widgery, "by a majority of 19, including the president [Hancock] whose very Name is an Honour to the State, for by his coming in and offering Som Amendments which furnished many with Excuses to their Constituants, it was adopted to the great Joy of all Boston."[1] The triumphant Constitutionalists kept up their mellowing tactics of conciliation after their victory and with good results, as appears by Mr. Widgery's account.

The "great bone" which had been thrust into his throat had not stuck there as he had feared it would. The Constitutionalists furnished materials to wash it down. "After Taking a parting Glass at the Expense of the Trades men in Boston we Disolved";[2] but not before the mollified Widgery announced that the Constitution "had been carried by a majority of wise and understanding men. . . . After expressing his thanks for the civility which the inhabitants of this town [Boston] have shown to the Convention, . . . he concluded by saying that he should support the . . . Constitution" with all his might.[3]

"One thing I mus menchen," relates Widgery, "the Gallerys was very much Crowded, yet on the Desition of so emportant a Question as the present you might have heard a Copper fall on the Gallery

---

[1] Widgery to Thatcher, Feb. 8, 1788; *Hist. Mag.* (2d Series), vi, 270.
[2] *Ib.*   [3] Elliott, ii, 218.

THE STRUGGLE FOR RATIFICATION 351

floor, their was Sush a profound Silance; on thirs Day we got throw all our Business and on Fry Day, there was a federal Ship Riged and fix^d on a Slead, hald by 13 Horses, and all Orders of Men Turn^d out and formed a procession in the following ordor Viz first the Farmers with the plow and Harrow Sowing grain, and Harrowing it in as they went Som in a Cart Brakeing and Swingeing Flax . . . Tradesmen of all sorts, . . . the Bakers [with] their Bread peal . . . the Federal Ship ful Riged . . . the Merchants . . . a nother Slead, Halled by 13 Horses on which was a Ship yard, and a Number of smaul Ships &c. on that. in this order thay march^d to the House of Each of their Delegates in the Town of Boston, and returned to Fanuels Aall where the Merchants gave them 3 or 4 Hogsheads of Punch and as much wine cake & cheese as they could make way with . . . one thing more Notwithstanding my opposition to the Constitution, and the anxiety of Boston for its adoption I most Tel you I was never Treated with So much politeness in my Life as I was afterwards by the Treadesmen of Boston Merchants & every other Gentleman." [1]

Thus did the Massachusetts Constitutionalists take very human and effective measures to prevent such revolt against the Constitution, after its ratification, as the haughty and harsh conduct of their Pennsylvania brothers had stirred up in the City and State of Brotherly Love. "The minority are in good temper," King advises Madison; "they have the

[1] Widgery to Thatcher, Feb. 8, 1788; *Hist. Mag.* (2d Series), vi, 270-71.

magnanimity to declare that they will devote their lives and property to support the Government." [1] While there was a little Anti-Constitutionalist activity among the people after the Convention adjourned, it was not virulent. Gerry, indeed, gave one despairing shriek over departing "liberty" which he was sure the Constitution would drive from our shores; but that lament was intended for the ears of New York. It is, however, notable as showing the state of mind of such Anti-Constitutionalists as the Constitution's managers had not taken pains to mollify.

Gerry feared the "Gulph of despotism. . . . On these shores freedom has planted her standard, diped in the purple tide that flowed from the veins of her martyred heroes" which was now in danger from "the deep-laid plots, the secret intrigues, . . . the bold effrontery" of those ambitious to be aristocrats, some of whom were "speculating for fortune, by sporting with public money." Only "a few, a very few [Constitutionalists] . . . were . . . defending their country" during the Revolution, said Gerry. "Genius, Virtue, and Patriotism seems to nod over the vices of the times . . . while a supple multitude are paying a blind and idolatrous homage to . . . those . . . who are endeavouring . . . to betray the people . . . into an acceptance of a most complicated system of government; marked on the one side with the *dark, secret* and *profound intrigues* of the statesman, long practised in the purlieus of despotism; and on the other, with the ideal projects

[1] King to Madison, Feb. 6, 1788; King, i, 320.

THE STRUGGLE FOR RATIFICATION

of *young ambition*, with its wings just expanded to soar to a summit, which imagination has painted in such gawdy colours as to intoxicate the *inexperienced votary* and send *him* rambling from State to State, to collect materials to construct the ladder of preferment." [1]

Thus protested Gerry; but if the people, in spite of his warnings, *would* "give their voices for a voluntary dereliction of their privileges" — then, concluded Gerry, "while the statesman is plodding for power, and the courtier practicing the arts of dissimulation without check — while the rapacious are growing rich by oppression, and fortune throwing her gifts into the lap of fools, let the sublimer characters, the philosophic lovers of freedom who have wept over her exit, retire to the calm shades of contemplation, there they may look down with pity on the inconsistency of human nature, the revolutions of states, the rise of kingdoms, and the fall of empires." [2]

Such was the resistance offered to the Constitution in Massachusetts, such the debate against it, the management that finally secured its approval with recommendations by that Commonwealth,[3] and the after effects of the Constitutionalists' tactics.

[1] Gerry, in Ford: *P. on C.*, 1–23.
[2] *Ib.*, 23. When a bundle of copies of Gerry's pamphlet was received by the New York Anti-Constitutionalists in Albany County, they decided that it was "in a style too sublime and florid for the common people in this part of the country." (*Ib.*, 1.)
[3] During the debates the *Boston Gazette* published the following charge that bribery was being employed to get votes for the Constitution: —
    BRIBERY AND CORRUPTION ! ! !
"The most diabolical plan is on foot to corrupt the members of the Convention, who oppose the adoption of the new Constitution. Large

In New Hampshire a majority of the Convention was against the Constitution. "Almost every man of property and abilities . . . [was] for it," wrote Langdon to Washington; but "a report was circulated . . . that the liberties of the people were in danger, and the great men . . . were forming a plan for themselves; together with a thousand other absurdities, which frightened the people almost out of what little senses they had." [1]

Very few of the citizens of New Hampshire knew anything about the Constitution. "I was surprised to find . . . that so little information respecting the Constitution had been diffused among the people," wrote Tobias Lear. "The valuable numbers of *Pub-*

sums of money have been brought from a neighboring state for that purpose, contributed by the wealthy. If so, is it not probable there may be collections for the same accursed purpose nearer home? CENTINEL." (Elliott, ii, 51.)

The Convention appointed a committee to investigate (*ib.*); it found that the charge was based on extremely vague rumor. (Harding, 103.) There the matter appears to have been dropped.

More than eighty years afterward, Henry B. Dawson, the editor of the *Historical Magazine*, a scholar of standing, asserted, personally, in his publication: "It is very well known — indeed, the son and biographer of one of the great leaders of the Constitutionalists in New York has frankly admitted to us — that *enough members of the Massachusetts Convention were bought with money* from New York *to secure the ratification of the new system by Massachusetts.*" (*Hist. Mag.* (2d Series), vi, 268, footnote, referring to Savage's letter to Thatcher telling of the charge in the *Boston Gazette*.)

Professor Harding discredits the whole story. (Harding, 101-05.) It is referred to only as showing the excited and suspicious temper of the times.

[1] Langdon to Washington, Feb. 28, 1788; *Cor. Rev.*: Sparks, iv, 212. "At least three fourths of the property, and a large proportion of the abilities in the State are friendly to the proposed system. The opposition here, as has generally been the case, was composed of men who were involved in debt." (Lear to Washington, June 22, 1788; *ib.*, 224-25.)

THE STRUGGLE FOR RATIFICATION 355

lius are not known. . . . The debates of the Pennsylvania and Massachusetts Conventions have been read by but few persons; and many other pieces, which contain useful information have never been heard of."[1]

When the New Hampshire Convention assembled, "a great part of whom had positive instructions to vote against it," the Constitutionalists, after much argument and persuasion, secured an adjournment on February 22 until June.[2] Learning this in New York, nine days later, Madison wrote Pendleton that the adjournment had been "found necessary to prevent a rejection."[3] But, "notwithstanding our late Disappointments and Mortification," the New Hampshire Constitutionalists felt that they would win in the end and "make the people happy in spight of their teeth."[4]

When, therefore, Virginia's great Convention met on June 2, 1788, the Nation's proposed fundamental law had not received deliberate consideration in any quarter; nor had it encountered weighty debate from those opposed to it. New York's Convention was not to assemble until two weeks later and that State was known to be hostile. The well-arranged plan was working to combine the strength of the leading enemies of the Constitution in the various States so that a new Federal Convention should be called.[5]

[1] Lear to Washington, June 2, 1788; *Cor. Rev.*: Sparks, iv, 220.
[2] Langdon to King, Feb. 23, 1788; King, i, 321-22.
[3] Madison to Pendleton, March 3, 1788 (*Writings:* Hunt, v, 110), and to Washington, March 3, 1788 (*ib.*, 111); and to Randolph; March 3, 1788 (*ib.*, 113).
[4] Langdon to King, May 6, 1788; King, i, 328.
[5] Washington to Lafayette, Feb. 7, 1788; *Writings:* Ford, xi, 220.

"Had the influence of character been removed, the intrinsic merits of the instrument [Constitution] would not have secured its adoption. Indeed, it is scarcely to be doubted, that in some of the adopting States, a majority of the people were in the opposition," writes Marshall many years afterwards in a careful review of the thorny path the Constitution had had to travel.[1] Its foes, says Marshall, were "firmly persuaded that the cradle of the constitution would be the grave of republican liberty."[2]

In Virginia's Convention, the array of ability, distinction, and character on both sides was notable, brilliant, and impressive. The strongest debaters in the land were there, the most powerful orators, and some of the most scholarly statesmen. Seldom, in any land or age, has so gifted and accomplished a group of men contended in argument and discussion at one time and place. And yet reasoning and eloquence were not the only or even the principal weapons used by these giant adversaries. Skill in political management, craft in parliamentary tactics, intimate talks with the members, the downright "playing of politics," were employed by both sides. "Of all arguments that may be used at the convention," wrote Washington to Madison, more than four months before the Convention, "the most prevailing one . . . will be that nine states *at least* will have acceded to it."[3]

---

[1] Marshall, ii, 127. [2] *Ib.*
[3] Washington to Madison, Jan. 10, 1788; *Writings:* Ford, xi, 208.

CHAPTER X

IN THE GREAT CONVENTION

There is no alternative between the adoption of it [the Constitution] and anarchy. (Washington.)

I look on that paper as the most fatal plan that could possibly be conceived to enslave a free people. (Henry.)

MORE, much more, went forward in the Virginia struggle than appeared upon the surface. Noble as was the epochal debate in Virginia's Constitutional Convention, it was not so influential on votes of the members as were other methods[1] employed by both sides. Very practical politicians, indeed, were these contending moulders of destiny.

Having in mind the Pennsylvania storm; with the picture before them of the delicate and skillful piloting by which alone the Constitution had escaped the rocks in the tempestuous Massachusetts seas; with the hurricane gathering in New York and its low thunders heard even from States that had ratified — the Virginia Constitutionalists took no chances, neglected no precaution. Throughout the country the Constitutionalists were now acting with disciplined dispatch.

Intelligence of the New Hampshire Convention, of their success in which the Constitutionalists finally had made sure, was arranged to be carried by swift riders and relays of horses across country to Hamilton in New York; and "any expense which you may incur will be cheerfully repaid," King

[1] Though "practical," these methods were honorable, as far as the improper use of money was concerned.

assured Langdon.[1] As to Virginia, Hamilton wrote Madison to send news of "*any decisive* question . . . if favorable . . . by an express . . . with pointed orders to make all possible diligence, by changing horses etc."; assuring Madison, as King did Langdon, that "all expense shall be thankfully and liberally paid." [2]

The Constitutionalists, great and small, in other States were watching Virginia's Convention through the glasses of an infinite apprehension. "I fear that overwhelming torrent, Patrick Henry," General Knox confided to King.[3] Even before Massachusetts had ratified, one Jeremiah Hill thought that "the fate of this Constitution and the political Salvation of the united States depend cheifly on the part that Virginia and this State [Massachusetts] take in the Matter." [4] Hamilton's lieutenant, King, while in Boston helping the Constitutionalists there, wrote to Madison: "You can with difficulty conceive the real anxiety experienced in Massachusetts concerning your decision." [5] "Our chance of success depends on you," was Hamilton's own despairing appeal to the then leader of the Southern Constitutionalists. "If you do well there is a gleam of hope; but certainly I think not otherwise." [6] The

---

[1] King to Langdon, June 10, 1788; King, i, 331.
[2] Hamilton to Madison, May 19, 1788; *Works:* Lodge, ix, 430. See also *ib.*, 432.
[3] Knox to King, June 19, 1788; King, i, 335.
[4] Hill to Thatcher, Jan. 1, 1788; *Hist. Mag.* (2d Series), vi, 261.
[5] King to Madison, May 25, 1788; King, i, 329.
[6] Hamilton to Madison, June 27, 1788; *Works:* Lodge, ix, 436. Virginia had ratified the Constitution two days before Hamilton wrote this letter, but the news did not reach New York until long afterward.

worried New York Constitutionalist commander was sure that Virginia would settle the fate of the proposed National Government. "God grant that Virginia may accede. The example will have a vast influence."[1]

Virginia's importance justified the anxiety concerning her action. Not only was the Old Dominion preëminent in the part she had taken in the Revolution, and in the distinction of her sons like Henry, Jefferson, and Washington, whose names were better known in other States than those of many of their own most prominent men; but she also was the most important State in the Confederation in population and, at that time, in resources. "Her population," says Grigsby, "was over three fourths of all that of New England; ... not far from double that of Pennsylvania; ... or from three times that of New York ... over three fourths of all the population of the Southern States; ... and more than a fifth of the population of the whole Union." [2]

The Virginia Constitutionalists had chosen their candidates for the State Convention with painstaking care. Personal popularity, family influence, public reputation, business and financial power, and everything which might contribute to their strength with the people, had been delicately weighed. The people simply would not vote against such men as Pendleton, Wythe, and Carrington; [3] and these and

---

[1] Hamilton to Madison, June 8, 1788; *Works:* Lodge, ix, 432-34.

[2] Grigsby, i, 8. About three eighths of Virginia's population were slaves valued at many millions of dollars.

[3] Grigsby, i, footnote to 50; also 32; and see examples given by Judge Scott, in Scott, 235-38.

others like them accordingly were selected by the Constitutionalists as candidates in places where the people, otherwise, would have chosen antagonists to the Constitution.

More than one fourth of the Virginia Convention of one hundred and seventy members had been soldiers in the Revolutionary War; and nearly all of them followed Washington in his desire for a strong National Government. Practically all of Virginia's officers were members of the Cincinnati; and these were a compact band of stern supporters of the "New Plan."[1] Some of the members had been Tories, and these were stingingly lashed in debate by Mason; but they were strong in social position, wealth, and family connections, and all of them were for the Constitution.[2]

No practical detail of election day had been overlooked by the Constitutionalists. Colonel William Moore wrote to Madison, before the election came off: "You know the disadvantage of being absent at elections. . . . I must therefore entreat and conjure you — nay, command you, if it were in my power — to be here."[3] The Constitutionalists slipped in members wherever possible and by any device.

Particularly in Henrico County, where Richmond was situated, had conditions been sadly confused. Edmund Randolph, then Governor of the State, who next to Washington was Virginia's most conspicuous delegate to the Federal Convention, had refused to sign the Constitution and was, therefore, popularly

[1] Grigsby, i, footnote to 36; and see 29, 62, 339.
[2] Henry, ii, 339; and Rowland, ii, 223 *et seq.*   [3] Rives, ii, 549.

supposed to be against it. October 17, 1787, he wrote a letter to the Speaker of the House of Delegates explaining his reasons for dissent. He approved the main features of the proposed plan for a National Government but declared that it had fatal defects, should be amended before ratification, a new Federal Convention called to pass upon the amendments of the various States, and, thereafter, the Constitution as amended again submitted for ratification to State Conventions.[1] Randolph, however, did not send this communication to the Speaker "lest in the diversity of opinion I should excite a contest unfavorable to that harmony with which I trust that great subject will be discussed." [2] But it was privately printed in Richmond and Randolph sent a copy to Washington. On January 3, 1788, the letter was published in the *Virginia Gazette* together with other correspondence. In an additional paragraph, which does not appear in Randolph's letter as reproduced in Elliott, he said that he would "regulate himself by the spirit of America" and that he would do his best to amend the Constitution prior to ratification, but if he could not succeed he would accept the "New Plan" as it stood.[3] But he had declared to Richard Henry Lee that "either a monarchy or aristocracy will be generated" by it.[4]

[1] Randolph to the Speaker of the House of Delegates, Oct. 10, 1787; Elliott, i, 482-91; also Ford: *P. on C.*, 261-76.
[2] Randolph to Page and others, Dec. 2, 1787; *American Museum*, iii, 61 *et seq.*
[3] *Ib.*
[4] Lee to Randolph, Oct. 16, 1787; Elliott, i, 503. Upon the publication of this correspondence a young Richmond attorney, Spencer Roane, the son-in-law of Patrick Henry, in an article signed "Plain

Thus Randolph to all appearances occupied middle ground. But, publicly, he was in favor of making strenuous efforts to amend the Constitution as a condition of ratification, and of calling a second Federal Convention; and these were the means by which the Anti-Constitutionalists designed to accomplish the defeat of the "New Plan." The opponents of the proposed National Government worked hard with Randolph to strengthen his resolution and he gave them little cause to doubt their success.[1]

But the Constitutionalists were also busy with the Governor and with greater effect. Washington wrote an adroit and persuasive letter designed to win him entirely over to a whole-hearted and unqualified advocacy of the Constitution. The question was, said Washington, the acceptance of the Constitution or "a dissolution of the Union."[2] Madison,

Dealer," published in the *Virginia Gazette*, attacked Randolph for inconsistency. "Good God! How can the first magistrate and father of a pure republican government ... before his proposed plan of amendment has been determined upon, declare that he will accept a Constitution which is to beget a monarchy or an aristocracy? ... Can he foretell future events? How else can he at this time discover what the 'spirit of America' is? ... How far will this principle carry him? Why, ... if the dominion of Shays, instead of that of the new Constitution, should be generally accepted, and become 'the spirit of America,' his Excellency would turn Shayite." (Plain Dealer to Randolph, Feb. 13, 1788; Ford: *Essays on the Constitution*, 385; also *Branch Hist. Papers*, 47.) Roane's letter is important as the first expression of his hostility to the Constitution. He was to become the determined enemy of Marshall; and, as the ablest judge of the Virginia Court of Appeals, the chief judicial foe of Marshall's Nationalism. (See vol. III of this work.)

[1] "The importunities of some to me in public and private are designed to throw me unequivocally and without condition, into the opposition." (Randolph to Madison, Feb. 29, 1788; Conway, 101.)

[2] Washington to Randolph, Jan. 8, 1788; *Writings:* Ford, xi, 204–06.

IN THE GREAT CONVENTION

in a subtle mingling of flattery, argument, and insinuation, skillfully besought his "dear friend" Randolph to come out for the Constitution fully and without reserve. If only Randolph had stood for the Constitution, wrote Madison, "it would have given it a decided and unalterable preponderancy," and Henry would have been "baffled."

The New England opposition, Madison assured Randolph, was from "that part of the people who have a repugnance in general to good government ... a part of whom are known to aim at confusion and are suspected of wishing a reversal of the Revolution. ... Nothing can be further from your [Randolph's] views than the principles of the different sets of men who have carried on their opposition under the respectability of your name." [1]

Randolph finally abandoned all opposition and resolved to support the Constitution even to the point of resisting the very plan he had himself proposed and insisted upon; but nobody, with the possible exception of Washington, was informed of this Constitutionalist master-stroke until the Convention met; [2] and, if Washington knew, he kept the secret. Thus, although the Constitutionalists were not yet sure of Randolph, they put up no candidate against him in Henrico County, where the people were very much opposed to the Constitution. To

---

[1] Madison to Randolph, Jan. 10, 1788; *Writings:* Hunt, v, 79–84; and see same to same, Jan. 20, 1788 (*ib.*, 86–88); and March 3, 1788 (*ib.*, 113–14).

[2] "If he [Randolph] approves it at all, he will do it feebly." (Washington to Lafayette, April 28, 1788; *Writings:* Ford, xi, 255; and see Madison to Jefferson, April 22, 1788; *Writings:* Hunt, v, 121.)

have done so would have been useless in any event; for Randolph could have been elected almost unanimously if his hostility to the proposed Government had been more vigorous, so decided were the people's dislike and distrust of it, and so great, as yet, the Governor's popularity. He wrote Madison a day or two before the election that nothing but his personal popularity "could send me; my politicks not being sufficiently strenuous against the Constitution."[1] The people chose their beloved young Governor, never imagining that he would appear as the leading champion of the Constitution on the Convention floor and actually oppose amending it before ratification.[2]

But the people were not in the dark when they voted for the only candidate the Constitutionalists openly brought out in Henrico County. John Marshall was for the proposed National Government, outright and aboveboard. He was vastly concerned. We find him figuring out the result of the election in northern Virginia and concluding "that the question will be very nice."[3] Marshall had been made the Constitutionalist candidate solely because of his personal popularity. As it was, even the people's confidence in him barely had saved Marshall.

"Marshall is in danger," wrote Randolph; "but F. [Dr. Foushee, the Anti-Constitutionalist candidate] is not popular enough on other scores to be

[1] Randolph to Madison, Feb. 29, 1788; quoted in Conway, 101.
[2] "Randolph was still looked upon as an Anti-Federalist by the uninitiated." But his "position . . . was evidently no secret to Washington." (Rowland, ii, 210. See also *ib.*, 225, 227, 231.)
[3] *Ib.*

IN THE GREAT CONVENTION 365

elected, altho' he is perfectly a Henryite."[1] Marshall admitted that the people who elected Randolph and himself were against the Constitution; and declared that he owed his own election to his individual strength with the people.[2] Thus two strong champions of the Constitution had been secured from an Anti-Constitutionalist constituency; and these were only examples of other cases.

The Anti-Constitutionalists, too, straining every nerve to elect their men, resorted to all possible devices to arouse the suspicions, distrust, and fears of the people. "The opposition to it [the Constitution] . . . is addressed more to the passions than to the reason," declared Washington.[3]

Henry was feverishly active. He wrote flaming letters to Kentucky that the Mississippi would be lost if the new plan of government were adopted.[4] He told the people that a religious establishment would be set up.[5] The Reverend John Blair Smith, President of Hampden Sidney College, declared that Henry "has descended to lower artifices and management . . . than I thought him capable of."[6] Writing to Hamilton of the activities of the opposition, Washington asserted that "their assiduity stands unrivalled";[7] and he informed Trumbull

[1] Randolph to Madison, Feb. 29, 1788; Conway, 101. [2] Scott, 160.
[3] Washington to Carter, Dec. 14, 1787; *Writings:* Ford, xi, footnote to 210.
[4] Smith to Madison, June 12, 1788; Rives, ii, footnote to p. 544.
[5] *Ib.* "The Baptist interest . . . are highly incensed by Henry's opinions and public speeches." (Randolph to Madison, Feb. 29, 1788; Conway, 101.)
[6] Smith to Madison, June 12, 1788; Rives, ii, 544.
[7] Washington to Hamilton, Nov. 10, 1787; *Writings:* Ford, xi, footnote to p. 181.

that "the opponents of the Constitution are indefatigable."[1]

"Every art that could inflame the passions or touch the interests of men have been essayed; — the ignorant have been told that should the proposed government obtain, their lands would be taken from them and their property disposed of; — and all ranks are informed that the prohibition of the Navigation of the Mississippi (their favorite object) will be a certain consequence of the adoption of the Constitution."[2]

Plausible and restrained Richard Henry Lee warned the people that "by means of taxes, the government may command the whole or any part of the subjects' property";[3] and that the Constitution "promised a large field of employment to military gentlemen, and gentlemen of the law; and in case the government shall be executed without convulsions, it will afford security to creditors, to the clergy, salary-men and others depending on money payments."[4]

Nor did the efforts of the Virginia opponents of a National establishment stop there. They spread

---

[1] Washington to Trumbull, Feb. 5, 1788; *Writings:* Ford, 212. From the first Washington attributed much of the opposition throughout the country to the fact that popular leaders believed that the new National Government would lessen their importance in their respective States. "The governors elect or to be elected, the legislators, with a long tribe of others whose political importance will be lessened if not annihilated" were, said Washington, against a strong central Government. (Washington to Knox, Feb. 3, 1787; Sparks, ix, 230; and see Graydon, 340.)

[2] Washington to Lincoln, April 2, 1788; *ib.*, xi, footnote to 239-40.
[3] "Letters of a Federal Farmer," no. 3; Ford: *P. on C.*, 301.
[4] *Ib.*, no. 5, 319.

IN THE GREAT CONVENTION 367

the poison of personal slander also. "They have attempted to vilify & debase the characters who formed" the Constitution, complained Washington.[1] These cunning expedients on one side and desperate artifices on the other were continued during the sitting of the Virginia Convention by all the craft and guile of practical politics.

After the election, Madison reported to Jefferson in Paris that the Northern Neck and the Valley had elected members friendly to the Constitution, the counties south of the James unfriendly members, the "intermediate district" a mixed membership, with Kentucky divided. In this report, Madison counts Marshall fifth in importance of all Constitutionalists elected, and puts only Pendleton, Wythe, Blair, and Innes ahead of him.[2]

When the Convention was called to order, it made up a striking and remarkable body. Judges and soldiers, lawyers and doctors, preachers, planters, merchants, and Indian fighters, were there. Scarcely a field fought over during the long, red years of the Revolution but had its representative on that historic floor. Statesmen and jurists of three generations were members.[3]

From the first the Constitutionalists displayed better tactics and discipline than their opponents, just as they had shown greater skill and astuteness in selecting candidates for election. They arranged everything beforehand and carried their plans out

[1] Washington to Armstrong, April 25, 1788; *Writings:* Ford, xi, 252; and to Petit, Aug. 16, 1788; *ib.*, 300.
[2] Madison to Jefferson, April 22, 1788; *Writings:* Hunt, v, 120-22.
[3] Grigsby, i, 34-35; and footnote to 49.

with precision. For the important position of President of the Convention, they agreed on the venerable Chancellor, Edmund Pendleton, who was able, judicial, and universally respected. He was nominated by his associate, Judge Paul Carrington, and unanimously elected.[1]

In the same way, Wythe, who was learned, trusted, and beloved, and who had been the teacher of many members of the Convention, was made Chairman of the Committee of the Whole. The Anti-Constitutionalists did not dare to oppose either Pendleton or Wythe for these strategic places. They had made the mistake of not agreeing among themselves on strong and influential candidates for these offices and of nominating them before the Constitutionalists acted. For the first time in Virginia's history, a shorthand reporter, David Robertson, appeared to take down a stenographic report of the debates; and this innovation was bitterly resented and resisted by the opposition[2] as a Constitutionalist maneuver.[3] Marshall was appointed a member of the committee[4] which examined the returns of the elections of members and also heard several contested election cases.[5]

At the beginning the Anti-Constitutionalists did not decide upon a plan of action — did not carefully weigh their course of procedure. No sooner had rules been adopted, and the Constitution and official

---

[1] Grigsby, i, 64–66; and Elliott, iii, 1.
[2] Rowland, ii, 222.
[3] Henry, ii, 345. So angered were the Anti-Constitutionalists that they would not correct or revise Robertson's reports of their speeches. (*Ib.*)
[4] Elliott, iii, 1.   [5] *Ib.*, 5–6; also, Journal of the Convention, 7–11.

GEORGE WYTHE

IN THE GREAT CONVENTION

documents relating to it laid before the Convention, than their second tactical mistake was made; and made by one of their very ablest and most accomplished leaders. When George Mason arose, everybody knew that the foes of the Constitution were about to develop the first move in their order of battle. Spectators and members were breathless with suspense. Mason was the author of Virginia's Constitution and Bill of Rights and one of the most honorable, able, and esteemed members of the Legislature.

He had been a delegate to the Federal Convention and, with Randolph, had refused to sign the Constitution. Sixty-two years old, his snow-white hair contrasting with his blazing dark eyes, his commanding stature clad in black silk, his full, clear voice deliberate and controlled, George Mason was an impressive figure as he stood forth to strike the first blow at the new ordinance of Nationality.[1] On so important a subject, he did not think any rules should prevent "the fullest and clearest investigation." God's curse would be small compared with "what will justly fall upon us, if from any sinister views we obstruct the fullest inquiry." The Constitution, declared Mason, should be debated, "clause by clause," before any question was put.[2]

---

[1] Grigsby, i, 69–70. In the descriptions of the dress, manners, and appearance of those who took part in the debate, Grigsby's account has been followed. Grigsby took infinite pains and gave many years to the gathering and verifying of data on these picturesque subjects; he was personally intimate with a large number of the immediate descendants of the members of the Convention and with a few who were eye-witnesses; and his reconstruction of the scenes in the Convention is believed to be entirely accurate. [2] Elliott, iii, 3.

The Constitutionalists, keen-eyed for any strategic blunder of their adversaries, took instant advantage of Mason's bad generalship. Madison suavely agreed with Mason,[1] and it was unanimously resolved that the Constitution should be "discussed clause by clause through all its parts,"[2] before any question should be put as to the instrument itself or any part of it. Thus the opposition presented to the Constitutionalists the very method the latter wished for, and had themselves planned to secure, on their own initiative.[3] The strength of the foes of the proposed National Government was in attacking it as a whole; their weakness, in discussing its specific provisions. The danger of the Constitutionalists lay in a general debate on the large theory and results of the Constitution; their safety, in presenting in detail the merits of its separate parts.

While the fight over the Constitution was partly an economic class struggle, it was in another and a larger phase a battle between those who thought nationally and those who thought provincially. In hostile array were two central ideas: one, of a strong National Government acting directly on men; the other, of a weak confederated league merely suggesting action to States. It was not only an economic

---

[1] Mason's clause-to-clause resolve was, "contrary to his expectations, concurred in by the other side." (Madison to Washington, June 4, 1788; *Writings:* Hunt, v, footnote to 124.) And see Washington's gleeful report to the New York Constitutionalists of Mason's error: "This [Mason's resolve] was as unexpected as acceptable to the federalists, and their ready acquiescence seems to have somewhat startled the opposite side for fear they had committed themselves." (Washington to Jay, June 8, 1788; *Writings:* Ford, xi, 271.)

[2] Elliott, iii, 4.   [3] Grigsby, i, 77.

contest, but also, and even more, a conflict by those to whom "liberty" meant unrestrained freedom of action and speech, against those to whom such "liberty" meant tumult and social chaos.

The mouths of the former were filled with those dread and sounding words "despotism" and "arbitrary power"; the latter loudly denounced "enemies of order" and "foes of government." The one wanted no bits in the mouth of democracy, or, at most, soft ones with loose reins and lax hand; the other wished a stout curb, stiff rein, and strong arm. The whole controversy, on its popular side, resounded with misty yet stirring language about "liberty," "aristocracy," "tyranny," "anarchy," "licentiousness"; and yet "debtor," "creditor," "property and taxes," "payment and repudiation," were heard among the more picturesque and thrilling terms. In this fundamental struggle of antagonistic theories, the practical advantage for the hour was overwhelmingly with those who resisted the Constitution.

They had on their side the fears of the people, who, as has appeared, looked on all government with suspicion, on any vital government with hostility, and on a great central Government as some distant and monstrous thing, too far away to be within their reach, too powerful to be resisted, too high and exalted for the good of the common man, too dangerous to be tried. It was, to the masses, something new, vague, and awful; something to oppress the poor, the weak, the debtor, the settler; something to strengthen and enrich the already strong and opulent, the merchant, the creditor, the financial interests.

True, the people had suffered by the loose arrangement under which they now lived; but, after all, had not they and their "liberties" survived? And surely they would suffer even more, they felt, under this stronger power; but would they and their "liberties" survive its "oppression"? They thought not. And did not many of the ablest, purest, and most trusted public characters in the Old Dominion think the same? Here was ammunition and to spare for Patrick Henry and George Mason, Tyler and Grayson, Bland and Harrison — ammunition and to spare, with their guns planted on the heights, if they could center their fire on the Constitution as a single proposition.

But they had been sleeping and now awoke to find their position surrendered, and themselves compelled, if Mason's resolutions were strictly followed, to make the assault in piecemeal on detached parts of the "New Plan," many of which, taken by themselves, could not be successfully combated. Although they tried to recover their lost ground and did regain much of it, yet the Anti-Constitutionalists were hampered throughout the debate by this initial error in parliamentary strategy.[1]

And now the Constitutionalists were eager to push the fighting. The soldierly Lee was all for haste. The Anti-Constitutionalists held back. Mason protested "against hurrying them precipitately." Harrison said "that many of the members had not yet arrived."[2] On the third day, the Convention went

[1] For a discussion of this tactical blunder of the opponents of the Constitution, see Grigsby, i, 72.   [2] Elliott, iii, 4.

IN THE GREAT CONVENTION 373

into committee of the whole, with the astute and venerable Wythe in the chair. Hardly had this brisk, erect little figure — clad in single-breasted coat and vest, standing collar and white cravat, bald, except on the back of the head, from which unqueued and unribboned gray hair fell and curled up from the neck [1] — taken the gavel before Patrick Henry was on his feet.

Henry moved for the reading of the acts by authority of which the Federal Convention at Philadelphia had met,[2] for they would show the work of that Convention to be illegal and the Constitution the revolutionary creature of usurped power. If Henry could fix on the advocates of stronger law and sterner order the brand of lawlessness and disorder in framing the very plan they now were championing, much of the mistake of yesterday might be retrieved.

But it was too late. Helped from his seat and leaning on his crutches, Pendleton was recognized by Wythe before Henry could get the eye of the chair to speak upon his motion; and the veteran jurist crushed Henry's purpose before the great orator could make it plain. "We are not to consider," said Pendleton, "whether the Federal Convention exceeded their powers." That question "ought not to influence our deliberations." Even if the framers of the Constitution had acted without authority, Virginia's Legislature afterwards had referred it to the people who had elected the present Convention to pass upon it.[3] Pendleton's brief

[1] Grigsby, i, 75.   [2] Elliott, iii, 6.   [3] *Ib.*

speech was decisive;[1] Henry withdrew his motion; the preamble and the first two sections of the first article of the Constitution were laid before the committee and the destiny-determining debate began.

The Constitutionalists, who throughout the contest never made a mistake in the men they selected to debate or the time when they should speak, had chosen skillfully the parliamentary artillerist to fire their opening gun. They did not wait for the enemy's attack, but discharged the first shot themselves. Quickly there arose a broad, squat, ungainly man, "deformed with fat," shaggy of brow, bald of head, gray-eyed, with a nose like the beak of an eagle, and a voice clear and emotionless.[2] George Nicholas had been a brave, brilliant soldier and was one of the ablest and best-equipped lawyers in the State. He was utterly fearless, whether in battle on the field or in debate on the floor. His family and connections were powerful. In argument and reasoning he was the equal if not the superior of Madison himself; and his grim personality made the meek one of Madison seem tender in comparison. Nothing could disconcert him, nothing daunt his cold courage. He probably was the only man in the Convention whom Henry feared.[3]

Nicholas was glad, he said, that the Convention was to act with the "fullest deliberation." First he thrust at the method of the opposition to influence members by efforts outside the Convention itself; and went on with a clear, logical, and informed exposition of the sections then under consideration.

[1] Grigsby, i, 77.   [2] Ib., 79.   [3] Ib., 78, 79, 140, 141, 246, 247.

He ended by saying "that he was willing to trust his own happiness, and that of his posterity, to the operation of that system."[1]

The Constitution's enemies, thus far out-pointed by its perfectly trained and harmonious supporters, could delay no longer. Up rose the idol and champion of the people. Although only fifty-two years old, he had changed greatly in appearance since the days of his earlier triumphs. The erect form was now stooped; spectacles now covered the flashing eyes and the reddish-brown hair was replaced by a wig, which, in the excitement of speech, he frequently pushed this way and that. But the wizard brain still held its cunning, the magic tongue which, twenty-three years ago had trumpeted Independence, still wrought its spell.[2] Patrick Henry began his last great fight.

What, asked Henry, were the reasons for this change of government? A year ago the public mind was "at perfect repose"; now it was "uneasy and disquieted." "A wrong step now . . . and our republic may be lost." It was a great consolidated Government that the Constitutionalists proposed, solemnly asserted Henry. What right, he asked, had the framers of the Constitution to say, "*We, the people*, instead of *We, the states*"? He demanded the cause of that fundamental change. "Even from that illustrious man [Washington] who saved us by his valor, I would have a reason for his conduct." The Constitution-makers had no authority except to amend the old system under which the people were

[1] Elliott, iii, 7–21. [2] Grigsby, i, 76.

getting along very well. Why had they done what they had no power to do?[1]

Thus Henry put the Constitutionalists on the defensive. But they were ready. Instantly, Randolph was on his feet. He was thirty-seven years of age, fashioned on noble physical lines, with handsome face and flowing hair. His was one of Virginia's most distinguished families, his connections were influential, and he himself was the petted darling of the people. His luxuriant mind had been highly trained, his rich and sonorous voice gave an added charm to his words.[2] He was the ostensible author[3] of the plan on the broad lines of which the Constitution finally had been built. His refusal to sign it because of changes which he thought necessary, and his conversion to the extreme Constitutionalist position, which he now, for the first time, was fully to disclose, made him the strongest single asset the Constitutionalists had acquired. Randolph's open, bold, and, to the public, sudden championship of the Constitution was the explosion in the opposition's camp of a bomb which they had hoped and believed their own ammunition.

Never before, said Randolph, had such a vast event come to a head without war or force. It might well be feared that the best wisdom would be unequal to the emergency and that passion might prevail over reason. He warned the opposition that the chair "well knows what is order, how to command obedience, and that political opinions may be as

[1] Elliott, iii, 21-23. [2] Grigsby, i, 83-84.
[3] Madison was the real designer of the Virginia plan. (Rives, ii, chap. xxvii.)

honest on one side as on the other." Randolph then tried to explain his change. "I had not even the glimpse of the genius of America," said he of his refusal to sign the report of the Federal Convention. But it was now so late that to insist on amendments before ratification would mean "inevitable ruin to the Union"; [1] and he would strike off his arm rather than permit that.

Randolph then reviewed the state of the country under the Confederation: Congress powerless, public credit ruined, treaties violated, prices falling, trade paralyzed, "and justice trampled under foot." The world looks upon Americans "as little wanton bees, who had played for liberty, but had no sufficient solidity or wisdom" to keep it. True, the Federal Convention had exceeded its authority, but there was nothing else to be done. And why not use the expression "We, the people"? Was the new Government not for them? The Union is now at stake, and, exclaimed he, "I am a friend to the Union." [2]

The secret was out, at last; the Constitutionalists' *coup* was revealed. His speech placed Randolph openly and unreservedly on their side. "The Governor has ... thrown himself fully into the federal scale," gleefully reported the anxious Madison to the supreme Nationalist chieftain at Mount Vernon.[3]

[1] This was the point Washington had made to Randolph. It is interesting that, throughout the debate, Randolph, over and over again, used almost the exact language of Washington's letter.

[2] Elliott, iii, 23–29. Randolph's speech was apologetic for his change of heart. He was not "a candidate for popularity": he had "satisfied his conscience," etc.

[3] Madison to Washington, June 4, 1788; *Writings:* Hunt, v, 124.

"The G[overno]r exhibited a curious spectacle to view. Having refused to sign the paper [the Constitution] everybody supposed him against it," was Jefferson's comment on Randolph's change of front.[1] Washington, perfectly informed, wrote Jay in New York that "Mr. Randolph's declaration will have considerable effect with those who had hitherto been wavering."[2] Theodoric Bland wrote bitterly to Arthur Lee that, "Our chief magistrate has at length taken his party and appears to be reprobated by the honest of both sides. . . . He has openly declared for posterior amendments, or in other words, unconditional submission."[3]

All of Randolph's influence, popularity, and prestige of family were to be counted for the Constitution without previous amendment; and this was a far weightier force, in the practical business of getting votes for ratification, than oratory or argument.[4] So "the sanguine friends of the Constitution counted upon a majority of twenty . . . which number they imagine will be greatly increased."[5]

Randolph's sensational about-face saved the Constitution. Nothing that its advocates did during these seething three weeks of able discussion and skillful planning accomplished half so much to secure ratification. Washington's tremendous influence,

[1] Jefferson to Short, Sept. 20, 1788; quoting a private letter from Virginia of July 12; *Works:* Ford, v, 431.
[2] Washington to Jay, June 8, 1788; *Writings:* Ford, xi, 271.
[3] Bland to Lee, June 13, 1788; Rowland, ii, 243-44. Evidently the opposition was slow to believe that Randolph had irrevocably deserted them; for Bland's letter was not written until Randolph had made his fourth extended speech ten days later.   [4] Scott, 160.
[5] Washington to Jay, June 8, 1788; *Writings:* Ford, xi, 271.

aggressive as it was tactful, which, as Monroe truly said, "carried" the new National plan, was not so practically effective as his work in winning Randolph. For, aside from his uncloaked support, the Virginia Governor at that moment had a document under lock and key which, had even rumor of it got abroad, surely would have doomed the Constitution, ended the debate abruptly, and resulted in another Federal Convention to deal anew with the Articles of Confederation.

By now the Anti-Constitutionalists, or Republicans as they had already begun to call themselves, also were acting in concert throughout the country. Their tactics were cumbersome and tardy compared with the prompt celerity of the well-managed Constitutionalists; but they were just as earnest and determined. The Society of the Federal Republicans had been formed in New York to defeat the proposed National Government and to call a second Federal Convention. It opened correspondence in most of the States and had agents and officers in many of them.

New York was overwhelmingly against the Constitution, and her Governor, George Clinton, was the most stubborn and resourceful of its foes. On December 27, 1787, Governor Randolph, under the formal direction of Virginia's Legislature, had sent the Governors of the other States a copy of the act providing for Virginia's Convention, which included the clause for conferring with her sister Commonwealths upon the calling of a new Federal Convention. The one to Clinton of New York was delayed in the mails for exactly two months and eleven days, just long enough to prevent New York's Legislature from acting on it.[1]

After pondering over it for a month, the New York leader of the Anti-Constitutionalist forces wrote Governor Randolph, more than three weeks before the Virginia Convention assembled, the now famous letter stating that Clinton was sure that the New York Convention, to be held June 17, "will, with great cordiality, hold a communication with any sister State on the important subject [a new Federal Convention] and especially with one so respectable in point of importance, ability, and patriotism as Virginia"; and Clinton assumed that the Virginia Convention would "commence the measures for holding such communications." [2]

When Clinton thus wrote to Randolph, he supposed, of course, that the Virginia Governor was against the Constitution. Had the New York Executive known that Randolph had been proselyted by the Constitutionalists, Clinton would have written to Henry, or Mason, or taken some other means of getting his letter before the Virginia Convention. Randolph kept all knowledge of Clinton's fatal communication from everybody excepting his Executive Council. He did not make it public until after the long, hard struggle was ended; when, for the first time, too late to be of any effect, he laid the

[1] From this delay Randolph's enemies have charged that his letter to Clinton was not posted in time. Much as Randolph had to answer for, this charge is unjust. Letters between Richmond and New York sometimes were two or three months on the way. (See *supra*, chap. VII.)

[2] Clinton to Randolph, May 8, 1788; Conway, 110-12.

IN THE GREAT CONVENTION

New York communication before the Virginia Legislature which assembled just as the Convention was adjourning.[1]

Weighty as were the arguments and brilliant the oratory that made the Virginia debate one of the noblest displays of intellect and emotion which the world ever has seen, yet nothing can be plainer than that other practices on both sides of that immortal struggle were more decisive of the result than the amazing forensic duel that took place on the floor of the Convention hall.

When one reflects that although the weight of fact and reason was decisively in favor of the Constitutionalists; that their forces were better organized and more ably led; that they had on the ground to help them the most astute politicians from other States as well as from Virginia; that Washington aggressively supported them with all his incalculable moral influence; that, if the new National Government were established, this herculean man surely would be President with all the practical power of that office, of which patronage was not the least — when one considers that, notwithstanding all of these and many other crushing advantages possessed by the Constitutionalists, their majority, when the test vote finally came, was only eight out of a total vote of one hundred and sixty-eight; when one takes into account the fact that, to make up even this slender majority, one or two members violated their instructions and several others voted

[1] Clinton to Randolph, May 8, 1788; Conway, 110–12; Henry, ii, 363; Rowland, ii, 276–79; and see *infra*, chap. XII.

against the known will of their constituents, it becomes plain how vitally necessary to their cause was the Constitutionalists' capture of the Virginia Governor.[1]

The opponents of the proposed National Government never forgave him nor was his reputation ever entirely reëstablished. Mason thereafter scathingly referred to Randolph as "young A[rno]ld." [2]

Answering Randolph, Mason went to the heart of the subject. "Whether the Constitution be good or bad," said he, "it is a national government and no longer a Confederation . . . that the new plan provides for." The power of direct taxation alone "is

[1] Randolph's change was ascribed to improper motives. Mason was almost offensive in his insinuations during the debate and Henry openly so, as will appear. Randolph's last words to the Convention were explanatory and defensive.

Washington made Randolph his first Attorney-General and he exercised great power for a time. "The Government is now solely directed by Randolph," complained Jefferson. (Conway, 140.) While Washington certainly did not appoint Randolph as a reward for his conduct in the struggle over the Constitution, it is a reasonable inference that he would not have been made a member of the Cabinet if he had not abandoned his opposition, supported the Constitution, and suppressed Clinton's letter.

Virginia had the head of the Cabinet in Jefferson as Secretary of State; Washington himself was from Virginia; and since there were numerous men from other States as well as or better equipped than Randolph for the Attorney-Generalship, his selection for that place is, at least, noteworthy. It gave Virginia the Presidency and two members of a Cabinet which numbered only four in all.

When the Attorney-Generalship was tendered to Randolph, he wrote to Madison bitterly resenting "the load of calumny which would be poured upon" him if he should accept. "For," writes Randolph, "it has been insinuated . . . that my espousal of the Constitution had alienated even its friends from me, who would not elect me to the house of representatives. The insinuation has been carried so far as to apply it to the disposal of offices under the government." (Randolph to Madison, July 19, 1789; Conway, 127-28.)

[2] Rowland, ii, 308.

calculated to annihilate totally the state governments." It means, said Mason, individual taxation "by two different and distinct powers" which "cannot exist long together; the one will destroy the other." One National Government is not fitted for an extensive country. "Popular governments can only exist in small territories." A consolidated government "is one of the worst curses that can possibly befall a nation." Clear as this now was, when the Convention came to consider the Judiciary clause, everybody would, Mason thought, "be more convinced that this government will terminate in the annihilation of the state governments."

But here again the author of Virginia's Bill of Rights made a tactical mistake from the standpoint of the management of the fight, although it was big-hearted and statesmanlike in itself. "If," said he, "such amendments be introduced as shall exclude danger... I shall most heartily make the greatest concessions... to obtain... conciliation and unanimity."[1] No grindstone, this, to sharpen activity — no hammer and anvil, this, to shape and harden an unorganized opposition into a single fighting blade, wielded to bring victory or even to force honorable compromise. The suggestion of conciliation before the first skirmish was over was not the way to arouse the blood of combat in the loose, undisciplined ranks of the opposition.

Swift as any hawk, the Constitutionalists pounced upon Mason's error, but they seized it gently as a dove. "It would give me great pleasure," cooed

[1] Elliott, iii, 29-34.

Madison, "to concur with my honorable colleague in any conciliatory plan." But the hour was now late, and he would postpone further remarks for the time being.[1]

So the Convention adjourned and the day ended with the Constitutionalists in high spirits.[2] Madison wrote to Washington that "Henry & Mason made a lame figure & appeared to take different and awkward ground. The Federalists [Constitutionalists][3] are a good deal elated by the existing prospect." Nevertheless, the timid Madison fluttered with fear. "I dare not," wrote he, "speak with certainty as to the decision. Kentucky has been extremely tainted and is supposed to be generally adverse, and every possible piece of address is going on privately to work on the local interests & prejudices of that & other quarters."[4]

The next day the building of the New Academy, where the Convention met, was packed with an eager throng. Everybody expected Madison to engage both Henry and Mason as he had intimated that he would do. But once more the excellent management of the Constitutionalists was displayed. Madison, personally, was not popular,[5] he was physically unimpressive, and strong only in his superb intellect. The time to discharge the artillery of that powerful

[1] Elliott, iii, 34–35. [2] Grigsby, i, 99.
[3] Those who supported the Constitution were called "Federalists" and its opponents "Anti-Federalists"; but, for sake of clearness, the terms "Constitutionalists" and "Anti-Constitutionalists" are employed in these chapters.
[4] Madison to Washington, June 4, 1788; *Writings:* Hunt, v, footnote to 123–24.
[5] Grigsby, i, footnote to 46.

IN THE GREAT CONVENTION

mind had not yet come. Madison was not the man for this particular moment. But Pendleton was, and so was "Light-Horse Harry" Lee. The Constitutionalists combined the ermine and the sword. Virginia's most venerated jurist and her most dashing soldier were ordered to the front. In them there was an appeal to much that the Old Dominion still reverenced and loved, in spite of the "levelling spirit" manifest there as well as in Massachusetts and other States. So when all eyes were turned on Madison's seat, they beheld it vacant. Madison had stayed away. Had he been present, he could not have avoided speaking.

Dramatic, indeed, appeared the white-haired, crippled jurist, as, struggling to his feet, he finally stood upon his crutches and faced the Convention. He had been unused to public debate for many years, and was thought to be so infirm that no one expected him to do more than make or decide points of order and give his vote. Yet there the feeble old man stood to answer the resistless Henry and the learned Mason. His ancient friend and brother justice, Wythe, leaned forward from his chair to catch the tones of the beloved voice. Tears rolled down the cheeks of some of the oldest members who for decades had been Pendleton's friends.[1] The Constitutionalists had set the stage to catch the

---

[1] Grigsby, i, 101–02. Scenes of a similar character occurred several times in both Senate and House between 1900 and 1911, when one of our elder statesmen, who plainly was nearing the end of life, rose to speak. More than one notable contest, during that decade, was decided by the sympathetic votes of aged friends who answered the call of long years of affection.

emotions which they affected to despise, with the very character whose strength was in that pure reasoning on which they pretended solely to rely.

Without wasting a word, Pendleton came to the point. Henry, he said, had declared that all was well before "this Federal system was thought of." Was that accurate? In a few short sentences he showed that it was not. There was, said Pendleton, "no quarrel between government and liberty; the former is shield and protector of the latter. The war is between government and licentiousness, faction, turbulence, and other violations of the rules of society to preserve liberty." Why are the words "We, the people," improper? "Who but the people have a right to form government? ... What have the state governments to do with it?" Had the Federal Convention exceeded its powers? No. Because those powers were "to propose, not to determine."

"Suppose," asked the venerable Pendleton, "the paper on your table [the Constitution] dropped from one of the planets; the people found it, and sent us here to consider whether it was proper for their adoption; must we not obey them?" Of course. "Then the question must be between this government and the Confederation," which "is no government at all." The Confederation did not carry us through the war; "common danger and the spirit of America" did that. The cry "United we stand — divided we fall," which "echoed and reëchoed through America — from Congress to the drunken carpenter" — saved us in that dark hour. And Pendleton clearly, briefly, solidly, answered every objection which Mason and Henry had made. Nothing could have been more practically effective than his close. He was of no party, Pendleton avowed; and his "age and situation" proved that nothing but the general good influenced him.[1]

The smouldering fires in Henry's blood now burned fiercely. This was the same Pendleton who had fought Henry in his immortal resolution on the Stamp Act in 1765 and in every other of those epochal battles for liberty and human rights which Henry had led and won.[2] But the Constitutionalists gave the old war horse no chance to charge upon his lifelong opponent. A young man, thirty-two years of age, rose, and, standing within a few feet of the chair, was recognized. Six feet tall, beautiful of face, with the resounding and fearless voice of a warrior, Henry Lee looked the part which reputation assigned him. Descended from one of the oldest and most honorable families in the colony, a graduate of Princeton College, one of the most daring, picturesque, and attractive officers of the Revolution, in which by sheer gallantry and military genius he had become commander of a famous cavalry command, the gallant Lee was a perfect contrast to the venerable Pendleton.[3]

Lee paid tribute to Henry's shining talents; but, said he, "I trust that he [Henry] is come to judge, and not to alarm." Henry had praised Washington; yet Washington was for the Constitution. What was there wrong with the expression "We, the

[1] Elliott, iii, 35-41.
[2] See *infra*, chap. III; also Grigsby, i, 105-06.   [3] *Ib.*, 106-09.

people," since upon the people "it is to operate, if adopted"? Like every Constitutionalist speaker, Lee painted in somber and forbidding colors the condition of the country, "all owing to the imbecility of the Confederation." [1]

At last Henry secured the floor. At once he struck the major note of the opposition. "The question turns," said he, "on that poor little thing — the expression, 'We, the *people;* instead of the *states.*'" It was an "alarming transition ... a revolution [2] as radical as that which separated us from Great Britain.... Sovereignty of the states ... rights of conscience, trial by jury, liberty of the press, ... all pretensions of human rights and privileges" were imperiled if not lost by the change.

It *was* the "despised" Confederation that had carried us through the war. Think well, he urged, before you part with it. "Revolutions like this have happened in almost every country in Europe." The new Government may prevent "licentiousness," but also "it will oppress and ruin the people," thundered their champion. The Constitution was clear when it spoke of "sedition," but fatally vague when it spoke of "privileges." Where, asked Henry, were the dangers the Constitutionalists conjured up? Purely imaginary! If any arose, he depended on "the American spirit" to defend us.

---

[1] Elliott, iii, 41–43.

[2] Elliott, iii, 44. The word "revolution" is printed "resolution" in Elliott's *Debates*. This is a good example of the inaccuracy of Elliott's reprint of Robertson's stenographic report. In Robertson's *Debates*, published in 1805, the word is correctly printed "revolution." I have cited Elliott only because it is accessible. Even Robertson's report is admittedly meager and unsatisfactory; all the more, therefore, is it to be regretted that Elliott's reprint should be so inaccurate.

The method of amendment provided in the Constitution, exclaimed Henry, was a mockery — it shut the door on amendment. "A contemptible minority can prevent the good of the majority." "A standing army" will "execute the execrable commands of tyranny," shouted Henry. And who, he asked, will punish them? "Will your mace-bearer be a match for a disciplined regiment?" If the Constitution is adopted, "it will be because we like a great splendid" government. "The ropes and chains of consolidation" were "about to convert this country into a powerful and mighty empire." The Constitution's so-called checks and balances, sneered Henry, were "rope-dancing, chain-rattling, ridiculous . . . contrivances."

The Constitutionalists talked of danger if the Confederation was continued; yet, under it, declared Henry, "peace and security, ease and content" were now the real lot of all. Why, then, attempt "to terrify us into an adoption of this new form of government? . . . Who knows the dangers this new system may produce? They are out of sight of the common people; they cannot foresee latent consequences." It was the operation of the proposed National Government "on the middling and lower classes of people" that Henry feared. "This government" [the Constitution], cried he, "is not a Virginian but an American government."

Throughout Henry's speech, in which he voiced, as he never failed to do, the thought of the masses, a National Government is held up as a foreign power — even one so restricted as the literal words of the

Constitution outlined. Had the Constitutionalists acknowledged those Nationalist opinions which, in later years, were to fall from the lips of a young member of the Convention and become the law of the land, the defeat of the Constitution would have been certain, prompt, and overwhelming.

In the Constitution's chief executive, Henry saw "a great and mighty President" with "the powers of a King . . . to be supported in extravagant magnificence." The National Government's tax-gatherers would "ruin you with impunity," he warned his fellow members and the people they represented. Did not Virginia's own "state sheriffs, those unfeeling blood-suckers," even "under the watchful eye of our legislature commit the most horrid and barbarous ravages on our people? . . . Lands have been sold," asserted he, "for 5 shillings which were worth one hundred pounds." What, then, would happen to the people "if their master had been at Philadelphia or New York?" asked Henry. "These harpies may search at any time your houses and most secret recesses." Its friends talked about the beauty of the Constitution, but to Henry its features were "horribly frightful. Among other deformities, it has an awful squinting; it squints toward monarchy."

The President, "your American chief," can make himself absolute, dramatically exclaimed the great orator. "If ever he violates the laws . . . he will come at the head of his army to carry everything before him; or he will give bail, or do what Mr. Chief Justice will order him." But will he submit to punishment? Rather, he will "make one bold push for the

American throne," prophesied Henry. "We shall have a king; the army will salute him monarch: your militia will leave you, and assist in making him king and fight against you." [1] It would be infinitely better, he avowed, to have a government like Great Britain with "King, Lords, and Commons, than a government so replete with such insupportable evils" as the Constitution contained.

Henry spoke of the danger of the power of Congress over elections, and the treaty-making power. A majority of the people were against the Constitution, he said, and even "the adopting states have already heart-burnings and animosity and repent their precipitate hurry. . . . Pennsylvania has been tricked into" ratification. "If other states who have adopted it have not been tricked, still they were too much hurried.[2] . . . I have not said the one hundred thousandth part of what I have on my mind and wish to impart" — with these words of warning to the Constitutionalists, Henry closed by apologizing for the time he had taken. He admitted that he had spoken out of order, but trusted that the Convention would hear him again.[3]

Studying this attack and defense of master swordsmen, following the tactical maneuvers of America's ablest politicians, a partisan on one side, yet personally friendly with members of the other, John

[1] At this point the reporter, unable to follow Henry's speech, notes that he "strongly and pathetically expatiated on the probability of the President's enslaving America and the horrid consequences that must result." (Elliott, iii, 60.)
[2] Henry had not heard of the Constitutionalists' bargain with Hancock in Massachusetts.
[3] Elliott, iii, 43-64.

Marshall was waiting for the call that should bring him into the battle and, by the method which he employed throughout his life, preparing to respond when the Constitutionalist managers should give the word. He was listening to the arguments on both sides, analyzing them, and, by that process of absorption with which he was so peculiarly and curiously gifted, mastering the subjects under discussion. Also, although casual, humorous, and apparently indifferent, he nevertheless was busy, we may be sure, with his winning ways among his fellow members.

Patrick Henry's effort was one of the two or three speeches made during the three weeks of debate which actually may have had an effect upon votes.[1] The Constitutionalists feared that Henry would take the floor next morning to follow up his success and deepen the profound impression he had made. To prevent this and to break the force of Henry's onslaught, they put forward Governor Randolph, who was quickly recognized by the chair. Madison and Nicholas were held in reserve.[2]

But in vain did Randolph employ his powers of oratory, argument, and persuasion in the great speech beginning "I am a child of the Revolution," with which he attempted to answer Henry. There is no peace; "the tempest growls over you. . . . Jus-

---

[1] General Posey, a Revolutionary officer, who was for the Constitution, afterwards said that Henry's speech made him believe that the Constitution would destroy liberty. Another intelligent man who heard Henry's speech said that when the great orator pictured the President at the head of the army, he felt his own wrists for the shackles, and that his place in the gallery suddenly seemed like a dungeon. (Grigsby, i, 118-19.)

[2] Grigsby, i, 121.

IN THE GREAT CONVENTION 393

tice is suffocated," he said; legal proceedings to collect debts are "obscured by legislative mists." As an illustration of justice, consider the case of Josiah Philips, executed without trial or witness, on a bill of attainder passed without debate on the mere report of a member of the Legislature: "*This made the deepest impression on my heart and I cannot contemplate it without horror.*"[1] As to "the American spirit" expressed through the militia being competent to the defense of the State, Randolph asked: "Did ever militia defend a country?"

Randolph's speech was exhaustive and reached the heights of real eloquence. It all came to this, he said, Union or Dissolution, thus again repeating the argument Washington had urged in his letter to Randolph. "Let that glorious pride which once defied the British thunder, reanimate you again," he cried dramatically.[2] But his fervor, popularity, and influence were not enough.

[1] Elliott, iii, 64–86. In the debate, much was made of this famous case. Yet Philips was not executed under the provisions of the law Randolph referred to. When arrested, he was indicted, tried, and convicted in the General Court; and he was hanged by sentence of the court, December 4, 1778.

Although, at that time, Randolph was Attorney-General of Virginia and actually prosecuted the case; and although Henry was Governor and ordered the arrest of Philips (Henry, i, 611–13), yet, ten years later, both had forgotten the facts, and Randolph charged, and Henry in reply admitted, that Philips had been executed under the bill of attainder without trial. (Jefferson to Wirt, Oct. 14, 1814; *Works:* Ford, xi, 407.) The bill of attainder was drawn by Jefferson. It appears in *ib.*, ii, 330–36.

Marshall, when he came to speak later in the debate, made the same mistake. No more striking illustration exists of how public men, in the hurry and pressure of large affairs, forget the most important events, even when they themselves were principal actors in them.

[2] Again, Randolph's speech was marred by the note of personal

Although the time had not properly come for the great logician of the Constitution to expound it, the situation now precipitated the psychological hour for him to strike. The chair recognized a slender, short-statured man of thirty-seven, wearing a handsome costume of blue and buff with doubled straight collar and white ruffles on breast and at wrists. His hair, combed forward to conceal baldness, was powdered and fell behind in the long beribboned queue of fashion. He was so small that he could not be seen by all the members; and his voice was so weak that only rarely could he be heard throughout the hall.[1] Such was James Madison as he stood, hat in hand and his notes in his hat, and began the first of those powerful speeches, the strength of which, in spite of poor reporting, has projected itself through more than a hundred years.

At first he spoke so low that even the reporter could not catch what he said.[2] He would not, remarked Madison, attempt to impress anybody by "ardent professions of zeal for the public welfare." Men should be judged by deeds and not by words. The real point was whether the Constitution would be a good thing or a bad thing for the country. Henry had mentioned the dangers concealed in the Constitution; let him specify and prove them. One explanation that pervaded it. "The rectitude of my intentions"; "ambition and popularity are no objects with me"; "I expect, in the course of a year, to retire to that private station which I most sincerely and cordially prefer to all others," — such expressions gave to his otherwise aggressive and very able appeal a defensive tone.

[1] Grigsby, i, 130. Madison's apparel at this Convention was as ornate as his opinions were, in his opponents' eyes, "aristocratic."

[2] Elliott, iii, 86. See entire speech, *ib.*, 86-96.

IN THE GREAT CONVENTION 395

by one he caught and crushed Henry's points in the jaws of merciless logic.

What, for the gentle Madison, was a bold blow at the opposition shows how even he was angered. "The inflammatory violence wherewith it [the Constitution] was opposed by designing, illiberal, and unthinking minds, begins to subside. I will not enumerate the causes from which, in my conception, the heart-burnings of a majority of its opposers have originated." His argument was unanswerable as a matter of pure reason and large statesmanship, but it made little headway and had only slight if any influence. "I am not so sanguine," reported Washington's nephew to the General at Mount Vernon, "as to . . . flatter myself that he made many converts." [1]

The third gun of the powerful battery which the Constitutionalists had arranged to batter down the results of Henry's speech was now brought into action. George Nicholas again took the floor. He was surprised that Mason's resolution to debate the Constitution clause by clause had not been followed. But it had not been, and therefore he must speak at large. While Nicholas advanced nothing new, his address was a masterpiece of compact reasoning. [2]

Age and middle age had spoken for the Constitution; voices from the bench and the camp, from the

[1] Bushrod Washington to Washington, June 6, 1788; *Writings:* Sparks, ix, 378. But Madison gave Henry an opening through which that veteran orator drove like a troop of horse, as far as practical and momentary effect was concerned. Madison described the new government as partly National and partly Federal. (Elliott, iii, 94; and see Henry's use of this, *ib.*, 171; also *infra.*)

[2] Elliott, iii, 97–103.

bar and the seats of the mighty, had pleaded for it; and now the Constitutionalists appealed to the very young men of the Convention through one of the most attractive of their number. The week must not close with Henry's visions of desolation uppermost in the minds of the members. On Saturday morning the chair recognized Francis Corbin of Middlesex. He was twenty-eight years old and of a family which had lived in Virginia from the early part of the seventeenth century. He had been educated in England at the University of Cambridge, studied law at the Inner Temple, was a trained lawyer, and a polished man of the world.

Corbin made one of the best speeches of the whole debate. On the nonpayment of our debts to foreign nations he was particularly strong. "What!" said he, "borrow money to discharge interest on what was borrowed? . . . Such a plan would destroy the richest country on earth." As to a Republican Government not being fitted for an extensive country, he asked, "How small must a country be to suit the genius of Republicanism?" The power of taxation was the "lungs of the Constitution." His defense of a standing army was novel and ingenious. The speech was tactful in the deference paid to older men, and so captivating in the pride it must have aroused in the younger members that it justified the shrewdness of the Constitutionalist generals in putting forward this youthful and charming figure.[1]

Of course Henry could not follow a mere boy. He cleverly asked that Governor Randolph should

[1] Elliott, iii, 104–14.

finish, as the latter had promised to do.[1] Randolph could not avoid responding; and his speech, while very able, was nevertheless an attempt to explode powder already burned.[2] Madison saw this, and getting the eye of the chair delivered the second of those intellectual broadsides, which, together with his other mental efforts during the Constitutional period, mark him as almost the first, if not indeed the very first, mind of his time.[3] The philosophy and method of taxation, the history and reason of government, the whole range of the vast subject were discussed,[4] or rather begun; for Madison did not finish, and took up the subject four days later. His effort so exhausted him physically that he was ill for three days.[5]

Thus fortune favored Henry. The day, Saturday, was not yet spent. After all, he could leave the last impression on the members and spectators, could apply fresh color to the picture he wished his hearers to have before their eyes until the next week renewed the conflict. And he could retain the floor so as to open again when Monday came. The art of Henry in this speech was supreme. He began by stating the substance of Thomas Paine's terrific sentence about government being, at best, "a neces-

[1] Elliott, iii, 114. [2] Ib., 114-28.
[3] Madison was equaled only by Hamilton in sheer intellectuality, but he was inferior to that colossus in courage and constructive genius.
[4] Ib., 128-37.
[5] Madison to Hamilton, June 9, 1788; Hamilton MSS., Lib. Cong. Madison's four famous speeches in this Convention, are properly parts of one comprehensive exposition. (See Madison's own notes for the third of these speeches in *Writings:* Hunt, v, 148.) Mr. Hunt also prints accurately Robertson's report of the speeches themselves in that volume. They cannot be summarized here, but should be read in full.

sary evil"; and aroused anew that repugnance to any sturdy rule which was a general feeling in the breasts of the masses.

Both the Confederation and the proposed Constitution were "evils," asserted Henry, and the only question was which was the less. Randolph and Madison incautiously had referred to maxims. Henry seized the word with infinite skill. "It is impiously irritating the avenging hand of Heaven ... to desert those maxims which alone can preserve liberty," he thundered. They were lowly maxims, to be sure, "poor little, humble republican maxims"; but "humble as they are" they alone could make a nation safe or formidable. He rang the changes on the catchwords of liberty.

Then Henry spoke of Randolph's change of front. The Constitution "was once execrated" by Randolph. "It seems to me very strange and unaccountable that that which was the object of his execration should now receive his encomiums. Something extraordinary must have operated so great a change in his opinion." Randolph had said that it was too late to oppose the "New Plan"; but, answered Henry, "I can never believe that it is too late to save all that is precious." Henry denied the woeful state of the country which the Constitutionalist speakers had pictured. The "imaginary dangers" conjured by them were to intimidate the people; but, cried Henry, "fear is the passion of slaves." The execution of Josiah Philips under the bill of attainder was justifiable. Philips had been a "fugitive murderer and an outlaw" leader of "an infamous banditti," perpetrator of "the most cruel and shocking barbarities . . . an enemy to human nature." [1]

It was not true, declared Henry, that the people were discontented under the Confederation — at least the common people were not; and it was the common people for whom he spoke. But, of course, sneered that consummate actor, "the middling and lower ranks of people have not those illuminated ideas" which the "well-born" are so happily possessed of; "they [the common people] cannot so readily perceive latent objects." It was only the "illuminated imaginations" and the "microscopic eyes of modern statesmen" that could see defects where there were none.

Henry hinted with great adroitness at the probable loss of the Mississippi, which was the sorest point with the members from Kentucky; and, having injected the poison, passed on to let it do its work against the time when he would strike with all his force. Then he appealed to state pride. "When I call this the most mighty state in the Union, do I not speak the truth? Does not Virginia surpass every state?" Of course! There was no danger, then, that Virginia would be left out of the Union, as the Constitutionalists had hinted might happen if Virginia rejected the Constitution; the other States would be glad to have her on her own terms.

Henry went over a variety of subjects and then returned to his favorite idea of the National Government as something foreign. Picking up a careless word of Randolph, who had spoken of the people

[1] See *supra*, footnote to 393.

as a "herd," Henry said that perhaps the words "We, the people," were used to recommend it to the masses, "to those who are likened to a *herd;* and by the operation of this blessed system are to be transformed from respectable, independent citizens, to abject, dependent subjects or slaves."[1] Finally, when he felt that he had his hearers once more under his spell, Henry, exclaiming that a Bill of Rights was vital, asked for adjournment, which was taken, the great orator still holding the floor.

[1] Elliott, iii, 137-50.

CHAPTER XI

THE SUPREME DEBATE

There will undoubtedly be a greater weight of abilities against the adoption in this convention than in any other state. (Washington.)

What are the objects of the National Government? To protect the United States and to promote the general welfare. (Marshall, in his first debate.)

Now appeared the practical political managers from other States. From Saturday afternoon until Monday morning there was great activity in both camps. The politicians of each side met in secret conference to plan the operations of the coming week and to devise ways and means of getting votes. For the Constitutionalists, Gouverneur Morris was on the ground from New York;[1] Robert Morris and probably James Wilson, both from Philadelphia, had been in Virginia at the time of the elections and the former remained for the Convention.[2] During the second week the Philadelphia financier writes Gates from Richmond, lamenting "the depre-

[1] "I am to acknowledge yours of the 19th of May, which reached me a few days since." (Gouverneur Morris from Richmond, June 13, 1788, to Hamilton in New York; Hamilton MSS., Lib. Cong.)

[2] Robert Morris to Horatio Gates, Richmond, June 12, 1788; MS., N.Y. Pub. Lib. "James [Wilson] the Caladonian, Leut. Gen. of the myrmidons of power, under Robert [Morris] the cofferer, who with his aid-de-camp, *Gouvero* [Gouverneur] the cunning man, has taken the field in Virginia." (*Centinel*, no. 10, Jan. 12, 1788; reprinted in McMaster and Stone, 631.)

Robert Morris was in Richmond, March 21, 1788. (Morris to *Independent Gazetteer* on that date; *ib.*, 787, denying the charge that paper had made against him. See *supra*, chap. x.) He was in Richmond in May and paid John Marshall four pounds, four shillings as a "retainer." (Account Book, May 2, 1788.) He had heavy business interests in Virginia; see Braxton *vs.* Willing, Morris & Co. (4 Call, 288). Marshall was his lawyer.

dations on my purse," but "inclined to think the Constitution will be adopted by Virginia." [1]

For the opposition, Oswald, publisher of the "Independent Gazetteer," came on from Philadelphia and arrived in Richmond at the close of the first week's debate. He at once went into secret conference with Henry, Mason, and the other Anti-Constitutionalist leaders. Madison reports to Hamilton that "Oswald of Phil[a] came here on Saturday; and he has closet interviews with the leaders of the opposition." [2] By the same mail Grayson advises the general Anti-Constitutionalist headquarters in New York that he is "sorry . . . that our affairs in the convention are suspended by a hair." Randolph's conduct "has not injured us," writes Grayson, thus proving how poorly the Anti-Constitutionalists estimated the real situation. But they were practical enough to know that "there are seven or eight dubious characters whose opinions are not known" and upon whose decisions the fate of the Constitution "will ultimately depend." Grayson cautions Lamb not to let this get into the newspapers.[3]

Just what was devised and decided by the leaders of both sides in these behind-the-doors meetings and

[1] Morris to Gates, June 12, 1788, *supra*. Morris's remark about depredations on his purse may or may not refer to the work of the Convention. He was always talking in this vein about his expenses; he had lost money in his Virginia business ventures; and, having his family with him, may, for that reason, have found his Southern trip expensive. My own belief is that no money was used to get votes; for Henry, Mason, and Grayson surely would have heard of and, if so, denounced such an attempt.

[2] Madison to Hamilton, June 9, 1788; Hamilton MSS., Lib. Cong.

[3] Grayson to Lamb, June 9, 1788; quoted in Leake: *Lamb*, 311.

what methods were used outside the Convention hall to influence votes, there is no means of learning exactly; though "the opposition" committee seems to have been occupied chiefly in drawing amendments.[1] But the frequent references, particularly of the Constitutionalist speakers on the floor, to improper conduct of their adversaries "out of doors" show that both sides were using every means known to the politics of the day to secure support. In the debate itself Henry certainly was making headway.[2]

On Monday, Henry and Mason made a dramatic entrance into the Convention hall. Walking arm in arm from their quarters in "The Swan,"[3] they stopped on the steps at the doors of the New Academy and conferred earnestly for some minutes; so great was the throng that the two Anti-Constitutionalist chieftains made their way to their seats with great difficulty.[4] When Henry rose to go on with his speech, the plan decided on during Sunday quickly was revealed. The great prize for which both sides now were fighting was the votes from Kentucky.[5] Henry held up before them the near forfeiture to the Spanish of our right to navigate the

---

[1] Grayson to Lamb, June 9, 1788; quoted in Leake: *Lamb*, 311.
[2] Grigsby, i, 149–50.
[3] The new tavern at Richmond — competitor of Formicola's inn.
[4] Grigsby, i, 151.
[5] Kentucky had fourteen members. On the final vote, the Constitution was ratified by a majority of only 10 out of 168 members present and voting. At the opening of the Convention, Grayson said that "the district of Kentucke is with us, and if we can get all of the four Counties, which lye on the Ohio between the Pennsylv[a] line and Big Sandy Creek, the day is our own." (Grayson to Dane, June 4, 1788; Dane MSS., Lib. Cong.) The Constitutionalists finally succeeded in getting four of these Kentucky votes.

Mississippi.[1] This, he said, was the work of seven Northern States; but under the Confederation they had been thwarted in their fell purpose by six Southern States; and the Mississippi still remained our own. But if the Constitution was adopted, what would happen? The Senate would be controlled by those same Northern States that had nearly succeeded in surrendering the great waterway and the West and South would surely be deprived of that invaluable commercial outlet. He asked the members of Congress who were in the Convention to tell the facts about the Mississippi business. Jefferson, he avowed, had counseled Virginia to "reject this government."[2]

Henry answered the Constitutionalists' prophecy of foreign war, ridiculed danger from the Indians, proved that the Constitution would not pay Virginia's debts; and, in characteristic fashion, ranged at large over the field. The Constitution, he asserted, would "operate like an ambuscade ... destroy the state governments ... swallow the liberties of the people without" warning. "How are our debts to be discharged unless taxes are increased?" asked he; and demonstrated that under the Constitution taxes surely would be made heavier. Time and again he warned the Convention against the loss of liberty: "When the deprivation of our liberty was attempted, what did ... the genius of Virginia tell us? '*Sell all and purchase liberty!*' ... Repub-

[1] The Jay-Gardoqui agreement.
[2] Jefferson to Donald, Feb. 7, 1788; Jefferson's *Writings:* Washington, ii, 355; and see Monroe to Jefferson, July 12, 1788; *Writings:* Hamilton, i, 186–87.

lican maxims, ... and the genius of Virginia landed you safe on the shore of freedom."

Once more he praised the British form of government — an oversight which a hawk-eyed young member of the Convention, John Marshall, was soon to use against him. Henry painted in darkest colors the secrecy of the Federal Convention. "*Look at us — hear our transactions!* — if this had been the language of the Federal Convention," there would have been no Constitution, he asserted, and with entire accuracy. Yet, the Constitution itself authorized Congress to keep its proceedings as secret as those of the Constitution's makers had been kept: "The transactions of Congress," said Henry, "may be concealed a century from the public." [1]

Seizing Madison's description of the new Government as partly National and partly Federal, Henry brought to bear all his power of satire. He was "amused" at Madison's "treatise of political anatomy. ... In the brain it is national; the stamina are federal; some limbs are federal, others national." Absurd! The truth was, said Henry, that the Constitution provided for "a great consolidation of government." Why not abolish Virginia's Legislature and be done with it? This National Government would do what it liked with Virginia.

As to the plan of ratifying first and amending afterwards, Henry declared himself "at a loss what to say. You agree to bind yourselves hand and foot — for the sake of what? Of being unbound. You go

[1] Elliott, iii, 170–71. The reporter noted that "Mr. Henry in a very animated manner expatiated on the evil and pernicious tendency of keeping secret the common proceedings of government." (*Ib.*, 170.)

into a dungeon — for what? To get out. ... My anxiety and fears are great lest America by the adoption of this system [the Constitution], should be cast into a fathomless bottom."

Tradition has it that during this speech Henry, having frozen his hearers' blood by a terrific description of lost "liberty," with one of his sudden turns set both Convention and spectators into roars of laughter by remarking with a grimace, and as an aside, "why, *they'll free your niggers*."[1] And then, with one of those lightning changes of genius, which Henry alone could make, he solemnly exclaimed, "I look on that paper [the Constitution] as the most fatal plan that could possibly be conceived to enslave a free people."[2]

Lee, in reply, spoke of the lobbying going on outside the Convention. "Much is said by gentlemen out of doors," exclaimed Lee; "they ought to urge all their objections here." He taunted Henry, who had praised the militia, with not having been himself a soldier. "I saw what the honorable gentleman did not see," cried Lee, "our men fight with the troops of that King whom he so much admires."[3]

When the hot-blooded young soldier had finished his aggressive speech, Randolph could no longer restrain himself. Henry's bold challenge of Randolph's change of front had cut that proud and sen-

[1] Grigsby, i, footnote to 157. [2] Elliott, iii, 150–76.
[3] Lee, while pretending to praise the militia, really condemned it severely; and cited the militia's panic and flight at Guilford Court-House, which lost the battle to the Americans. "Had the line been supported that day," said he, "Cornwallis, instead of surrendering at Yorktown, would have laid down his arms at Guilford." (Elliott, iii, 178.)

sitive nature to the heart. "I disdain," thundered
he, "his aspersions and his insinuations." They
were "warranted by no principle of parliamentary
decency, nor compatible with the least shadow of
friendship; and if our friendship must fall, *let it fall,
like Lucifer, never to rise again!*" It was not to answer Henry that he spoke, snarled Randolph, "but
to satisfy this respectable audience." Randolph then
explained his conduct, reading part of the letter [1]
that had caused all the trouble, and dramatically
throwing the letter on the clerk's table, cried "that
it might lie there for *the inspection of the curious and
malicious.*" [2] Randolph spoke for the remainder of
the day and consumed most of the next forenoon.[3]

No soldier had yet spoken for the Anti-Constitutionalists; and it perhaps was Lee's fling at Henry
that now called a Revolutionary officer to his feet
against the Constitution. A tall, stiff, raw-boned
young man of thirty years arose. Poorly educated,
slow in his mental processes,[4] James Monroe made
a long, dull, and cloudy speech, finally declaring of
the Constitution, "I think it a dangerous government"; and asking "why . . . this haste — this
wild precipitation?" Long as Monroe's speech was,
he reminded the Convention that he had "not yet

[1] Randolph's letter explaining why he had refused to sign the Constitution.
[2] This was the only quarrel of the Convention which threatened
serious results. A duel was narrowly averted. Colonel William Cabell,
as Henry's friend, called on Randolph that night; but matters were
arranged and the tense situation relieved when it was learned, next
morning, that no duel would take place. (Grigsby, i, 162-65.)
[3] Elliott, iii, 187-207.
[4] Grigsby, i, 167-68.

said all that I wish upon the subject" and that he would return to the charge later on.[1]

Monroe did not help or hurt either side except, perhaps, by showing the members that all the Revolutionary veterans were not for the Constitution. Neither members nor spectators paid much attention to him, though this was no reflection on Monroe, for the Convention did not listen with patience to many speakers except Henry. When Henry spoke, every member was in his seat and the galleries were packed. But only the most picturesque of the other speakers could hold the audience for longer than half an hour; generally members walked about and the spectators were absent except when Henry took the floor.[2]

As usual, the Constitutionalists were ready with their counter-stroke. Wythe in the chair recognized a tall, ungainly young man of thirty-two. He was badly dressed in a loose, summer costume, and his blazing black eyes and unkempt raven hair made him look more like a poet or an artist than a lawyer or statesman.[3] He had bought a new coat the day the Convention met; but it was a most inexpensive addition to his raiment, for it cost but one pound, Virginia currency, then greatly depreciated.[4] He

[1] Elliott, iii, 207-22.

[2] "When any other member spoke, the members of the audience would, in half an hour, be going out or moving from their seats." (Winston to Wirt, quoted in Henry, ii, 347.) Henry spoke every day of the twenty-two days' debate, except five; and often spoke several times a day. (*Ib.*, 350.)

[3] Grigsby, i, 176.

[4] Marshall's Account Book. The entry is: "[June] 2 Paid for coat for self 1." Two months earlier Marshall paid "for Nankin for breeches for self 1.16." (*Ib.*, April 1, 1788.) Yet about the same time he spent one pound, nine shillings at a "barbecue."

probably was the best liked of all the members of the Convention. Sociable to extreme good-fellowship, "his habits," says Grigsby, "were convivial almost to excess";[1] and it is more than likely that, considering the times, these habits in his intimate social intercourse with his fellow members helped to get more votes than his arguments on the floor, of which he now was to make the first.[2] His four years' record as a soldier was as bright and clean as that of any man from any State who had fought under Washington.

So when John Marshall began to speak, he was listened to with the ears of affection; and any point the opposition had made by the fact that Monroe the soldier had spoken against the Constitution was turned by Marshall's appearance even before he had uttered a word. The young lawyer was also accounted an "orator" at this time,[3] a fact which added to the interest of his fellow members in his speech.

The question, Marshall said, was "whether democracy or despotism be most eligible."[4] He was sure that the framers and supporters of the Constitution "intend the establishment and security of the former"; they are "firm friends of the liberty and

[1] Grigsby, i, 176.
[2] Marshall had provided for entertaining during the Convention. His Account Book shows the following entry on May 8, 1788: "Paid McDonald for wine 20" (pounds); and "bottles 9/" (shillings). This was the largest quantity of wine Marshall had purchased up to that time.
[3] Marshall's reputation for "eloquence" grew, as we shall see, until his monumental work on the Supreme Bench overshadowed his fame as a public speaker.
[4] Elliott, iii, 222.

the rights of mankind." That was why they were for the Constitution. "We, sir, idolize democracy." The Constitution was, said he, the "best means of protecting liberty." The opposition had praised monarchy, but, deftly avowed Marshall, "We prefer this system to any monarchy"; for it provides for "a well regulated democracy."

He agreed with Henry that maxims should be observed; they were especially "essential to a democracy." But, "what are the ... maxims of democracy? ... A strict observance of justice and public faith, and a steady adherence to virtue. These, Sir, are the principles of a good government," [1] declared the young Richmond Constitutionalist.

"No mischief, no misfortune, ought to deter us from a strict observance of justice and public faith," cried Marshall. "Would to Heaven," he exclaimed, "that these principles had been observed under the present government [the Confederation]." He was thinking now of his experience in the Legislature and appealing to the honesty of the Convention. If the principles of justice and good faith had been observed, continued he, "the friends of liberty would not be so willing now to part with it [the Confederation]."

Could Virginians themselves boast that their own Government was based on justice? "Can we pretend to the enjoyment of political freedom or security,

[1] Marshall's idea was that government should be honest and efficient; a government by the people, whether good or bad, as a method of popular self-development and progress did not appeal to him as much as excellence in government.

when we are told that a man has been, by an act of Assembly, struck out of existence without a trial by jury, without examination, without being confronted with his accusers and witnesses, without the benefits of the law of the land?"[1] Skillfully he turned against Henry the latter's excuse for the execution of Philips, and dramatically asked: "Where is our safety, when we are told that this act was justifiable because the person was not a Socrates? . . . Shall it be a maxim that a man shall be deprived of his life without the benefit of the law?"

As to the navigation of the Mississippi, he asked: "How shall we retain it? By retaining that weak government which has hitherto kept it from us?" No, exclaimed Marshall, but by a Government with "the power of retaining it." Such a Government, he pointed out, was that proposed in the Constitution. Here again the Constitutionalist managers displayed their skill. Marshall was the best man they could have chosen to appeal to the Kentucky members on the Mississippi question. His father, mother, and his family were now living in Kentucky, and his relative, Humphrey Marshall, was a member of the Convention from that district.[2] Marshall himself was the legislative agent of the District of Kentucky in Richmond. The development of the West became a vital purpose with John Marshall, strengthening with the years; and

[1] Marshall here referred to the case of Josiah Philips, and fell into the same error as had Randolph, Henry, and others. (See *supra*, 393, footnote 1.)
[2] Humphrey Marshall, i, 254. Humphrey Marshall finally voted for the Constitution, against the wishes of his constituents. (Scott, 135-38.)

this was a real force in the growth of his views on Nationality.[1]

Henry's own argument, that amendments could not be had after adoption, proved, said Marshall, that they could not be had before. In all the States, particularly in Virginia, there were, he charged, "many who are decided enemies of the Union." These were inspired by "local interests," their object being "disunion." They would not propose amendments that were similar or that all could agree upon. When the Federal Convention met, said Marshall, "we had no idea then of any particular system. The formation of the most perfect plan was our object and wish"; and, "it was imagined" that the States would with pleasure accept that Convention's work. But "consider the violence of opinions, the prejudices and animosities which have been since imbibed"; and how greatly they "operate against mutual concessions."

Marshall reiterated that what the Constitutionalists were fighting for was "a well-regulated democracy." Could the people themselves make treaties, enact laws, or administer the Government? Of course not. They must do such things through agents. And, inquired he, how could these agents act for the people if they did not have power to do so? That the people's agents might abuse power was no argument against giving it, for "the power of doing good is inseparable from that of doing some evil." If power were not given because it might be misused, "you can have no government."

---
[1] See vol. III of this work.

Thus Marshall stated that principle which he was to magnify from the Supreme Bench years later.

"Happy that country," exclaimed the young orator, "which can avail itself of the misfortunes of others . . . without fatal experience!" Marshall cited Holland. The woes of that country were caused, said he, by "the want of proper powers in the government, the consequent deranged and relaxed administration, the violence of contending parties" — in short, by such a government, or rather absence of government, as America then had under the Confederation. If Holland had had such a government as the Constitution proposed, she would not be in her present sorry plight. Marshall was amused at Henry's "high-colored eulogium on such a government."

There was no analogy, argued he, between "the British government and the colonies, and the relation between Congress and the states. We *were not* represented in Parliament. Here [under the Constitution] we are represented." So the arguments against British taxation "do not hold against the exercise of taxation by Congress." The power of taxation by Congress to which Henry objected was "essentially necessary; for without it there will be no efficiency in the government." That requisitions on the States could not be depended on had been demonstrated by experience, he declared; the power of direct taxation was, therefore, necessary to the very existence of the National Government.

"The possibility of its being abused is urged as an

argument against its expediency"; but, said Marshall, such arguments would prevent all government and result in anarchy. "All delegated powers are liable to be abused." The question was, whether the taxing power was "necessary to perform the objects of the Constitution? . . . What are the objects of national government? To protect the United States, and to promote the general welfare. Protection, in time of war, is one of its principal objects. Until mankind shall cease to have ambition and avarice, wars will arise."

Experience had shown, said Marshall, that one State could not protect the people or promote general welfare. "By the national government only" could these things be done; "shall we refuse to give it power to do them?" He scorned the assertion "that we need not be afraid of war. Look at history," he exclaimed, "look at the great volume of human nature. They will foretell you that a defenseless country cannot be secure. The nature of men forbids us to conclude that we are in no danger from war. The passions of men stimulate them to avail themselves of the weakness of others. The powers of Europe are jealous of us. It is our interest to watch their conduct and guard against them. They must be pleased with our disunion. If we invite them by our weakness to attack us, will they not do it? If we add debility to our present situation, a partition of America may take place."

The power of National taxation, therefore, was necessary, Marshall asserted. "There must be men and money to protect us. How are armies to be raised? Must we not have money for that purpose?" If so, "it is, then, necessary to give the government that power in time of peace, which the necessity of war will render indispensable, or else we shall be attacked unprepared." History, human nature, and "our own particular experience, will confirm this truth." If danger should come upon us without power to meet it, we might resort to a dictatorship; we once were on the point of doing that very thing, said he — and even Henry and Mason did not question this appeal of Marshall to the common knowledge of all members of the Convention.

"Were those who are now friends to this Constitution less active in the defense of liberty, on that trying occasion, than those who oppose it?" scathingly asked Marshall. "We may now . . . frame a plan that will enable us to repel attacks, and render a recurrence to dangerous expedients unnecessary. If we be prepared to defend ourselves, there will be little inducement to attack us. But if we defer giving the necessary power to the general government till the moment of danger arrives, we shall give it then, and with an *unsparing hand.*"

It was not true, asserted Marshall, that the Confederation carried us through the Revolution; "had not the enthusiasm of liberty inspired us with unanimity, that system would never have carried us through it." The war would have been won much sooner "had that government been possessed of due energy." The weakness of the Confederation and the conduct of the States prolonged the war. Only "the extreme readiness of the people to make their utmost exertions to ward off solely the pressing danger, supplied the place of requisitions." But when this danger was over, the requisition plan was no longer effective. "A bare sense of duty," said he, "is too feeble to induce men to comply with obligations."

It was plain, then, Marshall pointed out, that "the government must have the sinews of war some other way." That way was by direct taxation which would supply "the necessities of government . . . in a peaceable manner"; whereas "requisitions cannot be rendered efficient without a civil war."

What good would it do for Congress merely to remonstrate with the States, as Henry had proposed, if we were at war with foreign enemies? There was no danger that Congress, under the Constitution, would not lay taxes justly, asserted Marshall; for if members of Congress laid unjust taxes, the people would not reëlect them. Under the Constitution, they were chosen by the same voters who elected members of the State Legislature. These voters, said he, "have nothing to direct them in the choice but their own good." Men thus elected would not abuse their power because that would "militate against their own interest. . . . To procure their reëlection, it will be necessary for them to confer with the people at large, and convince them that the taxes laid are for their own good."

Henry had asked whether the adoption of the Constitution "would pay our debts." "It will compel the states to pay their quotas," answered Marshall. "Without this, Virginia will be unable to pay. Unless all the states pay, she cannot. . . . Economy and industry are essential to our happiness"; but the Confederation "takes away the incitements to industry, by rendering property insecure and unprotected." The Constitution, on the contrary, "will promote and encourage industry."

The statement of the Anti-Constitutionalists that the extent of the country was too great for a strong National Government was untrue, argued Marshall. Also, said he, this objection was from writers who criticized those governments "where representation did not exist." But, under the Constitution, representation would exist.

Answering Henry's objection, that there were no effective checks in the Constitution, Marshall inquired, "What has become of his enthusiastic eulogium on the American spirit?" There, declared Marshall, was the real check and control. "In this country, there is no exclusive personal stock of interest. The interest of the community is blended and inseparably connected with that of the individual. When he promotes his own, he promotes that of the community. When we consult the common good, we consult our own." In such considerations were found the greatest security from an improper exercise of power.

"Is not liberty secure with us, where the people hold all powers in their own hands, and delegate them cautiously, for short periods, to their servants, who are accountable for the smallest mal-administration? . . . We are threatened with the loss of our liberties by the possible abuse of power, notwithstanding the maxim that those who give may take away. It is the people that give power, and can take it back. What shall restrain them? They are the masters who give it, and of whom their servants hold it."

Returning to the subject of amendments, "what," asked Marshall, "shall restrain you from amending it, if, in trying it, amendments shall be found necessary. . . . When experience shall show us any inconvenience, we can then correct it. . . . If it be necessary to change government, let us change that government which has been found to be defective." The Constitution as it stood filled the great objects which everybody desired — "union, safety against foreign enemies, and protection against faction [party] — against what has been the destruction of all republics."

He turned Henry's unhappy praise of the British Constitution into a weapon of deadly attack upon the opposition. The proposed Constitution, said Marshall, was far better than the British. "I ask you if your House of Representatives would be better than it is, if a hundredth part of the people were to elect a majority of them? If your senators were for life, would they be more agreeable to you? If your President were not accountable to you for his conduct, — if it were a constitutional maxim, that he could do no wrong, — would you be safer than you are now? If you can answer, Yes, to these questions, then adopt the British constitution. If not, then, good as that government may be, this [Constitution] is better."

Referring to "the confederacies of ancient and

modern times" he said that "they warn us to shun their calamities, and place in our government those necessary powers, the want of which destroyed them." The ocean does not protect us from war; "Sir," exclaimed Marshall, "the sea makes them neighbors to us. . . . What dangers may we not apprehend to our commerce! Does not our naval weakness invite an attack on our commerce?" Henry had said "that our present exigencies are greater than they will ever be again." But, asked he, "Who can penetrate into futurity?"

Henry's objection that the National Government, under the Constitution, would "call forth the virtue and talents of America," to the disadvantage of the States, was, Marshall said, the best guarantee that the National Government would be wisely conducted. "Will our most virtuous and able citizens wantonly attempt to destroy the liberty of the people? Will the most virtuous act the most wickedly?" On the contrary, "the virtue and talents of the members of the general government will tend to the security instead of the destruction of our liberty. . . . The power of direct taxation is essential to the existence of the general government"; if not, the Constitution was unnecessary; "for it imports not what system we have, unless it have the power of protecting us in time of war." [1]

This address to the Virginia Convention is of historic interest as John Marshall's first recorded utterance on the Constitution of which he was to become the greatest interpreter. Also, it is the first report

[1] See entire speech in Elliott, iii, 223-36.

of Marshall's debating. The speech is not, solely on its merits, remarkable. It does not equal the logic of Madison, the eloquence of Randolph or Lee, or the brilliancy of Corbin. It lacks that close sequence of reasoning which was Marshall's peculiar excellence. In provoking fashion he breaks from one subject when it has been only partly discussed and later returns to it. It is rhetorical also and gives free rein to what was then styled "Marshall's eloquence."

The warp and woof of Marshall's address was woven from his military experience; he forged iron arguments from the materials of his own soldier life. Two thirds of his remarks were about the necessity of providing against war. But the speech is notable as showing, in their infancy, those views of government which, in the shaggy strength of their maturity, were to be so influential on American destiny.[1] It also measures the growth of those ideas of government which the camp, the march, and the battlefield had planted in his mind and heart. The practical and immediate effect of the speech, which was what the Constitutionalists, and perhaps Marshall himself, cared most about, was to strengthen the soldier vote for the Constitution and to cause the Kentucky members to suspend judgment on the Mississippi question.

For the Anti-Constitutionalists there now arose a big-statured old man "elegantly arrayed in a rich suit of blue and buff, a long queue tied with a black

[1] Some of the sentences used in this unprepared speech are similar to those found in the greatest of his opinions as Chief Justice. (See vol. III of this work.)

John Marshall
From a painting by Martin in the Robe Room of the U. S. Supreme Court.

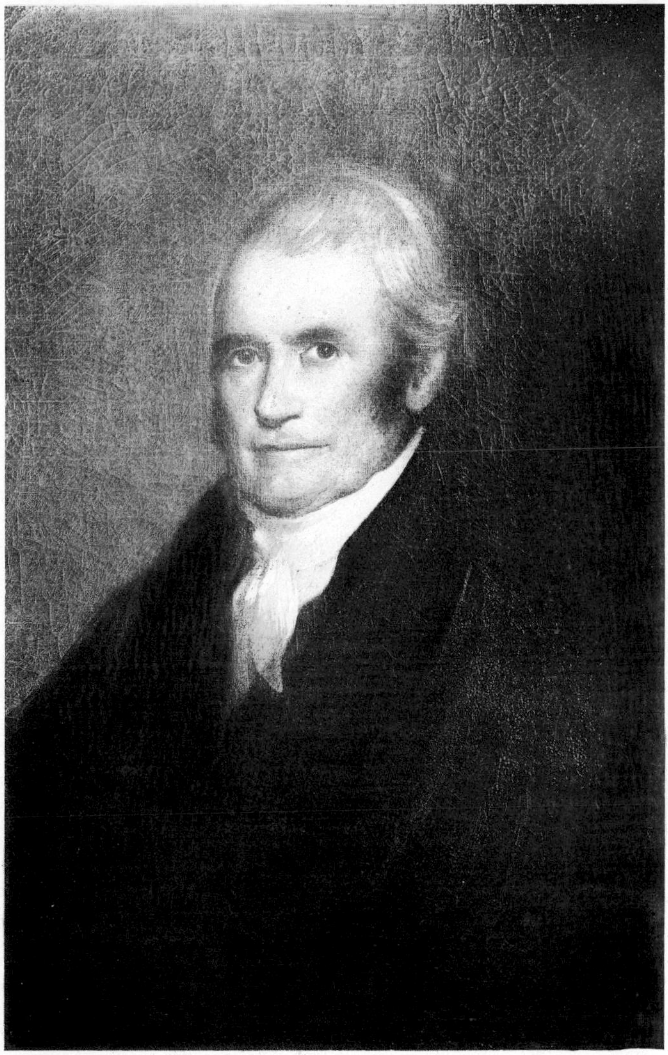

ribbon dangling from his full locks of snow, and his long black boots encroaching on his knees." [1] His ancestors had been Virginians even before the infant colony had a House of Burgesses. When Benjamin Harrison now spoke he represented the aristocracy of the Old Dominion, and he launched all his influence against the Constitution. For some reason he was laboring "under high excitement," and was almost inaudible. He lauded the character of the Virginia Legislature, of which he had been a member. The Constitution, insisted Harrison, "would operate an infringement of the rights and liberties of the people." [2]

George Nicholas answered at length and with characteristic ability and learning.[3] But his speech was quite unnecessary, for what Harrison had said amounted to nothing. On the morning of the ninth day of the Convention Madison continued his masterful argument, two sections of which he already had delivered.[4] He went out of his way to praise Marshall, who, said Madison, had "entered into the subject with a great deal of ability." [5]

Mason, replying on taxation, said that under the Constitution there were "some land holders in this state who will have to pay twenty times as much [taxes] as will be paid for all the land on which Philadelphia stands." A National excise tax, he declared, "will carry the exciseman to every farmer's house, who distills a little brandy where he may search and ransack as he pleases." And what men, asked

---

[1] Grigsby, i, 183–85. [2] Elliott, iii, 236. [3] *Ib.*, 236–47.
[4] *Ib.*, 247–62. [5] *Ib.*, 254.

Mason, would be in Congress from Virginia? Most of them would be "chosen . . . from the higher order of the people — from the great, the wealthy — the *well-born* — the *well-born*, Mr. Chairman, that aristocratic idol — that flattering idea — that *exotic* plant which has been lately imported from the ports of Great Britain, and planted in the luxurious soil of this country."

It is significant to find the "well-born," wealthy, learned, and cultivated Mason taking this tone. It shows that the common people's dislike of a National Government was so intense that even George Mason pandered to it. It was the fears, prejudices, and passions of the multitude upon which the enemies of the Constitution chiefly depended; and when Mason stooped to appeal to them, the sense of class distinction must have been extreme. His statement also reveals the economic line of cleavage between the friends and foes of the Constitution.

It was in this speech that Mason made his scathing "cat and Tory" comparison. He knew those who were for the Constitution, "their connections, their conduct, their political principles, and a number of other circumstances. There are a great many wise and good men among them"; but when he looked around and observed "who are the warmest and most zealous friends to this new government," it made him "think of the story of the cat transformed to a fine lady: forgetting her transformation and happening to see a rat, she could not restrain herself, but sprang upon it out of the chair." [1]

[1] This caustic reference was to the members of the Convention who

THE SUPREME DEBATE 423

Mason denounced Randolph for the latter's apostasy. "I know," said Mason, "that he once saw as great danger in it as I do. What has happened since this to alter his opinion?" Of course, the Confederation was defective and reform needed; but the Constitution was no reform. Without previous amendments, "we never can accede to it. Our duty to God and to our posterity forbids it," [1] declared the venerable author of Virginia's Bill of Rights and the Constitution of the State.

Henry Lee answered with fire and spirit, first rebuking "the irregular and disorderly manner" in which the opposition had carried on the debate. As to the cat story, Mason ought to know "that ridicule is not the test of truth. Does he imagine that he who can raise the loudest laugh is the soundest reasoner?" And Mason's "insinuations" about the "well-born" being elected to Congress were "unwarrantable." He hoped that "we shall hear no more of such groundless aspersions." Lee's speech is valuable only as showing the rising spirit of anger which was beginning to appear even in Virginia's well-conducted, parliamentary, and courteous debate.[2]

The Anti-Constitutionalists were now bringing all their guns into action. The second Revolutionary soldier to speak for the opposition now arose. William Grayson was almost as attractive a military

had been Tories. (Grigsby, i, 193; Elliott, iii, 269; also Rowland, ii, 240.) As we have seen most of the Tories and Revolutionary soldiers were united for the Constitution. These former enemies were brought together by a common desire for a strong National Government.

[1] Elliott, iii, 262-72.   [2] Ib., 272-73.

figure as Henry Lee himself. He had been educated at Oxford, had studied law in the Inner Temple; and his style of speech was the polished result of practice in the English political clubs, in Congress, and at the bar.[1] There were few men in America with more richly stored or better trained minds. He was a precise Latinist and a caustic wit. When, during the debate, some of the Constitutionalist speakers used Latin phrases with a wrong pronunciation, Grayson, *sotto voce*, would correct them. Once he remarked, loud enough to be heard by the other members whom he set roaring with laughter, that he was not surprised that men who were about to vote away the liberties of a living people should take such liberties with a dead language.

Grayson now brought into action the heaviest battery the Anti-Constitutionalists had in reserve. He did not blame Virginia's delegates to the Federal Convention, said Grayson suavely. It was unfortunate "that they did not do more for the general good of America"; but "I do not criminate or suspect the principles on which they acted." Of course, the Confederation had defects; but these were "inseparable from the nature of such [Republican]

[1] Grigsby, i, 194-205. William Grayson was one of the strongest men in Virginia. He became Virginia's first Senator under the Constitution. (See *infra*, vol. II, chap. II.) He filled and satisfied the public eye of his day as a soldier, scholar, and statesman. And yet he has dropped out of history almost completely. He is one of those rare personalities whom the whims of time and events have so obscured that they are to be seen but dimly through the mists. His character and mind can be measured but vaguely by fragments buried in neglected pages. William Grayson's talents, work, and vanished fame remind one of the fine ability, and all but forgotten career of Sir James Mackintosh.

governments." The Constitutionalists had conjured up "phantoms and ideal dangers to lead us into measures which will ... be the ruin of our country." He argued that we were in no danger from our default in paying foreign loans; for most European nations were friendly. "Loans from nations are not like loans from private men. Nations lend money ... to one another from views of national interest. France was willing to pluck the fairest feather out of the British crown. This was her hope in aiding us" — a truth evident to every man in the Convention. Such loans were habitually delayed, — for instance, "the money which the Dutch borrowed of Henry IV is not yet paid"; these same Dutch "passed Queen Elizabeth's loan at a very considerable discount," and they "made their own terms with that contemptible monarch," James I.

The people had no idea, asserted Grayson, that the Federal Convention would do more than to give the National Government power to levy a five per cent tariff, but since then "horrors have been greatly magnified." He ridiculed Randolph's prophecy of war and calamity. According to Randolph, "we shall be ruined and disunited forever, unless we adopt this Constitution. Pennsylvania and Maryland are to fall upon us from the north, like the Goths and Vandals of old; the Algerines, whose flat-sided vessels never came farther than Madeira, are to fill the Chesapeake with mighty fleets, and to attack us on our front; the Indians are to invade us with numerous armies on our rear, in order to convert our cleared lands into hunting-grounds; and the Carolinians, from the South (mounted on alligators, I presume), are to come and destroy our cornfields, and eat up our little children! These, sir, are the mighty dangers which await us if we reject [the Constitution] — dangers which are merely imaginary, and ludicrous in the extreme!"

At bottom, thought Grayson, the controversy was between two opinions — "the one that mankind can only be governed by force; the other that they are capable" of governing themselves. Under the second theory, which Grayson favored, all that was necessary was to "give congress the regulation of commerce" and to "infuse new strength and spirit into the state governments."

This, he remarked, was the proper course to pursue and to maintain "till the American character be marked with some certain features. We are yet too young to know what we are fit for." If this was not to be done and we must have a government by force, then Grayson "would have a President for life, choosing his successor at the same time; a Senate for life, with the powers of the House of Lords; and a triennial House of Representatives, with the powers of the House of Commons in England."[1] Consider the Judiciary. Suppose a man seized at the same time under processes from Federal and State Courts: "Would they divide the man in two, as Solomon directed the child to be divided who was claimed by two women?"

Evidently Grayson was making a strong impres-

[1] Elliott, iii, 279.

sion as the day grew to a close, for Monroe, seconded by Henry, moved that the Convention adjourn that Grayson might go on next day; and Madison, plainly nervous, "insisted on going through the business regularly, according to the resolution of the house." Grayson consumed most of the next forenoon, displaying great learning, but sometimes drawing the most grotesque conclusions. For example, he said that Congress might grant such privileges that "the whole commerce of the United States may be exclusively carried on by merchants residing within the seat of government [now the District of Columbia] and those places of arms which may be purchased of the state legislature." The Constitution did not give equality of representation; for "the members of Delaware will assist in laying a tax on our slaves, of which they will pay no part whatever." In general, Grayson's conclusion was that "we have asked for bread and they have given us a stone."[1]

Pendleton answered. Henry's treatment of Randolph's unhappy reference to the people as a "herd" seems to have had some effect; for Pendleton regretted its use and tried to explain it away. Henry and he differed "at the threshold" on government. "I think government necessary to protect liberty. ... Licentiousness" was "the natural offspring of liberty"; and "therefore, all free governments should endeavor to suppress it, or else it will ultimately overthrow that liberty of which it is the result." Henry "professes himself an advocate for the middling and lower classes of men, I profess to be a

[1] Elliott, iii, 273-93 (especial passage, 280).

friend to the equal liberty of all men, from the palace to the cottage."

The appeal to class hatred, said Pendleton, had been made by the opposition exclusively; the Constitutionalists knew no distinction among men except that of good and bad men. Why did the opposition make "the distinction of *well-born* from others? ... Whether a man be great or small, he is equally dear to me." He wished "for a regular government in order to secure and protect ... honest citizens ... the industrious farmer and planter." The purpose of the proposed National Government was to cherish and protect industry and property. Pendleton spoke at great length, but frequently his voice was so feeble that he could not be understood or reported.[1]

Madison followed with the fourth section of what might properly be called his treatise on government. Henry replied, striking again the master chord of the people's fears — that of a National Government as something alien. "The tyranny of Philadelphia may be like the tyranny of George III." That the Constitution must be amended "re-echoed from every part of the continent"; but that could not be done "if we ratify unconditionally." Henry remade his old points with his consummate art.

He mentioned a new subject, however, of such high practical importance that it is astonishing that he had not advanced it at the beginning and driven it home persistently. "There are," he said, "thousands and thousands of contracts, whereof equity

[1] Elliott, iii, 293-305.

forbids an exact literal performance. . . . Pass that government [the Constitution] and you will be bound hand and foot. . . . An immense quantity of depreciated Continental paper money . . . is in the hands of individuals to this day. The holders of this money may call for the nominal value, if this government be adopted. This State may be compelled to pay her proportion of that currency, pound for pound. Pass this government and you will be carried to the federal court . . . and you will be compelled to pay, shilling for shilling."

Returning to this point later on, Henry said: "Some of the states owe a great deal on account of paper money; others very little. Some of the Northern States have collected and barrelled up paper money. Virginia has sent thither her cash long ago. There is little or none of the Continental paper money retained in this State. Is it not their business to appreciate this money? Yes, and it will be your business to prevent it. But there will be a majority [in Congress] against you and you will be obliged to pay your share of this money, in its nominal value."[1]

Referring to Pendleton's assertion that the State Court had declared void legislative acts which violated the State Constitution, Henry exclaimed:

[1] Elliott, iii, 319-22; and see chap. II, vol. II, of this work. Although this, like other economic phases of the contest, was of immediate, practical and serious concern to the people, Henry touched upon it only twice thereafter and each time but briefly; and Mason mentioned it only once. This fact is another proof of the small place which this grave part of the economic problem occupied in the minds of the foes of the Constitution, in comparison with that of "liberty" as endangered by a strong National Government.

"Yes, sir, our judges opposed the acts of the legisature. We have this landmark to guide us. They had the fortitude to declare that they were the judiciary and would oppose unconstitutional acts. Are you sure your federal judiciary will act thus? Is that judiciary as well constructed, and as independent of the other branches, as our state judiciary? Where are your landmarks in this government? I will be bold to say you cannot find any in it. I take it as the highest encomium on this country [Virginia] that the acts of the legislature, if unconstitutional, are liable to be opposed by the judiciary." [1]

As usual, Henry ended with a fearsome picture and prophecy, this time of the danger to and destruction of Southern interests at the hands of the Northern majority. This, said he, "is a picture so horrid, so wretched, so dreadful, that I need no longer dwell upon it"; and he "dreaded the most iniquitous speculation and stock-jobbing, from the operation of such a system" as the Constitution provided.[2] Madison replied — the first spontaneous part he had taken in the debate.[3]

The next morning the opposition centered their fire on the Mississippi question. Henry again demanded that the members of the Convention who had been in Congress should tell what had been done.[4] The members of Congress — Lee, Monroe,

---

[1] Elliott, iii, 325. At this time the fears of the Anti-Constitutionalists were principally that the powers given the National Government would "swallow up" the State Governments; and it was not until long afterward that objection was made to the right and power of the National Supreme Court to declare a law of Congress unconstitutional. (See vol. III of this work.)

[2] *Ib.*, 313-28. [3] *Ib.*, 328-32. [4] *Ib.*, 332-33.

Grayson, and Madison — then gave their versions of the Jay-Gardoqui transaction.[1]

The Constitutionalists rightly felt that "the whole scene has been conjured by Henry to affect the ruin of the new Constitution,"[2] and that seasoned gladiator now confirmed their fears. He astutely threw the blame on Madison and answered the charge of the Constitutionalists that "we [the opposition] are scuffling for Kentucky votes and attending to local circumstances." With all of his address and power, Henry bore down upon the Mississippi question. Thus he appealed for Kentucky votes: "Shall we appear to care less for their interests than for that of distant people [the Spaniards]?"

At Henry's word a vision rose before all eyes of the great American valley sustaining "a mighty population," farms, villages, towns, cities, colleges, churches, happiness, prosperity; and "the Mississippi covered with ships laden with foreign and domestic wealth" — a vision of a splendid West "the strength, the pride, and the flower of the Confederacy." And then quickly succeeded on the screen the picture of the deserted settlers, the West a wilderness, the Father of Waters flowing idly to the sea, unused by commerce, unadorned by the argosies of trade. Such, said he, would be the Mississippi under the Constitution "controlled by those who had no interest in its welfare."[3]

At last the Constitutionalists were stunned. For a while no one spoke. Pendleton, "his right hand

---

[1] Elliott, iii, 333–51. [2] Grigsby, i, 230 and 243.
[3] *Ib.*, 245; Elliott, iii, 251–56. This, the real vote-getting part of Henry's speech, is not reported by Robertson.

grasping his crutch, sat silent and amazed."[1] Nicholas, the dauntless, was first to recover himself, and repeated Marshall's argument on the Mississippi question. Evidently the opposition had lobbied effectively with the Kentucky members on that sore point; for, exclaimed Nicholas, "we have been alarmed about the loss of the Mississippi, in and *out* of doors."[2]

The Constitutionalists strove mightily to break the force of Henry's *coup* on the Kentucky delegates. He had "seen so many attempts made," exclaimed Randolph, "and so many wrong inducements offered to influence the delegation from Kentucky," that he must speak his mind about it.[3] Corbin called the Mississippi trick "reprehensible." And well might the Constitutionalists tremble; for in spite of all they could do, ten out of fourteen of the Kentucky delegates voted against ratifying the Constitution.

That night Pendleton fell ill and John Tyler, "one of the staunchest opponents of the new Constitution," was elected Vice-President.[4] The Mississippi question was dropped for the moment; the Constitutionalists rallied and carried Corbin's motion to debate the new Government clause by clause in accordance with the original resolution. Several sections of the first article were read and debated, Henry, Mason, and Grayson for the opposition; Madison bearing the burden of the debate for the Constitutionalists.

The rich man and the poor, the State Govern-

[1] Grigsby, i, 245.
[2] Elliott, iii, 356.
[3] *Ib.*, 361-65.
[4] Grigsby, i, 248.

ment a thing of the "people" and the National Government something apart from the "people," were woven throughout the Anti-Constitutionalists' assaults. "Where," exclaimed Henry, "are the purse and the sword of Virginia? They must go to Congress. What has become of your country? The Virginian government is but a name. ... We are to be consolidated." [1]

The second week's debate closed with the advantage on the side of the opposition. Gouverneur Morris, the New York Constitutionalist, who, still on the ground, was watching the fight in Richmond and undoubtedly advising the Virginia Constitutionalists, reported to Hamilton in New York that "matters are not going so well in this State as the Friends of America could wish." The Anti-Constitutionalists had been making headway, not only through Henry's tremendous oratory, but also by other means; and the Constitutionalists acknowledged that their own arguments in debate were having little or no effect.

"If, indeed, the Debates in Convention were alone attended to," wrote Gouverneur Morris, "a contrary Inference would be drawn for altho M^r. Henry is most warm and powerful in Declamation being perfectly Master of 'Action Utterrance and Power of Speech to stir Men's Blood' yet the Weight of Argument is so strong on the Side of Truth as wholly to destroy even on weak Minds the Effects of his Eloquence But there are as you well know certain dark Modes of operating on the Minds of Members which

[1] Elliott, iii, 366–410.

like contagious Diseases are only known by their Effects on the Frame and unfortunately our moral like our phisical Doctors are often mistaken in their Judgment from Diagnostics Be of good Chear. My Religion steps in where my Understanding falters and I feel Faith as I loose Confidence. Things will yet go right but when and how I dare not predicate. So much for this dull Subject." [1]

"We have conjectured for some days," Madison advised Hamilton, "that the policy is to spin out the Session in order to receive overtures from your [New York's] Convention: or if that cannot be, to weary the members into a adjournment without taking any decision. It [is] presumed at the same time that they do not despair of carrying the point of previous amendments which is preferable game. The parties continue to be nearly balanced. If we have a majority at all, it does not exceed three or four. If we lose it Kentucke will be the cause; they are generally if not unanimously against us." [2]

On the back of Madison's letter, Henry Lee wrote one of his own to the New York Constitutionalist chieftain. "We possess as yet," said Lee, "in defiance of great exertions a majority, but very small indeed. A correspondence has certainly been opened thro a Mr. O.[swald] of Philad^a from the Malcontents of B. & N. Y. to us — it has its operation, but I believe we are still safe, unless the question of adjournment should be introduced, & love of home may

[1] Gouverneur Morris from Richmond to Hamilton in New York, June 13, 1788; Hamilton MSS., Lib. Cong.

[2] Madison to Hamilton, June 16, 1788; Hamilton MSS., Lib. Cong.

induce some of our friends to abandon their principles."[1]

"The business is in the most ticklish state that can be imagined," Madison informed Washington; "the majority will certainly be very small on whatever side it may finally lie; and I dare not encourage much expectation that it will be on the favorable side. Oswald of Philadª has been here with letters for the anti-Federal leaders from N. York and probably Philadª He Staid a very short time here during which he was occasionally closeted with H⸺y M⸺s⸺n &c."[2]

On Monday the Anti-Constitutionalists were first in the field. They were by now displaying improved tactics. Henry opened on the dangers of a standing army. "If Congress shall say that the general welfare requires it, they may keep armies continually on foot. . . . They may billet them on the people at pleasure." This is "a most dangerous power! Its principles are despotic."[3] Madison followed,[4] and Mason, Corbin, and Grayson also spoke,[5] the latter asserting that, under the Constitution, the States could not "command the militia" unless by implication.

---

[1] Lee to Hamilton; Hamilton MSS., Lib. Cong. The first paragraph of Lee's letter to Hamilton shows that the latter was helping his friend financially; for Lee wrote, "God bless you & your efforts to save me from the manifold purse misfortunes which have & continue to oppress me, whenever I attempt to aid human nature. You will do what you think best, & whatever you do I will confirm — Hazard has acted the part of a decided rascal, & if I fail in my right, I may not in personal revenge." (*Ib.*)

[2] Madison to Washington, June 13, 1788; *Writings:* Hunt, v, 179 and footnote.

[3] Elliott, iii, 410–12.   [4] *Ib.*, 412–15.   [5] *Ib.*, 415–18.

Here Marshall again took part in the debate.[1] He asked whether Grayson was serious in stating that the Constitution left no power in the States over the militia unless by implication. Under the Constitution, State and National Governments "each derived its powers from the people, and each was to act according to the powers given it." Were "powers not given retained by implication?" asked Marshall. Was "this power [over the militia] not retained by the states, as they had not given it away?"

It is true, he admitted, that "Congress may call forth the militia" for National purposes — "as to suppress insurrections and repel invasions"; but the power given the States by the people "is not taken away, for the Constitution does not say so." The power of Congress over the ten miles square where the National Capital was to be located is "exclusive . . . because it is expressed [in the Constitution] to be exclusive." Marshall contended that any power given Congress which before was in the States remained in both unless the Constitution said otherwise or unless there was incompatibility in its exercise. So the States would have the same control over the militia as formerly. "When invaded or in imminent danger they [the States] can engage in war."

Grayson had said, declared Marshall, that if the National Government disciplined the militia, "they will form an aristocratic government, unsafe and unfit to be trusted." Grayson interrupted Marshall in an unsuccessful attempt to squirm out of the posi-

[1] Elliott, iii, 419-20.

tion in which the latter had placed him. He had only said that in its military features the Constitution "was so constructed as to form a great aristocratic body."

Marshall retorted that "as the government was drawn from the people, the feelings and interests of the people would be attended to"; and, therefore, there would be no military aristocracy. "When the government is drawn from the people and depending on the people for its continuance, oppressive measures will not be attempted," argued Marshall, "as they will certainly draw on their authors the resentment of those on whom they depend." No! cried he: "On this government, thus depending on ourselves for its existence, I will rest my safety."

Again Marshall expressed his military experience and instincts. If war should come "what government is able to protect you?" he asked. "Will any state depend on its own exertions?" No! If the National Government is not given the power "state will fall after state and be a sacrifice to the want of power in the general government." Uttering the motto of American Nationalism, which, long years afterward, he declared to have been the ruling maxim of his entire life, Marshall cried, "*United we are strong, divided we fall.*" If the National militia cannot "draw the militia of one state to another ... every state must depend upon itself. ... It requires a superintending power, ... to call forth the resources of all to protect all."

Replying to Grayson's assertion that "a general regulation [of the militia] may be made to inflict punishments," Marshall asked whether Grayson imagined that a militia law would be "incapable of being changed?" Grayson's idea "supposes that men renounce their own interests." And "if Congress neglect our militia, we can arm them ourselves. Cannot Virginia import arms . . . [and] put them into the hands of her militia men?" Marshall summed up with the statement that the States derived no powers from the Constitution "but retained them, though not acknowledged in any part of it." [1]

Marshall's speech must have been better than anything indicated in the stenographer's report; for the resourceful Grayson was moved to answer it at once [2] and even Henry felt called upon to reply to it.[3] Henry was very fond of Marshall; and this affection of the mature statesman for the rising young lawyer saved the latter in a furious political contest ten years afterwards.[4] The debate was continued by Madison, Mason, Nicholas, Lee, Pendleton, and finally ended in a desultory conversation,[5] but nothing important or notable was said in this phase of the debate. One statement, however, coming as it did from Mason, flashes a side-light on the prevailing feeling that the proposed National Government was something apart from the people. Mason saw the most frightful dangers from the unlimited power of Congress over the ten miles square provided for the National Capital.

[1] Elliott, iii, 419-21.   [2] *Ib.*, 421-22.   [3] *Ib.*, 422-24.
[4] Henry turned the tide in Marshall's favor in the latter's hard fight for Congress in 1798. (*Infra*, vol. ii, chap. x.)
[5] Elliott, iii, 434.

"This ten miles square," cried Mason, "may set at defiance the laws of the surrounding states, and may, like the custom of the superstitious days of our ancestors, become the sanctuary of the blackest crimes. Here the Federal Courts are to sit.... What sort of a jury shall we have within the ten miles square?" asked Mason, and himself answered, "The immediate creatures of the government. What chance will poor men get? ... If an attempt should be made to establish tyranny over the people, here are ten miles square where the greatest offender may meet protection. If any of the officers or creatures [of the National Government] should attempt to oppress the people or should actually perpetrate the blackest deed, he has nothing to do but to get into the ten miles square." [1]

The debate then turned upon amending the Constitution by a Bill of Rights, the Constitutionalists asserting that such an amendment was not necessary, and the opposition that it was absolutely essen-

[1] Elliott, iii, 431. Throughout the entire debate Henry often sounded his loudest alarms on the supreme power of Congress over the ten miles square where the National Capital was to be located; and, indeed, this seems to have been one of the chief sources of popular apprehension. The fact that the people at large looked upon the proposed National Government as something foreign, something akin to the British rule which had been overthrown, stares the student in the face wherever he turns among the records of the Constitutional period. It is so important that it cannot too often be repeated.

Patrick Henry, of course, who was the supreme popular orator of our history and who drew his strength from his perfect knowledge of the public mind and heart, might have been expected to make appeals based on this general fear. But when such men as George Mason and William Grayson, who belonged to Virginia's highest classes and who were carefully educated men of conservative temper, did the same thing, we see how deep and strong was the general feeling against any central National power.

tial. The question was "whether rights not given up were reserved?" Henry, as usual, was vivid. He thought that, without a Bill of Rights, "excisemen may come in multitudes ... go into your cellars and rooms, and search, and ransack, and measure, everything you eat, drink, and wear." And the common law! The Constitution did not guarantee its preservation. "Congress may introduce the practice of the civil law, in preference to that of the common law; ... the practice of ... torturing, to extort a confession of the crime. ... We are then lost and undone."[1]

The slavery question next got attention, Mason, Madison, Tyler, Henry, and Nicholas continuing the discussion.[2] Under the first clause of the tenth section of article one, Henry again brought up the payment of the Continental debt. "He asked gentlemen who had been high in authority, whether there were not some state speculations on this matter. He had been informed that some states had acquired vast quantities of that money, which they would be able to recover in its nominal value of the other states." Mason said "that he had been informed that some states had speculated most enormously in this matter. Many individuals had speculated so as to make great fortunes on the ruin of their fellow-citizens." Madison in reply assured the Convention that the Constitution itself placed the whole subject exactly where it was under the Confederation; therefore, said he, it is "immaterial who holds those great quantities of paper money, ... or at what value

[1] Elliott, iii, 447–49.   [2] *Ib.*, 452–57.

THE SUPREME DEBATE 441

they acquired it."[1] To this extent only was the point raised which became most vital when the National Government was established and under way.[2]

Madison's point, said Mason, was good as far as it went; but, under the Confederation, Congress could discharge the Continental money "at its depreciated value," which had gone down "to a thousand for one." But under the Constitution "we must pay it shilling for shilling or at least at the rate of one for forty"; which would take "the last particle of our property. ... We may be taxed for centuries, to give advantage to a few particular states in the Union and a number of rapacious speculators." Henry then turned Madison's point that "the new Constitution would place us in the same situation with the old"; for Henry saw "clearly" that "this paper money must be discharged shilling for shilling."[3] Then Henry brought up the scarecrow of the British debts, which had more to do with the opposition to the Constitution in Virginia[4] than any other specific subject, excepting, perhaps, the threatened loss of the Mississippi and the supreme objection

[1] Elliott, iii, 473.

[2] It is exceedingly strange that in the debates on the Constitution in the various State Conventions, so little, comparatively, was made of the debt and the speculations in it. The preciousness of "liberty" and the danger of "monarchy," the security of the former through State sovereignty and the peril of the latter through National Government, received far more attention than did the economic problem.

[3] Elliott, 472-74. And see vol. II, chap. II, of this work.

[4] "The recovery of the British debts can no longer be postponed and there now seems to be a moral certainty that your patrimony will all go to satisfy the unjust debt from your papa to the Hanburys." (Tucker to his stepsons, June 29, 1788, quoted in Conway, 106; and see comment, *ib.*)

that a National Government would destroy the States and endanger "liberty."

The opposition had now come to the point where they were fighting the separate provisions of the Constitution one by one. When the first section of the second article, concerning the Executive Department, was reached, the opposition felt themselves on safe ground. The Constitution here sapped the "great fundamental principle of responsibility in republicanism," according to Mason.[1] Grayson wanted to know how the President would be punished if he abused his power. "Will you call him before the Senate? They are his counsellors and partners in crime."[2]

The treaty-making power, the command of the army, the method of electing the President, the failure of the Constitution to provide for his rotation in office, all were, to the alarmed Anti-Constitutionalists, the chains and shackles of certain and inevitable despotism. The simple fears of the unlettered men who sullenly had fought the Constitution in the Massachusetts Convention were stated and urged throughout the great debate in Virginia by some of her ablest and most learned sons. Madison was at his best in his exposition of the treaty-making power. But if the debate on the Executive Department had any effect whatever in getting votes for or against the Constitution, the advantage was with the enemies of the proposed new Government.

Grayson wrote to Dane: "I think we got a Vote by debating the powers of the President. This, you will

[1] Elliott, iii, 484.   [2] *Ib.*, 491.

observe, is confidential." But this was cold comfort, for, he added, "our affairs . . . are in the most ticklish situation. We have got ten out of thirteen of the Kentucke members but we wanted the whole: & I don't know that we have got one yet of the four upper counties: this is an important point & which both sides are contending for by every means in their power. I believe it is absolutely certain that we have got 80 votes on our side which are inflexible & that eight persons are fluctuating & undecided." [1]

[1] Grayson to Dane, June 18, 1788; Dane MSS., Lib. Cong. This shows the loose management of the Anti-Constitutionalist politicians: for Kentucky had fourteen votes in the Convention, instead of thirteen, as Grayson declared; and so uncertain was the outcome that to omit a single vote in calculating the strength of the contending forces was unpardonable in one who was, and was accounted to be, a leader.

CHAPTER XII

THE STRATEGY OF VICTORY

Washington's influence carried this government [Virginia's ratification of the Constitution]. (Monroe to Jefferson, July 12, 1788.)

If I shall be in the minority, I shall have those painful sensations which arise from a conviction of *being overpowered in a good cause.* Yet I will be a peaceable citizen. (Henry, in his last debate.)

Now came the real tug-of-war. The debate on the Judiciary was the climax of the fight. And here John Marshall was given the place of chief combatant. The opposition felt that again they might influence one or two delegates by mere debate, and they prepared to attack with all their might. "Tomorrow the Judiciary comes on when we [Anti-Constitutionalists] shall exert our whole force. It is expected we shall get two Votes if the point is conducted in an able & masterly manner," Grayson advised the opposition headquarters in New York.[1]

The Judiciary was, indeed, the weakest part of the Constitutionalists' battle line. The large amount of the British debts; the feeling, which Virginia's legislation against the payment of them had fostered, that the day would be far distant and perhaps would never come when those debts would have to be paid; the provision of the Constitution concerning the making of treaties, which were to be the supreme law of the land; the certainty that the Treaty of Peace would be covered by the new fundamental law; the fear that another treaty would be negotiated governing the British obligations more specifically, **if**

[1] Grayson to Dane, June 18, 1788; Dane MSS., Lib. Cong.

the Constitution were adopted; the fact that such a treaty and all other National laws would be enforced by National Courts — all these and many other germane considerations, such as land grants and confused titles, were focused on the fears of the planters.

The creditor class were equally anxious and alarmed. "If the new Constitution should not be adopted or something similar, we are of the opinion that such is the interest and influence of Debtors in our State that every thing ... will be at Risk" was the opinion of the legal representatives in Virginia of the Collins mercantile house.[1]

Great quantities of land granted under the Royal Government by Great Britain, but which the State had confiscated, had been bought and settled by thousands of men whose families now lived upon this land; and these settlers felt that, in some way, their titles would be in danger if they were dragged before a National Court.[2]

The Constitutionalists did not underestimate their peril, and at no point during the three weeks' debate did they prepare for battle with greater care. They returned to their original tactics and delivered the first blow. Pendleton, of course, was the ideal man to lead the Constitutionalist attack. And never in his whole life did that extraordinary man make a more convincing argument.[3] Mason tried his best to

[1] Logan and Story to Stephen Collins, Petersburg, Nov. 2, 1787; Collins MSS., Lib. Cong.
[2] See Grigsby, i, 278-79, for an able and sympathetic account from the point of view of the settler and debtor.
[3] *Ib.*, 280-84; Elliott, iii, 517-21.

answer Pendleton, although he admitted that the Judiciary "lies out of my line." Still he was clear, in his own mind, that the National Judiciary was "so constructed as to destroy the dearest rights of the community," and thought it would "destroy the state governments, whatever may have been the intention."

While Mason spoke with uncertainty, it was in this brief speech that this eminent Virginian uncovered the hidden thought and purpose of many of the Constitutionalists; and uttered an unconscious prophecy which it was the destiny of John Marshall to realize. "There are," said Mason, "many gentlemen in the United States who think it right that we should have one great, national, consolidated government, and that it was better to bring it about slowly and imperceptibly rather than all at once. This is no reflection on any man, for I mean none. To those who think that one national, consolidated government is best for America, this extensive judicial authority will be agreeable"; and he further declared, "I know from my own knowledge many worthy gentlemen" of this opinion. Madison demanded of Mason "an unequivocal explanation." Mason exonerated Madison, personally, and admitted that "neither did I ever hear any of the delegates from this state advocate it." Thus did the extreme courtesy of the Virginia debate cause the opposition to yield one of its most effective weapons.[1]

[1] Elliott, iii, 522; Grigsby, i, 284. So overwhelming was the popular feeling against a strong National Government that, if the Anti-Constitutionalists had concentrated their attack upon this secret purpose of the leading Constitutionalists to make it such by easy stages,

But Mason made the most out of the Constitution's proposed Judiciary establishment. Take it at its best, said he: "Even suppose the poor man should be able to obtain judgment in the inferior court, for the greatest injury, what justice can he get on appeal? Can he go four or five hundred miles? Can he stand the expense attending it?"[1] As to the jurisdiction of National Courts in controversies between citizens of different States, "Can we not trust our state courts with a decision of these?" asked Mason. "What!" cried he, "carry me a thousand miles from home — from my family and business — to where, perhaps, it will be impossible for me to prove that I paid" the money sued for.

"Is not a jury excluded absolutely?" by the Constitution, asked Mason. And even if a jury be possible in National Courts, still, under the Constitution, where is there any right to challenge jurors? "If I be tried in the Federal Court for a crime which may effect my life, have I a right of challenging or excepting to the jury?" This omission was a serious and immediate peril to great numbers of Virginians, said he. "I dread the ruin that will be wrought on thirty thousand of our people [deriving their titles through Fairfax] with respect to disputed lands. I am personally endangered as an inhabitant of the Northern Neck." Under the Constitution "the people of that part will be obliged . . . to pay the quit rent of their lands." This was to Mason, "a most serious alarm. . . ."

it is more than probable that the Constitution would have been defeated.

[1] Elliott, iii, 524.

"Lord Fairfax's title was clear and undisputed," he continued. The State had "taxed his lands as private property"; but "after his death" Virginia, in 1782, "sequestered the quit rents due at his death, in the hands of his debtors. The following year" they were restored to his executor. Then came the Treaty of Peace providing against "further confiscation"; but, "after this, an act of Assembly passed, confiscating his [Fairfax's] whole property."

So, concluded Mason, "as Lord Fairfax's title was indisputably good, and as treaties [under the Constitution] are to be the supreme law of the land, will not his representatives be able to recover all in the federal court? How will gentlemen like to pay an additional tax on lands in the Northern Neck?" Yet that was what they would be compelled to do if the Constitution were adopted. Thus they would be "doubly taxed." "Were I going to my grave, I would appeal to Heaven that I think it [this] true," fervently avowed the snowy-haired Mason.

Thus Mason made one of the cleverest appeals of the whole debate to the personal and pecuniary interests of a considerable number of the people and to several members of the Convention. In this artful and somewhat demagogic argument he called attention to the lands involved in other extensive land grants. As we have seen, John Marshall was then personally interested in the Fairfax title,[1] and he was soon to possess it; in after years, it was to develop one of the great legal contests of history; and

---

[1] His own and his father's lands in Fauquier County were derived through the Fairfax title.

the court over which Marshall was to preside was to settle it definitively.

Although not a lawyer,[1] Madison now made an argument which was one of the distinguished intellectual performances of the Convention. But he did not comprehend the sweep of the National Judiciary's power. "It is not in the power of individuals," said Madison, "to call any state into court." It may be that this statement influenced John Marshall, who soon followed, to repeat it.[2]

But it was Henry who gave the subject of the Judiciary that thrill, anticipation of which filled every seat on the floor and packed the galleries. "Mournful," to Henry, were the recollections which the debate already had produced. "The purse is gone; the sword is gone," and now the scales of Justice are to be given away. Even the trial by jury is to be abandoned. Henry spoke long and effectively; and, extravagant as most of his statements were, his penetrating mind was sometimes more nearly right in its forecast than even that of Madison.

As he closed, the daring of the Patrick Henry of 1765 and 1775 displayed itself. "Shall Americans give up that [jury trial] which nothing could induce the English people to relinquish?" he exclaimed. "The idea is abhorrent to my mind. There was a time when we should have spurned at it. . . . Old as I am, it is probable I may yet have the appellation of *rebel*. . . . As this government [Constitution]

---

[1] Grigsby, i, 290.
[2] Elliott, iii, 530–39. For Marshall's repetition see *ib.*, 551–62.

stands, I despise and abhor it," cried the unrivaled orator of the people.[1]

Up now rose John Marshall, whom the Constitutionalist leaders had agreed upon for the critical task of defending the Judiciary article. Marshall, as we have seen, had begun the practice of law in Richmond only five years before; and during much of this period his time and attention had been taken by his duties as a delegate in the Legislature. Yet his intellectual strength, the power of his personality, his likableness, and all the qualities of his mind and character had so impressed every one that, by common consent, he was the man for the hour and the work at hand. And Marshall had carefully prepared his speech.[2]

The Judiciary provided by the Constitution was, said Marshall "a great improvement on that system from which we are now departing. Here [in the Constitution] are tribunals appointed for *the decision of controversies* which were before either not at all, or improperly, provided for. That many benefits will result from this to the members of the collective society, every one confesses." The National Judiciary deserved the support of all unless it was "defectively organized and so constructed as to injure, instead of accommodate, the convenience of the people."

After the "fair and able" discussion by its supporters, Marshall supposed that its opponents "would be convinced of the impropriety of some of their objections. But," he lamented, "they still continue the same opposition." And what was their

[1] Elliott, iii, 539-46.   [2] Grigsby, i, 297.

complaint? This: That National Courts would not be as fair and impartial as State Courts.

But why not? asked Marshall. Was it because of their tenure of office or the method of choosing them? "What is it that makes us trust our [State] judges? Their independence in office and manner of appointment."[1] But, under the Constitution, are not National judges "chosen with as much wisdom as the judges of the state governments? Are they not equally, if not more independent? If so," will they not be equally fair and impartial? "If there be as much wisdom and knowledge in the United States as in a particular state," will they "not be equally exercised in the selection of [National] judges?" Such were the questions which Marshall poured upon the Anti-Constitutionalists.

The kernel of the objection to National Courts was, declared Marshall, "a belief that there will not be a fair trial had in those courts." But it was plain, he argued, that "we are as secure there as anywhere else. What mischief results from some causes being tried there [in the National Courts]?" Independent judges "wisely appointed . . . will never countenance an unfair trial." Assuming this to be true "what are the subjects of the jurisdiction" of National Courts? To Mason's objection that Congress could create any number of inferior courts it might deem necessary, Marshall replied that he had supposed that those who feared Congress would say that "*no inferior courts*" would be established, "but that we

[1] Virginia judges were, at this period, appointed by the General Assembly. (Constitution, 1776.)

should be dragged to the centre of the Union." On the contrary, the greater the number of these inferior courts, the less danger "of being dragged to the centre of the United States."

Mason's point, that the jurisdiction of National Courts would extend to all cases, was absurd, argued Marshall. For "has the government of the United States power to make laws on every subject? ... laws affecting the mode of transferring property, or contracts, or claims, between citizens of the same state? Can" Congress "go beyond the delegated powers?" Certainly not. Here Marshall stated the doctrine which, fifteen years later, he was to announce from the Supreme Bench:—

"If," he asserted, "they [Congress] were to make a law not warranted by any of the powers enumerated, it would be considered by the [National] judges as an infringement of the Constitution which they are to guard. They would not consider such a law as coming under their jurisdiction. *They would declare it void.* ... To what quarter will you look for protection from an infringement of the Constitution, if you will not give the power to the judiciary? There is no other body that can afford such a protection."

The National Courts would not supplant the State tribunals. The Constitution did not "exclude state courts" from those cases which they now possess. "They have concurrent jurisdiction with the Federal courts in those cases in which the latter have cognizance," expounded the nascent jurist. "Are not controversies respecting lands claimed under the grants of different states the only controversies between citizens of the same state which the Federal Judiciary can take [exclusive] cognizance of?"

The work of the National Courts would make the State Courts more efficient because it would relieve them of a mass of business of which they were not able to dispose. "Does not every gentleman know that the causes in our [State] courts are more numerous than they can decide?" asked Marshall. "Look at the dockets," he exclaimed. "You will find them crowded with suits which the life of man will not see determined.[1] If some of these suits be carried to other courts, will it be wrong? They will still have business enough."

How vain and fanciful, argued Marshall, the contention that National judges would screen "officers of the [National] government from merited punishment." Does anybody really believe that "the Federal sheriff will go into a poor man's house and beat him or abuse his family and the Federal court will protect him," as Mason and Henry had said would be the case? Even if a law should be passed authorizing "such great insults to the people . . . it would be void," declared Marshall. Thus he stated for the second time the doctrine which he was, from the Supreme Bench, to put beyond controversy.

Why, asked Marshall, "discriminate [in the Con-

[1] "There are upwards of 4,000 suits now entered on the docket in the General Court; and the number is continually increasing. Where this will end the Lord only knows — should an Act pass to extend the term of the Courts sitting — it is thought that the number of Executors [executions] that would issue . . . would be too heavy for our government to bear and that such a rapid transfer of Property would altogether stop the movement of our Machine." (Logan and Story, to Stephen Collins, Petersburg, Nov. 2, 1787; Collins MSS., Lib. Cong.)

stitution] between ... chancery, admiralty and the common law" as the Anti-Constitutionalists insisted upon doing? "Why not leave it to Congress? They ... would not wantonly infringe your rights." If they did, they would "render themselves hateful to the people at large." Therefore, "something may be left to the legislature [Congress] freely chosen by ourselves from among ourselves, who are to share the burdens imposed upon the community and who can be changed at our pleasure. Where power may be trusted and there is no motive to abuse it, it ... is as well to leave it undetermined as to fix it in the Constitution."

These sentences had prophecy in them. Indeed, they were to be repeated almost without change by the same man that now uttered them in debate, when he should ascend to the ultimate place of official interpretation of our fundamental law. While Hamilton's immortal state papers profoundly impressed Marshall, as we shall see, they were not, as many have supposed, the source of his convictions. In the Virginia Constitutional Convention of 1788 Marshall stated in debate the elements of most of his immortal Nationalist opinions.

But there was one exception. As to "disputes between *a state and the citizens of another state*," Marshall hoped "that no gentleman will think that a state will be called at the bar of a Federal court. . . . It is not rational to suppose that the Sovereign power should be dragged before a court. The intent is to enable states to recover claims of individuals residing in other states." If there were partiality in

THE STRATEGY OF VICTORY

this — "if an individual cannot ... obtain judgment against a state, though he may be sued by a state" — it was a difficulty which could "not be avoided"; let the claimant apply to the State Legislature for relief.

The objection to suits in the National Courts between citizens of different States went "too far," contended Marshall. Such actions "may not in general be absolutely necessary," but surely in some such cases "the citizen ... ought to be able to recur to this [National] tribunal." What harm could it do? "Will he get more than justice there? What has he to get? Justice! Shall we object to this because the citizen of another state can obtain justice without applying to our state courts?" Indeed, "it may be necessary" in causes affected by "the laws and regulations of commerce" and "in cases of debt and some other controversies." ... "In claims for land it is not necessary — but it is not dangerous."

These suits between citizens of different States "will be instituted in the state where the defendant resides, and nowhere else," expounded the youthful interpreter of the Constitution; and the case "will be determined by the laws of the state where the contract was made. According to those laws, and those only, can it be decided." That was no "novelty," but "a principle" long recognized in the jurisprudence of Virginia. "The laws which governed the contract at its formation, govern it in its decision." National Courts, in such controversies, would "preserve the peace of the Union," because if courts of different States should not give justice between citizens of those States, the result would be "disputes between the states." Also the jurisdiction of National Courts in "controversies between a state and a foreign state ... will be the means of preventing disputes with foreign nations"; for since "the previous consent of the parties is necessary ... each party will acquiesce."

As to "the exclusion of trial by jury, in this case," Marshall asked, "Does the word *court* only mean the judges? Does not the determination of the jury necessarily lead to the judgment of the court? Is there anything" in the Constitution "which gives the [National] judges exclusive jurisdiction of matters of fact? What is the object of a jury trial? To inform the court of the facts." If "a court has cognizance of facts," it certainly "can make inquiry by a jury," dryly observed Marshall.

He ridiculed Mason's and Henry's statement that juries, in the ten miles square which was to be the seat of the National Government, would be "mere tools of parties with which he would not trust his person or property." "What!" exclaimed Marshall, "Will no one stay there but the tools and officers of the government? ... Will there not be independent merchants and respectable gentlemen of fortune ... worthy farmers and mechanics" in the National Capital just as there were in Richmond? And "will the officers of the government become improper to be on a jury? What is it to the government whether this man or that man succeeds? It is all one thing."

As to jury trial not being guaranteed by the

National Constitution in civil cases, neither did Virginia's Constitution, said Marshall, "direct trials by jury"; and the provision was "merely recommendatory" concerning jury trials in the Bill of Rights, which, as everybody knew, was no part of the State Constitution. "Have you a jury trial when a judgment is obtained on a replevin bond or by default?" Or "when a motion is made by the Commonwealth against an individual ... or by one joint obligor against another, to recover sums paid as security." Of course not! "Yet they are all civil cases.... The Legislature of Virginia does not give a trial by jury where it is not necessary, but gives it wherever it is thought expedient." And Congress would do the same, he reassured the Convention.

Mason's objection, that the right to challenge jurors was not guaranteed in the Constitution, was trivial, said Marshall. Did Virginia's Constitution make such a guaranty? Did the British Constitution do so by any express provision? Was jury challenge secured by Magna Charta? Or by the Bill of Rights?[1] Every Virginian knew that they were not. "This privilege is founded in their [English people's] laws," Marshall reminded the Convention. So why insert it in the American Constitution?

Thus the inhabitants of the Northern Neck or anybody else were not in danger on that score. Neither were they placed in jeopardy in any other way by the Constitution. Here Marshall made a curious argument. Mason, he said, had "acknowl-

[1] This form of argument by asking questions to which the answers must needs be favorable to his contention was peculiarly characteristic of Marshall.

edged that there was no complete title [1] [in Fairfax]. . . . Was he [Mason] not satisfied that the right of the legal representatives of the proprietor [to collect quitrents] did not exist at the time he mentioned [the date of the Treaty of Peace]? If so, it cannot exist now," declared Marshall. "I trust those who come from that quarter [the Northern Neck] will not be intimidated on this account in voting on this question" he pleaded; for let them remember that there was "a law passed in 1782 [sequestration of quitrents] which secured this."

Let the "many poor men" who Mason had said might "be harassed by the representatives of Lord Fairfax" rest assured on that point; for "if he [Fairfax] has no right," they could not be disturbed. "If he has this right [to collect quitrents] and comes to Virginia, what laws will his claims be determined by?" By Virginia's laws. "By what tribunals will they be determined? By our state courts." [2] So the "poor man" who was "unjustly prosecuted" would "be abundantly protected and satisfied by the temper of his neighbors." [3]

[1] The reporter makes Mason assert the reverse.

[2] It is hard to see how Marshall arrived at this conclusion. But for the fact that Marshall prepared this speech, one would think the reporter erred.

[3] See Marshall's argument in Hite *vs.* Fairfax, chap. v, *supra;* and see vol. III of this work.

Randolph made the clearest statement of the whole debate on the Fairfax question: —

"Lord Fairfax . . . died during the war. In the year 1782, an act passed sequestering all quitrents, then due, in the hands of the persons holding the lands, until the right of descent should be known, and the General Assembly should make final provision therein. This act directed all quitrents, thereafter becoming due, to be paid into the public treasury; so that, with respect to his descendants, this act con-

THE STRATEGY OF VICTORY

The truth was, said Marshall, that justice would be done in all cases by both National and State Courts. Laws would not be "tyrannically executed" as the opposition feared; the "independency of your judges" would prevent that. "If," he argued, "a law be exercised tyrannically in Virginia, to whom can you trust? To your Judiciary! What security have you for justice? Their independence! Will it not be so in the Federal court?"

Like other objections to the power of Congress and the conduct of National Courts, the criticism that men might be punished for their political opinions was, declared Marshall, groundless and absurd; for, "the good opinion of the people at large must be consulted by their representatives — otherwise mischiefs would be produced which would shake the government to its foundations." Of course, then, he contended, neither Congress nor the courts would abuse their power. The charge that "unjust claims will be made, and the defendant had better pay them than go to the Supreme Court" was unthinkable. Would anybody incur great expense to oppress another? "What will he gain by an unjust demand?

fiscated the quitrents. In the year 1783, an act passed restoring to the legal representative of the proprietor the quitrents due to him at the time of his death. But in the year 1785 another act passed, by which the inhabitants of the Northern Neck are exonerated and discharged from paying composition and quitrents to the commonwealth." But Randolph then asserted that: "This last act has completely confiscated this property. It is repugnant to no part of the treaty, with respect to the quitrents confiscated by the act of 1782." So, continued he, "I ask the Convention of the free people of Virginia if there can be honesty in rejecting the government because justice is to be done by it? I beg the honourable gentleman to lay the objection to his heart." (Elliott, iii, 574–75.)

Does a claim establish a right? He must bring his witnesses to prove his claim"; otherwise "the expenses must fall on him." Will he take the chances that the injured man will not appear and defend the unjust suit? "Those who know human nature, black as it is," sarcastically observed Marshall, "must know that mankind are too attached to their own interest to run such a risk."

"The Federal Government," exclaimed Marshall, "has no other motive, and has every reason for doing right which the members of our state legislature have. Will a man on the eastern shore be sent to be tried in Kentucky, or a man from Kentucky be brought to the eastern shore to have his trial? A government, by doing this, would destroy itself." [1]

This, in effect, was John Marshall's exposition of the second section of article three of the Constitution. Although Grigsby, whose accuracy on such details is not questioned, says that the speech was prepared, Robertson's report would not indicate that such was the case. The address is wanting in that close-knit continuity of reasoning and in that neatness of thought and expression which were Marshall's peculiar excellence. Like his first debate in the Convention, his speech on the Judiciary is disjointed. A subject is half treated in one part of his remarks and resumed in another.[2] But he makes his

[1] Elliott, iii, 551-62.
[2] In summarizing Marshall's speech, it is necessary to collect his arguments on any given point, and present them consecutively. In Robertson's (Elliott) report Marshall scatters his points in distracting fashion.

principal points with clearness and power. His argument is based on the independence of the courts as the best guaranty against unjust decisions; the responsibility of Congress to the people as the strongest safeguard against oppressive laws; and the similarity of Virginia's Constitution and Courts to the National Constitution and Courts as proof of the security, fairness, and justice of the National Judiciary.

Marshall's effort really closed the case for the Constitution on the Judiciary. That night Madison wrote to Hamilton that "a great effort is making" against the Judiciary. "The retrospection to cases antecedent to the Constitution, such as British debts and an apprehended revival of Fairfax — Indiana, Vandalia, &c., claims are also brought into view in all the terrific colours which imagination can give them. ... Delay & an adjournment will be tried if the adverse party find their numbers inferior. ... At present it is calculated that we still retain a majority of 3 or 4; and if we can weather the storm agst." the Judiciary, "I shall hold the danger to be pretty well over. There is nevertheless a very disagreeable uncertainty in the case; and the more so as there is a possibility that our present strength may be miscalculated." [1]

Marshall's speech alarmed the opposition, and Grayson used all his learning, wit, and cleverness in an attempt to break its force. Randolph replied. Thus the second week closed. Neither side was certain of the exact number of votes it had, though every member was observed with the politician's

[1] Madison to Hamilton, June 20, 1788; Hamilton MSS., Lib. Cong.

anxiety and care.[1] The Constitutionalists had the greater confidence. Madison wrote his father that "The calculations on different sides do not accord; ... I think however, the friends of the Constitution are most confident of superiority. ... It is not probable that many proselytes will be made on either side." [2]

On Sunday Madison made his weekly report to Hamilton: "The Judiciary Department has been on the anvil for several days; and I presume will still be a further subject of disquisition. The attacks on it have apparently made less impression than was feared. But they may be secretly felt by particular interests that would not make the acknowledgment, and w^d chuse to ground their vote agst the Constitution on other motives." [3]

The Anti-Constitutionalists were becoming desperate. If they could not amend the Constitution as a condition of ratifying it, their game now was either an adjournment or a delay until the Legislature, scheduled to meet on the following Monday and known to be, in the main, opposed to the Constitution, should afford them relief.

If these expedients should fail, there was open talk of secession.[4] The Constitutionalists arranged for the utmost dispatch and planned to "withhold, by a studied fairness in every step on the side of the

[1] The members of the Convention were carefully watched and each side made, every night, a minute estimate of its votes.

[2] Madison to his father, June 20, 1788; *Writings:* Hunt, v, footnote to 216.

[3] Madison to Hamilton, June 22, 1788; Hamilton MSS., Lib. Cong

[4] *Ib.*

Constitution, every pretext for rash experiments." They hoped to avoid previous amendment by proposing "to preface the ratification with some plain & general matters that cannot effect the validity of the" Constitution. They felt that "these expedients are rendered prudent by the nice balance of members, and the scruples entertained by some who are in general well affected." But whether these devices "will secure us a majority," wrote Madison, "I dare not positively to declare."

So small was their expected majority likely to be, that the Constitutionalists felt that "ordinary casualties . . . may vary the result." They were exceedingly alarmed over the coming to town of the members of the Legislature who "as individuals . . . may have some influence and as coming immediately from the people at large they can give any colour they please to the popular sentiments at this moment, and may in that mode throw a bias on the representatives of the people in Convention." [1]

From the adjournment on Saturday until the Convention again assembled on the following Monday, June 23, the opposition decided that something more must be done to counteract Marshall's exposition of the Judiciary article. For this purpose their leader and strongest men took the floor. The shorthand reporter was not present on this day, but the printer of the debates took notes.[2]

Nothing so well shows the esteem in which Marshall's ability was held as Patrick Henry's compli-

[1] Madison to Hamilton, June 22, 1788; Hamilton MSS., Lib. Cong.
[2] Elliott, iii, 576.

ment to his young associate. "I have," said Henry, "the highest veneration and respect for the honorable gentleman, and I have experienced his candor on all occasions"; but "in this instance" Henry felt that Marshall was mistaken. "It is not on that paper before you we have to rely. . . . It is on those who may be appointed under it. It will be an empire of men, and not of laws."

Marshall interrupted Henry to explain that the latter had not clearly understood him as to the trial by jury. Henry responded that "the gentleman's candor, sir, as I informed you before, I have the highest opinion of, and am happy to find he has so far explained what he meant; but, sir, has he mended the matter?" Then Henry enlarged upon what he thought was the Constitution's sacrifice of rights of trial by jury. What would become of this, that, and the other? What would be the end of this contract and that? And "what is to become of the *purchases of the Indians?* — those unhappy nations who . . . by being made drunk, have given a thousand, nay I might say, ten thousand acres, for the trifling sum of sixpence!" And what of those who owed the British debts? — they will "be ruined by being dragged into Federal courts and the liberty and happiness of our citizens gone, never again to be recovered." [1]

The Constitutionalists had anticipated that Henry would touch on his hobby, the Indians; and they were ready with an answer far more effective on the votes of the members than any argument, however weighty. Hardly had Henry closed when a giant old

[1] Elliott, iii, 577–80.

man got upon his feet. For more than thirty years this bluff and ancient veteran had been a soldier. Since 1755 he had been one of the boldest and ablest of Virginia's famous Indian fighters and often had commanded the Virginia rangers that defended the frontier from the savages. His utter fearlessness and tremendous physical strength had made him the terror of the red man, and his name was a household word throughout Virginia as a bulwark against the savages. Throughout the Revolution he had borne himself as a hero. So when Colonel Adam Stephen spoke, his words were sword-thrusts.[1]

Henry, growled Stephen, "means to frighten us by his bugbears of hobgoblins, his sale of lands to pay taxes, Indian purchases and other horrors that I think I know as much about as he does." Colonel Stephen then described the Indian country, the Indian tribes, and Indian trade. He also knew "of several rich mines of gold and silver in the western country" which would pay the taxes Henry was so worried about. "If the gentleman [Henry] does not like this government, let him go and live among the Indians. I know of several nations that live very happily; and I can furnish him with a vocabulary of their language."[2]

Nothing can be plainer than that this personal assault on Henry was prearranged; for George Nich-

[1] Grigsby, i, 300. See Washington's letters to Stephen during the year of Marshall's birth, when Stephen, under Washington, was fighting the French and Indians. (*Writings:* Ford, i, 227, 322, 332, 360; also *Proceedings*, Council of War, Oct. 30, 1756; *ib.*, 364-71; in which Colonel Adam Stephen was presiding officer.)

[2] Elliott, iii, 580.

olas followed it up with what came near being an open insult. Answering Henry's insinuation about Indian lands being fraudulently purchased, Nicholas retorted, looking directly at Henry, "there are gentlemen who have come by large possessions that it is not easy to account for." This was taken as a reflection on some of Henry's land speculations. The latter felt the sting; for "here Mr. Henry interfered and hoped the honorable gentleman meant nothing personal." Nicholas snapped back, "I mean what I say, sir."

The extremes to which the opposition went in lobbying with members and the nature of their conversation are shown by an acid sentence of Nicholas in this speech. He referred to "an observation I have heard out of doors; which was that, because the New England men wore black stockings and plush breeches, there can be no union with them."

Henry was instantly on his feet when Nicholas finished. He thought the Convention floor "an improper place" to make "personal insinuations, or to wound my private reputation. . . . As to land matters, I can tell how I came by what I have . . . I hold what I hold in right, and in a just manner." Henry was most courteous and dignified in this discussion, disclaiming any intention to offend any one. Nicholas responded that he "meant no personality . . . nor . . . any resentment." But, said he, "If such conduct meets the contempt of that gentleman [Henry] I can only assure him it meets with an equal degree of contempt from me."

Here the President of the Convention interfered

and "hoped the gentlemen would not be personal; that they would proceed to investigate the subject calmly, and in a peaceable manner." Thereupon Nicholas admitted that he had not referred to Henry when he first spoke, but to "those who had taken up large tracts of land in the western country"; Nicholas had not, however, explained this before because he felt that Henry had said some things that one gentleman ought not to say to another. Thus ended the second of the only two instances in Virginia's long and masterful debate which approached a personal quarrel or displayed even the smallest discourtesy.[1]

The debate now drew swiftly to a close. Excitement ran high. The Anti-Constitutionalists, tense and desperate, threatened forcible opposition to the proposed National Government if it should be established. Mason "dreaded popular resistance" to the Constitution and was "emphatic" in his fears of "*the dreadful effects* . . . should the people resist." Gentlemen should pause before deciding "a question which involved such awful consequences." This so aroused Lee that he could "no longer suppress" his "utterance." Much as he liked and admired Mason, Lee asked him "if he has not pursued the very means to bring into action the horrors which he deprecates?"

"Such speeches within these walls, from a character so venerable and estimable," declared Lee, "easily progress into overt acts, among the less thinking and the vicious." Lee implored that the "God of heaven avert from my country the dreadful

[1] Elliott, iii, 581-82.

curse!" But, he thundered, "if the madness of some and the vice of others" should arouse popular resistance to the Constitution, the friends of that instrument "will meet the afflicting call"; and he plainly intimated that any uprising of the people against the proposed National Government would be met with arms.[1] The guns of Sumter were being forged.

On the night of June 23, the Constitutionalists decided to deliver their final assault. They knew that it must be a decisive one. The time had arrived for the meeting of the Legislature which was hostile to the Constitution;[2] and if the friends of the proposed new Government were to win at all, they must win quickly. A careful poll had shown them that straight-out ratification without amendment of some kind was impossible. So they followed the plan of the Massachusetts Constitutionalists and determined to offer amendments themselves — but amendments merely by way of recommendation and subsequent to ratification, instead of previous amendments as a condition of ratification. The venerable Wythe was chosen to carry out the programme. On Tuesday morning, June 24, Pendleton called to the chair Thomas Mathews, one of the best parliamentarians in the Convention, a stanch Constitutionalist, a veteran of the Revolution, and a popular man.

[1] Elliott, iii, 585-86.
[2] "Virginia is the only instance among the ratifying states in which the Politics of the Legislature are at variance with the sense of the people, expressed by their Representatives in Convention." (Madison to Washington, Nov. 5, 1788; *Writings:* Hunt, v, 302.)

Instantly Mathews recognized Wythe; for Henry was ready with his amendments, and, had an Anti-Constitutionalist been in the chair, would have been able to offer them before Wythe could move for ratification. Wythe, pale and fatigued, was so agitated that at first he could not speak plainly.[1] After reviewing the whole subject, he said that to insist on previous amendments might dissolve the Union, whereas all necessary amendments could easily be had after ratification. Wythe then moved the Constitutionalists' resolution for ratification.

In a towering rage, Henry rose for what, outside of the courtroom, was the last great speech of his life.[2] He felt that he had been unjustly forestalled and that the battle against the Constitution was failing because of the stern and unfair tactics of his foes.[3] The Constitutionalists admitted, said Henry, that the Constitution was "capitally defective"; yet they proposed to ratify it without first remedying its conceded faults. This was so absurd that he was "sure the gentleman [Wythe] meant nothing but to amuse the committee. I know his candor," said Henry. "His proposal is an idea dreadful to me. . . . The great body of yeomanry are in decided opposition" to the Constitution.

Henry declared that of his own personal knowledge "nine tenths of the people" in "nineteen coun-

---

[1] Grigsby, i, 307.
[2] The two amazing speeches which Henry made that day should be taken together. While both were inspired by what happened on the floor, yet they are in reality one. The reports give no idea of the tremendous effect which those who heard Henry tell us these speeches had.
[3] Grigsby, i, 307-08.

ties adjacent to each other" were against the proposed new National Government. The Constitutionalists' plan of "subsequent amendments will not do for men of this cast." And how do the people feel even in the States that had ratified it? Look at Pennsylvania! Only ten thousand out of seventy thousand of her people were represented in the Pennsylvania Convention.

If the Constitution was ratified without previous amendments, Henry declared that he would "have nothing to do with it." He offered the Bill of Rights and amendments which he himself had drawn, proposing to refer them to the other States "for their consideration, previous to its [Constitution's] ratification."[1] Henry then turned upon the Constitutionalists their own point by declaring that it was their plan of ratification without previous amendments which would endanger the Union.[2] Randolph followed briefly and Dawson at great length. Madison for the Constitutionalists, and Grayson for the opposition, exerted themselves to the utmost. Nature aided Henry when he closed the day in an appeal such as only the supremely gifted can make.

"I see," cried Henry, in rapt exaltation, "the awful immensity of the dangers with which it [the Constitution] is pregnant. I see it. I feel it. I see beings of a higher order anxious concerning our decision. When I see beyond the horizon that bounds

[1] Henry's amendments were practically the same as those which the Convention finally adopted as recommendations subsequent to ratification instead of previous amendment on which ratification was conditioned.
[2] Elliott, iii, 587-96.

PATRICK HENRY

human eyes, and look at the final consummation of all human things, and see those intelligent beings which inhabit the ethereal mansions reviewing the political decisions and revolutions which, in the progress of time, will happen in America, and the consequent happiness or misery of mankind, I am led to believe that much of the account, on one side or the other, will depend on what we now decide. Our own happiness alone is not affected by the event. All nations are interested in the determination. We have it in our power to secure the happiness of one half of the human race. Its adoption may involve the misery of the other hemisphere." [1]

In the midst of this trance-like spell which the master conjurer had thrown over his hearers, a terrible storm suddenly arose. Darkness fell upon the full light of day. Lightnings flashed and crashing thunders shook the Convention hall. With the inspiration of genius this unrivaled actor made the tempest seem a part of his own denunciation. The scene became insupportable. Members rushed from their seats.[2] As Henry closed, the tempest died away.

The spectators returned, the members recovered their composure, and the session was resumed.[3] Nicholas coldly moved that the question be put at

[1] Elliott, iii, 625. This extract is badly mangled. The reporter confesses that he could take only a little of Henry's peroration. Elliott's reprint of Robertson's reports gives scarcely a suggestion of its dramatic appeal. We are indebted to Grigsby's patient work in collecting from eye and ear witnesses first-hand accounts, for a reasonably accurate description of the scene.

[2] Grigsby, i, 316–17; also Wirt, 313; Henry, ii, 370–71; and Conway, 113.

[3] Grigsby, i, 316–17.

nine o'clock on the following morning. Clay and Ronald opposed, the latter declaring that without such amendments "as will secure the happiness of the people" he would "though much against his inclination vote against this Constitution."

Anxious and prolonged were the conferences of the Constitutionalist managers that night. The Legislature had convened. It was now or never for the friends of the Constitution. The delay of a single day might lose them the contest. That night and the next morning they brought to bear every ounce of their strength. The Convention met for its final session on the historic 25th of June, with the Constitutionalists in gravest apprehension. They were not sure that Henry would not carry out his threat to leave the hall; and they pictured to themselves the dreaded spectacle of that popular leader walking out at the head of the enraged opposition.[1]

Into the hands of the burly Nicholas the Constitutionalists wisely gave command. The moment the Convention was called to order, the chair recognized Nicholas, who acted instantly with his characteristically icy and merciless decision. "The friends of the Constitution," said Nicholas, "wish to take up no more time, the matter being now fully discussed. They are convinced that further time will answer no end but to serve the cause of those who wish to destroy the Constitution. We wish it to be ratified and such amendments as may be thought necessary to be subsequently considered by a committee in order to be recommended to Congress."

[1] Grigsby, i, 317.

Where, he defiantly asked, did the opposition get authority to say that the Constitutionalists would not insist upon amendments after they had secured ratification of the Constitution? They really wished for Wythe's amendments;[1] and would "agree to any others which" would "not destroy the spirit of the Constitution." Nicholas moved the reading of Wythe's resolution in order that a vote might be taken upon it.[2]

Tyler moved the reading of Henry's proposed amendments and Bill of Rights. Benjamin Harrison protested against the Constitutionalists' plan. He was for previous amendment, and thought Wythe's "measure of adoption to be unwarrantable, precipitate, and dangerously impolitic." Madison reassured those who were fearful that the Constitutionalists, if they won on ratification, would not further urge the amendments Wythe had offered; the Constitutionalists then closed, as they had begun, with admirable strategy.

James Innes was Attorney-General. His duties had kept him frequently from the Convention. He was well educated, extremely popular, and had been one of the most gifted and gallant officers that Virginia had sent to the front during the Revolution. Physically he was a colossus, the largest man in that State of giants. Such was the popular and imposing champion which the Constitutionalists had so well

[1] Very few of the Constitutionalists wanted any amendments; and Madison sorrowfully offered in Congress the following year those that were reluctantly adopted. See vol. II, chap. II, of this work.
[2] Elliott, iii, 627.

chosen to utter their parting word.[1] And Innes did his utmost in the hardest of situations; for if he took too much time, he would endanger his own cause; if he did not make a deep impression, he would fail in the purpose for which he was put forward.[2]

Men who heard Innes testify that "he spoke like one inspired." [3] For the opposition the learned and accomplished Tyler closed the general debate. It was time wasted on both sides. But that nothing might be left undone, the Constitutionalists now brought into action a rough, forthright member from the Valley. Zachariah Johnson spoke for "those who live in large, remote, back counties." He dwelt, he said, "among the poor people." The most that he could claim for himself was "to be of the middle rank." He had "a numerous offspring" and he was willing to trust their future to the Constitution.[4]

Henry could not restrain himself; but he would better not have spoken, for he admitted defeat. The anxious Constitutionalists must have breathed a sigh of relief when Henry said that he would not leave the hall. Though *overpowered in a good cause, yet I will be a peaceable citizen.*" All he would try to do would be "to remove the defects of that system [the Constitution] in a constitutional way." And so, declared the scarred veteran as he yielded his sword to the victors, he would "patiently wait in expectation of seeing that government changed, so as to be compatible with the safety, liberty, and happiness, of the people."

[1] Grigsby, i, 323-29.
[2] *Ib.*, 328.
[3] *Ib.*, 332.
[4] Elliott, iii, 644-49.

THE STRATEGY OF VICTORY 475

Wythe's resolution of ratification now came to a vote. No more carefully worded paper for the purposes it was intended to accomplish ever was laid before a deliberative body. It reassured those who feared the Constitution, in language which went far to grant most of their demands; and while the resolve called for ratification, yet, "in order to relieve the apprehensions of those who may be solicitous for amendments," it provided that all necessary amendments be *recommended* to Congress. Thus did the Constitutionalists, who had exhausted all the resources of management, debate, and personal persuasion, now find it necessary to resort to the most delicate tact.

The opposition moved to substitute for the ratification resolution one of their own, which declared "that previous to the ratification . . . a declaration of rights . . . together with amendments . . . should be referred by this Convention to the other states . . . for their consideration." On this, the first test vote of the struggle, the Constitutionalists won by the slender majority of 8 out of a total of 168. On the main question which followed, the Anti-Constitutionalists lost but one vote and the Constitution escaped defeat by a majority of only 10.

To secure ratification, eight members of the Convention voted against the wishes of their constituents,[1] and two ignored their instructions.[2] Grayson openly but respectfully stated on the floor that the

[1] Henry, ii, 377. "At least ten members voted, either in disobedience of positive instructions of their constituents, or in defiance of their well known opinions." (Grigsby, i, 41.)
[2] Scott, 235-38.

vote was the result of Washington's influence. "I think," said he, "that, were it not for one great character in America, so many men would not be for this government." [1] Followers of their old commander as the members from the Valley were, the fear of the Indians had quite as much to do with getting their support for a stronger National Government as had the weight of Washington's influence.[2]

Randolph "humbly supplicated one parting word" before the last vote was taken. It was a word of excuse and self-justification. His vote, he said, would be "ascribed by malice to motives unknown to his breast." He would "ask the mercy of God for every other act of his life," but for this he requested only Heaven's justice. He still objected to the Constitution, but the ratification of it by eight States had now "reduced our deliberations to the single question of *Union* or no *Union*." [3] So closed the greatest debate ever held over the Constitution and one of the ablest parliamentary contests of history.

A committee was appointed to report "a form of ratification pursuant to the first resolution"; and another was selected "to prepare and report such amendments as by them shall be deemed neces-

[1] Elliott, iii, 616. Madison frankly admitted that only the prominence of the framers of the Constitution secured even a consideration of it by many of its warmest friends, much less by the people. "Had the Constitution been framed and recommended by an obscure individual," wrote Madison, "instead of a body possessing public respect and confidence, there cannot be a dcubt, that, although it would have stood in the identical words, it would have commanded little attention from those who now admire its wisdom." (Madison to Randolph, Jan. 10, 1788; *Writings:* Hunt, v, 81.)

[2] Grigsby, i, footnote to 110.

[3] Elliott, iii, 652.

sary."[1] Marshall was chosen as a member of both these important committees.

The lengths to which the Constitutionalists were driven in order to secure ratification are measured by the amendments they were forced to bring in. These numbered twenty, in addition to a Bill of Rights, which also had twenty articles. The ten amendments afterwards made to the Constitution were hardly a shadow of those recommended by the Virginia Convention of 1788.

That body actually proposed that National excise or direct tax laws should not operate in any State, in case the State itself should collect its quota under State laws and through State officials; that two thirds of both houses of Congress, present, should be necessary to pass navigation laws or laws regulating commerce; that no army or regular troops should be "raised or kept up in time of peace" without the consent of two thirds of both houses, present; that the power of Congress over the seat of the National Government should be confined to police and administrative regulation. The Judiciary amendment would have imprisoned the Supreme Court within limits so narrow as to render that tribunal almost powerless and would have absolutely prevented the establishment of inferior National Courts, except those of Admiralty.[2] Yet only on such terms could ratification be secured even by the small and uncertain majority that finally voted for it.

On June 25, Clinton's suppressed letter to Randolph was laid before the House of Delegates which

[1] Elliott, iii, 653–63. [2] *Ib.*, 659–61.

had just convened.[1] Mason was so furious that he drew up resolutions for an investigation of Randolph's conduct.[2] But the deed was done, anger was unavailing, and the resolutions never were offered.[3]

So frail was the Constitutionalist strength that if the news of the New Hampshire ratification had not reached Virginia, it is more than probable that Jefferson's advice would have been followed and that the Old Dominion would have held back until all the amendments desired by the opposition had been made a part of the fundamental law;[4] and the Constitution would have been a far different and infinitely weaker instrument than it is.

Burning with wrath, the Anti-Constitutionalists held a meeting on the night of the day of the vote for ratification, to consider measures for resisting the new National Government. The character of Patrick Henry never shone with greater luster than when he took the chair at this determined gathering of furious men. He had done his best against the Constitution, said Henry, but he had done it in the "*proper place*"; the question was settled now and he advised his colleagues that "as true and faithful republicans, they had all better go home!"[5] Well might Washington write that only "conciliatory con-

[1] Clinton's letter was not read, however, because all the members of the Legislature had gone to hear Henry's last great speech. (Conway, 112.)

[2] Conway, 114; Henry, ii, 363.

[3] For Mason's resolutions and a careful review of the incident, see Rowland, ii, 274-80.

[4] Henry, ii, 377.

[5] *Southern Literary Messenger*, i, 332; also quoted in Rowland, ii, 274.

duct" got the Constitution through;[1] well might he declare that "it is nearly impossible for anybody who has not been on the spot (from any description) to conceive what the delicacy and danger of our situation have been."[2]

And Marshall had been on the spot. Marshall had seen it all. Marshall had been a part of it all. From the first careful election programme of the Constitutionalists, the young Richmond lawyer had been in every meeting where the plans of the managers were laid and the order of battle arranged. No man in all the country knew better than he, the hair's breadth by which the ordinance of our National Government escaped strangulation at its very birth. No one in America better understood how carefully and yet how boldly Nationalism must be advanced if it were to grow stronger or even to survive.

It was plain to Marshall that the formal adoption of the Constitution did not end the battle. That conflict, indeed, was only beginning. The fight over ratification had been but the first phase of the struggle. We are now to behold the next stages of that great contest, each as dramatic as it was vital; and we shall observe how Marshall bore himself on every field of this mighty civil strife, note his development and mark his progress toward that supreme station for which events prepared him. We are to witness his efforts to uphold the National Government, not only with argument and

[1] Washington to Pinckney, June 28, 1788; *Writings:* Ford, xi, 285.
[2] Washington to Jefferson, Aug. 31, 1788; *ib.*, 321.

political activity, but also with a readiness to draw the sword and employ military force. We shall look upon the mad scenes resulting in America from the terrific and bloody convulsion in Europe and measure the lasting effect the French Revolution produced upon the statesmen and people of the United States. In short, we are to survey a strange swirl of forces, economic and emotional, throwing to the surface now one "issue" and now another, all of them centering in the sovereign question of Nationalism or States' Rights.

END OF VOLUME I

APPENDIX

APPENDIX

I

WILL OF THOMAS MARSHALL, "CARPENTER"

IN THE NAME OF GOD AMEN! I, Thomas Marshall of the County of Westmoreland of Washington Parish, Carpenter, being very weak but of perfect memory thanks be to God for it doth ordain this my last will and testament in manner and form following, first I give and bequeath my soul into the hands of my blessed Creator & Redeemer hoping through meritts of my blessed Saviour to receive full pardon and remission of all my sins and my body to the Earth to be decently bur-yed according to the discretion of my Executrix which hereafter shall be named. Imps. I make and ordain my well beloved wife Martha Marshall to be my full and whole Executrix — Item, I will that my estate shall remain in the hands of my wife as long as she remain single but in case she marrys then she is to have her lawful part & the rest to be taken out of her hands equally to be divided among my children — Item, I will that if my wife marry, that David Brown Senr. and Jno. Brown to be guardians over my children and to take the estate in their hands bringing it to appraisement giving in good security to what it is valued and to pay my children their dues as they shall come to age. Item — I will that Elizabeth Rosser is to have a heifer delivered by my wife called White-Belly to be delivered as soon as I am deceast — Item, I will that my son William Marshall shall have my plantation as soon as he comes to age to him and his heirs forever, but in case that my son William die before he comes to age or die without issue then my plantation is to fall to the next heir apparent at law.

THOMAS MARSHALL (Seal)

Test EDW: TAYLOR, JOHN HEARFORD,
JOHN TAYLOR.

WESTMORLD: ss. { At a Court held for the said County the 31st day of May 1704.

The last will and testament of Thomas Marshall within written was proved by the oaths of John Oxford and John Taylor two of the witnesses thereto subscribed and a Probat thereof granted to Martha Marshall his relict and Executrix therein named.

         Test
         IA: WESTCOMB Cler. Com. Ped.

Record aty: sexto die Juny:
1704. Pr.
Eundm Clerum.

A Copy. Teste:
 ALBERT STUART, Clerk.
  By:
   F. F. CHANDLER, Deputy Clerk.

[A Copy. Will of Thomas Marshall. Recorded in the Clerk's Office of the Circuit Court of Westmoreland County, in Deed and Will Book no. 3 at page 232 *et seq.*]

II
WILL OF JOHN MARSHALL "OF THE FOREST"

THE LAST will and testament of John Marshall being very sick and weak but of perfect mind and memory is as followeth.

First of all I give and recommend my soul to God that gave it and my Body to the ground to be buried in a Christian like and Discent manner at the Discretion of my Executors hereafter mentioned? Item I give and bequeath unto my beloved daughter Sarah Lovell one negro girl named Rachel now in possession of Robert Lovell. Item I give and bequeath unto my beloved daughter Ann Smith one negro boy named Danniel now in possession of Augustine Smith. Item I give and bequeath unto my beloved daughter Lize Smith one negro boy named Will now in possession of John Smith. Item I give and bequeath unto my well beloved wife Elizabeth Marshall one negro fellow named Joe and one negro woman named Cate and one negro woman named pen after Delivering the first child next born of her Body unto my son John until which time she shall remain in the possession of my wife Likewise I leave my Corn and meat to remain unappraised for the use of my wife and children also I give and bequeath unto my wife one Gray mair named beauty and side saddle also six hogs also I leave her the use of my land During her widowhood, and afterwards to fall to my son Thomas Marshall and his heirs forever. Item I leave my Tobacco to pay my Debts and if any be over for the clothing of my small children. Item I give and bequeath unto my well Beloved son Thomas Marshall one negro woman named hanno and one negroe child named Jacob? Item I give and bequeathe unto my well beloved son John Marshall one negroe fellow named George and one negroe child named Nan. Item. I give and bequeathe unto my beloved son Wm. Marshall one negro woman named Sall and one negro boy named Hanable to remain in the possession of his mother until he come to the age of twenty years. Item I give and Bequeath unto my Beloved son Abraham Marshall one negro boy named Jim and one negroe girl named bett to remain in the possession of his mother until he come to the age of twenty years. Item I give and Bequeath unto my Beloved daughter Mary Marshall one negro girl named Cate and negro boy Gus to remain in possession of her mother until she come to the age of Eighteen years or until marriage. Item, I give and Bequeath unto my beloved Daughter Peggy Marshall one negro boy named Joshua and one negro girl named Liz to remain in possession of her mother until she come to the age of Eighteen or until marriage! Item. I leave my personal Estate Except the legacies abovementioned to be equally Divided Between my wife and six children last above mentioned. Item I constitute and appoint my wife and my two sons Thos. Marshall and John Marshall Executors of this my last will & testament In witness hereof I have hereunto set my hand and fixed my seal this first day of April One thousand seven hundred and fifty two.

Interlined before assigned.

BENJAMIN RALLINS }
WILLIAM HOUSTON }
AUGUSTINE SMITH }

JOHN MARSHALL (Seal)

WESTMORLAND SCT. { At a Court held for the said County the 26th day of May 1752.

This Last will and testament of John Marshall decd. was presented into Court by Eliza. his relict and Thomas Marshall two of his Executors therein named who made oath thereto and being proved by the oaths of Benja. Rallings and Augustine Smith two of the witnesses thereto is admitted to record, and upon the motion of the said Eliza. & Thos. and their performing what the Law in such cases require Certificate is granted them for obtaining a probate thereof in due form.

Test

GEORGE LEE C. C. C. W.

Recorded the 22d. day of June 1752.
Per
    G. L. C. C. W. C.

A Copy. Teste:
    FRANK STUART, Clerk of the Circuit Court of Westmoreland County, State of Virginia.

[A copy. John Marshall's Will. Recorded in the Clerk's Office of Westmoreland County, State of Virginia, in Deeds and Wills, no. 11, at page 419 *et seq.*]

III

DEED OF WILLIAM MARSHALL TO JOHN MARSHALL "OF THE FOREST"

THIS INDENTURE made the 23d day of October in ye first year of ye reign of our sovereign Lord George ye 2d. by ye. grace of God of Great Brittain France & Ireland King defendr. of ye faith &c. and in ye year of our Lord God one thousand seven hundred & twenty seven, between William Marshall of ye. County of King & Queen in ye. Colony of Virginia planter of the one part & John Marshall of ye. County of Westmoreland Virginia of the other part: WITNESSETH that ye sd. William Marshall for and in consideration of ye. sum of five shillings sterling money of England to him in hand paid before ye sealing & delivery hereof ye. receipt whereof he doth hereby acknowledge & thereof & of every part thereof doth hereby acquit & discharge ye. sd John Marshall his heirs Exectrs & administrators by these presents, hath granted bargained & sold & doth hereby grant bargain & sell John Marshall his heirs Exectrs administrs & assigns all that tract or parsel of land (except ye parsel of land wch was sold out of it to Michael Hulburt) scitute lying & being in Westmoreland County in Washington parish on or near Appamattox Creek & being part of a tract of land containing 1200 acres formerly granted to Jno: Washington & Tho: Pope gents by Patent dated the 4th Septbr. 1661 & by them lost for want of seating & since granted to Collo. Nicholas Spencer by Ordr. Genll. Court dated Septbr. ye 21st 1668 & by ye said Spencer assign'd to ye. sd. Jno: Washington ye 9th of Octobr. 1669 which sd. two hundred acres was conveyed & sold to Thomas Marshall by Francis Wright & afterwards acknowledged in Court by John Wright ye. 28th day of May 1707 which sd two hundred acres of land be ye. same more or less and bounded as follows beginning at a black Oak standing in ye. southermost line of ye sd. 1200 acres & being a corner tree of a line that divideth this two hundred acres from One hundred acres of Michael Halbarts extending along ye. sd southermost lines west two hundred poles to a marked red Oak, thence north 160 poles to another marked red Oak thence east 200 poles to a black Oak of ye sd. Halberts to ye place it began, with all houses outhouses Orchards water water courses woods under woods timbers & all other things thereunto belonging with the revertion & revertions remainder & remainders rents issues & yearly profits & every part & parcell thereof. To have and to hold ye. sd. land & premises unto ye. sd John Marshall his heirs Executors Administrs & assignes from ye. day of ye date thereof for & during & untill the full end & term of six months from thence next ensuing fully to be compleat & ended to ye. end that by virtue thereof & of the statutes for transferring uses into possessions ye. sd John Marshall might be in actual possession of ye premises & might be enabled to take and accept of a grant release of the same to him ye. sd John Marshall his heires & assignes forever. In Witness whereof the parties to these present Indentures interchangeably have set —— hands & seals ye. day & year first above written.

WM MARSHALL (seal)

Signd. Seald & d'd in sight & presence of —
FRANCIS LACON, JANE LACON, THOMAS THOMPSON

WESTMORLD. SS. At a Court held for the sd. County the 27th day of March 1728.

William Marshall personally acknowledged this lease of land by him passed to John Marshall to be his proper act and deed, which at the instance of the sd. John Marshall is admitted to record.

Test
G. TURBERVILE, C. C. W.

Recorded the 29th day of March 1728.
Pr.
G. T. C C W.

A Copy. Teste:
FRANK STUART, Clerk of tne Circuit Court of Westmoreland County, State of Virginia.

[A copy. William Marshall to John Marshall. Deed. Recorded in the Clerk's Office of Westmoreland County, State of Virginia, in Deeds and Wills, no. 8–1, at page 276.]

IV
MEMORIAL OF THOMAS MARSHALL FOR MILITARY EMOLUMENTS

To the Honorable the Speaker and members of the house of Delegates, the Memorial of Thomas Marshall humbly sheweth.

That your Memorialist in Augt 1775 was appointed Major to the first minute Battalion raisd within this Commonwealth and early in October the same year enterd into actual service in which he continued during the following winter campaign. That while your memorialist commanded at the Great Bridge he was appointed Major to the 3^d Virginia Continental Regim^t he did not however retire from service but retaind his command and continued at his post till the latter end of March 1776 when the troops under his command were relieved by those of the continent rais'd in this State, by which time the 3^d Virginia Regim^t was rais'd and your Memorialist immediately called on to take command in it. That in Augt 1776 he together with the regiment to which he belonged in obedience to the orders they had rec^d began their march to New York, where they join'd the Grand-Army. That your Memorialist continued in hard and unremitting service from this time till the close of the campaign of 1777. That in the latter end of November 1777 your Memorialist was informed by an official letter from the then Governor, of his haveing been appointed by the General Assembly of Virginia to the command of the State regiment of Artillery; — a command he was only induced to take by a preference he ever felt for Artillery Service. That your Memorialist however retain'd his command and continued his service in the Northern Army till the end of the Campaign when the Troops were ordered into winter quarters. That your Memorialist then return'd to Virginia and about the middle of January following took command of his Regim^t of Artillery, which command he rataind till the 26th of February 1781 at which time, the term of enlistment of most of the soldiers of the Regim^t having expired, they were discharged and your Memorialist became a reduced officer. Your Memorialist conceived from the Laws existing at the time he enter'd into the particular service of this State and from the different acts respecting the State Troops which have since passd the Legislature, that he should be intitled to every emolument to which he would have had a just claim had he remaind in the Continental Service. If however only particular discriptions of State Officers are to receive such emoluments as Continental are intitled to, your Memorialist humbly presumes to hope that his haveing made three of the severest campaigns in the last war before he took command of the State Regim^t of Artillery, his haveing rendered, as he trusts, some services as commanding officer of that Regiment, his haveing remaind in service till there was no longer a command fcr him, his having held himself in readiness to return to service, had his regiment been recruited, give him as fair a claim to military emoluments as any officer who has been in the particular service of this State. Your memorialist therefore humbly prays that your honorable house will take his services into consideration and allow him those emoluments which may be given to other State Officers whose services may not be superior to his.

T. MARSHALL.

A true copy
  H. R. McILWAIN,
    State Librarian.
      June 20, 1916.
[Marshalls Pet^n Nov. 25th 1784 Referred to Propositions Props. discharged and ref^d to whole on Bill for giving Commutation to Officers of 1st and 2d State Regiments.]

WORKS CITED IN THIS VOLUME

WORKS CITED IN THIS VOLUME

The material given in parentheses and following certain titles indicates the form in which those titles have been cited in the footnotes.

ADAMS, CHARLES FRANCIS, editor. See Adams, John. Works.
ADAMS, HENRY. The Life of Albert Gallatin. Philadelphia. 1879. (Adams: *Gallatin.*)
    See also Gallatin, Albert. Writings.
ADAMS, JOHN. Works. Edited by Charles Francis Adams. 10 vols. Boston. 1856. (*Works:* Adams.)
—— Old Family Letters. Copied from the originals for Alexander Biddle. Philadelphia. 1892. (*Old Family Letters.*)
ALLEN, ETHAN. Narrative of the Capture of Ticonderoga, and his Captivity in England, written by himself. Burlington. 1854. (Ethan Allen.)
ALLEN, GARDNER WELD. A Naval History of the American Revolution. 2 vols. New York. 1913. (Allen: *Naval History of Revolution.*)
—— Our Navy and the Barbary Corsairs, Boston. 1905. (Allen: *Our Navy and the Barbary Corsairs.*)
AMBLER, CHARLES HENRY. Sectionalism in Virginia, from 1776 to 1861. Chicago. 1910. (Ambler.)
American Historical and Literary Curiosities. See Smith, John Jay, and Watson, John Fanning, *joint editors.*
American Historical Review. Managing editor, J. Franklin Jameson. Vols. 1–21. New York. 1896–1916. (*Amer. Hist. Rev.*)
American Journal of Education. Edited by Henry Barnard. Vols. 1–30. Hartford. 1856–80.
American Museum or Repository of Ancient and Modern Fugitive Pieces, Philadelphia. 1788. (*American Museum.*)
ANBUREY, THOMAS. Travels through the Interior Parts of America, in a Series of Letters, by An Officer. 2 vols. London. 1789. (Anburey.)
AVERY, ELROY MCKENDREE. A History of the United States and its people. 7 vols. Cleveland. 1904–10. (Avery.)

494   WORKS CITED IN THIS VOLUME

BAILY, FRANCIS. Journal of a Tour in Unsettled Parts of North America, in 1796 and 1797. London. 1856. (Baily's *Journal.*)

BASSETT, JOHN SPENCER, editor. *See* Byrd, Colonel William, of Westover. Writings.

BAYARD, JAMES A. Papers, from 1796 to 1815. Edited by Elizabeth Donnan. Washington. 1915. (Volume 2 of *Annual Report of the American Historical Association* for 1913.) (*Bayard Papers:* Donnan.)

BEARD, CHARLES A. An Economic Interpretation of the Constitution of the United States. New York. 1913. (Beard: *Econ. I. C.*)

—— Economic Origins of Jeffersonian Democracy. New York. 1915. (Beard: *Econ. O. J. D.*)

BELCHER, ROBERT HENRY. The First American Civil War. 2 vols. London. 1911. (Belcher.)

BINNEY, HORACE. Eulogy on John Marshall, reprinted. *See* Dillon, John F.

BOLTON, CHARLES KNOWLES. The Private Soldier Under Washington. New York. 1902. (Bolton.)

BOUDINOT, ELIAS. Journal of Events in the Revolution, or Historical Recollections of American Events during the Revolutionary War. Philadelphia. 1894. (Boudinot's *Journal.*)

BRANCH, JOHN P. Historical Papers, issued by the Randolph-Macon College, Ashland, Virginia. Richmond. 1901. (*Branch Historical Papers.*)

BRISSOT DE WARVILLE, JEAN PIERRE. New Travels in the United States of America, performed in 1788. Dublin. 1792. (De Warville.)

BROGLIE, *Duc* DE, editor. *See* Talleyrand, Prince de. Memoirs.

BRUCE, PHILIP ALEXANDER. Economic History of Virginia in the Seventeenth Century. 2 vols. New York. 1896. (Bruce: *Econ.*)

—— Institutional History of Virginia in the Seventeenth Century. 2 vols. New York. 1910. (Bruce: *Inst.*)

BURGESS, JOHN WILLIAM. Political Science and Comparative Constitutional Law. 2 vols. Boston. 1890.

BURK, JOHN DALY. The History of Virginia, from its First Settlement to the Present Day. Continued by Skelton Jones and Louis Hue Girardin. 4 vols. Richmond. 1804–16. (Burk.)

WORKS CITED IN THIS VOLUME

BURKE, JOHN, *and* Sir JOHN BERNARD. Peerages of England, Ireland, and Scotland, Extinct, Dormant, and in Abeyance. London. 1846. (Burke: *Extinct Peerages*.)

BURKE, Sir JOHN BERNARD. Dictionary of Peerage and Baronage. Edited by Ashworth P. Burke. New York. 1904. (Burke: *Peerage*.)

BURNABY, ANDREW. Travels Through North America. [Reprinted from the Third Edition of 1798.] New York. 1904. (Burnaby.)

BUTLER, MANN. A History of the Commonwealth of Kentucky. Louisville. 1834. (Butler: *History of Kentucky*.)

BYRD, *Colonel* WILLIAM, of Westover. Writings. Edited by John Spencer Bassett. New York. 1901. (Byrd's *Writings:* Bassett.)

CABOT, GEORGE. *See* Lodge, Henry Cabot. Life and Letters of George Cabot.

Calendar of Virginia State Papers and Other Manuscripts. Preserved in the Capitol at Richmond. Vols. 1–11. Richmond. 1875–1893. (*Cal. Va. St. Prs.*)

CAMPBELL, CHARLES. History of the Colony and Ancient Dominion of Virginia. Philadelphia. 1860. (Campbell.)

CARLYLE, THOMAS. History of Friedrich II of Prussia, called Frederick the Great. 6 vols. London. 1858–65. (Carlyle: *Frederick the Great*.)

CHALKLEY, LYMAN. Chronicles of the Scotch-Irish Settlement in Virginia, Extracted from the Original Court Records of Augusta County [Virginia], 1745–1800. 3 vols. Rosslyn, Virginia. 1912–13. (*Chalkley's Augusta County (Va.) Records*.)

CHANNING, EDWARD. A History of the United States. [Vols. 1–3.] New York. 1912–16. (Channing.)

CHASTELLUX, *Marquis* F. J. DE. Travels in North America in the years 1780–81–82. New York. 1828. (Chastellux.)

CHEETHAM, JAMES. Letters, From 1801 to 1806. Printed in Proceedings of the Massachusetts Historical Society, April and May, 1907.

CHRISTIAN WILLIAM ASBURY. Richmond, Her Past and Present. Richmond. 1912. (Christian.)

COLLINS, LEWIS. History of Kentucky. Enlarged by his son, Richard H. Collins. 2 vols. Covington, Kentucky, 1874. (Collins: *History of Kentucky*.)

CONWAY, MONCURE DANIEL. Omitted Chapters of History, disclosed in the Life and Papers of Edmund Randolph. New York. 1888. (Conway.)
—— Also see Paine, Thomas. Writings.
CRÈVECŒUR, MICHEL GUILLAUME SAINT JOHN DE. Letters from an American Farmer. By J. Hector St. John Crèvecœur. [*pseud.*] New York. 1904. (Crèvecœur.)

DANDRIDGE, DANSKE. American Prisoners of the Revolution. Richmond. 1911. (Dandridge: *American Prisoners of the Revolution.*)
DAVIS, JOHN. Travels of Four Years and a half in the United States of America. 1798–1802. London. 1803. (Davis.)
DAWSON, HENRY B. The Assault on Stony Point by General Anthony Wayne. Morrisania. 1863. (Dawson.)
DEFOE, DANIEL. Novels and Miscellaneous Works. Preface and Notes attributed to Sir Walter Scott. Moll Flanders [vol. 3.] [Bohn's British Classics.] 7 vols. London. 1854–66. (Defoe: *Moll Flanders.*)
DILLON, JOHN F., *compiler*. John Marshall, Life, Character, and Judicial Services. (Including the Classic Orations of Binney, Story, Phelps, Waite, and Rawle.) 3 vols. Chicago. 1903. (Story, in Dillon; and Binney, in Dillon.)
DODD, WILLIAM E. Statesmen of the Old South, or From Radicalism to Conservative Revolt. New York. 1911. (Dodd.)
DONNAN, ELIZABETH, *editor*. See Bayard, James A. Papers.
DOUGLAS, *Sir* ROBERT. Peerage of Scotland. Edinburgh. 1764. (Douglas: *Peerage of Scotland.*)

ECKENRODE, H. J. The Revolution in Virginia. Boston. 1916. (Eckenrode: *R. V.*)
—— Separation of Church and State in Virginia. A Study in the Development of the Revolution. Richmond. 1910. [Special Report of the Department of Archives and History of the Virginia State Library.] (Eckenrode: *S. of C. and S.*)
Eighty Years' Progress of the United States, from the Revolutionary War to the Great Rebellion. [By Eminent Literary Men.] New York. 1864. (*Eighty Years' Progress.*)
ELLIOTT, JONATHAN, *compiler*. The Debates in the Several

WORKS CITED IN THIS VOLUME

State Conventions of the Adoption of the Federal Constitution. 5 vols. Philadelphia. 1896. (Elliott.)

FITHIAN, PHILIP VICKERS. Journal and Letters, 1767–1774. Edited by John Rogers Williams. Princeton University Library. 1900. (Fithian.)

FLANDERS, HENRY. The Lives and Times of the Chief Justices of the Supreme Court of the United States. 2 vols. Philadelphia. 1881. (Flanders.)

FOOTE, REV. WILLIAM HENRY. Sketches of Virginia, Historical and Biographical. 2 vols. Philadelphia. 1850–55. (Foote: *Sketches of Virginia*.)

FORD, PAUL LEICESTER, *editor*. Essays on the Constitution of the United States. New York. 1892. (Ford: *Essays on the Constitution*.)

—— Pamphlets on the Constitution of the United States. New York. 1888. (Ford: *P. on C.*)

See also Jefferson, Thomas. Works.

FORD, WORTHINGTON CHAUNCEY, *editor*. See Jefferson, Thomas. Correspondence.

Also see Washington, George. Writings.

FRANKLIN, BENJAMIN. Writings. Edited by Albert Henry Smyth. 10 vols. New York. 1907. (*Writings:* Smyth.)

FRENEAU, PHILIP. Poems of Philip Freneau. Edited by Fred Lewis Pattee. 3 vols. Princeton. 1902–07. (Freneau.)

GALLATIN, ALBERT. Writings. Edited by Henry Adams. 3 vols. Philadelphia. 1879. (Gallatin's *Writings:* Adams.)

See also Adams, Henry. Life of Albert Gallatin.

GARLAND, HUGH A. Life of John Randolph of Roanoke. 2 vols. New York. 1851. (Garland: *Randolph*.)

GIBBS, GEORGE, *editor*. See Wolcott, Oliver. Memoirs of the Administrations of Washington and John Adams. (Gibbs.)

GOODRICH, SAMUEL G. Recollections of a Lifetime, or Men and Things I Have Seen. 2 vols. New York. 1856. (Goodrich.)

GOSSE, EDMUND. A History of Eighteenth Century Literature. London. 1889. (Gosse: *History of Eighteenth Century Literature*.)

GRAYDON, ALEXANDER. Memoirs of His Own Time, with Reminiscences of the Men and Events of the Revolution. Edited by John Stockton Littell. Philadelphia. 1846. (Graydon.)

498   WORKS CITED IN THIS VOLUME

Green Bag, The; an Entertaining Magazine for Lawyers. Edited by Horace W. Fuller. Vols. 1–26. Boston. 1889–1914. [After 1914 consolidated with *The Central Law Journal.*] (*Green Bag.*)

GRIGSBY, HUGH BLAIR. The History of the Virginia Federal Convention of 1788. Virginia Historical Society. Richmond. 1815. [Volume 1 is volume 9, new series. Volume 2 is volume 10, new series.] (Grigsby.)

HALSEY, FRANCIS WHITING. The Old New York Frontier. New York. 1901. (Halsey: *Old New York Frontier.*)

HAMILTON, ALEXANDER. Works. Edited by John C. Hamilton. 7 vols. New York. 1851. (*Works:* Hamilton.)

—— Works. Edited by Henry Cabot Lodge. [Federal Edition.] 12 vols. New York. 1904. (*Works:* Lodge.)

HAMILTON, JOHN C., editor. History of the Republic of the United States, as traced in the Writings of Alexander Hamilton and his Contemporaries. 6 vols. New York. 1857–60. (Hamilton: *History of the Republic.*)

See also Hamilton, Alexander. Works.

HAMILTON, STANISLAUS MURRAY, editor. See Monroe, James. Writings.

HARDING, SAMUEL BANNISTER. The Contest over the Ratification of the Federal Constitution in the State of Massachusetts. New York. 1896. (Harding.)

HART, ALBERT BUSHNELL. American History told by Contemporaries. 4 vols. New York. 1897–1901. (Hart.)

HATCH, LOUIS CLINTON. Administration of the American Revolutionary Army. New York. 1904. (Hatch.)

HAZEN, CHARLES DOWNER. Contemporary American Opinion of the French Revolution. Baltimore. 1897. (Hazen.)

HEITMAN, FRANCIS BERNARD. Historical Register of Officers of the Continental Army, during the War of the Revolution. Washington, D.C. 1893.

—— Same. Revised and Enlarged Edition. Washington. 1914. (Heitman.)

HENING, WILLIAM WALLER. See Virginia. Laws.

HENRY, PATRICK. Life, Correspondence, and Speeches. Edited by William Wirt Henry. 3 vols. New York. 1891. (Henry.)

See also Wirt, William. Sketches of Life and Character of Patrick Henry.

WORKS CITED IN THIS VOLUME

HENRY, WILLIAM WIRT, editor. *See* Henry, Patrick. Life, Correspondence, and Speeches.

HINSDALE, B. A. The Old Northwest. 2 vols. New York. 1891. (Hinsdale.)

Historical Magazine and Notes and Queries Concerning the Antiquities, History, and Biography of America. [1st Series.] Vols. 1–10. New York. 1857–75. (*Hist. Mag.*)

History of William and Mary College, from its foundation, 1693, to 1870. Baltimore. 1870.

HOWE, HENRY. Historical Collections of Virginia. Charleston, S.C. 1845. (Howe.)

HUDSON, FREDERIC. Journalism in the United States from 1690 to 1872. New York. 1873. (Hudson: *Journalism in the United States.*)

HUNT, GAILLARD, editor. *See* Madison, James. Writings.

IREDELL, JAMES. *See* McRee, Griffith J. Life and Correspondence of James Iredell.

IRVING, WASHINGTON. The Life of George Washington. 5 vols. New York. 1855. (Irving.)

JAMESON, J. FRANKLIN, editor. Essays in the Constitutional History of the United States, 1775–1789, by Graduates and Former Members of Johns Hopkins University. Boston. 1889. (Jameson.)

JAY, JOHN. Correspondence and Public Papers. Edited by Henry P. Johnston. 4 vols. New York. 1890. (*Jay:* Johnston.)

JEFFERSON, THOMAS. Correspondence, from originals in the collections of William K. Bixby. Edited by Worthington Chauncey Ford. Boston. 1916. (*Thomas Jefferson Correspondence:* Ford.)

—— Works. Edited by Paul Leicester Ford. Federal Edition. 12 vols. New York. 1904. (*Works:* Ford.)

—— Writings. Edited by H. A. Washington. 9 vols. Washington, D.C. 1853–54. (Jefferson's *Writings:* Washington.)

See Morse, John T. Thomas Jefferson.

And see Randall, Henry S. Life of Thomas Jefferson.

Also see Tucker, George. Life of Thomas Jefferson.

JOHNSTON, HENRY P., editor. *See* Jay, John. Correspondence and Public Papers.

JONES, HUGH. The Present State of Virginia. London. 1724. (Jones.)

KAPP, FRIEDRICH. Life of Major-General Von Steuben. New York. 1859. (Kapp.)
KEITH, Sir WILLIAM, Bart. The History of the British Plantations in America, Part I, containing the History of Virginia. London. 1738. (Keith: *History of Virginia.*)
KING, CHARLES R., editor. See King, Rufus. Life and Correspondence.
KING, RUFUS. Life and Correspondence. Edited by Charles R. King. 6 vols. New York. 1894. (King.)

LAMB, General JOHN. Memoir and Life. See Leake, Isaac Q.
LANG, ANDREW. History of English Literature. New York. 1912. [2d edition.] (Lang: *History of English Literature.*)
LA ROCHEFOUCAULD-LIANCOURT, FRANÇOIS ALEXANDRE FRÉDÉRIC, Duc DE. Travels through the United States of North America. 4 vols. London. 1800. (La Rochefoucauld.)
LEAKE, ISAAC Q. Memoir of the Life and Times of General John Lamb, an Officer of The Revolution, and his Correspondence with Washington, Clinton, Patrick Henry, and other Distinguished Men. Albany. 1850. (Leake: *Lamb.*)
LEE, EDMUND JENNINGS. Lee of Virginia. 1642–1892. Biographical and Genealogical Sketches of the Descendants of Colonel Richard Lee. Philadelphia. 1895. (Lee: *Lee of Virginia.*)
LEE, Colonel RICHARD. Lee of Virginia. See Lee, Edmund Jennings.
LODGE, HENRY CABOT. Life and Letters of George Cabot. Boston. 1878. (Lodge: *Cabot.*)
——— George Washington. 2 vols. Boston. 1889. [American Statesmen.] (Lodge: *Washington.*)
See also Hamilton, Alexander. Works.
LOSSING, BENSON J. The Pictorial Field-Book of the Revolution. 2 vols. New York. 1851. (Lossing.)
See also Washington, George. Diary.
LOWDERMILK, WILL H. History of Cumberland (Maryland). Washington, D.C. 1878. (Lowdermilk.)

M'CLUNG, JOHN ALEXANDER. Sketches of Western Adventure. Philadelphia. 1832. (M'Clung: *Sketches of Western Adventure.*)

McCRADY, EDWARD. The History of South Carolina. 4 vols. New York. 1897-1902. (McCrady.)
McHENRY, JAMES. Life and Correspondence. *See* Steiner, Bernard C.
McMASTER, JOHN BACH, *and* STONE, FREDERICK D. Pennsylvania and the Federal Constitution. Philadelphia. 1888. (McMaster and Stone.)
McREE, GRIFFITH, J. Life and Correspondence of James Iredell. 2 vols. New York. 1857. (McRee.)
MADISON, JAMES. Writings. Edited by Gaillard Hunt. 9 vols. New York. 1900. (*Writings:* Hunt.)
  See also Rives, William C. History of Life and Times.
Magazine, The, of American History, with Notes and Queries. Vols. 1-42. New York. 1877-1913. (*Mag. Am. Hist.*)
Magazine of Western History. Cleveland, Ohio. Edited by William W. Williams. Vols. 1-14. 1885-94. (*Mag. Western Hist.*)
MARSHALL, HUMPHREY. The History of Kentucky. 2 vols. Frankfort. 1824. (Humphrey Marshall.)
MARSHALL, JOHN. Autobiography. *See* Smith, John Jay *and* Watson, John Fanning, *joint editors.* American Historical and Literary Curiosities. (*Autobiography.*)
—— Same. In National Portrait Gallery of Eminent Americans. Paintings by Alonzo Chappel, and Biographical and Historical Narratives by Evert A. Duyckinck. 2 vols. New York. 1862.
—— Same, reprinted. *See* Dillon, John F.
—— Life of George Washington. [1st Edition.] 5 vols. Philadelphia. 1805. [2d Edition.] 2 vols. Philadelphia. 1840. [The 2d Edition is cited in this work unless otherwise stated in the notes.] (Marshall.)
  See also Thayer, James Bradley. John Marshall.
  And see Flanders, Henry. Lives of the Chief Justices.
  Also see Van Santvoord, George. Sketches of the Lives of the Chief-Justices.
MASON, GEORGE. Life. *See* Rowland, Kate Mason.
MEADE, *Bishop* WILLIAM. Old Churches, Ministers, and Families of Virginia. 2 vols. Richmond. 1910. (Meade.)
MINER, CHARLES. History of Wyoming, in a series of letters, from Charles Miner, to his son, William Penn Miner, Esq. Philadelphia. 1845. (Miner: *History of Wyoming.*)
MINOT, GEORGE RICHARDS. The History of the Insurrections

502 WORKS CITED IN THIS VOLUME

in Massachusetts, in 1786, and the Rebellion consequent thereon. Boston. 1810. (Minot: *History of the Insurrections in Massachusetts.*)

MONROE, JAMES. Writings. Edited by Stanislaus Murray Hamilton. 7 vols. [Unfinished work.] New York. 1898–1903. (Monroe's *Writings:* Hamilton.)

MOORE, FRANK. Diary of the American Revolution, from Newspapers and Original Documents. 2 vols. New York. 1809. (Moore's *Diary.*)

MORDECAI, SAMUEL. Richmond in By-Gone Days, Being Reminiscences of An Old Citizen. Richmond. 1856. (Mordecai.)

MORRIS, GOUVERNEUR. Diary and Letters. Edited by Anne Cary Morris. 2 vols. London. 1889. (Morris.)

MORSE, JOHN T. Thomas Jefferson. Boston. 1795. [American Statesmen.] (Morse.)

MUNFORD, WILLIAM. *See* Virginia, Law Reports.

New Jersey Historical Society. Proceedings. Vols. 1–10. Newark. 1847–1905. (*Proc.*, N.J. Hist. Soc.)

NILES, HEZEKIAH. Centennial Offering, Republication of the Principles and Acts of the Revolution in America. New York. 1876. (Niles: *Principles and Acts of the Revolution.*)

NOTT, ELIPHALET. Memoirs. *See* Van Santvoord, C.

PAINE, THOMAS. Writings. Edited by Moncure Daniel Conway. 4 vols. New York. 1894–96. (*Writings:* Conway.)

PAXTON, WILLIAM M. The Marshall Family, or a Genealogical Chart of the Descendants of John Marshall and Elizabeth Markham. Cincinnati. 1885. (Paxton.)

PECQUET DU BELLET, LOUISE. Some Prominent Virginia Families. 4 vols. Lynchburg, Va. 1909. (Pecquet du Bellet.)

Pennsylvania Magazine of History and Biography. Published by the Historical Society of Pennsylvania. Vols. 1–40. Philadelphia. 1877–1916. (*Pa. Mag. Hist. and Biog.*)

PICKERING, OCTAVIUS. Life of Timothy Pickering, by his son and continued by Charles W. Upham. 4 vols. Boston. 1867–73. (Pickering: *Pickering.*)

PICKERING, TIMOTHY. Life. *See* Pickering, Octavius.

QUINCY, JOSIAH. Figures of the Past, from the leaves of Old Journals. Boston. 1883. (Quincy: *Figures of the Past.*)

WORKS CITED IN THIS VOLUME 503

RANDALL, HENRY S. Life of Thomas Jefferson. 3 vols. New York. 1858. (Randall.)
RANDOLPH, EDMUND. Life and Papers. *See* Conway, Moncure Daniel.
RANDOLPH, JOHN. Life. *See* Garland, Hugh A.
RIVES, WILLIAM C. The History of the Life and Times of James Madison. 3 vols. Boston. 1859. (Rives.)
ROWLAND, KATE MASON. Life of George Mason. 2 vols. New York. 1892. (Rowland.)

SARGENT, WINTHROP. The History of an Expedition against Fort Du Quesne, in 1755, under Major-General Edward Braddock. Philadelphia. 1855. (Sargent.)
SCHOEPF, JOHANN DAVID. Travels in the Confederation, 1783–1784. Translated and edited by Alfred J. Morrison. 2 vols. Philadelphia. 1911. (Schoepf.)
SCOTT, JOHN, of Fauquier County, Va. The Lost Principle. By "Barbarossa" [*pseud.*]. Richmond. 1860. (Scott.)
SLAUGHTER, Rev. PHILIP. A History of St. Mark's Parish, Culpepper County, Virginia. Baltimore. 1877. (Slaughter.)
—— A History of Bristol Parish, Virginia. Richmond. 1879. (Slaughter: *Bristol Parish*.)
SMITH, JOHN JAY, *and* WATSON, JOHN FANNING, *joint editors*. American Historical and Literary Curiosities. New York. 1852. (*Am. Hist. and Lit. Curiosities*.)
SMYTH-STUART, J. FERDINAND D. A Tour in the United States of America. 2 vols. London. 1784. (Smyth: *Tour of the United States*.)
Southern Literary Messenger. Vols. 1–38. New York and Washington. 1834–64.
SPARKS, JARED. The Life of George Washington. Boston. 1839. [Same plates, 1842.] (Sparks.)
—— Correspondence of the American Revolution [being letters of eminent men to George Washington]. 4 vols. Boston. 1853. (*Cor. Rev.*: Sparks.)
See also Washington, George. Writings.
STANARD, MARY NEWTON. The Story of Bacon's Rebellion. New York. 1907. (Stanard: *Story of Bacon's Rebellion*.)
STEINER, BERNARD C. The Life and Correspondence of James McHenry. Cleveland. 1907. (Steiner.)
STEPHEN, LESLIE. Alexander Pope. New York. 1880. (Stephen: *Alexander Pope*.)

STEUBEN, FREIDRICH WILHELM AUGUST HEINRICH FERDINAND, *Baron* VON. Life. *See* Kapp, Friedrich.
STILLÉ, CHARLES J[ANEWAY]. Major-General Anthony Wayne, and the Pennsylvania Line in the Continental Army. Philadelphia. 1893. (Stillé.)
STORY, JOSEPH. Discourse on John Marshall, reprinted.
See Dillon, John F.
Also see Story, William Wirt.
STORY, WILLIAM WIRT. Life and Letters of Joseph Story. 2 vols. Boston. 1851. (Story.)

TALLEYRAND-PÉRIGORD, CHARLES MAURICE DE, *Prince* DE BÉNÉVENT. Memoirs. Edited by the Duc de Broglie. 5 vols. New York. 1891. (*Memoirs of Talleyrand:* Broglie's Ed.)
TERHUNE, MARY VIRGINIA HAWES. Some Colonial Homesteads and their Stories. By Marion Harland [*pseud.*]. 2 vols. New York. 1912. (Terhune: *Colonial Homesteads.*)
THAYER, JAMES BRADLEY. John Marshall. Boston. 1904. [Riverside Biographical Series, No. 9.] (Thayer.)
TRAILL, H. D., *editor*. Social England. A Record of the Progress of the People. By Various Writers. 7 vols. London. 1896. (Traill: *Social England.*)
TREVELYAN, *Sir* GEORGE OTTO, *Bart*. The American Revolution. 4 vols. New York. 1907. (Trevelyan.)
TUCKER, GEORGE. Life of Thomas Jefferson. 2 vols. Philadelphia. 1837. (Tucker.)
TURNER, FREDERICK JACKSON. The Old West. [Printed in Wisconsin Historical Society, *Proceedings* for 1908.] Madison, Wis. 1909. (Turner: *The Old West.*)
TYLER, LYON G. Letters and Times of the Tylers. 2 vols. Richmond. 1884. (Tyler.)
—— Williamsburg, the Old Colonial Capital. Richmond. 1907. (Tyler: *Williamsburg.*)

VAN BUREN, MARTIN. Inquiry into the Origin and Course of Political Parties in the United States. New York. 1867. (Van Buren.)
VAN SANTVOORD, C. Memoirs of Eliphalet Nott. New York. 1876. (Van Santvoord: *Memoirs of Eliphalet Nott.*)

WORKS CITED IN THIS VOLUME 505

VAN SANTVOORD, GEORGE. Sketches of the Lives and Judicial Services of the Chief-Justices of the Supreme Court of United States. New York. 1854. (Van Santvoord.)

Virginia Historical Papers. Manuscripts now in the Virginia Historical Society Library, at Richmond. (*Va. Hist. Prs.*)

VIRGINIA. House of Burgesses. Journal of the Virginia House of Burgesses. 1619–1776. Now in the Archives of the Virginia State Library. (Journal, H.B.)

VIRGINIA. House of Delegates. Journal of the Virginia House of Delegates. 1776–1916. Now in the Archives of the Virginia State Library. (Journal, H.D.)

VIRGINIA. Laws. Hening, William Waller. The Statutes at Large. Being a Collection of the Laws of Virginia from 1619 to 1808. 13 vols. New York. 1819–23. (Hening.)

VIRGINIA. Law Reports. Call, Daniel. Reports of Cases Argued and Adjudged in the Court of Appeals of Virginia. 6 vols. Richmond. 1824–33. (Call.)

—— Munford, William. Reports of Cases Argued and Determined in the Supreme Court of Appeals, of Virginia. 15 vols. New York. 1812. (Munford).

Virginia Magazine of History and Biography. Published by the Virginia Historical Society. Vols. 1–24. Richmond. 1893–1916. (*Va. Mag. Hist. and Biog.*)

WALDO, *Surgeon* ALBIGENCE. Diary at Valley Forge from Nov. 1, 1777 to Jan. 15, 1778. [In *Historical Magazine*, vol. 5, pp. 129–34, 169–72.]

WALLACE, DAVID DUNCAN. The Life of Henry Laurens, with Sketch of the Life of Lieutenant-Colonel John Laurens. New York. 1915. (Wallace.)

WARVILLE. *See* Brissot de Warville.

WASHINGTON, GEORGE. Diary from 1789 to 1791. Edited by Benson J. Lossing. New York. 1860. (Washington's *Diary:* Lossing.)

—— Writings. Edited by Worthington Chauncey Ford. 14 vols. New York. 1889–1893. (*Writings:* Ford.)

—— Writings. Edited by Jared Sparks. 12 vols. Boston. 1834–1837. (*Writings:* Sparks.)

 See Irving, Washington. Life of George Washington.
 And Lodge, Henry Cabot. George Washington.
 Also Marshall, John. Life of George Washington.
 Also see Sparks, Jared. Life of George Washington.

WASHINGTON, H. A., *editor*. *See* Jefferson, Thomas. Writings.

WATSON, WINSLOW C. Men and Times of the Revolution, or Memoirs of Elkanah Watson, by his son. New York. 1856. (Watson.)

WEEDON, *General* GEORGE. Valley Forge Orderly Book. New York. 1902. (Weedon.)

WELD, ISAAC. Travels Through the States of North America, and the Provinces of Upper and Lower Canada During the Years 1795, 1796, and 1797. [3d Edition.] 2 vols. London. 1800. (Weld.)

WERTENBAKER, THOMAS J. Patrician and Plebeian in Virginia, or the Origin and Development of the Social Classes of the Old Dominion. Charlottesville, Va. 1910. (*Wertenbaker: P. and P.*)

—— Virginia Under the Stuarts, 1607–1688. Princeton University. 1914. (Wertenbaker: *V. U. S.*)

WILD, EBENEZER. Diary in the Revolutionary War from 1776 to 1781. [In Massachusetts Historical Society, *Proceedings* (2d Series), vol. 6, pp. 78–160.]

WILKINSON, *General* JAMES. Memoirs of my Own Times. 3 vols. Philadelphia. 1816. (Wilkinson: *Memoirs*.)

William and Mary College Quarterly Historical Magazine. Richmond. Vols. 1–16. 1892–1908. (*W. and M. C. Q.*)

WIRT, WILLIAM. The Letters of the British Spy. [9th Edition.] Baltimore. 1831. (Wirt: *British Spy*.)

—— Sketches of the Life and Character of Patrick Henry. Philadelphia. 1818. (Wirt.)

WISE, JENNINGS CROPPER. Ye Kingdome of Accawmacke, or the Eastern Shore of Virginia, in the Seventeenth Century. Richmond. 1911. (Wise.)

WOLCOTT, OLIVER. Memoirs of the Administrations of Washington and John Adams. Edited from the papers of Oliver Wolcott, by George Gibbs. 2 vols. New York. 1846. (Gibbs.)

WOOD, WILLIAM. The Fight for Canada. Westminster, 1904. (Wood.)

DATE DUE

WITHDRAWN
from
Funderburg Library